A.N. Wilson
VICTORIANS

TED SMART

First published in Great Britain in 2005
This edition produced for The Book People Limited, Hall Wood Avenue,
Haydock, St Helens WA11 9UL

10 9 8 7 6 5 4 3 2 1

Hutchinson
The Random House Group Limited
20 Vauxhall Bridge Road, London SW1V 2SA

www.randomhouse.co.uk

Addresses for companies within The Random House Group Limited
can be found at: www.randomhouse.co.uk/offices.htm

The Random House Group Limited Reg. No. 954009

A CIP catalogue record for this book
is available from the British Library

ISBN 9780091796228

The Random House Group Limited makes every effort to ensure that
the papers used in its books are made from trees that have been legally
sourced from well-managed and credibly certified forests. Our paper
procurement policy can be found at: www.randomhouse.co.uk/paper.htm

Typeset in 10 on 14pt Century Expanded
Designed by Peter Ward

Printed and bound in China
by C & C Offset Printing Co., Ltd

Previous pages: Derby Day by William Powell Frith
This page: Margate Beach, 1900
Following pages: Oxford Circus, London, *c.* 1880

Contents

Early Victorian

The Eighteen-Fifties

The Eighteen-Sixties

The Eighteen-Seventies

The Eighteen-Eighties

The Eighteen-Nineties

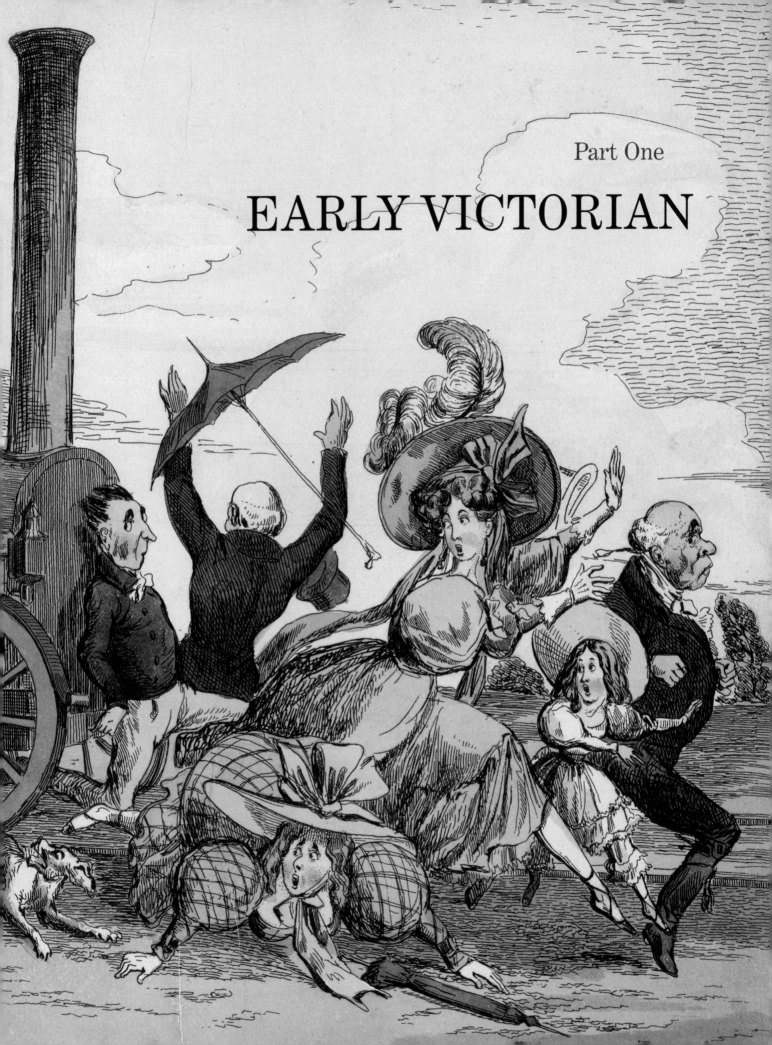

Part One

EARLY VICTORIAN

Chapter One

The Little Old Woman Britannia

On 16 October 1834, two visitors arrived at the Palace of Westminster and asked to be shown the chamber of the House of Lords. Parliament was in recess: sessions were much shorter in those days than now. The Speaker of the Lords, the Clerk of the Parliament, the Gentleman Usher of Black Rod, the Sergeant-at-Arms – all those charged with the responsibility for the safety and upkeep of the Houses of Parliament – were away, in the country. The place was in the charge of a housekeeper called Mrs Wright.[1]

When, at four o'clock that afternoon, Mrs Wright showed the visitors into the chamber of the Lords, they could scarcely make out the magnificent tapestries on the walls. There was smoke everywhere. The visitors complained that the stone floor was so hot that they could feel it through the soles of their feet. The throne, the grand centrepiece of the chamber, where sat the constitutional monarch when opening and proroguing their Lordships' assemblies, was invisible because of smoke. The house was, Mrs Wright agreed, in 'a complete smother'.

The workmen in the crypt who had started the blaze had been charged, in the absence of the parliamentarians, with the task of burning the wooden tallies used by the Exchequer for centuries as a means of computing tax. These were modern times and these wooden tabs were to be replaced by figures written down in paper ledgers.

> The sticks were housed at Westminster, and it would naturally occur to any intelligent person that nothing could be easier than to allow them to be carried away for firewood, by some of the many miserable creatures in that neighbourhood. However, they never had been useful, and official routine could not endure that they ever should be useful, and so the order went forth that they were to be privately and confidentially burnt. It came to pass that they were burnt in a stove in the House of Lords. The stove over-gorged with these preposterous sticks, set fire to the panelling; the panelling set fire to the House of Lords; the House of Lords set fire to the House of Commons; the two houses were reduced to ashes; architects were called in to build two more; and we are now in the second million of the cost thereof; the national pig is not nearly over the style yet; and the little old woman, Britannia, hasn't got home tonight.[2]

The voice, unmistakably, is that of Charles Dickens (1812–70), speaking years after the fire. There was, as he half implied, a fittingness about the fire. The Reform Bill of 1832 had selfconsciously ushered in a new era; when the emperor of Russia heard of the Westminster fire he thought it was heavenly punishment for the Whiggish abolition of rotten boroughs – boroughs which, with only a handful of voters, could nevertheless return a member of Parliament. That was perhaps because he saw the passing of the Reform Bill as the first stage of the

Among the immense crowd gathered to watch the blaze was Joseph Mallord William Turner (1775–1851), who stayed up all night doing innumerable pencil sketches. Afterwards he rushed home to Queen Anne Street to do so many watercolour studies, based on immediate memory, that the leaves of his sketchbook stuck together. In all likelihood Turner, who saw visual images as symbols, envisioned the fire as an emblem of the old world being done away with, purged and destroyed.

'The Pleasures of the Railroad – Caught in the Railway!' A satirical cartoon on the pace of industrial expansion at the beginning of the Victorian age, c. 1840.

The homes of the London poor as depicted in an issue of The Builder Magazine *from 1854. The Reverend Thomas Malthus believed that human population grows at a 'geometric rate', as in the series, 1, 2, 4, 8, 16, whereas means of subsistence must grow at an arithmetical rate – 1, 2, 3, 4, 5. The inevitable consequence of this, he believed, was starvation – and before that the misery, belligerence and social disruption which hunger brings to human societies.*

Fig. 2.—View of Wild-court, as seen from Great Wild-street.

modernizing of the British political system, the first unpicking of an old-fashioned system of hierarchy, and deference, the first stage in a hand-over of political power from the aristocracy to the bourgeoisie. This, however, was hardly how it appeared at the time. Few, if any, of the Whig aristocrats who had reformed the parliamentary system were believers in democracy. All deplored the notion of universal suffrage. The extension of the suffrage, which diehards so regretted, was limited wholly to persons of property.

Even with the abolition of rotten boroughs, the new Parliament was representative of the people only in the most notional sense. That was not how it conceived its purpose. What was new about the political classes

Fig. 3.—*Front View of the House No. 2.*

Fig. 4.—*View of Back-yard in House No. 2.*

in the so-called Age of Reform was their desire, a successful desire, to exercise control over the populace. There was no divide in the Parliament of the 1830s and 1840s between what a modern person would conceive of as Left and Right. The problem for the political classes was all seen as the same problem: how to control a rapidly expanding population. How to feed it, how to

keep it busy, how, if it was Irish, or Scottish, to restrain it from open rebellion, how, if it was poor and discontented, to discourage it from sedition, how, if it was French, to prevent it from invading Great Britain, how, if it was Jamaican or Canadian, to stop it seceding from the British Crown. Hence the development in this era of the first police force, of tight controls over paupers, and of the workhouses in which to incarcerate those incapable of feeding their families.

The statistics speak for themselves. Over the previous eighty years, the population of England, Wales and Scotland had doubled – 7,250,000 in 1751, 10,943,000 in 1801, 14,392,000 in 1821; by 1831, 16,539,000 – and in Ireland 4,000,000 had become 8,000,000.[3]

Economics and politics conceived in terms of population-growth was an inevitable development in the history of human thought. If the Reverend Thomas Malthus (1766–1834) had not existed it would have been necessary to invent him and someone else would have written *An Essay on the Principle of Population*, a work which he first wrote in 1798 and constantly revised.

Although seen immediately as a kind of monster – Shelley called him 'a eunuch and a tyrant', Dickens makes Scrooge a mouthpiece for Malthusianism by asking why the poor don't go away and die 'to decrease the surplus population' – it was in fact with the highest altruism that Malthus wrote his *Essay*. He wanted poor people not to be poor – or if inevitably poor, at least to be well fed. Paradoxically he saw that the existent Poor Laws – what we would call Welfare – encouraged a dependency-culture. Whereas the old Poor Laws had left to the discretion of local parishes the choice of to whom charitable provision should be made, the new Poor Laws – enacted by the last Parliament before the fire of 1834 – centralized the provision of Poor Relief. Rather than extending charity to the poor in their own homes, the Commissioners had built a chain of workhouses across the country. It could be said that no one had to go to the workhouse. When the alternative, however, was to watch children go hungry, it is not surprising that the hated places began to fill up.

Britain was changing, and changing more rapidly and more creatively than any other country in the world. Within three years of witnessing the destruction of the Palace of Westminster, the prime minister, Lord Melbourne (1779–1848), was to see the death of the old King William IV (1765–1837) and the accession of Queen Victoria (1819–1901). Melbourne was Queen Victoria's mentor, her father-figure. Together this somewhat unlikely pair, the world-weary cynical Whig peer and the plain, diminutive, teenaged monarch, gazed forward to a new world more populous, more competitive and more adaptable than the Reverend Thomas Malthus could have envisaged in his worst nightmares. His death in Bath in the very year of the New Poor Laws, and of the Westminster fire, could also be seen as emblematic.

What Malthus failed to predict was the colossal growth in wealth in the era which would be known as Victorian. The more people, the more wealth-producers there were. It was an era of paupers, pauperism, famine, disease, certainly. In this, his predictions were more than amply fulfilled in the first decade of the new reign. But it was also an era of prodigious energy, growth and expansion.

The two writers who stand at the beginning of the Victorian Age like choruses to the drama, one in tragic, the other in comic mask, are Thomas Carlyle (1795–1881) and Charles Dickens. Carlyle's *French Revolution*, after many adventures (which included the only manuscript of volume 1 being inadvertently burnt by John Stuart Mill's housemaid), was published in book form for the first time in 1837, the year of the Queen's accession. It was also the year which saw the final instalment of the serial publication of *The Posthumous Papers of the Pickwick Club*.

When we gasp with astonishment at the undemocratic nature of government (even after the Reform Bill) in the early decades of the nineteenth century; when we survey the Britain of workhouses, of coal mines worked by children, of grinding poverty and even starvation in town and country, it is a striking fact that two of the most distinctive voices of the age should not have come from privileged backgrounds. Dickens, the son of a government clerk imprisoned in the Marshalsea Prison for debt, had only rudimentary schooling and next to no money when, as a very young man, he began to report parliamentary debates in the *Monthly Magazine*. By modern standards, the poverty of the Carlyle family in Ecclefechan, Dumfriesshire, was little above a subsistence level; but by comparison with other Scotch peasants, Carlyle's parents, enterprising and thrifty, were prosperous. Thanks to the admirable educational system in Scotland by which a clever boy could rise, however poor he was, Carlyle went to Edinburgh University and immersed himself in contemporary European literature, language and philosophy. He was the great interpreter of German poetry and philosophy to the English-speaking world.

It was to France, however, that he went at the age of twenty-nine on a visit which was of crucial importance. It is difficult to overestimate the extent to which the British, after the defeat of Napoleon, continued to feel paranoia about France. Not only did Palmerston and Wellington fear the prospect of French invasion long after the very possibility of such an event had been extinguished; but France was also seen as the very object lesson of what could happen if a society imploded. We sow what we reap, both as individuals and as

Oliver being cared for by Mr Brownlow in an illustration by George Cruikshank from the first edition of Oliver Twist. *The* Edinburgh Review *in 1838, writing of Dickens, said: 'One of the qualities we most admire in him is his comprehensive spirit of humanity. The tendency of his writings is to make us practically benevolent – to excite our sympathy in behalf of the aggrieved and suffering in all classes; and especially those who are most removed from observation.'*

societies. This is the simple and compelling message of *The French Revolution.*

Carlyle demonstrates clearly and relentlessly how the *ancien régime* was bound to fall, how the relentlessly selfish aristocrats and royal family could expect nothing less than a destructive apocalypse. But he is no advocate of the Terror, and his seagreen Robespierre is one of the great monsters of literature. Carlyle's agonies in print were to become the inner torments, political, religious and philosophical, of his generation, which is why he was the greatest of its prophets in the English-speaking world. He could not believe in Christianity, but his was no Voltairean delight at having done away with the old superstitions. He mourned his absent Christ and he trembled for a society with no sense of the awesome, no reverence before the great mysteries. Above all, he

feared what would happen in a society which plainly could not sustain (morally or politically) a system of oligarchic privilege but which could so easily slither into something worse – anarchy, mayhem, butchery. The notion that the spiritual and political malaise of his times could be solved by parliamentary reforms was ludicrous to him.

He was not optimistic about the prospects of his contemporaries avoiding a revolution even worse than the French. But almost worse than this, in his view, was the horrifying effect on thousands of human lives of the industrial, capitalist revolution which made so many not merely economic slaves but dullards, incapable of seeing the sort of intellectual or spiritual truths which had been clear to his own pre-industrialized, though poverty-stricken, relations and family.

Carlyle, though a vigorously comic writer, and one of the great wits both on the acerbic page and in his own conversation, had an ultimately tragic vision of life and of the world. It would be hard to conceive of a more different temperament from that which created *The Pickwick Papers*.

The story, published between 1836 and 1837 in serial parts, was a rambling picaresque; its first audiences were drawn by a Janus-like double-appeal. On the one hand it celebrates and fantasizes about the holiday-freedoms of the swelling lower middle class from which Dickens himself sprang. In this sense, it is utterly modern. On the other hand it is a nostalgic snapshot, or series of snapshots, of an England which industry and the railways were to change forever.

Pickwick revealed (and perhaps in some senses created) the existence of a new public. Before it was published, the reading public was divided. Newspapers cost sevenpence. A three-volume novel cost £1. 11*s*. 6*d*. Only the substantial middle, upper middle and upper class bought what we should call broadsheet papers or hardback novels. Beneath this class of perhaps 50,000 readers there were those who read popular fiction purveyed not in book form but in cheap periodicals, loose paperbacks sold by travelling salesmen from door to door or at street markets. Ballad-sheets, satires and popular romances would be sold in this way by vendors not unlike Silas Wegg in *Our Mutual Friend*. Some of Dickens's contemporaries, such as William Harrison Ainsworth, the popular imitator of Sir Walter Scott, believed that the young journalist was making a grave mistake in writing fiction in this popular form, the loose-covered serial; a form hitherto reserved only for low trash. But within months, the sales of *Pickwick* had risen to tens of thousands. Hereafter, many of the great novels by Dickens, Thackeray, Trollope, George Eliot and others would be published serially in one of the many periodicals of the day.

Even as they read *The Pickwick Papers*, the first readers could indulge in instant nostalgia. The first railway terminus, Euston, was built in London in the year the book was published. The old era of the stagecoach – each with its name (*Defiance*, *True Blue*, *Wonder*, *Tantivy*, *Star of Brunswick*, *Isis*, *Irresistible*, *Tally Ho*, *Rocket*, *Zephyr*, *Ariel*, *Emerald*, *Flower of Kent*, *Mazeppa*) – was to give place to named steam engines, about which in later eras schoolboy enthusiasts would be no less sentimental.

The nostalgia of *Pickwick* is a large part of its appeal, and it is one of the most remarkable features of the collective Victorian consciousness. That is, while they were in every sense different from previous generations, and glad to be different, they also hankered after the past. Dickens had in common with most of his contemporaries a desire to put the old world of injustice, ignorance and disease behind him. He shared with them, too, however, a sentimentality about the past, a sense that industrialization was wrecking the world. This dichotomy, felt by all readers of *Pickwick*, is to be one of the defining features of nineteenth-century socio-political debates.

There is another obvious feature of *Pickwick* which makes an appeal to its admirers; and of all the qualities in its author it is perhaps both the strongest and the hardest with which to come to terms. It is benevolence. How can one talk about this quality without smugness, without being saccharine? Many of the 'benevolent' characters in Dickens will strike some readers as clumsily drawn and manipulative of our tear-ducts. One thinks of the brothers Cheeryble or of Mr Brownlow or Pickwick himself. It was well said that 'their facile charity forbids censoriousness; they are too busy being happy to think'. Yet each time one reads *A Christmas Carol*, it works. The ethics of Scrooge (which are the ethics of Adam Smith and Jeremy Bentham, the ethics of the mill-owners and factory-builders who created the wealth of Victorian England) are held in check by a tremendously simplified form of Christian charity.

Dickens admired and promoted the notion of benevolence, both in his person (for example in his work at Great Ormond Street Children's Hospital) and in his writings, to the point where he must be recognized as a hugely benign force in Victorian England. He is both the cause, and a symptom, of a benevolence which is palpable.

Dickens, partly because he is so consistently funny a writer, and so unpompous, reminds us of the existence of another Britain, in which the harshness of life is tempered by kindliness. His belief in the power of good-heartedness to triumph over evil is expressed in terms, not of a political programme, but of personality. His world, like the world of Victorian England, is not a Marxian *mass*: it is a teeming, moving screen of hilarious characters. He was in some senses the least realistic of all great geniuses; more than most writers, he created his own world. Such was his success, however, that we can almost say that the early nineteenth century in England was the England of Dickens.

Chapter Two

Victoria's Inheritance

Old William IV, dropsical, drunken, stupid, died two days after Waterloo Day, on 20 June 1837. He had been visibly sinking for some weeks. The Duke of Wellington, in the previous week, had offered to cancel the annual banquet commemorating the victory on 18 June, twenty-two years earlier, over the French emperor. William IV had robustly insisted that the banquet go ahead. He baffled everyone by exclaiming 'The Church, The Church!' just before he died. (He had shown no great interest in the Church when alive.)

William was the father of ten children by the celebrated comic actress Dorothea Jordan (1762–1816); but none of them were legitimate, so none could inherit the throne. When his niece Princess Charlotte died in 1817 – she was the only legitimate child of the future King George IV – the race had begun to determine which of George III's surviving children could produce an heir, and so become father of the new dynasty. It was the Duke of Kent, the fourth son of George III, who was destined to win 'Hymen's War Terrific' as contemporary gossips termed it.

The tiny figure of Archbishop Howley, clad in a wig, rochet and chimere, knelt early next morning in Kensington Palace to tell William IV's eighteen-year-old niece that she was now the Queen. He was accompanied by the lord chamberlain. The iconic moment had its own personal drama. Victoria, who had been brought up as a semi-hermit in the palace, with few friends, was going to display her own capacity for Darwinian survival and Samuel Smilesish Self-Help by effectually dismissing her domineering mother, the Duchess of Kent, and the sinister Sir John Conroy. This pair, who had so long planned to be the powers behind the throne, were banished like demons in a fairy tale. At nine that morning, the Queen received her prime minister, 'Of COURSE *quite* ALONE as I shall *always* do all my Ministers',[1] and there began that intense and mutually enjoyable *amitié amoureuse* between the tiny, plump, plain girl of eighteen and the languid, handsome fifty-eight-year-old Whig, a relationship likened by Melbourne's biographer to that sought by 'other girls . . . in some sympathetic schoolmaster or kindly clergyman'.[2]

At the Privy Council meeting, all the old men who had been governing England for years, Whig or Tory, were charmed by their new monarch. 'She not merely

The young Queen Victoria by F.X. Winterhalter.

'A Cabinet Lecture'– Queen Victoria with Lord Melbourne. In the company of this worldly Whig she played draughts, while he explained the Constitution.

A CABINET LECTURE.

London Published by J. M? Cormick, 147, Strand.

Aug. 1840

filled her chair,' said the Duke of Wellington, 'she filled the room.'[3]

Charles Greville (1794–1865), the greatest diarist of the age had, as clerk to the Privy Council, afforded a unique opportunity of observing the Queen at first hand, noted, 'Everything is new and delightful to her. She is surrounded with the most exciting and interesting enjoyments, her occupations, her pleasures, her business, her Court, all present an unceasing round of gratifications.'[4]

Cynical, worldly Lord M. amazed courtiers like Greville by the evident delight with which he gave himself up to his new sovereign lady, playing draughts with her while he explained the Constitution. The man who, within the previous decade, had scandalized London by his very public affair with a married woman, Caroline Norton, seems in the company of the young Queen to have discovered qualities of innocence in himself which he did not know existed.

Nevertheless, as you read of their conversations, Victoria and her beloved Lord M., the question which comes most often to mind is – why was there no revolution in Britain in the late 1830s and the 1840s? In 1848, the Year of Revolutions on the European continent, crowns and aristocracies were sent packing. How does it come about that Queen Victoria was destined to survive not only the troubles of 1848 but all the subsequent years? When she died, nominal head of the largest, wealthiest and most aggressively powerful empire the world had ever known, her prime minister was the impeccably aristocratic figure of Lord Salisbury (1830–1903). Of all her prime ministers only three were non-aristocratic – Sir Robert Peel (1788–1850), William Ewart Gladstone (1809–98) and Benjamin Disraeli (1804–81). Gladstone was a millionaire, whose father and brother owned vast family estates in Scotland; Disraeli was an aristocrat by adoption. How did they all survive not merely the tumbril and the guillotine but – when it was eventually introduced – the ballot-box? Many readers of these pages, particularly if British, might consider it axiomatic both that Victorian political institutions would adapt themselves to survive, and that they would maintain sufficient popularity not to be exchanged for some thoroughgoing form of democracy. But nothing about political history is contingent. There is an inexorability about events and their consequences.

When Queen Victoria asked Lord Melbourne if he could recommend the newly published novel *Oliver Twist* (serialized 1837–8), which was attracting much fame, he replied that he did not want her to read it. 'It's all among workhouses and Coffin Makers and Pickpockets . . . I don't *like* these things; I wish to avoid them; I don't like them in reality, and therefore I don't wish to see them represented.'[5] This airy unwillingness to confront one of the more displeasing aspects of contemporary existence might have been regarded as merely self-protective if Lord Melbourne's remark had been made by any rich nobleman of the period. Coming from the lips, however, of the prime minister who brought in the New Poor Laws of 1834, who was, in direct fact, responsible for the existence of the workhouses in such dimensions and numbers, the words have a chilling amorality.

The years 1837–44 brought the worst economic depression that had ever afflicted the British people. It is estimated – and we are speaking here of the years before the Irish famine – that more than a million paupers starved from simple lack of employment.[6] Many of the nation's businesses came to a halt. The workhouses whose existence Lord Melbourne found so distressing to contemplate could not conceivably house the influx of paupers. *Oliver Twist* had inspired shocked and indignant reactions from the public. The Poor Law Amendments initiated by Melbourne's administration were not popular with the educated middle classes. In

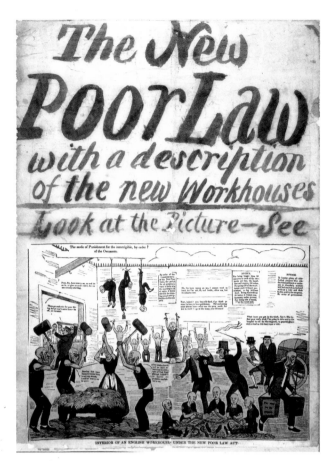

A Poor Law poster from 1832.

particular *The Times*, which reprinted *Oliver Twist*, took upon itself to print innumerable horror-stories about life in the workhouses. Many of the stories turn out in examination to be either untrue or exaggerated.[7] Enough of them sank into the public consciousness for the ostrich attitude of Melbourne to seem unendurable.

What shocked the early Victorians was the disparity between rich and poor, the visible unfairness of it all, made all the more visible in the railway age, when communications between the big manufacturing cities became so easy. In the rural, pre-railway age many of the more prosperous strata could avoid contact with the poor. In the 1840s they became much more visible because there were so many more of them, and the question could be asked, were such gross and obvious unfairnesses avoidable by acts of charity, or were the unfairness and competitiveness actually ineradicable ingredients in the capitalistic success-story in which that society was caught up?

In Fareham, in Hampshire, the workhouse had a large school; three of its pupils, bastard boys called Withers, Cook and Warren, aged between three and a half and five, were sent for special tuition from Bishop's Warren. Eight weeks later they were returned, so weakened by diarrhoea and disease that they could barely stand. What had happened? On their arrival at Fareham they had been placed together. One of the disturbed children had wet the bed. Their punishment was a cut of 50 per cent in the weekly food ration of 2 lb 10 oz of bread, 5 oz of mutton, 1 lb potatoes, 3½ oz cheese and 12 oz of pudding. The starvation diet did not cure the bedwetting. The children were then placed in specially designed stocks – imagine being the man who designed children's stocks! – and made to watch the other children having their meals. Since they now smelt intolerable they were made to sleep in an unheated shed in the yard, in the depth of winter.

Similar cases were the almost daily diet for readers of *The Times*. This situation continued for at least the first ten years of the Queen's reign, until a scandal too far led to the resignation, and eventual abolition, of the Poor Law Commission in London. This was the scandal of the Andover Workhouse.

From the very start of the New Poor Laws in 1834 the local chairman of the Board, Charles Dodson, and the pair who ran the Andover workhouse, Mr and Mrs Colin McDougal, applied the screw, the dreaded Prohibitory Order. In this parish all relief of the poor in their own homes was stopped. Single women with bastard children were obliged, if they wished to eat, to wear the yellow stripe of shame sewn across their coarse grey workhouse gown. The boys and men were set to the smelly work of bone-grinding, making fertilizer out of the bones of dead farm animals. They were so hungry they fell to gnawing the rotten bones and putrid horseflesh which came from the slaughterhouse.

Colin McDougal, the workhouse supervisor, was a rough Scotsman, born in 1793, who had fought at Waterloo and been discharged from the service as a staff sergeant in 1836. He was a drunkard who frequently got into fights with his no less horrible wife. He regularly thrashed children as young as three for messing their beds and he kept his paupers on such short rations that some survived by eating candles. Charles Lewis of Weyhill remembered his children eating the potato peelings thrown out for Mr McDougal's chickens. The scandal broke in 1845 when Ralph Etwall, the member for Andover, rose in the House of Commons and demanded an inquiry into the administration of the Andover Workhouse, and by implication into the Poor Law Commission. In July 1847 the Commission was finally abolished – and in the very same week John Walter (1776–1847), the editor of *The Times* who had campaigned so tirelessly against it, also died. Yet, in spite of the shaming of the Poor Law Commission, and the resolution of Parliament to improve conditions in workhouses, these institutions remained grim for many decades to come.

Chapter Three

The Charter

A society's attitude to disease reveals more than the state of its medical knowledge. Victorian England, destined to become so densely populous, so politically powerful throughout the world, so dirty and so rich, poured much of its paranoia and its ambivalence concerning Mammon-worship into its feelings about cholera. The disease came from India, source of so much British wealth and guilt. It did not break out of the Indian subcontinent until the nineteenth century, the first major pandemic being in 1817. The extent of the outbreak was a direct consequence of trade, of the increase of traffic between European, chiefly British, merchants in Bengal and the armies sent to protect them.

The Privy Council in London immediately addressed itself to the question of whether traded goods could be contagious. Thus, from the beginning, cholera became a metaphor for the contagion of Mammon. The society which based itself entirely on profits from trade would invent arcane hierarchies and etiquettes in which to be 'in trade' was to be untouchable. Within the questions about contagious imported goods were also fears of the foreign and the foreigner.

After 1832, there were to be three major cholera epidemics in Britain: 1848–9, 1853–4 and 1866. The first of these killed 53,000 in England and Wales, 8,000 in Scotland; the next killed 26,000 – but 10,000 in London alone; the 1866 outbreak killed 17,000 – 6,000 in London. It should not be supposed that any British government was so reckless as to use plague as a political weapon. It terrified rich and poor alike, but their responses, not merely in Britain but throughout Europe, revealed the differences in attitude between the classes which were themselves the creation of capitalism. The propertied classes half feared the foreign import of plague which came as the sting in the tail of their new-found wealth. They feared it too as the outward and visible sign of that physical contagion which social division had created in the slums. The poor in most previous ages could perhaps, as the old Tory Sir Walter Scott had urged, be 'left alone', un-'bothered'.

Doctors, like policemen, were seen by the early Victorian poor as representatives of a hated governing class, come to keep the poor from doing what in the circumstances might have seemed reasonable: erupting, rebelling, looting,

JOHN BULL BETWEEN TWO HUMBUGS

In 1818 cholera engulfed the whole of the Indian subcontinent. By 1831 it had spread to the Baltic ports. Thomas Wakley (1795–1862), founder of The Lancet, *remarked of the government's plans to create a cordon sanitaire: 'Sagacious legislators who cannot prevent the spread of cholera from traversing the ocean, yet can keep it from penetrating a hedge or crossing a field.'*

'Peelers' circa 1835.

destroying – not necessarily with any fixed or focused aim in view, but merely as the political equivalent of a scream. The Metropolitan Police Force was established in 1829. Comparable gendarmeries grew up on the continental mainland as a simple response to the population explosion. They had two principal tasks, to protect property (and life), and to curb liberty.[1] From its inception, the police force was seen as a Benthamite organ of social control. Radicals such as Edwin Chadwick believed that the consolidation of police forces would actually prevent crime – his *Preventive Policing* (1829) was received with rapture by his philosophical radical friends, such as James and John Stuart Mill, and was even praised by old Jeremy Bentham himself.[2]

Jeremy Bentham (1748–1832) looks an unlikely godfather of the British or any state. And when one refers to his looks, these may be verified since, ardent rationalist that he was, he specified that he should not be buried with religious ceremonial but preserved in a glass case, an everlasting reminder to nineteenth-century humankind of the non-resurrection of the body and the life, far from everlasting but terrestrial, fact-based and empirical.

His spiritual journey from High Tory absolutist to darling of the radicals, from churchman to unbeliever, was dynamoed by high intelligence and independence of mind, lubricated by enormous inherited wealth. (It was in origin a pawnbroking fortune.) He had the leisure, time, health and money to devote laborious hours to considering the whole nature of society, what makes it function and what, in revolutionary periods, makes it break down. His 'utilitarian' doctrine – the phrase was popularized by the son, John Stuart, of Bentham's most ardent follower, James Mill – of the greatest happiness of the greatest number led in one direction to radical libertarianism and in another to rigid notions of control. His 'Panopticon' in prisons and workhouses was the architectural expression of his political outlook – central control must depend on keeping an eye on the dissident or recalcitrant elements in a state. Because of his huge expertise in the field of what we should call sociology and economics, Bentham was in fact consulted by politicians with whom no one would expect him to be in sympathy. Robert Peel corresponded with him about the setting up of a police force. The judicial reforms of Henry Brougham, from the suppression of special pleading to the setting up of local courts, followed Bentham to the letter. Wider yet and wider – Bentham's ideas about governing India, which seemed fantastic in the 1820s when the East India Company held its sway, were all put in force by the time of Imperial Expansion in the 1860s.[3]

Bentham therefore in fact as well as in spirit may be seen as the father of Victorian realpolitik. The 'greatest happiness of greatest numbers' theory was based on the callous but realistic view that pleasing everyone is impossible. The secret of a stable society is to isolate and emasculate the miserable.

Whereas in the aristocratically dominated hierarchical world of eighteenth-century England life and property were largely protected by law, meted out with great severity from magistrates or the judicial bench, the Age of Reform substituted for the concept of law the concept of preventive policing. Eighteenth-century England got by without a police force partly because the population was so small, partly because there were, by the time of the 1820s, over 200 capital offences. England had the harshest criminal code in Europe. By 1841, only eight offences remained on the statute book for which an individual could be hanged. In effect the only capital

Drawing of the Panopticon prison design from Jeremy Bentham's Management of the Poor, *1796. Bentham's design shows a prison where each prisoner is housed in such a way as to prevent them from being aware whether or not they are under observation at any given moment.*

PANOPTICON

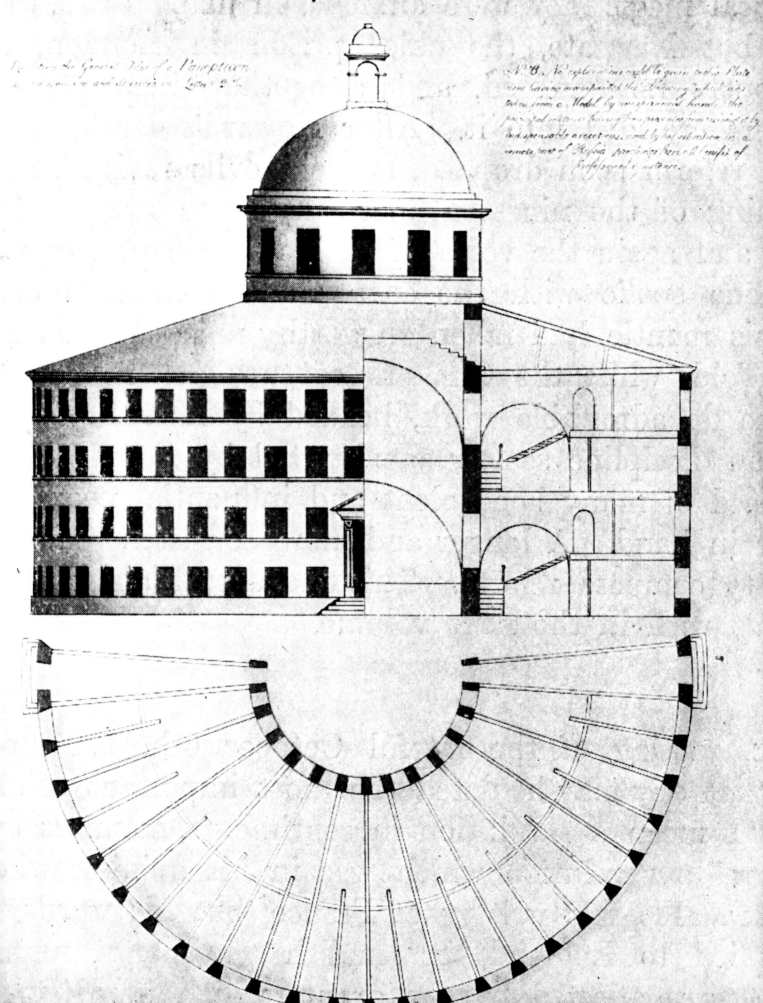

Exhibiting the General Idea of a Panopticon
the several parts are described in Letter 2d.

N.B. No explanation ought to be given to this Plate
now having accompanied the Drawing which was
taken from a Model by inexperienced hands, the
principal entrance having been previously omitted by
an oversight of the architect, and by its situation in a
remote part of Russia precluded from all benefit of
professional assistance.

offence was murder. These reforms were the delight of liberals, happy to escape the *Beggar's Opera* world of the gallows. But the working classes were the chief opponents of introduction of the police force. Liberalism, using the term in its loosest sense, extended certain political rights to a wider group of propertied individuals, but it sharply reduced personal liberty. The establishment of a centralized police force, abolishing the local 'watch', the Dogberrys and Elbows who had kept the peace since Tudor times, tightened the hold of the state.[4]

There was, incidentally, no noticeable reduction in crimes against property after the establishment of the Met.[5] Peel's force of 3,000 men had a very largely political function in the first twenty years of its life. Almost to a man – this in itself was a sign of the times – they were agricultural labourers, drawn to the work by poverty, but detached from the urban proletariat whom they were enlisted to control. ('I have refused to employ gentlemen', Peel explained, 'as superintendents and inspectors, because I am certain they would be above their work.')[6] Though all the talk, when they were established, was of their supposed efficacy in stemming the loss of £900,000 worth of property by theft and violence, it was not long before the Metropolitan Police were being used to put down the rising tide of Chartist agitations.[7]

It is possible to view the phenomenon of Chartism as a premature harbinger of twentieth-century leftists, though the links are tenuous and it is often hard to find much in the way of an apostolic succession being passed from surviving Chartist groups or individuals to incipient Labour-ites. Chartism is perhaps more helpfully seen as a phenomenon of its time. Its aspirations, the hopes and fears which it inspired in differing parts of the populace, its near victories and its muted defeat form the most consistently interesting backdrop to the political history of Victoria's reign in its first ten years.

Those who hoped that the Reform Bill of Lord Grey (1764–1845) and Lord John Russell (1792–1878) would usher in an era of democracy, or even of government by the bourgeoisie, were to find their hopes disappointed. Grey's Cabinet was almost entirely aristocratic. The first act of Grey's government, after the passage of the Reform Bill, was to create two dukes.[8] The reforms of 1832 perhaps extended the suffrage to some propertied persons who had hitherto been excluded, but many of the old ways persisted. 'Proprietary boroughs' still existed for example, parliamentary seats which were effectively in the possession of one patron. Nor should we imagine that the extension of the franchise in 1832 affected more than a handful of the populace. In terms of actual votes cast the Reform Act made no difference at all in many regions. Very many of the smaller seats, particularly those owned by aristocrats, were uncontested at elections, and the bribing of voters was an accepted part of the procedure – not merely accepted but necessary, in order to persuade those eligible to vote at all. As for voting in secret, many perhaps would share the view of Lord Palmerston, that 'to go sneaking to the ballot-box, and poking in a piece of paper, looking round to see that no one could read it, is a course which is unconstitutional and unworthy of the character of straightforward and honest Englishmen'.[9]

At the meeting of Queen Victoria's first Parliament, Thomas Wakley, the radical member for Finsbury, had suggested extending the suffrage still further, and introducing a secret ballot to make elections less vulnerable to abuse. He provoked the acknowledged Master Craftsman of the Great Reform Bill, Lord John Russell, to make his celebrated 'Finality' speech in the House of Commons. Lord John did not rule out the possibility of Reform being taken further at some future date; but if 'the people of England did not care for Lord John's moderate reforms, they may reject me. They can prevent me from taking part either in the Legislature or in the councils of the Sovereign; they can place others there who may have wider and more extended, more enlarged, and more enlightened views, but they must not expect me to entertain these views.' Quite how 'the people of England' could have any effect at all on the political fortunes of Lord John Russell when he considered 'unwise' the very notion of offering any more of them the vote, His Lordship did not on that occasion vouchsafe.

It was largely in response to this intransigent Whig mindset, at a time of unprecedented economic hardship, made worse by the Liberals' workhouses and police forces, that the movement known as Chartism came into being.

'There is verily a "rights of man" let no man doubt. An ideal of right does dwell in all men in all arrangements, actions and procedures of men: it is to this ideal of right, more and more developing itself as it is more approximated to, that human society forever tends and struggles.'[10] So affirmed the great Carlyle, and others must have felt that there was something apocalyptic in the air, a change which had to happen merely because the gross disparities between rich and poor were so glaring, and the absence of political representation for the majority of the population was in the very nature of things wrong.

In 1837 *The Northern Star*, the Chartist newspaper, was founded in Leeds, using machinery and type brought from London. The comparative cheapness and speed of producing a newspaper, and the ease of disseminating its ideas by means of newly built railways, are important features of the Chartist story. The half-starved labourer in Andover was now in touch, in a manner impossible or inconceivable in previous generations, with the radical weaver of Spitalfields in London, the potter of Staffordshire choked on china clay, the overworked miner of Nottinghamshire, loom-hand of Yorkshire, cotton-spinner of Lancashire, iron-worker of South Wales, docker of Harwich. The working classes began for the first time to have a sense of solidarity. From the beginning, though its leaders were not working-class, Chartism was essentially a working-class movement because the only 'radicals' in the House of Commons represented the interests of factory-owners and industrialists who would oppose such reforms as the Christian Tory Lord Ashley's (1801–85) – from 1851 7th Earl of Shaftesbury – attempts to protect children and women from working more than ten hours a day or in dangerous conditions. The New Poor Law, believed the Chartists, placed the labouring classes 'at the feet of the rich assassins, who rob, brutalize, and enslave the population . . . It is in the nature of things that the middle classes must be worse than any other part of the community.'[11]

Carlyle believed that for the working-class movement to succeed, it needed 'not misgovernment, but veritable government'; not democracy or 'clattering of ballot-boxes' but firm leadership. It was the undoing of the Chartist cause that no such People's King arose. James Bronterre O'Brien (1805–64), the thirty-two-year-old son of an Irish wine merchant who read for the Bar in London, presented the first petition to the Parliament in 1837 – 'THAT THE POOR OF ENGLAND SHALL BE HEARD BY COUNCIL AT THE BAR OF THE HOUSE OF COMMONS AGAINST THE LATE TYRANNICAL AND INHUMAN ENACTMENT MISCALLED THE POOR LAW AMENDMENT ACT.'[12] He effectually passed over the leadership of the movement – as far as its parliamentary life was concerned – to Feargus O'Connor (1794–1855), the member of Parliament for Cork.

From the beginnings, however, there was always a division among Chartists between the emphasis of O'Connor, who called, in often fiery language, for working-class resistance and if necessary the use of force against their oppressors, and those who believed with William Lovett (1800–77) that the strength of their position lay in 'moral force'. Feargus O'Connor, brought up on his father's estates in Dangan Castle, Co. Cork, educated at Trinity, Dublin, called to the Bar, belonged to the colourful and noisy tradition of radical Irish gentry – though he represented in Parliament the English seat of Oldham, vacated by the death of Cobbett. Lovett, a failed cabinet-maker who became a pastry-cook and small-time shopkeeper in London, had founded the London Working Men's Association to 'draw into one bond of unity the intelligent and influential portion of the working classes in town and country, and to seek by every legal means to place all classes of society in possession of equal political and social rights'.[13]

Whether they looked to O'Connor, who was called 'an English Marat',[14] or to the peaceable Lovett, the Chartists shared a conviction (drawn from the socialist ideas of Robert Owen) that labour, being the source of value, was a form of wealth. The labourer, therefore, just as much as the man of property, was entitled to a stake in the political life of the nation. They weren't looking, as Carlyle thought they should have been, for one dynamic figurehead who could bring justice to them. Rather they believed that if every man had the vote, as opposed to the mere 8,000 property-owners of Liverpool, or the 179 of Totnes, then it would follow automatically that the interests of justice and equality would be dispensed from the parliamentary system. Electoral systems, even when the franchise had become universal, were so designed as to moderate, if not actually to thwart, the unruly majority; and to leave as unshaken as was consistent with the principles of decency the small oligarchy who in fact governed, and govern, the nation. In Victorian times this was a largely aristocratic oligarchy, evolving in time into a system of prime ministerial patronage, Cabinet government and a tightly run Civil Service. This system still obtains, so we have no means of knowing whether the ideals of the Chartists, if put into practice, would have brought universal felicity or social anarchy.

William Lovett favoured true universal suffrage, which meant, logically, the extension of the vote to women as well as to men. Other Chartists such as John La Mont and W.J. Linton shared the ideal, but it was not made part of the original Charter – which gives the movement its name – since they did not trust the Spirit of the time. It was felt to be too 'extreme' to suggest that women could vote. Another error. It would probably have made no difference to the eventual fate of the Movement, but there was no shortage of women prepared to support Feargus O'Connor, Lovett and the others.

The Charter itself – The People's Charter and National Petition – was published in May 1838. It had six points, asking for annual parliaments, universal male suffrage, equal electoral districts (to iron out the disparity between Totnes and Liverpool), the removal of the property qualification for membership of Parliament, a secret ballot, and payment for members. The impressiveness of the Charter was in the purity of its political language. That is, Chartism spoke, from first to last, in political terms and for political ends. Though embracing the cause of the disadvantaged and speaking up for the poor, it wasn't a glorified trade union. It was not asking Parliament as then constituted for higher wages or shorter working hours or better housing. It was asking for what it deemed to be a just and a logical political representation, confident that these other benefits would flow inexorably therefrom.

It is important to recognize that Chartism was largely a political reaction to the Whig–Radical alliance which brought in the Reform Act, the new Poor Laws, the police and all the other paraphernalia of control which were to be necessary in a successful liberal economy. In some regards therefore, the Chartists were not so much revolutionaries, still less prototypes of later collectivist solutions to social difficulties, as they were old-fashioned libertarians. Suffrage was the only possible weapon against what felt, if you lived at the bottom end of society, like a repressive coup d'état by the Whigs. In the many riots which the movement provoked, throughout the country, during the first decade of Victoria's reign, the demonstrators usually singled out for aggressive attacks those noted in the locality for their obnoxious political views. In the riots in the Potteries, for instance, it was not so much the employers and the pot banks which were the objects of violence as the Poor Law Commissioners, the unpopular magistrates and the workhouses which were besieged.

The Chartists were occasionally violent – those who favoured O'Connor more than they who read Lovett – but they remained, even when forming themselves into peaceable associations or angry mobs, committed to a belief in an individualism which the growth of industrial cities was itself to undermine.

Their real enemy, therefore, were the big capitalists. *The Northern Star* of 1838 spoke of the Corn Laws (protecting artificially the wealth of the big landed aristocrats) and the horrors of the factory system. 'All have the same end, viz the making of the working classes beasts of burden – hewers of wood and drawers of water – to the aristocracy, Jewocracy, Millocracy,

Shopocracy and every other Ocracy that feeds on human vitals.'[15]

By the end of 1838 the number of public meetings at which O'Connor had made threats or incitements to physical violence had grown so much that there was no hope of the Commons giving the Charter a fair hearing. On 12 July the Commons refused by 235 to 46 votes to consider the national petition, which contained 1,200,000 signatures. Sir Charles Napier (1782–1853) was appointed by Parliament to command of the North of England. Having toured Nottingham, Leeds, Newcastle and Manchester, he lost no time in assembling the Chartist

leaders and telling them that he would 'maul them with cannon and musketry' at the first signs of violence.

The most violent of the outbursts in that eventful and violent year of 1839 – which saw riots in Birmingham, Lovett and O'Connor imprisoned, and the hardening of government hearts against the Charter – came in Newport, South Wales. Several thousand men from the Welsh mining and ironworking valleys marched on the town in an attempt to take it over. The leaders included a linen draper named John Frost, who was a former magistrate and mayor of Newport. The invaders were beaten off by troops firing from the Westgate Hotel, with the loss of at least twenty-two lives, and the dispersal of the workers' army was followed by a large number of arrests. Frost and other ringleaders were sentenced to death for high treason.[16]

No one who read the news from Newport or from Birmingham could doubt the resolve of the propertied classes to protect their own. This would persist, even when Lord Melbourne was voted from office in 1839 – on a matter which also had bearings on the rights of humankind, but which concerned another vital ingredient in the Victorian success story: the colonies.

*Two British officers
of the East India Company
entertained by music,
c. 1820.*

Typhoon Coming On

Whether the British Empire grew up by accident or design or by the inexorable movement of economic force is one of the questions which the reader of these pages will have decided by the end of the Victorian period. The heyday of Imperial colonization belongs to a later generation than the one we are considering here. At the beginning of the reign the East India Company, rather than the government in Westminster, still took responsibility for the administration of 'British India'. The huge expanses of Africa which would be painted red on the Imperial map were still uncharted. The attitude in London towards the colonies was both looser and less formal than would be the case at the close of the nineteenth century.

The importance of Jamaica, the largest island in the British West Indies, was both emblematic and commercial. It had been a British colony since 1655, when the Cromwellian navy, led by Admirals Penn and Venables, had taken the island from the Spanish. Jamaica had a bloody history. Its peaceable native inhabitants, the Arawak Indians, had been systematically annihilated by the conquistadors in 1509. Thereafter, its rich and exotic harvests, primarily of sugar, but also of coffee, cocoa, pimento and ginger, were cultivated by slave labour, imported from West Africa. Thus, from the beginning of British involvement with this Caribbean island it had been a source of wealth purveyed by the hands of the oppressed.

One fact which united almost all British shades of opinion in the years after the Napoleonic wars was pride in having abolished the slave trade. But although, thanks to the philanthropic enterprise of William Wilberforce and the other campaigners, the trade had been banned in all lands that were co-signatories to the Congress of Vienna (1814–15), the *ownership* of slaves persisted for another eighteen years in British colonies such as Jamaica. In 1832, when they heard a Reform Bill had been passed in London, the Jamaican slaves believed that they were at last free, and there was a rebellion. Emancipation came two years later.

British self-congratulation on the subject was tempered by commercial self-interest. The abolition of slavery had already, even before the emancipation of the Demerara slaves, led to a disparity in world sugar prices. The price of sugar in Great Britain was 7½d. per lb, while Cuban or Brazilian sugar of higher quality, harvested by slaves, sold abroad for 4½d. per lb.[1] Logically, a nation which was converting itself to an out-and-out belief in Free Trade should have recognized this as the luck of the draw. The fact that the South Americans were undercutting British planters and traders, however, added a keen edge to the British moral outrage against Brazilian slavers. The foreign secretary, Lord Palmerston, who was not noted for his championship of human rights on his own Irish estates for example, had no hesitation in sending British warships into Brazilian ports and flushing out any ships they found being fitted for the slave trade.[2] Biffing the Brazilians, damaging their sugar and coffee trade while maintaining a high moral tone, was good for morale.

Palmerston, who would become one of Victoria's prime ministers at the age of seventy, was hugely popular with a certain type of Englishman.[3] His swashbuckling, vulgar belief in British intervention in every corner of the globe – now in Egypt, now in China – was largely driven by commerce. Expansion abroad, which would turn into the full-scale Imperial expansion seen in the mid-1850s onwards, went hand in hand with the rapid growth of industry at home.

Meanwhile, disguising beneath a genuine moral self-belief the venality of their commercial interests, the British took on the role of global policemen. The Royal Navy went in pursuit of slave ships partly no doubt with the fervour of moral liberators, partly influenced by the fact that they could earn 'head money' for the number of slaves liberated. The slavers in turn could claim insurance for cargo – i.e. slaves – lost at sea, but not for slaves who died on board. It was therefore a common occurrence, if a Royal Navy vessel pursued a slaver, that she would cast her 'cargo' into the ocean, still in chains, as a feast for the sharks. Turner's *Slavers Throwing Overboard the Dead and Dying – Typhoon Coming On*, exhibited at the Academy in 1840, depicts just such a gruesome scene. The great sunset blaze reflects on a heaving sea. The writhing forms of slaves in the foreground could be sea-serpents. They are part of the cruelty of nature itself. There is an Homeric pitilessness about the canvas, though the fiery decline of the sun tells its own tale of endings and finishings behind the old masts of the obsolescent sailing ship. The sun is going down violently and angrily on the old world. The coming typhoon boils as it contemplates the horror of what the ship, and the sea, contain.[4] The picture is in a sense a companion-piece to Turner's canvas of the burning of the Parliament buildings.

Doubts there were aplenty – in individuals, in groups, in society at large – about the Condition of England question (Carlyle's phrase from *Past and Present*), about the relations between Britain and the rest of the world, about religion and science, about social justice: but we who live in a fragmented society have become like an individual addicted to psychoanalysis, struggle with our uncertainties, pick at our virtues and vices as if they were scabs. The Victorian capacity *not* to do this, to live,

Slavers Throwing Overboard the Dead and Dying – Typhoon Coming On ('The Slave Ship') *by J.M.W. Turner. 'I believe,' wrote John Ruskin, 'if I were reduced to rest Turner's immortality upon any single work, I should choose this.'*

very often, with double standards, is what makes so many of them – individually and collectively – seem to be humbugs and hypocrites.

All these things bubbled beneath the surface when Lord Melbourne, in 1839, found himself faced with an intransigent Jamaica Assembly. Eight hundred thousand negroes on the island became fully and unconditionally free on 1 August 1838.[5] The planters were offered £15 million in compensation. The British government tried to take things further and insist upon an improvement in the conditions in Jamaican prisons. This the assembly in Kingston, Jamaica (overwhelmingly made up of white planters but containing some 'coloureds'),[6] refused to do. It became, in effect, an issue of confidence. Melbourne put it to the vote in Parliament and the Tory Party defeated the Whigs by five votes. Melbourne resigned.

Historians of the period tend, as did newspapers of the time, to turn with some relief from the trivial fate of 800,000 emancipated men and women in the Caribbean – how they should work, eat, earn their livings, how their former owners could be expected to make a living in an increasingly competitive world market – and to concentrate on the high drama of the Bedchamber Crisis. Jamaica, as far as history is concerned, can be forgotten for another quarter-century before it awakens anyone's attention when Governor Eyre (1815–1901) split British opinion by the severity with which he suppressed a negro rebellion.

Queen Victoria, in 1839, was far more troubled by the thought of being deprived of her hours of playing draughts with Lord Melbourne. Sir Robert Peel was a very different sort of man. The Queen failed to understand that it was perfectly normal for incoming prime ministers to propose new members of the royal household. As a mark of confidence, Peel asked her to replace some of the Whig ladies of the bedchamber with the wives of Tory noblemen. She refused, and Peel declined to take office. The Melbourne administration therefore hobbled on towards a disastrous election defeat in 1841 – by which time the young Queen had further demeaned the monarchy in the public eye by falsely accusing one of her ladies-in-waiting, Lady Flora Hastings, of being pregnant. (Her swollen appearance was owing to cancer.) Small wonder that the House of Commons, particularly on the Tory side, enjoyed baiting the Queen when she chose as her husband Prince Albert of Saxe-Coburg.

Albert, only six months short of his twenty-first birthday when he married, was a highly cultivated person, of well above average intelligence, with an impressive range of gifts and interests. Baron Stockmar's approving comment was: 'He shows not the slightest interest in politics . . . while declaring that the Augsburg *Allgemeine Zeitung* is the only paper one wants or that is worth reading, he does not even read it.'[7] Such indifference to politics made Albert an ideal consort in a constitutional monarchy. In a broader sense however, he was highly aware of politics, intelligently conscious of the enormous changes which had come about in modern society as a result of the French Revolution and its aftermath, and of industrialization. He and his brother had studied at Bonn University. Old Beethoven had not long since walked its streets – Albert was an impressive musician whose *Lieder* stand comparison with many minor composers. (He's certainly better than Parry or Vaughan Williams.) He was taught literature by A.W. von Schlegel and attended Fichte's philosophy classes, absorbing perhaps that Idealism (in the philosophical sense) which was to be a marked feature of the English intellectual scene a generation later. He was also – thanks to the dreadful emotional chaos in which he had grown up – deeply committed to the notion of loyal family life. He was energetic. He was ardently desirous to do good. No wonder it took him some time to settle in.

Monuments to Albert's range of abilities remain visible to this day: first of which was the glorious Italianate palazzo on the Isle of Wight – Osborne, with its impressive sculpture-gallery and its collection of Winterhalter masterpieces. (The interiors were much cluttered and spoilt in the long years of Victoria's widowhood.) Then there was the Gothic baronial of Balmoral, an allusion to the beloved Schloss Rosenau where Albert had grown up. Both these residences, fascinating in themselves as tributes to the eclecticism and intelligence of Albert's taste, are also embodiments of his wise attitude to modern constitutional monarchy. He saw that as well as having official residences where they were always on display, always at the mercy of politicking, they should cultivate private lives and private virtues.

Albert's improvements at Windsor, his reordering and management of the estates and the farms, his building of a beautiful and efficient dairy, still operative to this day, are further tributes to his good taste. His model housing in Kennington, built on the very site of the last Chartist demonstration, and the huge museum complex in Kensington which some call the Albertopolis, are further reminders of the depth and range of his contribution to English public life.

His first two gifts to the British people were more

personal. Primarily and most importantly, he made Victoria a happy woman. She was highly sexed and she worshipped her husband. From the first 'gratifying and bewildering night' as she described it to Lord Melbourne, the Queen was crazy about Albert. 'YOU CANNOT IMAGINE HOW DELIGHTFUL IT IS TO BE MARRIED. I COULD NOT HAVE DREAMED THAT ANYONE COULD BE SO HAPPY IN THIS WORLD AS I AM,' she wrote in her childish capitals to her cousin Victo (Victoria Augusta Antoinetta).[8]

Albert made her value private life. Although she did take an interfering interest in political affairs, he ensured that for most of the century she was at home, a private individual – until his death she was at the centre of family life, after it she retreated into the shadows for decades. Constitutional monarchy thrives on this low-key approach.

In so far as she did take a political interest in her early married life, Albert – and this was his second great early gift to the nation – persuaded her to drop her girlish tendresse for the Whigs and to see that by far the most important and intelligent political figure of the age was not Lord M. with his charming drawing-room manners, but Sir Robert Peel.

Chapter Five

The Age of Peel

Sir Robert Peel was the last prime minister of whom no photograph was ever taken.[1] Even the Duke of Wellington sat to a daguerreotypist. Sir Robert Peel remains discreetly in the shadows of the past. It seems characteristic. He was unshowy, sensible, brilliant. He was, in what he did and in his own person, a transitional figure of crucial importance. At the beginning of his premiership England, for all the changes which had been taking place since the battle of Waterloo, was still of the old world. By the time he left office, after his dramatic volte-face over the Corn Laws, the new world had come into being. Britain had become an out-and-out free-trading nation. Partly because the tariffs were lifted, and capitalism was given a free rein, partly because the economic cycle was in any event moving into a phase of quite unprecedented and extraordinary stability, fifty or sixty years of sound money were about to be ushered in. Private investors placed their money with the disciples of expanding industry and reaped not merely unparalleled riches but unprecedented leisure.

Peel is a Janus figure at this crucial and exciting pivot of time. On the one hand, what could be more *ancien régime* than his parliamentary career, seen solely from the position of *representation*? From 1830 he sat for his small home borough of Tamworth, which his father had earlier represented. The electorate stood at only 528 in 1832. Twenty years later, Peel himself was dead and the electorate had fallen to 307. Yet many of the innovations which we should most associate with the political progress of the nineteenth century – Catholic Emancipation for example in 1829, Free Trade in 1846 – came about because of Peel's own distinctive vision of things. The paradox of English political history is that the most radical changes are often introduced by Conservatives. Janus Peel, a very rich baronet who led a party which was in effect a coalition – one destined most dramatically to split asunder over the question of Free Trade – was the heir to fortunes made not from generations of landowning, but from capitalism. It was a cotton fortune. Peel belonged to the thriving, thrusting, Darwinian new class. His grandfather had pioneered calico-printing in Blackburn; and with the money made in this great Northern industrial enterprise Peel's father, the first Baronet, had acquired the estate of Drayton Manor in Staffordshire, near Tamworth.

There were, however, some formidable obstacles in the path of his, and Britain's, success. They make the period of his premiership so eventful that almost every month brought some form or another of crisis. There were four fundamental factors in play. The first, broadly, was the Condition of England question, the seething discontent of the poor and in particular the apparent successes and popularity, so alarming to the ruling powers, of the Chartist movement. The second was the Irish question, a lingering political problem which all British governments, in all areas, have had a tendency to bungle, but which in Peel's day

Queen Victoria in the House of Lords. Pugin was an inspired decorator – the House of Cards effect of the Chamber of the House of Lords, particularly when filled for a State Opening with peers in scarlet robes, the Sovereign in a crown, heralds in tabards and the rest, makes the spectator gasp.

was exacerbated by a calamity of Biblical proportions – that is, the famine. The third, deeply connected to both these issues, to the position of Britain in the world, and to all the social changes we have been discussing, was the issue of Free Trade in general, the Corn Laws in particular; and the fourth, obviously consequent on these three, and other issues, was the political composition of the two Houses of Parliament, the actual men who in one House by inheritance, in the other by a very exclusive voting system, were taking their seats. For it was after all the parties within Parliament who determined the success or otherwise of Sir Robert Peel's ambitions and enterprises.[2] We shall consider them in the reverse of the order just listed, but it is important to remember how much they all interconnected.

The new Parliament building which, very slowly, was a-building during this period was satisfyingly symbolic of some of the multi-stranded themes which come together in any consideration of the period. After the fire, the Lords were squeezed into the surviving Painted Chamber at Westminster, and the Commons sat in the Court of Requests.[3] Both these magnificent rooms were destined to be demolished when Charles Barry's (1795–1860) winning designs for the new Palace of Westminster were put into effect. The very Painted Chamber where Edward the Confessor had died and Charles I's death warrant had been signed would be replaced by neo-Tudor Gothic, bright as a stage set.

The committee that set the competition for the new Houses of Parliament had specified that the designs should be in a Gothic or Elizabethan style. Clearly, as one whose infant eyes had first focused on the Gothic traceries of Westminster Abbey and who was as familiar with medieval Westminster as had been the infant William Blake, Barry favoured a Gothic style.

Having won the competition in 1836, he faced a series of problems before the building could so much as begin. First, there was opposition in the Commons at the proposed expense (£800,000 over six years). Barry's unsuccessful rivals in the competition then got up a petition to change the specifications to the Greek or Roman style.

There is no doubt that the British would think of themselves differently if their parliamentary buildings resembled the Assemblée Nationale in Paris or the Senate in Washington DC. Barry's solid Tudor Gothic, embellished (one is tempted to say camped up) by the florid ornamentations of Augustus Welby Northmore Pugin (1812–52), makes, as they say, a statement. These buildings say, on the one hand, we are new as paint. We are so self-confidently new that we are prepared to pull down some of the historic old rooms which survived the fire. On the other hand they say that, like the lineage of Sir Leicester Dedlock, we are old as the hills and infinitely more respectable.

More than an aesthetic statement is being made by the choice of late Gothic, with many Tudor elements. Most parliamentarians, and perhaps most men and women in the Age of Peel, believed that to be British was *ipso facto* to be Protestant. (Here was one of the sticking points in the whole tragic story of failed understanding between England and Ireland.) As Edward White Benson helpfully explained when a Birmingham schoolboy to his fellow scholar Lightfoot, 'you must know that the Roman Church may be a true church in Italy but in England it is not only in error but in heresy and schismatical'.[4] Anthony Froude spoke for the huge majority of his compatriots when he said that the Reformation was the decisive, the key event in English history. Tennyson saw it as 'the dawning of a new age; for after the era of priestly domination comes the era of the freedom of the individual'.[5]

Barry's Parliament buildings had to suggest, therefore, not so much the monastic past of the Middle Ages as the world of new families – Horners, Cecils – who took their lands from the old monastic foundations: a world when Britain, led by a young Queen and standing independent of Europe, sent forth its adventurers on the seas to discover new territories, poised for its golden age of mercantile property, religious freedom, literary flowering. That was the world, semi-mystical, half true, that Barry had to summon up. He also had to bring to life the one element of medieval tradition of which the Parliamentary Committees who paid his fees heartily approved – the medieval peerage. His Palace of Westminster was therefore to evoke a Middle Ages gutted of its central ideological *raison d'être* – namely Catholicism. The post-1689 oligarchic system of government, the Whiggish idea of an aristocracy importing and sustaining its own constitutional monarch, could be dressed up in the fancy dress of Pugin and Barry to portray a continuity with feudal times.

To a twenty-first-century reader, such notions perhaps seem bizarre, even comic. So they did to the more facetious of Barry's contemporaries. But political realities are reflected here. Immediately opposite the

One of Pugin's floor designs for the Houses of Parliament, making a modern building possess instant, ready-made medieval 'tradition'.

Green 1.
Pink 2
White 3
Blue 4
Red 5
Brown 6

swampy building site on which Barry proposed to build his political sermon in stones, on the other side of Westminster Bridge, was Astley's famous Amphitheatre, where shows which were part circus, part historical *tableaux vivants* showed to packed audiences. As well as such exciting shows as *The Storming of Seringapatam and the Death of Tippoo Sahib* or *The Conquest of Mexico* there were medieval extravaganzas – *The Battle of Agincourt* or the tournament from Sir Walter Scott's *Ivanhoe*. Wildly popular too with the public in the early years of the reign was the newly opened museum at the Tower of London, showing Queen Elizabeth I's armoury, twenty gleaming knights arranged historically in their armour from Henry VI in 1450 to James II in 1685. This genuine nostalgia for some medieval fantasy-past was reflected in Peel's Parliament with the presence of the Young England movement.[6]

They were mainly aristocrats, just down from Cambridge: George Smythe, later 7th Viscount Strangford; Lord John Manners, later 6th Duke of Rutland; Alexander Cochrane-Baillie, later ennobled as Lord Lamington. They were not perhaps very serious figures in themselves but they became the friends and allies of Benjamin Disraeli, now thirty-five years old, intensely ambitious, and not so lucky as Gladstone, whom Peel had made a junior minister. Disraeli had written to Peel begging for office, but he had been humiliatingly rebuffed. He was to have his revenge, being an incessant enemy of Peel's in the House of Commons and mobilizing that opposition which prime ministers most dread – opposition from his own ranks.

What a Parliament that was! Peel had the Earl of Aberdeen as foreign secretary, Lord Stanley as colonial secretary, and young W.E. Gladstone as his vice president of the Board of Trade and master of the Mint – that is three future prime ministers in the government, and the old Duke of Wellington still active for the Tories in the Lords. Then, just look at the benches of the House of Commons! Liberal Radicals represented by figures as various and impressive as Richard Cobden, the great apostle of Free Trade, or Henry Labouchere who (with Bradlaugh) was to have so momentous an effect on the perception of the established religion and its place in parliamentary life; the glorious eccentric 'Ultra' Tory Colonel Sibthorp in his white nankeen trousers, large white hat, and huge top-boots, thundering against every innovation, from railways to the Prince Consort; Dr Thomas Wakley, founder of *The Lancet*; Thomas Babington Macaulay, representing Edinburgh; Richard Monckton Milnes – friend of Swinburne, and keeper of

Keats's flame; Lord Palmerston; Lord Ashley (better known to history as the 7th Earl of Shaftesbury), Tory champion of the poor! This isn't to mention Daniel O'Connell, representing the seats of both Meath and Cork – which must somehow be a version of the Irish electoral principle to vote early, vote often; Alexander Pringle; Sir Charles Napier.

A galaxy of stars who make our modern parliaments seem very undistinguished indeed. In this Parliament, Disraeli saw Young England as rallying the country diehards against Peel, and perhaps even attracting some of the Radicals. He reckoned that out of Peel's majority of 90 seats there were 'between 40 and 50 agricultural malcontents' – country Tories who distrusted Peel even before his volte-face on the Corn Laws, who were Protestant bigots to a man and who might have been prepared to wound or dethrone Peel on a number of issues.

Disraeli's feelings for Young England – so much younger and more nobly born than himself – have an element of romanticism, perhaps even (for all his early love affairs and his devoted marriage to a widow, Mary Anne Wyndham Lewis, years older than himself) tinged with a hint of homoeroticism, and are poured out in his trilogy of novels *Coningsby*, *Sybil* and *Tancred*.

It was always the Tory contention that the Whigs ruled by a sleight of hand, holding together an unpleasant alliance of Nonconformist killjoys and big landowners. The vision of Disraeli's novels is substantially the same as in his *Vindication of the English Constitution*, where he wrote that 'the Tory party in this country is the national party; it is the really democratic party of England. It supports the institutions of the country, because they have been established for the common good, and because they secure the equality of civil rights, without which, whatever may be its name, no government can be free, and based upon which principle, every government, however it may be styled, is in fact a Democracy.'[7]

The great difficulty with the Romantic–Aristocratic point of view was a religious one. Barry could imply with an architectural sleight of hand that Catholicism did not exist. Perhaps it was even possible to do so when discussing England in the 1840s. Where Ireland was in question, however, it was less easy. So it was that while Disraeli managed in the early sessions of Peel's Parliament to persuade his young friends that he could manipulate votes ('*Most private*' – Smythe wrote to Manners in 1842 – 'Dizzy has much more parliamentary power than I had any notion of . . .'), by 1845 the Young

POPERY OR NO POPERY? THAT IS THE QUESTION! OR JOHN BULL IN A FIX.

LONDON: PUBLISHED BY E. LLOYD, 12, SALISBURY-SQUARE, FLEET-STREET.

A no-Popery cartoon of 1850. Instinctive English distrust of Catholicism was enormously exacerbated by fear of Ireland.

England alliance largely came unstuck over the (by twenty-first-century standards) unlikely and arcane issue of a government grant to the Roman Catholic seminary of Maynooth. The Young Englanders who had fantasized about the recreation of a medieval past, and who had even praised a scheme (more optimistic than realistic) for the reunion of the two Churches, Rome and Canterbury, voted separate ways over Maynooth and thereafter, as a political entity, were finished.

The controversy over the Maynooth grant was one of the more striking examples provided by history of the English political classes working themselves into a fury of ignorance and prejudice over a matter which seemed trivial with hindsight. Maynooth, or to give it its full name, the Royal College of St Patrick at Maynooth, had been established when Pitt was prime minister. It was called a Royal College at the special request of George

III. It was – and is – the chief training-college for priests in Ireland. The grant of £9,000 per annum which had been given it by the Irish Parliament in 1795 was annually renewed by the Westminster Parliament after the Irish one was suspended, but in 1845 it was seriously inadequate. The priests and students lived in considerable hardship there and Peel was sensible enough to see – given the influence these young men would have in Ireland when they went out to become priests or bishops – that maltreating the seminarians was not a very good way of improving Anglo–Irish relations.

Considerations such as this, and of simple justice, prompted Peel to propose backing up his reforms of Irish schools, to which he granted more money in his Academic Institutions (Ireland) Act, with a decent annual grant to Maynooth – £26,360[8] annually, with a further £30,000 for upkeep of the buildings, and with a commitment that the grant would be steady. The college would not have to come to Parliament each year cap in hand.[9]

Peel got this measure through, but not without a tremendous fight. He admitted that he was surprised by the intensity of the hostility. The opponents, who had not mounted a campaign in any of the previous fifty years of the college's existence, behaved and spoke as if Peel had encroached upon some matter of principle. Anti-Catholic prejudice, rank and sour, rose into the public air.

'No Popery' was deep in the English psyche, but like most prejudices it was capable of selectivity. When the British annexed Corsica in 1794 they had declared that 'the Roman Catholic is the only national religion of Corsica'. Here was an island which George III had actually insisted be Catholic![10] In Malta, Mauritius and French-speaking Canada, the Crown had given money to the Church.

The Maynooth controversy exposed the peculiar nature of English attitudes to the Irish. To concede the fact that the Irish were predominantly of a different Christian denomination undermined the confidence of the British and their Church. Gladstone, full of High Church zeal, had written a book, first published in 1839, entitled *The State in its Relations with the Church* in which he argued vehemently that it was the function of the British state to propagate the practice of the Anglican faith. Macaulay in a devastating review reduced the young Etonian bigot's arguments to a nonsense.

Ridiculously, Gladstone resigned from Peel's government over the issue of the Maynooth Grant on a point of principle so obscure that no one understood it. Between the years 1839 and 1845 he had seen the error of his *Church and State*. He was in favour of Maynooth getting its increased grant in 1845 but, because he had written in the terms so ridiculed by Macaulay in 1839, he felt he must resign in 1845.

*

Sir Robert Peel's common-sense conservatism was based on such a creed as Sydney Smith's – that the object of good government was a contented, well-fed and well-behaved populace. That, quite simply, explains why he was prepared to take on his own party in Parliament, and in effect to destroy the Tories' electoral fortunes for twenty years. To his supporters Peel would always seem a fundamentally decent, sensible man, a man of principle, perhaps the last truly sensible prime minister until the rise of Salisbury. For Peel's High Tory opponents he would always be the ultimate opportunist, changing one

of the cardinal doctrines of the party in order to stay in office. Parallels with modern political struggles flicker in any commentator's mind; one thinks naturally of the agonies of the Conservative Party in the last decade of the twentieth, the opening decade of the twenty-first centuries, over their membership of the European Union. The greatest historian of the Conservative Party, Lord Blake, says that it was one of those extraordinary moments in English history, such as the Abdication of Edward VIII or the Munich crisis, when the whole nation was divided. Families split over it, friendships were broken. Once Peel's decision had been made, the Tory Party, 'The party of Pitt, Perceval, Liverpool, Canning, Wellington and Peel vanished in "smoke and confusion".'[11] Afterwards, the parties reformed. The Peelites either drifted with nowhere to go, or joined up with the Liberal Party which had emerged from an alliance of Whigs and Radicals. The diehards who had persisted in wanting the price of bread to be kept artificially high were led in the Lords by Lord Stanley, in the Commons by Lord George Bentinck, with Benjamin Disraeli as his rather improbable campaigner and lieutenant.

For ten years at least, there had been an active campaign against the protectionist laws designed to subsidize the English rural economy and keep out the import of cheap foreign corn. The movement centred on Manchester, John Bright, a textile manufacturer from Rochdale, being one of its leading lights, the other Richard Cobden, MP for Manchester and one of the first aldermen in the city. From the outset, the Anti-Corn Law League which they formed had aimed its sights at the political power of the aristocracy. Corn Law Repeal was much more important in this respect than the electoral reforms of 1842. 'The sooner,' said Cobden in one of his speeches, 'the sooner the power in this country is transferred from the landed oligarchy, which has so misused it, and is placed absolutely – mind I say absolutely – in the hands of the intelligent middle and industrious classes, the better for the condition and destinies of this country.'[12] Cobden believed that wars had been the sport of aristocrats, and that Free Trade would bring not merely wealth to Britain but peace to the world.

Not everyone agreed. The Chartists, on the whole, inclined to the view that British agriculture needed government aid and subsidies by means of keeping the price of wheat – hence of bread – artificially high. They suspected the Free Traders' motives, believing that Northern capitalists like Bright only wanted cheap bread so that they could lower the wages of their workers.

Peel, like his ultra-Tory backbenchers, had fought the election of 1841 as an opponent of the repeal of the Corn Laws, but he had never been an anti-Free Trade fanatic; his budgets were all in the direction of Free Trade. All the economic arguments began to pile up on the side of repealing the Corn Laws.

Given the social, economic and political situation of England in the mid-1840s it was inevitable that at some stage protectionism would be abandoned and Free Trade would win, as the market so often does. The vast increases in productivity and manufacturing which were happening while the Corn Laws were being debated were changing the nature of England. Railway mania had struck. By 1848, around 5,000 miles of line were working in the United Kingdom – only 400 of them in Ireland, a fact of dire omen. Five railway companies had built lines to Brighton, three to Norwich. The combination of private investment and improved means of production and transport prepared for an astonishing boom which would inevitably have the long-term effect of improving the cost of living for all but agricultural labourers and those whose livelihood came solely from native-grown crops.[13] Even within agriculture itself there was some economic buoyancy, with new fertilizers – nitrate of soda and guano – now in common use, and new crops: the swede and the mangel-wurzel came to be used increasingly, an invaluable feed, far more frost-resistant than other root crops. As for the wheat harvests – they had not been good – 1842, 1843 and 1844 saw a fall in the price of corn of 14s., momentarily halting the demand to lift the tariff and bring in foreign grain at a cheaper price.

But then came 1845, a disastrously wet summer and the rains which, as it was said, washed the Corn Laws away. Peel took the ultimate risk – he waged war on his own party. Rather than resign and hand the 'poisoned chalice' of Corn Law repeal to the Liberal leader Lord John Russell, he did what he deemed honourable and proposed their repeal from his position as Conservative prime minister. So the Corn Laws were abolished. The 'Ultras', the country Tories egged on by Disraeli, took their revenge by voting Peel out of power over the Irish Coercion Bill. Wellington called the alliance against Peel – Whigs and Ultra Protectionists who in turn agreed on no matter of principle – the 'blackguard combination'.[14] Thus ended the old Tory Party and the career of the best leader that party had ever had.

By then the government was faced by a problem of much wider and more sinister significance than the breaking and mending of political alliances in Westminster. The greatest single human disaster to befall the European continent in that century had begun its mortal work.

Chapter Six

Famine in Ireland

While the human population of Europe, Asia – eventually the Americas – collapsed before the imperial invasion of King Cholera, another devastation was making its way to Europe: the fungal disease *Phytophthora infestans* or potato blight. It came to the Netherlands, to Belgium and to Scotland, all countries with a population of poor agrarian workers, but also with an expanding industrial life, comparatively sophisticated road or rail networks, and the will and capacity in case of hardship to help those afflicted. Of course there was hunger and wretchedness in those countries, particularly in Scotland. But it was nothing to compare in size or scale or horror with the Great Irish Famine. To the scale of the Irish disaster itself must be added the political aftermath of distrust and hatred, with us all to this day.

This view is largely endorsed by modern historians. No one doubts the scale of the calamity. Nor is it in question that successive British administrations were incompetent, even callous. Given the nature of Ireland in 1845, however, the actual physical, social and political situation, it is hard to see how the Famine could have been averted. The modern reader is aghast at the unfolding narratives of suffering which any account of the Famine will provide. But in the circumstances, and *at the time*, it is hard to see what a different government, even a government based in Dublin, could have done. True, good landlords (of whom there were all too few) could alleviate suffering *in some measure* on their estates. True, the continued trade in corn, when the famine was at its height, was avoidable, causes anguish to read about today, and caused worse than anguish to the starving who watched Irish corn being *exported* from Cork and elsewhere. But given the social hierarchies which existed at the time, and the political tensions which already overshadowed Anglo-Irish relations, one knows that it is as unrealistic to have expected a modern-style famine relief operation as it is to have expected Lord John Russell's government to take maize to County Kerry by helicopter.

The story of the famine is therefore truly tragic, the more so when we consider the fact that those very benefits for which the Liberals campaigned so vociferously on the British mainland were, as our historian implies, more nails in the Irish coffin. Early Victorian Liberalism was posited on the notion of less state interference, not more. The idea that states were responsible for the welfare of citizens was horrifying to laissez-faire economists. Combine the idea of laissez-faire with those of Malthus and you end up, as we have seen, with workhouses, designed specifically to encourage effort and self-help on the part of the poor.

The economic benefits, in terms of the overall enrichment of society, were already being seen in the industrialized North. By 1845, the Benthamites had influenced the political attitudes of a generation. They had a natural distrust of the idea of state aid. Create what would later be called a dependency culture and you

Irish tenant farmers in the Duke of Devonshire's photographic studio, Lismore Castle, County Waterford. This photograph was taken in 1853, a few years after the height of the Irish potato famine.

will end up with national bankruptcy. So, when the extent of the famine came to be known, there is found an instinctive reluctance on the part of the state to do anything – either in terms of welfare, or, still less, in terms of economic protectionism. Had they not just spent ten painful years campaigning for the lifting of protection on corn? Were they to throw that away because the Irish were hungry?

And here, the darker and quite undeniable fact of anti-Irish prejudice comes into play. The atavistic and irrational feelings which were provoked by the matter of the Maynooth Grant were not going to evaporate because of the sad stories which began to reach England in the late summer of 1845. In fact, the religious prejudices unearthed by the Maynooth affair only confirmed, for many English Protestants, their Malthusian hunches about the improvident and (as they believed) superstitious population of the Other Island.

> It is awful to observe how the Almighty humbles the pride of Nations. The Sword, the Pestilence and Famine are the instruments of his displeasure: the canker-worm and the locust are his armies, he gives the word: a single copy is blighted; and we see a Nation prostrate, stretching out its Hands for Bread. These are solemn warnings, and they fill me with reverence; they proclaim with a voice not to be mistaken, that 'doubtless there is a God who judgeth the Earth!'[1]

These are not the words of an Ulster demagogue preaching on a street corner, nor even of an evangelical bishop. They are the home secretary Sir James Graham writing to Sir Robert Peel. The Prime Minister broadly shared Graham's religious viewpoint. These were the *moderates* of the day. There were plenty who saw the Famine as a punishment for idolatry.

What is called the Great Famine was in fact a series of calamities continuing over a number of years. The basic facts are these. The first fungus struck the Irish potato crops in the summer of 1845. Some parts of Ireland escaped altogether, but about one-third of the overall potato crop was lost. By 1846, with the blight making deeper predations, three-quarters of the crop was lost. By 1847, yields were a little better, but little had been planted by the despairing population who had eaten their seed potatoes. By 1848, crops were back to about two-thirds of the normal, though it was not until 1850 that the worst was over.

During this period, the government changed. Peel, technically defeated over an Irish Coercion Bill in the House of Commons, had in reality, as we have seen, fallen foul of his own party over the repeal of the Corn Laws. His immediate reaction, on hearing of the failure of the 1845 potato crop, was to create schemes of public works. In this way 140,000 jobs were created, and he also spent £100,000 on imported maize from America to be sold cheaply to those in need. This did provide some relief, but for the relief to be effectual, it would have been necessary to get the grain to the mouths who needed it the most. Apart from the fact that there were only 400 miles of railways in the whole of Ireland,[2] ports on the west coast were non-existent. There were almost no harbours where a grain-ship could pull in.

Peel's comparatively charitable practical help was not followed up with much enthusiasm by the Liberal government of Lord John Russell, which came to power in the summer of 1846. After a year of untold sufferings in Ireland, there was, quite unrelated, a British banking crisis in 1847. The famine had now been afflicting Ireland for two years, killing hundreds of thousands of people and forcing others to emigrate. There *was* relief given to famine-sufferers by the British government – perhaps £7 million from a government which believed spending to be wicked and which had convinced itself that it was strapped for cash. It is only fair to note that seven years later the British government found £70 million to finance the Crimean War.[3]

How many died – and why? It is the second question which explains the gross, the truly terrible answer to the first. Indeed one needs to answer the question *why* the famine happened in at least two ways. It is very much not a simple question of one particular fungal disease destroying one tuber, though that is where one begins.

The population of Ireland by 1845 had probably reached some 8.3 million. True, it had increased dramatically over the years, as had the populations of other European countries, but apart from isolated cases of hunger in times of bad harvest, cases which could be (and usually had been) dealt with by the charity of landlords or others in the locality, there was no obvious sense in which this was an island incapable of feeding itself.

The way in which this population sustained itself, however, can be seen with the eyes of hindsight to be calamitous. The potato blight might have been a nuisance, or worse than a nuisance, to those farming twenty acres or more. The evidence suggests that none of these comparatively small farmers (still less the larger landowners) died of starvation. The big divide in Irish society was not so much between landlord and tenant as between those with at least twenty acres and those with less, or none. The great majority of Irish

This cartoon of the 1830s, mocking the state of Ireland, is chilling in the light of the later famine: 'It's starving we are.'

peasants farmed little strips of land, and their only crop was the potato. Few of them it would seem ever went fishing, on the plenteous inland waters of Ireland, nor did they put to sea as the Welsh, Scotch and Cornish had done, time out of mind, returning with plentiful supplies of fish. The potato was the ideal crop for a peasant economy, an agrarian world which had been unaffected by any of the momentous changes which had come upon the English countryside. The potato needed next to no maintenance, as a crop. You simply planted it, watched it grow, harvested and ate it.

The big landlords owned the place, the prosperous tenant farmers did well out of the arrangement. Inevitably, there was more thieving in this type of economy than there was in England, so Irish crime figures for the period are always higher than English. To English contemporaries this proved that the Irish were feckless, dishonest, potentially violent. The reality is that if you started from scratch and invented a society

such as that controlled by the Protestant Ascendancy in Ireland, in which the bottom 4 (out of 8+) million were given no educational or economic advantages or incentives, they would end up, very much as the Irish peasantry did end up, cultivating very small patches of land and doing little else besides. It was simply appalling bad luck that this very deprived and numerous group of people subsisted on one tuber alone which, since its introduction in the seventeenth century, had given no sign or indication that it would fail. It was the reliability of the spud, as well as the ease of growing it, which made it the favoured peasant food. Two million acres of Ireland were given over to potatoes. *Three million people ate nothing else*. Nothing. (Adult males consumed between twelve and fourteen pounds daily.)

All visitors to Ireland in pre-famine days were shocked by the poverty of the peasants. Froude, in 1841, saw, in Galway, 'the rags insufficient to cover the children and boys of twelve running about absolutely naked . . .

The inhabitants, except where they had been taken in hand and metamorphosed into police, seemed more like tribes of squalid apes than human beings.'[4] 'Only magnificent châteaux and miserable cabins are to be seen in Ireland,' said a French observer. All noted the mud floors, peat roofs and insanitary conditions in which the rural poor were housed.[5]

Comparable scenes were perhaps to be found in England, where the wages of agricultural labourers had started to fall badly behind those of the hired industrial workers in the factories. But England, because its economy was based on industry, and on the investment of the rentier class, was immeasurably richer and stronger than Ireland. The Irish landlords varied enormously. In areas where the landlord was compassionate, starvation was often averted. In many cases, however, landlords showed no mercy or were absent. Peasants who lived on estates with absentee landlords could often expect no pity from the small prosperous tenant farmers or the estate managers. Prosperous farmers continued, through the famine years, to prosecute starving labourers caught stealing food from their fields. They refused money wages to those unable to pay in advance for their 'conacre' portions of land.[6] (It was reckoned that half an acre of conacre would support a labourer's family.)[7] Many therefore simply did not have the money to buy the cheap imported corn. 'Conacre' rent was between £12 and £14 an acre, paid not in cash but in labour. A typical family of 4–7 people in Westmeath at this time was trying to subsist on 10d. a day. To earn the 10d. on one of the government's 'job creations', the labourer would have to walk 3½ miles to work and 3½ miles back, his sole meal of the day a small ration of oatmeal. No wonder violence broke out when the hungry were able to muster up the energy for it.

Deeply ingrained with the immediate horrors of the famine was the overall structure of Irish agrarian society, which placed Irish land and wealth in the hands of English (or in effect English) aristocrats. It was the belief of a Liberal laissez-faire economist such as Lord John Russell that the hunger of Irish peasants was not the responsibility of government but of landowners. No more callous example of a political doctrine being pursued to the death – quite literally – exists in the annals of British history. But Lord John Russell's government, when considering the Irish problem, were not envisaging some faraway island in which they had no personal concern. A quarter of the peers in the House of Lords had Irish interests.[8]

Of the three leading Whig ministers in 1848, only Russell himself had no direct economic interest in Ireland. Many of the English parliamentarians owned land there. Lord Palmerston for example – British foreign secretary in Russell's Cabinet – owned many acres of County Sligo. In common with many landowners he never went near his tenants in their plight, and certainly sent no relief, preferring to export them in their hundreds to Canada. When, in November 1847, the ship *Aeolus* arrived at St John with 428 passengers, almost all of them were Lord Palmerston's tenants. The following report was made of their condition:

> There are many aged persons of both sexes on board and a large population of women and children, the whole in the most abject state of destitution, with barely sufficient rags upon their persons to cover their nakedness . . . One boy, about ten years of age, was actually brought on deck stark naked.[9]

Eight passengers were dead on arrival at St John. The inhabitants of the Canadian port had nowhere to house them and demanded that the passengers of the *Aeolus* be given a free passage back to Ireland. The matter caused such scandal that Palmerston was called to make a statement in the House of Commons, blaming his agents. They in turn made the tenants write cruelly unconvincing letters to the St John newspapers expressing their deep gratitude to Lord Palmerston for rescuing them from the famine. They remained in the dockside slums there, struggling for some kind of existence. Many more went to New York. Some, risking the frequently violent anti-Irish feeling of the English working class, came to England, usually to work in the most menial capacities as navvies, often forcibly separated from their families. These were the survivors. In the five years of the famine the population of Ireland fell from a little over 8 million to a little over 6. About 1 million of that can be attributed to deaths by natural causes, and by (usually enforced) clearances of the land.

That leaves the eternally shaming statistic of 1.1 million deaths by starvation in Ireland between 1845 and 1850. Throughout this period, the viceroy in Dublin Castle continued to draw his salary of £20,000 per annum. (The prime minister's salary was £5,000.) While labourers in Westmeath struggled their seven miles a day to earn 10d. and while over a million died for want of anything to eat, anything at all, the viceroy kept up his lavish court. Lord Clarendon's household accounts for 1848 show £1,297 spent on wine; £1,868 on butcher's bills; £619 on poulterers, £352 on fishmongers and £562 on the butter man. Lord Clarendon as viceroy, supporting a government which had come into power on the Free

Trade ticket, had done nothing to check the profiteering which went on in the worst of the famine areas.[10] (Throughout the winter of '46–7, for instance, prices rocketed and speculators made a fortune selling imported maize – '£40,000 and £800,000 were spoken of as having been made by merchants in Cork', wrote one despondent contemporary.[11]

The riot police and troops were sent to quell the angry mobs, with the cynical promise of extra provisions. Trevelyan arranged for the provisioning of 2,000 riot troops with beef, pork and biscuit, to be mobilized at short notice in order to put down food riots.

It is all so horrible that one cannot and need not exaggerate the suffering of the hungry and the callousness of their governors. That should not prompt the distorted view that no one on the English side of St George's Channel was shocked by what was going on, nor offer cause to suppose that *all* the rich and powerful were (to use Bishop Berkeley's description of Irish landlords) 'vultures with iron bowels'.[12] Towards the end of 1846 a group of 'merchant princes' in the City of London, led by Baron Lionel de Rothschild and Mr Thomas Baring, set up 'The British Association for the relief of the extreme distress in the remote parishes of Ireland and Scotland'. Trevelyan did not believe the fund would do any good, but Queen Victoria donated £2,000, Rothschilds £1,000, the Duke of Devonshire (who in addition to his various English palaces also owned the castle of Lismore in Co. Waterford) £1,000 and Sir Charles Wood £200. The British Association appointed an anglicized Pole, Count Strzelecki, to administer distribution of the funds. Evangelical Christians and Quakers helped with their work.[13]

Yet these overtures from the English side were undoubtedly made against a tide of prejudice and bitterness. The hordes of Irish poor crowding into English slums did not evoke pity – rather, fear and contempt. The Whiggish Liberal *Manchester Guardian* blamed the famine quite largely on the feckless Irish attitudes to agriculture, family, life in general. Small English farmers, said this self-righteous newspaper, don't divide farms into four which are only sufficient to feed one family. (The economic necessities which forced the Irish to do this were conveniently overlooked by the *Manchester Guardian*: indeed economic weakness, in the Darwinian jungle, is the equivalent of sin.) Why weren't the English starving? Because 'they bring up their children in habits of frugality, which qualify them for earning their own living, and then send them forth into the world to look for employment'.

We are decades away from any organized Irish Republican Movement. Nevertheless, in the midst of the famine unrest, we find innumerable ripe examples of British double standards where violence is in question. An Englishman protecting his grossly selfish way of life with a huge apparatus of police and military, prepared to gun down the starving, is maintaining law and order. An Irishman retaliating is a terrorist. The marked increase in homicides during the years 1846 and 1847 filled these English liberals with terror. There were 68 reported homicides in Ireland in 1846, 96 in 1847, 126 shootings in the latter year compared with 55 the year before. Rather than putting these in the context of hundreds of thousands of deaths annually by starvation, John Bright, the Liberal Free Trader, blamed all the violence of these starving Celts on their innate idleness. 'Wherever a people are not industrious and are not employed, there is the greatest danger of crime and outrage. Ireland is idle, and therefore she starves; Ireland starves, and therefore she rebels.'

Both halves of this sentence are factually wrong. Ireland most astonishingly did *not* rebel in, or immediately after, the famine years; and we have said enough to show that though there was poverty, extreme poverty, before 1845, many Irish families survived heroically on potatoes alone. The economic structure of a society in which they could afford a quarter or half an acre of land on which to grow a spud while the Duke of Devonshire owned Lismore, Bolton (and half Yorkshire), Chatsworth (and ditto Derbyshire), the whole of Eastbourne and a huge palace in London was not of the Irish peasant's making.

By 1848/9 the attitude of Lord John Russell's government had become Malthusian, not to stay Darwinian, in the extreme. As always happens when famine takes hold, it was followed by disease. Cholera swept through Belfast and Co. Mayo in 1848, spreading to other districts. In the workhouses, crowded to capacity, dysentery, fevers and ophthalmia were endemic – 13,812 cases of ophthalmia in 1849 rose to 27,200 in 1850. Clarendon and Trevelyan now used the euphemism of 'natural causes' to describe death by starvation. The gentle Platonist–Hegelian philosopher Benjamin Jowett once said, 'I have always felt a certain horror of political economists, since I heard one of them say that he feared the famine of 1848 in Ireland would not kill more than a million people, and that would scarcely be enough to do much good.'[14] As so often Sydney Smith was right: 'The moment the very name of Ireland is mentioned, the English seem to bid adieu to common feeling, common prudence and common sense, and to act with the barbarity of tyrants and the fatuity of idiots.'[15]

The Monkey House at the Zoological Gardens, Regents Park, 1835,
when none of the beautifully-dressed visitors could guess that those
gambolling monkeys in the cage might actually be cousins.

Chapter Seven

Doubt

The phenomenon of the Zoo is characteristic of the Victorian Age, providing the chance of popular scientific inquiry, entertainment, and communal self-congratulation. *The Leisure Hour* of 1849, in an article entitled 'Saturday Afternoon at the Zoological Gardens', opined that 'it shows a high state of civilization when a great and overcrowded city devotes part of its energies and space to the preservation and kindly treatment of animals, which the savage looks upon as things made solely and on purpose to be hunted and destroyed'.[1] Opinions differed about the kindness and humaneness of the Zoo. In 1836 the *Quarterly Review* found something morally questionable about the notion of forcing animals to exchange their natural habitat for cages and pens. (It was making the same point nineteen years later – 'Why do we coop these noble animals in such nutshells of cages? What a miserable sight – to see them pace backwards and forwards in their box-like dens?')[2] Mortality rates were high. But from their inception, the Zoological Gardens in London's Regent's Park were enormously popular. The Zoological Society first moved there in 1828 to enclosures and grounds laid out by Decimus Burton. The original collection of 430 animals and birds was donated from the Royal Menagerie. In its first two decades of life the Zoo was an exclusive resort, open only to fellows of the Zoological Society or their guests and those prepared to pay a shilling's entrance fee. Nevertheless, it received 30,000 visitors within its first seven months of opening.[3]

Undoubtedly thrill was part of the appeal. Yet it was also recognized, as it is to this day, that the proximity of other species can bring consolation to the melancholy and solace to the depressed. It was more than the jolly atmosphere and the music playing from the bandstand that visitors found cheering.

The Zoological Society remained in principle a scientific organization, and a part of the fun, for those savouring a day's outing at the Zoo, was the notion that it was educative. As the clothed victors gawped at their encaged fellow creatures, and as the band played, however, it is possible that disturbing thoughts were beginning to dawn in the public mind about the nature of humanity in the scheme of things. At a deeper level of metaphysical awareness, was it not even more disturbing, as one viewed the apes' fingers and hands, their attentive expressions, so reminiscent of the more contemplative type of clergymen, their humourless but compulsive grins, their fussy attention to their young offspring, that they were not as alien as one could wish?

Progress was the watchword of the age: advance, improvement, struggle and climb. Thackeray in his *Book of Snobs* had chronicled with deadly accuracy how social climbers wish to kick away the ladder from beneath their feet – how those whom financial good fortune or professional skill have advanced could bitterly resent the reminder that only a generation or two ago, the forebears of the grandee were indulging in small trade, or ploughing fields. Consider the social journeys of – to take a random sample from differing rungs of the social ladder – the Reverend Patrick Brontë (born in the meanest hovel), Herbert Spencer, the Gladstone family . . . hundreds of examples could be adduced. Was the thought that Our Race could similarly be found to connect with 'lower' species on a comparable level of collective shame? If so, was that the reason that this was the decade, the first of Victoria's reign, when the idea took wing and became popular?

The commercial success of *Vestiges of the Natural History of Creation*, published anonymously in 1844, was both a symptom of how fascinating these matters had become to the public at large, and a cause of the growing obsession. It was a book which 'everybody' read. Fanny Kemble told Erasmus Darwin, 'its conclusions are utterly revolting to me – nevertheless they may be true' – thoughts which were echoed, more or less, by the 24,000 who bought the book. (Presumably you could multiply by five the numbers who read it.)[4]*

The author of *Vestiges* was not a scientist – a fact which was noted with scorn by the scientific establishment, though they did not know who he was. (Or she: Adam Sedgwick thought the book was so bad that it might be the work of a woman.) It was in fact Robert Chambers, who was born, the son of a Peebles cotton manufacturer, on 10 July 1802. The invention of the power-loom bankrupted his father James, compelling Chambers and his brother William to strike out on their own. Robert had set up in his own business as a bookseller by the age of sixteen; William, also a bookseller, founded *Chambers's Edinburgh Journal*, one of the innumerable new periodicals of the age catering for the ever-burgeoning inquiring classes. In the past, scholarship, book-learning and natural history had perhaps been the activities of the few. In the nineteenth century there was a tremendous growth of autodidacticism in all classes. In those days before science departments in universities, before films and 'natural history programmes' on television, men and women and children

could still look at the natural world about them and see. It was the great age of amateur botany – not just in the leisurely atmosphere of parsonage houses, though obviously the gentle existence of a country parson was ideal as a background for the natural historian, but in all classes of society.

A work such as *Vestiges* could be expected to make its appeal to a far wider circle than the scientific coteries of an earlier era. Chambers was not a professional scientist. Charles Darwin's view was that 'his geology strikes me as bad and his zoology far worse'.[5] One of the many blunders in the book is his belief that birds were the ancestors of the duck-billed platypus and the latter of mammals. He believed in botanical fables such as the possibility of converting oats into rye. But these were mere details. What Chambers did, as a fascinated layman, was to read as much as he could of evolutionary scientific literature. He read Buffon, Laplace, Monboddo, Erasmus Darwin, Lamarck. He provided the book-buying public with an image: that all life on this planet had a common origin,[6] and that life as we now observe it, and geology, had come about as a result of discernible or deducible evolutionary laws. *Vestiges*, as the great geologist Charles Lyell acknowledged, 'made the English public familiar with the leading views of Lamarck on transmutation and progression, but brought no new facts or original line of argument to support these views'.[7]

Chambers vehemently rejected atheism, though we must presume that the chief reason he chose to publish anonymously was fear of the religious backlash against his book. 'We advance from law to the cause of law, and ask, What is that? Whence have come all these beautiful regulations? Here science leaves us, but only to conclude, from other grounds, that there is a First Cause to which all others are secondary and ministrative . . .'[8] *Vestiges* takes a broadly deist view, thinking that the 'Almighty Deviser' has set in place those laws which it is the job of the scientist, not the theologian, to unearth. 'Are we to suppose the Deity adopting plans which harmonize only with the modes of procedure of the less enlightened of our race?'[9]

Evolutionary theory had been aired in scientific circles for at least a hundred years before this. Benoît de Maillet published posthumously in 1748 the theory that animal species transmuted into one another – the fish into birds, and so forth. Not only was such a notion condemned by theology (hence de Maillet waiting until dead before publishing, and then under the pseudonym of his name spelt backwards, Telliamed) – it was also ridiculed

*'Readers included Queen Victoria, Elizabeth Barrett Browning, Abraham Lincoln, William Ewart Gladstone, Arthur Schopenhauer, Francis Newman, John Stuart Mill, William Stanley Jeavons and Florence Nightingale. The co-discoverer of natural selection, Alfred Russel Wallace, began his search for a lawful explanation of species after reading *Vestiges* in 1845. The book had a profound effect on literature, most notably in the writings of Alfred Tennyson, Ralph Waldo Emerson and George Eliot.' James A. Secord, introduction to Robert Chambers (1994).

A cartoon published in 1830, 28 years before Darwin's Origin of the Species, *lampooning theories of evolution.*

by philosophy. Voltaire wrote that if such an idea were true, one species changing into another, why, 'The Metamorphoses of Ovid would be the best textbook of science that had ever been written.'[10] Diderot, however, and Maupertuis both put forward the view that there had once been one primeval animal and 'Nature lengthened, shortened, transformed multiplied or obliterated some of its organs' – according to need. Buffon began work on the kinship of asses and horses and realized that if a common equine ancestor could be found for them there was no logical reason to discount a common ancestor for men and apes.

The grandfather of Charles Darwin, Erasmus, concluded in *Zoönomia or the Laws of Organic Life*

(1794–6) that the species were mutable, but it was left to Lamarck to posit an actual genealogical tree, a theory of evolution, based on what is now universally seen as a fallacy, namely the notion that acquired characteristics can be passed on genetically. (Lyell was right to see Chambers as a popularizer of Lamarck *in general*, but *Vestiges* does in fact reject the possibility of inheriting acquired characteristics.)[11]

Vestiges did not merely popularize the developments in zoology. It recognized the pre-eminence of geologists, particularly the modern pioneers of the subject from Scotland – James Hutton, John Playfair and above all Charles Lyell, whose own *Principles of Geology*, published between 1830 and 1833 but constantly revised and updated, really laid the foundation for the destruction of 'creationist' thought in Britain, America and Northern Europe. The complexities of his arguments and the depth and range of his learning forbid any simplification or summary of its conclusions. Lyell was neither a religious unbeliever nor a controversialist, but the evidence of geology convinced him that the planet Earth, and the universe, were of infinitely greater antiquity than any simple-minded reading of the Book of Genesis might suggest.

Lyell, who was landed and affluent, also belonged very definitely to the inner circle of what passed for the early Victorian scientific establishment. They partly welcomed the success of *Vestiges*: it cleared the ground for their own work. Another part of them was wistful, frightened by the vehemence of religious prejudice and perhaps genuinely fearful that if unbelief became widespread, as in France, it would have revolutionary consequences.

Geology had only lately emerged as an independent discipline. It had to fight for its independence against those Biblical fundamentalists who, by counting back through the genealogies in the Old Testament to the point where 'in the beginning, God created the Heaven and the Earth', were able to date the momentous phenomenon at 4004 BC.[12]

All but crackpots now in the twenty-first century accept that these early to mid-nineteenth-century geologists were, if not precisely accurate in their conclusions, broadly speaking right. Independent scientific inquiry had taken the place of a blindly erroneous reading of Scripture, as the criterion for determining truth. If the jury is still out over the question of Darwin's theory of evolution, not published until fifteen years after *Vestiges*, it is because we can see how quintessentially it is of its time, whereas the antiquity of the Earth, hence of human prehistory, can be debated and determined on the basis of observable, tangible phenomena – geological specimens, strata, fossils and so forth. The theory of transmutation of species would find no comparable verification test until the development of electron microscopes and the whole science of molecular biology more or less a century later.

For the historian, then, the first and immediate importance of *Vestiges* and the phenomenon it represented is not whether it is true, but whether it aptly reflected a generation to itself. Robert Chambers read Lamarck, Buffon, Lyell and others to propound the notion that 'the whole train of animated beings, from the simplest and oldest up to the highest and most recent are . . . to be regarded as a series of *advances of the species of development*'[13] (his italics).

Many have noted that in the very months that Chambers was applying this notion to the phenomena of the visible world, John Henry Newman was completing *An Essay on the Development of Christian Doctrine*. 'Developments, reactions, reforms, revolutions, and changes of various kinds are mixed together in the actual history of states, as of philosophical sects, so as to make it very difficult to exhibit them in any scientific analysis.'[14] Taken to its extreme, this could lead to the view that religion itself is best understood in its sociological perspective, as an expression of the aspirations of different generations. That is not, on the surface at least, the conclusion of Newman's *Essay on Development*, though many would question, having accepted the premise, how any other conclusion was tenable.

Newman's career up to 1844 had been largely absorbed with the sometimes esoteric ecclesiastical controversies buzzing in the heads of his fellow academics at Oxford. The rallying cry for the Oxford Movement, so called, had been a sermon on 'National Apostasy' by the saintly professor of poetry, John Keble, who, together with his conservative-minded followers, saw the policy of successive governments, Whig and Peelite, in Ireland as profoundly regrettable. The reduction of the number of Protestant bishoprics in that largely Catholic land struck the Tractarians (so called after the Tracts they wrote in defence of their High Church doctrines) as worse than heretical. A typical mouthpiece of their viewpoint was Gladstone, who in his book on Church and state argued that any true believer in Anglicanism must believe in its absolute truth. For a Parliament whose function was to defend the Church, to hand over a part of the kingdom to a schismatic erroneous sect such as the Roman Catholic Church was indeed an 'apostasy'. Macaulay's robust review of this book must have led Gladstone to think again on the Irish question – as we know he did, by the time of the Maynooth Grant. Gladstone, however, remained High Church, that is a believer in the view that the true Catholic Church in England was that by law established.

The fact that very few Anglicans in history (and few of Queen Victoria's bishops) seemed to believe in the Catholicism of the Tractarians did not deter the dreamers of Oxford from their determination to make the solidly Protestant Church of England appear like a purified continuation of medieval Catholicism. Lord Blake has likened the Young England movement to the Oxford Movement. It would be even truer to see the matter the other way about and to view the intellectual contortions of Gladstone, Newman, Keble and friends as

ANIMAL MAGNETISM FOR THE MILLION.

Published by A Hays 15. G? Castle S? Regent S? & W Roxbrough Grays Place Brompton.

Satire on the gullibility of the public – a monkey mesmerises the audience while his assistant picks their pockets, c. 1830.

a form of mental Eglinton Tournament in which young men of the railway age tried to adopt the mentality of medieval monks or the Fathers of the Church in Late Antiquity. Newman was the most eminent of those who eventually found too burdensome the strain of defending the indefensible. He became a Roman Catholic in 1845, during one of those dark autumn rainstorms which had swept across northern Europe for weeks, destroying the crops. While the Irish starved, he worried his mind about Augustine's controversy in the fourth century with the Donatists. But his *Essay on Development* had opened doorways into new territories of thought which he was perhaps only half ready or willing to explore.

For most men and women, Tennyson was a surer guide to the crises of the age. He saw that what all this religious controversy threatened to remove (whether the Science vs Religion controversy or the esoteric tournaments played out in the Tracts) was the religion of

the inner life. He had this in common with the great hymn-writers of the age, of whom Newman was one. Most Christians have never heard of *The Essay in Development*, but many have been consoled by 'Lead Kindly Light'.

Even more, perhaps, have found comfort in the last verses of the Reverend H.F. Lyte, the vicar of All Saints' Church in the Devonshire fishing port of Brixham.[15] Ill health made him retire before he was fifty-two. He was sent abroad to cure his bronchitis and died at Nice in the autumn of 1847. He left behind one of the most haunting lyrics of the nineteenth century – 'Abide with Me'. Like Tennyson he could have claimed it was the cry of the whole human race. Intelligent people waited anxiously to see whether God Himself was to be withdrawn from the modern scheme of things and if so, how they would survive the bereavement.

I fear no foe with Thee at hand to bless

The repeated plea, throughout the hymn, that the Presence will not be removed has an undoubted pathos when we remember the date at which it was written, a time when so many, and with such heavy hearts, were taking leave of God.

While some investigators formed theories of a greater or lesser convincingness about the age of rocks or the evolution of species, others turned to the phenomenon of humanity itself – the nature of human personality, the question of whether 'mind' can be separated from brain, the nature of psychology. These matters cannot be studied in isolation, any more than can the work of the geologists and biologists.

The phenomenon of phrenology, for example, will seem bizarre to some readers of the twenty-first century, but there were many in its heyday who saw it as a serious science. Its various proponents divided up the skull into areas – twenty-six in one scheme, forty-three or more in another – in which it was purported that organs could be discovered explanatory of human behaviour. The lumps and bumps of the human cranium were seriously supposed to relate to propensities and characteristics such as amativeness, hope, wonder, wit and so on. The fact that no relation between brain functions and cranial formation could be demonstrated did not prevent serious people, many of them scientists, being wholly convinced by it. Phrenological ways of viewing human nature had a profound effect on the development not just of medicine but of anthropology, hence on the growth of imperialism.

The phrenological obsession with skulls was to be inherited by anthropologists of later generations. Many were influenced by Charles Caldwell's book *Thoughts on the Unity of the Human Species* which asserted, from skull evidence again, that negroes 'are no more competent to live orderly, prosperously, and happily, in a large and separate community, *under a government of laws*, prepared and administered by themselves, than is a *similar number* of buffaloes or beaters' (emphasis in original).[16]

One of the most enthusiastic disciples of phrenology in London was the professor of medicine at University College Hospital, John Elliotson. (He is the pioneer of the widespread use of the stethoscope.)[17] He was also to become, notoriously, one of the most vociferous champions of mesmerism, a practice which, like so many others engaging inquiring minds, appeared to its proponents as a science and to its critics (of whom there were plenty in Elliotson's lifetime) chicanery of the most transparent kind.

Franz Anton Mesmer (1734–1815), the Austrian medic and sage, had discovered, so he said, that the universe was penetrated and surrounded by a superfine magnetic fluid. By means which seem very close to hypnotism, he was able to put his patients into a trance, and by means of 'animal magnetism' to connect them up with the magnetic fluid of the universe.

Professor Elliotson, when he had become convinced not merely of the truth of the animal magnetism but of his own mesmeric powers, began his demonstrations in the wards of University College Hospital, Gower Street, in 1837. His success rate was remarkable. Elliotson himself records, among many a comparable case, hysterical epilepsy with spinal affection cured outright by mesmerism; in other epileptic cases, fits much reduced.

It is important to realize that much more than auto-suggestion was at work, as far as the mesmerists believed. Nor is it true that only hysterical or functional illnesses could be cured by mesmerism, though the great preponderance of reported cases *are* of such disorders. At the height of its popularity in the medical profession there were claims that it could cure not only neurasthenic conditions such as asthma but also deafness.

Elliotson, a combative man with a tendency to consider himself hard done by, was eventually hounded out by the medical 'establishment'. He resigned his chair of medicine and retired an embittered man.[18] His career might be seen as no more than a colourful interlude in the history of medicine, but mesmerism was peculiarly in tune with the spirit of the age, one of many forces inclining to suggest to the nineteenth-century mind that there could be naturalistic explanations for phenomena which had hitherto been seen as pure mysteries.

They were now able to look back at the Age of Miracles, at Christ himself, and see the supposedly implausible stories of pious legend explicable in terms of mesmeric fluid. Although the mesmerists claimed to be materialist through and through (and it was possible to practise even on birds or idiot children without their consciously joining their will to that of the mesmerist as he concentrated his energy upon them) it inevitably foreshadows that twentieth-century preoccupation with mind which can be seen in the psychology of Freud and Jung and the literary productions of Joyce and Proust.[19]

Chapter Eight

The Failed Revolution

There are, broadly, two responses to the question why there was no revolution in Britain and Ireland in 1848, as there was to be in so many other countries of Europe. The first is to suggest that there would have been some such uprising had not the British state learnt to exercise an iron authority over the masses, by means of law, policing, and military strength. The second is to imply that, hellish as life was for many British and Irish people in the 1840s, it could have been worse, that times of economic hardship were replaced by times of prosperity, and that, quite simply, not enough people would have been found to make a Chartist Parliament, still less a British socialist state, a viable proposition. Some historians, for either of these reasons, dismiss the so-called failure of the Chartist movement as risible, inevitable, insignificant. Yet it wasn't risible – in its own way, it could be viewed as tragic were it not for the peculiar composition and character of the English nation. The truly extraordinary lesson of 1848 in England is that, had the Chartists succeeded, and had their petition become law, with every adult male given the vote by secret ballot, it is perfectly possible that a majority of Englishmen would have voted to retain Queen Victoria as head of state, and Lord John Russell or Lord Stanley as prime minister.

It would be an absurdity to say that no English working-class people have ever supported either physical-force Chartism, or communism or other forms of potentially violent revolution in England. Yet it would seem from the evidence as if there had always been working-class English of a different persuasion – either gradualists or conservatives. Things might have been slightly different in Ireland, Wales or Scotland.

The newspaper placard announced that the French government (the 'July monarchy' of Louis-Philippe with his arch-conservative premier the historian Guizot) had been overthrown. A provisional government was set up. On 13 March Metternich, the chancellor of the Austrian empire, was overthrown. A little while before, Harney's German friends in exile had run off the press at 46, Liverpool Street in London, yards from the epicentre of the capitalist world, an anonymous pamphlet entitled *Manifest der Kommunistischen Partei*. Its authors were Friedrich Engels and Karl Marx (who had come to London on a visit and met Harney in November 1847). Engels was already living in England – in the unlikely role of a Northern capitalist. (His father had cotton manufactories in Lancashire –

NOT SO *VERY* UNREASONABLE!!! EH?

British Prime Minister John Russell greets a man who arrives with a bill from the Chartist Movement, 1848.

like Sir Robert Peel, Engels always spoke English with a pronounced Northern accent.) Marx would come to London as a refugee, his revolutionary journalism having made him an undesirable in Germany. He would never escape it, becoming *faute de mieux* a Londoner and British Museum habitué, until his death in 1883.

> A spectre is haunting Europe – the spectre of Communism. All the Powers of old Europe have entered into a holy alliance to exorcize this spectre: Pope and Czar, Metternich and Guizot, French Radicals and German police spies . . .

The quotation is from the 'authorized' English version of 1888, hastily, too hastily, revised by Engels himself, working on the English translation of a loyal plodder called Samuel Moore.[1]

There were many who shared the communist view that England would not be immune from the spectre's power. The 'physical force' Chartists, some of whom befriended, others of whom became, communists in late years, were to this extent at one with those – such as Macaulay, the great Whig historian – who saw antagonisms between the classes as absolutely inevitable. 'The history of all hitherto existing society is the history of class struggles.' In the mind of Macaulay, for whom the Whig Revolution of 1689 was the high point and defining moment of British history, Chartism was a disastrous idea. He saw the notion of giving the vote to the uneducated and unpropertied classes as a recipe for national suicide. When the Chartist riots had broken out in Newport in 1839 Macaulay had seen the spectre – civil war between the propertied and the unpropertied. The result would have been the destruction of property.

Marx saw the same truth of inevitable strife, and no doubt this inspired the more belligerent Chartists. There is equally no doubt that it scared many of them away from the movement, not because they were cowards, but because as tailors, small traders and craftsmen, even as factory workers, they did not wish to form themselves into a destructive mob.

The Chartist demonstration on Kennington Common, 10 April 1848. It is the first significant historical event to have been photographed, probably by police spies. The daguerreotypes record a scene of drizzly pathos. In the immediate foreground you can see the special officers, mounted on horseback and silk-hatted. Above and beyond the twenty thousand hopeful heads, a factory chimney stretches a defiant arm to the sky. Possibly it is Messrs Farmer's vitriol works. It seems to say that trade and capital are stronger than human dignity.

Fearing that a violent revolution was on its way, however, the Whig government took no chances, and when it was announced that the Third Chartist Petition would be presented to Parliament on 10 April 1848, both sides saw this as a day of the greatest significance, the day in which it would be determined whether the English revolution could come, or not.

The wilder radicals like Ernest Jones were optimistic, particularly since the Irish protest movements seemed prepared to join forces with the English working classes. Lord John Russell and his Cabinet took no chances. Though there were still Chartists after 10 April 1848, the government did effectively on that date crush Chartism.[2]

The Duke of Wellington was enlisted, less as an actual commander of operations than as an extremely useful piece of popular propaganda. Wellington, obsessed by the possibilities of mob violence, sent a list of proposals to Lord John suggesting provisions which should be made. He was certainly included, though or because a former Tory prime minister, in the discussions of security arrangements, but when he sent in his list of suggestions he found that Sir George Grey and the military secretary, Lord Fitzroy Somerset, had already pursued them. Nevertheless it did not do any harm to allow the potential rebels to believe that they would be fighting, if violence did break out, against the victor of Waterloo.

What had Grey and Somerset already arranged for 10 April? The royal family had been sent by train to the Isle of Wight. (Waterloo station was closed for hours beforehand and cordoned off by troops.) Wellington was afraid that Osborne House, a holiday palazzo, not a fort, was vulnerable from the Solent if the rebels got hold of a warship: this was the level of paranoia felt by the prevailing powers.

Mouchards brought word that the common soldiers, chatting to Chartist demonstrators as they began to assemble in London in the few days before the 10th, had promised to fire over the people's heads in the event of a riot.[3] The thought of the military showing class solidarity filled the Whigs with horror, but they could take comfort from the numbers who volunteered as special constables. Altogether, in London alone, Lord Fitzroy Somerset had mobilized 7,122 military, including cavalry; 1,231 military pensioners; 4,000 police, both City and metropolitan, and an astonishing 85,000 special constables. Comparable measures had been taken in all the major British cities.

The British Museum was barricaded – the director Sir Henry Ellis calculated that if invaded by 'disaffected persons it would prove to them a fortress capable of holding ten thousand men'. Somerset House in the Strand had a portcullis constructed in its entrance. The Bank of England was parapeted with sandbags, and guns mounted in every aperture. All the prisons were reinforced with heavily armed guards.[4] Comparable methods had been taken in Paris and they had not prevented the revolution. The difference between the two countries was that the presence of 100,000 troops outside Paris was resented by the petit-bourgeois downwards. In England, the urban middle and lower-middle class was proportionately far higher and they overwhelmingly supported all these measures. The sheer number of special constables is eloquent; even if we suppose a high proportion of them were domestic servants, this does not mean they did not prefer the status quo.

The show of strength undoubtedly had an enormous effect, both to boost the morale of the majority who did not want the Physical Force Chartists and the Irish revolutionaries to succeed, and on the reputation of Britain abroad, as the one nation in Europe which appeared to be immune from serious revolutionary upheaval.

On 10 April, the National Convention of Chartists assembled at 9 a.m. in John Street, just north of Gray's Inn, moved down Tottenham Court Road, passed via Holborn to Farringdon Street, crossed Blackfriars Bridge and reached Kennington Common by 11.30, where some 3,000 had congregated. Another contingent had assembled in the East End on Stepney Green, a crowd of some 2,000 with music, flags and an air of jamboree. The largest single group was in Russell Square, Bloomsbury. About 10,000 proceeded from here, down the Walworth Road, and eventually reached Kennington Green. They had hoped for hundreds of thousands: in the event, a mere 20,000 or so appeared, policed by a force nearly five times that number.

O'Connor addressed the gathering. Many of the historians of the movement blame him for its lack of success, his firebrand dissent from Lovett and the moral force Chartists in the beginning, his essential lack of sympathy with the urban population at the end of the decade since the Charter was composed. The Chartist Land Plan – in which O'Connor tried to establish systems of independent smallholdings on commonly held land – was probably never practicable and was irrelevant to the aspirations of the Alton Lockes who were the movement's core membership. 'The Charter was a means to an end –

the means was their political rights, and the end was equality' – as Harney had said at the outset.

The 10th of April appeared to demonstrate that capitalism was so powerful a machine that those who had become its cogs could not imagine things to be otherwise. Systems of universal education – like those of the communists, a Chartist dream – would not in reality come about for generations in Britain, and it is open to question whether the level of political interest required in a working democracy would ever have come to pass, Charter or no Charter. Democracy in the sense understood by O'Connor, Lovett or Ernest Jones has never been tried in Britain.

The truth is that the numbers supporting the Charter itself had been dwindling for some years before 1848. Region-by-region research shows that in 1,009 areas generally supportive of Chartism in 1839, only 207 had active Chartist organizations in 1848.[5] The aims and aspirations of the working people in these districts had been splintered. The government, as a result of pressure from the Tory Lord Ashley, had lately brought in the Ten Hours Act, limiting the hours of work in factories. Conditions in a number of places were improved, not wholly, not as much as people might wish. But they knew they had a government which no longer gave capitalism a totally free rein: children were not sent down the mines any more, mill-owners or factory-masters could not so easily exact slavishly long hours from employees. The slow, creakingly slow, improvement of working conditions could be seen, by optimists, to have begun. Meanwhile, Free Trade had begun to chug into prosperous action. Wages, with profits, were up in most manufacturing areas.

For some of us, though, the thought that the conditions of the labouring poor in 1848 were not so bad really, the claim that the Ten Hours Act and a few shillings a week destroyed the Chartist ideal, is just a little too smug. The truth is, as Marx saw very clearly, that there is a genuine difference of interest between the workers and the bourgeoisie. Any dissent from such a view – the view of Cobden and similar Manchester liberals that the urban proletariat had much chance to better themselves through evening classes and the like – is a gigantic con. In the years after they wrote the Manifesto, Marx and Engels were astounded to discover the sheer force of the British gendarmerie – Britain armed to the teeth both against the working class and against the Irish. That was the first lesson of 10 April 1848. Second, and more dispiriting, the sheer numbers of the *Kleinbürger* made any realignment of the political map impossible. The preparedness of Lord John Russell to *crush* the Chartists by force was *very popular indeed*.

The presenters of the Petition were allowed into three cabs to cross the river and to present the signatures to the House of Commons. Of the hoped-for signatories, there were only 1,200,000 (less than half of the expected 3 million),[6] two-thirds of which were said to be fraudulent.

April 10 demonstrated an alarming truth. Rather than being seen as a Chartist flop, it should be seen as the united front of the *Kleinbürger* – the petit-bourgeoisie – with the governing powers, the money powers, the aristocracy.

From now on, the Victorian story becomes an alarming triumph song, Great Britain growing richer and more powerful by the decade, coarsening in the process, and leaving the historian with a sense that only in its dissentient voices is redemption found.

Part Two

THE EIGHTEEN-FIFTIES

Crowds outside the Crystal Palace in Hyde Park for the Great Exhibition, 1851.

One of a series of illustrations by George Cruikshank in Henry Mayhew's novel Mr and Mrs Sandboys and Family *(1851). This facetious novel tells the story of a family who came up for the exhibition but, because of their provincial innocence, and the difficulty of finding their bearings in an overcrowded capital, never actually penetrated the Crystal Palace.*

Chapter Nine

The Great Exhibition

The statement that Britain 'survived' 1848, while the rest of the European continent was convulsed in revolutions (and counter-revolutions), requires at least a footnote, if not a qualification. If we look for signs of revolutionary disturbance only on Kennington Common on 10 April, then we might conclude that Britain had a peaceful year.

As so often in its history, Britain appeared to be going a way which was very different from that of the rest of Europe. In fact, Britain was not so very different, but it was undergoing its problems, and solving them, very much off home territory, and this is what gives us the sometimes false impression that things were stabler than they truly were. Two factors must be borne in mind. One was the extraordinary rate of imperial expansion abroad which accompanied the growth of the industrial economy at home. This enabled British governments to export many of their political and criminal dissidents where other nations had to look after them on domestic territory. But secondly, when we view the history of the colonies themselves, we remember that things were far from tranquil, either in 1848, or in the decades preceding or succeeding it.

An extraordinary expansion of British imperialism had marked the first decade of Victoria's reign. Hong Kong in the Far East – 1843, Labuan in Indonesia – 1846, Natal – 1843, Orange River in South Africa – 1848, Gambia on the West Coast of Africa – 1843. In 1842 the British fought the first of their disastrous Afghan wars, temporarily annexing that unconquerable country. Even the Russians in the twentieth century, or the Americans in the twenty-first, did not experience quite so cruelly the brutal indomitability of the Afghan guerrilla. Sir William Hay Macnaghten, through and through an old India hand, son of an Indian judge and an employee of the East India Company from adolescence, persuaded the governor-general of India, Auckland, that if the British did not move into Afghanistan the Russians would threaten British interests in India. There followed a period in which the British (just like the Russians and the Americans in a later age) backed first one and then another bunch of cut-throats who supposedly shared the interests of the foreign occupier. In November 1841, when Macnaghten was on the point of leaving Kabul to take up the governorship of Bombay, his successor, Sir Alexander Burnes, was murdered by a mob. Macnaghten himself was then assassinated by the leader of a rival Afghan faction to the one he had been supporting. The winter had begun. There was no chance of the British troops stationed at Kandahar getting through the snowy mountains to Kabul. After a series of negotiations with Afghan leaders, the British agreed to withdraw from Afghanistan. On 6 January, the entire garrison began the retreat to Jallalabad, with a huge number of Afghan camp-followers (afraid of reprisals from their hostile compatriots) and many British women and children. Akhbar Khan, the new

Afghan leader who had arranged for Macnaghten to be killed, would not give any assurance that the retreating forces would be immune from attack, though the women and children were allowed through. Sixteen thousand British troops made their last stand against the Afghans in the pass at Jagdallak. Of this number, only one, Dr Brydon, was allowed to limp his way to Jallalabad to tell the tale. When spring came, the British did send forces to occupy Kabul, but they were not there for long. They did not want to be.

The only positive result, for them, of the first Afghan war was that the East India Company greatly expanded its forces in North-West India. The conquest of Sind in 1843 was the direct consequence of the Afghan war. The Sikh wars led to the appropriation of the Punjab by 1849, as well as smaller states such as Satara (1848) and Sambalpur (1849). This was less part of some great plan than the need, here and there, to create the conditions of peace in which trade could flourish. Almost all English expansionism in India began like this, the putting down of this or that disturbance leading to the annexations of more and more territory.

The discontents which other European states experienced at home in 1848 could to a large measure be exported by Britain to the imperial territories. The Whigs knew that the key to retaining the support of the middle classes at home was to avoid tax increases. 'I believe we must keep our fingers out of the people's pockets; and try to keep down our expenditure' was what the chancellor of the Exchequer, Wood, told Grey. It had been Grey's own mission to save money on imperial troops. In India, this meant pensioning off European troops and having more and more native forces, a policy which many military observers could see to be fraught with hazard.

Sir Charles Napier is usually seen as one of the less sensitive wielders of military authority in India ('Were I Emperor of India for twelve years she should be traversed by railways and have her rivers bridged . . . No Indian Prince should exist').[1] Yet when he was sent to subdue the provinces of Northern India in the early 1840s he could easily foresee the problems which would ensue. He pointed out that the constant changes in the pay of the sepoys (native Indian soldiers) caused deep discontent. He thought the Brahmins and the Rajputs made 'admirable soldiers', and on the whole he took a very low view of the European officers in the Indian army, 'especially those of the higher ranks'.[2] He warned from Karachi, in March 1850, that the government could 'but look with feelings of alarm, upon so large a body of armed, able bodied and mutinous soldiery, clamorous and violent if their . . . demands are not complied with'.[3]

No one in government heeded his warning. The policy of squeezing the colonies to satisfy the middle classes in England was an essential part of Sir Charles Wood's budgets.[4] In India there were two aspects of this policy. One was to ride roughshod over the religious sensibilities of the native regiments if, for example, it came cheaper to disregard caste considerations and transport Brahmin sepoys with those of a lower caste or worse of a different faith altogether. Secondly there was a parsimonious tendency to reduce the sepoys' pay, which caused simmering resentment, frequent minor mutinies, and was an undoubted factor in provoking the Great Uprising of 1857.

In other parts of the Empire, the effects of Free Trade reforms caused hardship and near ruin, particularly in those places such as British Guiana and Jamaica whose economy was only just coming to terms with the emancipation of the slaves. Incendiarism and looting were widespread in the West Indian plantations throughout 1848. Similar troubles in Jamaica – there was simply no money to pay public officials – led to a British parliamentary loan being offered – of £100,000. As for Canada, the removal of the Corn Laws in England meant that Canadian wheat farmers no longer had a guaranteed market. The French Canadians in particular took it hard, organizing themselves into armed secret societies, rioting, pelting the governor with rotten eggs and conducting a series of incendiary raids in cities, particularly Toronto. In Ceylon, the attempt to raise a European-style peasant tax in 1848 led to a riot involving 60,000 men, an attack on prisons, with prisoners set free, and planters' estates being ransacked. At the Cape, the Boer leader Andries Pretorius led a small war against the settlement of British settlers in Natal and the Xhosa and Gaika peoples rebelled against the idea of a British police force being imposed on them. There was also a mutiny of the indigenous Cape Corps regiment.

In other words, in every corner of the globe the British were experiencing their own version of the 1848 revolutions, and if the dissidents of Canada, the West Indies, the Punjab, the Cape and Ceylon could by magic all have been concentrated on Kennington Common to assist the Chartists we can imagine a very different consequence to 10 April 1848. The problems thus scattered across the globe called for a new, vigorous imperial policy which, after the calamities a decade later in India, they would receive. For the time being, though, they could be dealt with piecemeal.

And meanwhile, the colonies also supplied Britain with a useful resource, and another explanation for the fact that 1848 was a quieter year for Londoners than it was for Parisians, Berliners or Viennese. Although in 1848 only thirty declaredly *political* prisoners were transported, there was a huge increase in the numbers, especially from Ireland, who were removed from their native soil and sent to the colonies out of harm's way. Once again, we sense here a problem deferred rather than solved forever. History does not eliminate grievances; it lays them down like landmines. Irish Fenianism and the Irish Republican movement really began among the exiles.

The modern reader, in post-colonial times, is inevitably made uneasy by the knowledge that the liberal state – and for many Europeans, England was the *ideal* liberal state – was underpinned by oppression and interference by Europeans in so many different quarters of the globe. For self-confident liberals of the time, perspectives were different. The internationalism of the Great Exhibition of 1851 was an outward and visible sign of how readily capitalism could conquer the globe, exporting its modernity to Asia, the Americas, Africa and Australia, and drawing, in turn, all nations to itself under the emblematic hothouse erected for the exotic plant of Free Trade in the very centre of Hyde Park. Not that the 'Free Trade' label was always used. The Tory weekly *John Bull* nicknamed the exhibition 'The Free Trade Festival', leading one of the organizers, none other than the apostle of Free Trade himself, Richard Cobden, to suggest avoiding the term, lest it appear the political propaganda exercise it actually was. By the time the leader of the Opposition, Lord Stanley, was selling the idea of the Exhibition in his Mansion House address, he had judiciously claimed that it would 'bring into harmonious concord the nations of the world' and 'give encouragement . . . to the industry of all nations'.[5]

In fact, as we have already seen, the imposition of Free Trade caused widespread unrest all over the globe, the expansionism which trade both fed and provoked leading to Asian wars. Cobden and Bright's belief that Free Trade, because it was bound to transcend national boundaries, would lead ineluctably to the death of war was to be severely challenged during the 1850s, which saw the first major European war for nearly forty years breaking out in 1854.

It was no doubt partly with a feeling of lucky escape – from the revolutions of '48, from the whole decade which had seen such volatile economic change, such alarming

social unease, such disease and such famine, against a background of industrial expansion and invention – that the organizers began to plan the exhibition.

Unquestionably, the galvanic force behind the whole enterprise, the man without whom it would not have left the ground, was Henry Cole. It was Cole who saw in the exhibitions held by the Society for the Encouragement of Arts, Manufacturers and Commerce (1844) or the Society of Arts (1846) models of a much bigger exhibition, which would both encourage enterprise and invention in the sphere of industrial design and advertise its success. As the pseudonymous Felix Summerly, Cole had designed a china tea service, made by Minton and Co., for the exhibition of 1846. He was the man who had been responsible for making a cataloguing system in the Public Record Office where he worked as a civil servant. With Rowland Hill, he had pioneered the Penny Post in 1838. He had campaigned for a single railway-gauge and for reforms in the patent law. He also invented the Christmas card.

Cole had first met Prince Albert during his work in the PRO, and it was he who persuaded the organizers of the earlier, smaller exhibitions to have wider ambitions and to enlist a royal patron. He also brought in Thomas Milner Gibson, the Liberal MP from Manchester who had been vice-president of the Board of Trade, Cobden, Scott Russell – a Glaswegian industrial designer and jack of all trades – and Thomas Cubitt, the London property-developer and self-taught architect who had redeveloped Belgravia, rebuilt Buckingham Palace and built Osborne House on the Isle of Wight to Prince Albert's designs. It was Cole who persuaded the Queen's husband to appoint a Royal Commission to plan the exhibition – a committee which included the Prince himself (president), the prime minister, Lord John Russell, the leader of the Opposition, Lord Stanley, the former prime minister, Robert Peel, the Duke of Buccleuch, Mr Gladstone, Charles Lyell the geologist, Richard Westmacott the sculptor, and other persons of eminence.

Cole's first battle was won – to make the pioneers of industrial design, whose previous exhibitions had felt like muted affairs, feel that they had been adopted by the mainstream of political life to which they contributed so much wealth and energy. The commission, which was formed by 3 January 1850, had just over a year to make the thing a success: to ensure that the exhibits were of sufficiently high quality, to canvass industrial opinion not only all over Britain but all over the world, and to find a design which would house the exhibition and give it identity. There was also a site to be determined, with

Regent's Park, Primrose Hill, Wormwood Scrubs and the Isle of Dogs all canvassed as possibilities.

The first design for the exhibition halls, submitted by the building committee, who had rejected 233 designs sent in by architects, resembled a brick engine-shed, surmounted with a disproportionate dome, several times larger than that of St Peter's. The committee clung to the design merely because time was not on their side and – though none of the commissioners liked it – no alternative was available.

Then transpired one of those happy chances which make one understand why so many Victorians believed in the Whiggish optimism of Macaulay. This really does seem like a society, for all the dreadful sufferings of its underclass, which is powered by ingenuity and luck, a nation with a strong wind behind it soaring from triumph to triumph. It is in such moments of good fortune uniting with sheer cleverness that the fascination of the Victorian period is found. Today we think of England as a place where nothing quite works properly, where great projects are seldom tried, and if attempted take laborious lengths of time to accomplish.

On 11 June, William Ellis MP, chairman of the Midland Railway, had a meeting at the House of Commons with Joseph Paxton, the landscape-architect of the 6th Duke of Devonshire. Paxton had been much more than that to the (heterosexual) 'bachelor' Duke, being in effect the best friend to that ingenious nobleman and the companion of his many schemes of beautification in his Derbyshire palace. Paxton, from his mid-twenties, had demonstrated extraordinary skills not only as a gardener but also as an engineer and architect. The model village of Edensor, the 'Emperor' Fountain and the 'Chatsworth Stove', a giant conservatory, were only some of the glories this working-class genius achieved for his ducal friend and patron.[6] The Stove was the largest glass building in the world. When the Queen and Prince Albert visited Chatsworth in 1843 Paxton and the Duke had lit the huge conservatory with 14,000 lamps – 'This really is wonderful – astonishing,' exclaimed the Duke of Wellington, who was one of the illustrious guests.[7]

And now, Paxton, in his fiftieth year, after a life of freelance displays of cleverness for a limitlessly rich patron, had become the sort of man who sat on the board of railway companies, and was meeting William Ellis MP at the Commons before they went on to a formal meeting of the Midland Railway. Sitting in the public gallery, Paxton could not hear the debate in progress that afternoon – Ellis complained that the acoustics in Barry's new chamber were inadequate. The two men fell to discussing other botched jobs, including the designs for the new exhibition hall.

During the meeting of the Midland Railway company that afternoon, Paxton doodled a better design on his blotter, and later that day he showed it to Ellis. What he had in mind was an even bigger version of the Chatsworth Stove, all glass and cast iron, which could, if required, be dismantled and relocated when the exhibition closed. Ellis gave the piece of blotting paper to Cole, who arranged an audience at once with Prince Albert. Within a week, Fox and Henderson, the Smethwick contracting firm, had costed the design to the nearest pound. On the very day that the building committee published (to general derision) its disastrous plan – the giant domed engine shed – Paxton showed his alternative to Lord Granville, nephew of the Duke of Devonshire, who was able to present the committee with this much more attractive alternative. There were still a number of hurdles to jump. Members of the commission offered to put up money themselves to pay for Paxton's scheme. Granville and the Radical cabinet minister Henry Labouchere offered £5,000 each and the financier Samuel Morton Peto offered £50,000 – a far cry from the committee of the Millennium Dome in 2000, who were only prepared to spend other people's money for their unpopular extravaganza. In spite of opposition, the Paxton glasshouse idea was accepted, and work began constructing the space, not in Regent's Park or the Isle of Dogs, but plumb in the middle of London – Hyde Park. This, said Sir Robert Peel – his last words to the commission on this or any subject – should be the site 'or none'.[8]

Those who criticized the Great Exhibition – Carlyle, Colonel Sibthorp, the *Mechanics Magazine* (a Radical periodical), the Chartists (what remained of them) – tended to be those who criticized Free Trade. *The Times* blew hot and cold, first supporting it, then claiming that the exhibition would ruin Hyde Park, finally compelled to acknowledge that in its own terms the exhibition was hugely successful. The sheer scale of it all makes any description, either of the opening ceremonies, or of the visitors, or of the 100,000 exhibits, become a catalogue of hyperboles. Twenty-five thousand season tickets were sold in advance, at 3 guineas each for gentlemen, 2 guineas for ladies. For ten days after the opening, admission cost £1 and was thereafter reduced to five

The first sketch for the design of Crystal Palace by Joseph Paxton, 1850, doodled on a blotter during a boring meeting of the Midland Railway company.

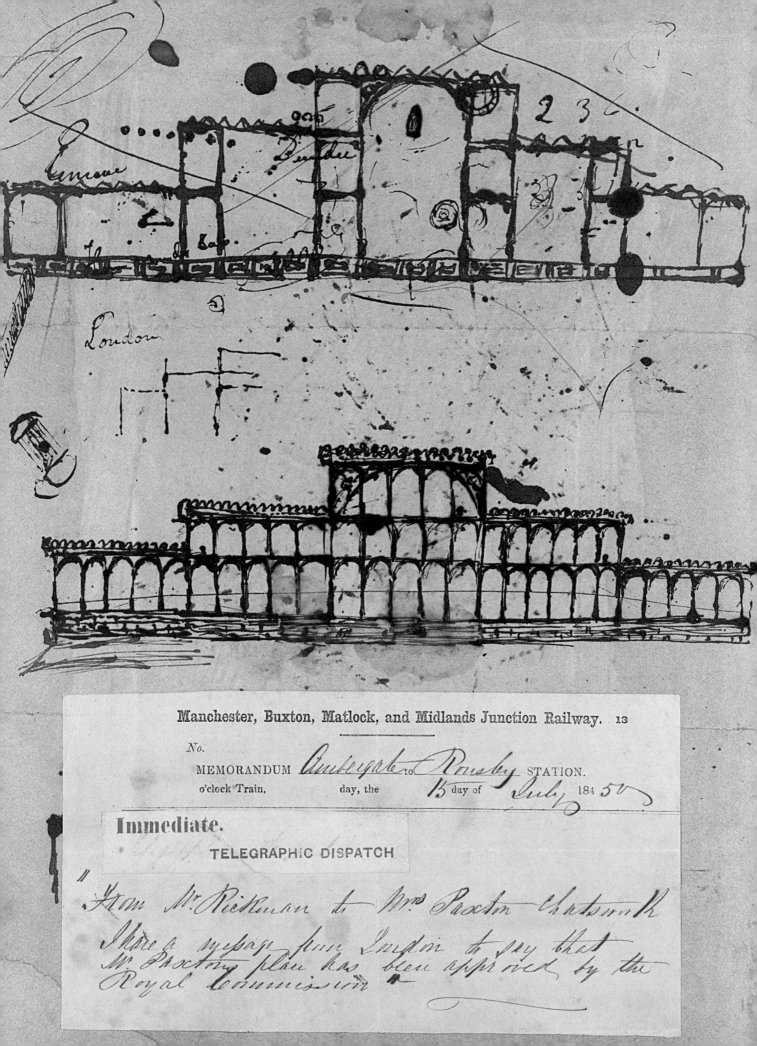

From Mr Rickman to Mr Paxton Chatsworth
I have a message from London to say that
Mr Paxton's plan has been approved by the
Royal Commission

A display of a portable steam engine corn threshing machine and a seed drill at the Great Exhibition in Hyde Park, 1851.

shillings. After 24 May, Mondays to Thursdays cost 1*s*., Fridays half a crown, Saturdays 5*s*. There was no opening on Sundays, no smoking, no alcohol and no dogs. On 1 May there were 6,000 extra police on duty and five cavalry regiments on standby in the Tower of London in case of trouble.

By 11 o'clock in the morning, 500,000 people had assembled in the Park to watch Charles Spencer the great aeronaut go up in his balloon at the moment the exhibition was declared open. The jam of cabs and carriages stretched back to the Strand – 1,500 cabs, 800 broughams, 600 post carriages, 300 clarences . . . At noon, the Queen and Prince Albert arrived and were saluted with guns. The great organ struck up 'God Save the Queen'. The archbishop of Canterbury offered a prayer and a choir sang Handel's Hallelujah chorus.

Albert had chosen as the motto 'The Earth is the Lord's and the fullness thereof'. *The Times* said it 'was the first morning since the creation of the world that all peoples have assembled from all parts of the world and done a common act'. The Queen was equally ecstatic:

The glimpse of the transept through the iron gates, the waving palms, flowers, statues, myriads of people filling the galleries and seats around, with the flourish of trumpets as we entered, gave us a sensation which I can never forget and I felt much moved . . . The sight as we came to the middle where the steps and a chair (which I did *not* sit on) were placed, with the beautiful crystal fountain just in front of it, was magical – so vast, so glorious, so touching. One felt – as so many did whom I have since spoken to – filled with devotion, more so than by any service I have ever heard. The tremendous cheers, the joy expressed in every face, the immensity of the building, the mixture of palms, flowers, trees, statues, fountains, the organ (with 200 instruments and 500 voices; which sounded like nothing) and my beloved husband, the author of this 'peace Festival' which united the industry of all nations of the earth – all this was moving indeed, and it was and is a day to live for ever.[9]

It would be fascinating to know how we, visitors from the twenty-first century, would have regarded the Great Exhibition had we joined the 20,000 visitors on that opening day, or the 6,039,195 visitors (more accurately one should say visits, since many, like the Queen, returned again and again) before the exhibition closed in October. Would we perhaps regard it as the very emblematic epitome of England in its time? The variety and ingenuity of the exhibits would no doubt astound us. Hibbert, Platt and Son's fifteen cotton-spinning machines demonstrated in anodyne, clean conditions, in a southern exhibition chamber, the kind of machinery which had done the home-weavers out of a living, and to which the northern working classes were now attached like slaves. But here, they seemed like gleaming incarnations of progress and progressivism. The machine section of the exhibition was always the most popular.[10] They were 'the epitome of man's industrial progress – of his untiring efforts to release himself from his material bondage', as James Ward wrote in *The World in its Workshops*. Here could be seen Nasmyth's steam hammer, invented ('after a few moments' thought')[11] to forge the proposed paddle shafts of the *Great Britain*; here were locomotives, talking telegraphs, steam turbines, printing machines, envelope machines; and a wide variety of scientific instruments – air pumps, microscopes, printing telegraphs, cameras and photographic equipment of the most up-to-date kind. J.A. Whipple, a Boston photographer, exhibited a daguerreotype of the Moon, the result of a collaboration with W.C. Bond at the Observatory at Harvard.

In all this, we visitors in a time machine from the twenty-first century would find harbingers of Victorian triumphs – we will see these great inventions used for good and ill in the coming years, cameras capturing for us everything from the Crimean War to Mrs Cameron's Arthurian fantasies; telegraphs playing a crucial role in the establishment of Empire. (The British use of the telegraph was vital in subduing the Indian uprisings in 1857–8.)

But as we have accustomed ourselves to seeing this exhibition as the symbol of nineteenth-century industrial progress and materialism, we turn the corner and – what is this? We are standing in the Medieval Court designed by Augustus Welby Pugin, in which we are confronted with Gothic High Altars, hanging lamps, and statues of the Virgin. So strongly did the Medieval Court offend Protestant sensibility that complaints were made to the Prince Consort and the prime minister and a flood of letters to *The Times* regarded the erection of a Crucifixion on the Rood Screen as an 'insult to the religion of the country'.[12]

While twenty-first-century time visitors, unless from Northern Ireland, would find such complaints bizarre, they might need to remind themselves that 'No Popery' was still a live issue for senior politicians in Britain in 1850–1.

Whatever the religious significance of all this, the visitor to the exhibition – particularly a twenty-first-century visitor coming to the Crystal Palace in Hyde Park in a time machine – might see the outbursts of irrational prejudice against Catholics less in meta-physical than in political terms. The paradox of the exhibition was that while being international in scope, it was fundamentally designed as a demonstration not merely of British superiority to other nations but, in some way, of British independence and isolationism.

We should not fail to notice the internationalism of the displays, and if we read the *Illustrated London News* of 26 April 1851, with its pictures of Bengalis busily carving ivory for the Great Exhibition, we might also see in it signs of colonial exploitation. We might gasp with delight at the stuffed elephant and howdah from India, or at the exoticism of the Tunis Room. As we wandered from the Turkish stalls, the Greek stalls, the French, German and Italian exhibits we might indeed feel that 'the exhibition turned the Crystal Palace into, in the words of so many visitors, a fairyland, a tour round the world'.

Yet it has to be said that the presence of so much exotic foreign material, and so many foreigners, did not diminish the natural xenophobia of the English. Quite the reverse. The Home Office, and the Duke of Wellington, seen as the natural defender of England against foreign foes, were inundated with paranoid letters. 'Woe to *England*. All the *French Socialists* it is understood are coming over to the Exhibition!!!! It will be *well* if *London* is not destroyed by *Fire*!!!! The Pope has successfully thrown the Apple of Discord *amongst us*!!!!' was one letter.

Broadly speaking the internationalist minority, including Prince Albert, rejoiced at the number of foreigners, and the xenophobic majority saw the exhibition as exacerbating trade rivalries rather than emphasizing the harmony between trading partners.

To most twenty-first-century eyes, the majority of artefacts in the exhibition would seem lumpen and hideous. For every laugh we might have at a stuffed

The many-tiered stalls at the Great Exhibition, 1851.

animal (and Plouquet's famous stuffed rabbits, squirrels, weasels playing cards, holding tea parties and playing the pianoforte were among the great losses when the Crystal Palace was destroyed by fire in the twentieth century) there would be dozens of Birmingham-made epergnes, overmantels, clocks and tables which would not seem beautiful to our contemporaries. The Jewel Cabinet designed for Elkington and Co. by Albert's artistic mentor Louis Gruner, and adorned with panels depicting the Queen and her consort in medieval costume, with silver statuettes at each corner, is a good example: can one ever envisage an age which thought it lovely? It is still treasured in the Royal Collection. As Ruskin bitterly but appositely reminded his readers, 'In the year 1851, when all that glittering roof was built, in order to exhibit the petty arts of our fashionable luxury-carved bedsteads of Vienna, glued toys of Switzerland and gay jewellery from France – in that very year, I say,

the greatest pictures of Venetian masters were rotting at Venice in the rain, for want of a roof to cover them, with holes made by cannon-shot through their canvas.'[13]

We should probably conclude if we had seen the original 1851 exhibition through twenty-first-century eyes that none of the exhibits could rival that 'glittering roof' itself.

The original conception of Paxton, so gloriously executed by the firm of Fox, Henderson and Co. of Smethwick, created a building which outsoared the Chatsworth Stove, a magnificent airy structure, entirely of iron and glass, modern, architecturally innovative and without the camp element of pastiche which characterizes almost all other great Victorian buildings. It was the largest greenhouse in the world, incorporating the very trees of Hyde Park. It was the world's first shopping mall, with tier upon tier of shops selling all manner of wares. It was infinitely adaptable to its purpose, containing an Aladdin's cave of variety, but it was also something of great beauty and worth in itself. When the exhibition closed on 11 October 1851, the net profit was more than £186,000 – money which was used to buy the plot of land in Kensington in which the permanent collections would be housed, and in which Prince Albert's memory was immortalized – in the Victoria and Albert Museum, the Imperial College of Science and Technology, and the Royal Albert Hall.

In spite of his misgivings about the exhibition, Wellington did visit the Crystal Palace for the opening, and went so often that he almost became part of the 'Shew'.[14] To the end of his days he took seriously his duties as warden of the Cinque Ports, the guardian of England against continental invasion. Long after the threat of a French invasion had become, to say the least, unlikely, he had strengthened fortifications on the south coast, and it was apt that he was to die in Walmer Castle, the warden's official residence. His funeral in London was an emblem of an old England which had vanished. The poet laureate in his eulogy 'Ode on the Death of the Duke of Wellington' used the funeral as a chance to beg

O Statesmen, guard us, guard the eye, the soul
Of Europe, keep our noble England whole,
And save the one true seed of freedom sown
Betwixt a people and their ancient throne.[15]

In fact, by then, Britain was involved with a French alliance, and not merely an entente with the nation that Wellington had fought so doughtily forty years since, but with a Bonaparte.

In December 1851, Louis Napoleon Bonaparte, who had been, a little shakily, elected as president of the new republic in 1848, staged a coup d'état and established himself as emperor of France. The foreign secretary, Lord Palmerston, whose antics over many an international incident had been so embarrassing to the government of which he was a part, told the French ambassador of his 'entire approbation' of Bonaparte's action.[16] He had not consulted the Queen, or the prime minister, and though he blusteringly claimed that he had only been speaking in a private capacity, such a defence in a foreign secretary was risible. Lord John Russell asked for his resignation. Victoria and Albert were cock-a-hoop. Albert did not believe that British public opinion was pro-Bonapartist and he was probably right – but Palmerston was not long gone from the political scene.[17]

When Lord John's government fell, the Tories came back into office and the Queen asked Lord Derby to form an administration. This was to be the famous 'Who? Who?' government, since when the Duke of Wellington was told the names of the new Cabinet, two months before he died, he had responded with those withering monosyllables.[18] Hindsight is chiefly interested in the *Who Who* administration because it contained Disraeli in his first role as chancellor of the Exchequer. Derby's government did not last the year, however, and by December, Lord Aberdeen had formed his Liberal–Peelite coalition Cabinet – with W.E. Gladstone replacing B. Disraeli as chancellor of the Exchequer, Lord John Russell as foreign secretary and Pam as home secretary. The Queen was not able to dismiss the 'two dreadful old men' as easily as she might have hoped. Moreover, though Pam lost control of the Foreign Office for the months of 1852, his policy – an alliance with the new French emperor – was still that of the government. Though the reasonable and unbelligerent figure of Aberdeen was the last man to want to break the forty years of European peace, this was the government which was to lead Britain to war.

Work by Ford Madox Brown. Notice in the foreground, to the right, Thomas Carlyle (in a hat) and F.D. Maurice.

Chapter Ten

Marx – Ruskin – The Pre-Raphaelites

The only cohesive opposition to the march of capitalism in the 1840s and 1850s came from communism – or its watered-down equivalents – and Christianity. But – this is one of the central questions facing the men and women of the age – were they believable? Their allure explains how such strange alliances could have been formed against the relentlessness of the factory-owners – a Bible Christian such as Ashley, motivated by reading the Gospels, standing alongside radicals and socialists whose views of other matters he might deplore, in his campaign to limit the hours worked by women and children in the cotton mills. It is a curious fact that the leader of the working men's cause in the House of Commons, until the Factory Act of 1850 finally did bring in the desired Ten Hours measure, was a high Tory aristocrat who believed in hierarchy, deference and the literal truth of every word of the Bible. His tireless campaigns to set up ragged schools for slum-dwellers, and to prick the conscience of laissez-faire economists, took over a decade. In the first years of Victoria's reign, the coal flickering cheerfully in your grate would, as like as not, have been dragged through underground tunnels too small for a grown man by child workers as young as six. This was brought to an end in 1844, against the fiercest opposition from the big colliery proprietors, such as Lord Londonderry. It took a further three years to persuade liberals such as Macaulay, Palmerston or Russell so much as to consider limiting the hours worked by women and children to ten hours a day. With their blinkered view of what constituted 'liberty' these liberals felt that legislation interfered with the personal freedoms of workers. Most of the child workers in the mills were employed not by the mill-owners themselves but by adult male spinners who subcontracted work. To make laws about such private arrangements was, in Palmerston's view, 'a vicious and wrong principle'.[1]

We shall fail to understand the Victorians if we do not take note of the word. Their principles were not ours. Some were candid enough to recognize that the greedy logic of their belief in laissez-faire economics was incompatible with a Christian witness. Others, perhaps a majority in the early to mid-Victorian period, tried to live with a double standard, being perfectly prepared to say that they believed the working classes were made in God's image and likeness, while treating them with a severity comparable to that of slave-owners in the West Indian plantations.

Sometimes we can learn more of a past generation by reading the authors who were popular at the time and have now sunk without trace, rather than reperusing the immortals. Harriet Martineau (1802–76) was one of the most highly esteemed journalists of the day, and her weathercock mind gives us the directions in which the mid-Victorian liberal wind was blowing. Born of a long line of (Huguenot) surgeons in Norwich, she was one of the most popular interpreters of the English-speaking nineteenth century to itself. A series of woodenly written short stories illustrative of the political economy of Malthus, James Mill and Ricardo would probably not reach the bestseller lists in the twenty-first century, but in the 1830s they made a very palpable hit, and as she tells us, 'the stern Benthamites' thanked her as a safe and faithful expositor of their doctrines. Her *Half a Century of the British Empire*, begun in 1848, was designed for the educated, self-educated or semi-educated bourgeoisie.

Wordy, authoritative, cliché-ridden, Miss Martineau had the know-all tone which so often wins journalism wide readership and short-term respect. Like many of her modern equivalents, she had all the right views – that is the views espoused by the metropolitan intelligentsia. She was a keen abolitionist – of slavery – but saw no reason why this concern for her oppressed fellow humans in American plantations should lead her to comparable feelings of compassion for English factory workers. In 1855 she penned *The Factory Controversy – A Warning Against Meddling Legislation*. Factory inspectors in 1853 had drawn the attention of the secretary of state to the 'enormous amount of accidents' in British factories, but clever journalist that she was, Martineau knew how to turn an obvious truth – that, in spite of the best endeavours of Ashley and others, the conditions in factories were still fairly appalling – into something absurd:

> The whole number of accidents from machinery, in three years, was reported to be 11,716 of which 3,434 were of a serious character. The serious are all that require any serious notice, as the others are of so slight a nature that they would not be noticed anywhere but in a special registration like that provided by The Factory Act. For instance, 700 are cases of cut fingers. Any worker who rubs off a bit of skin from finger or thumb, or sustains the slightest cut which interferes with the spinning process for a single day, has the injury registered under the Act.[2]

Turn to the chapter in *Capital* entitled 'The Working Day' – eighty of the finest pages ever written by Marx or anyone else on the plight of nineteenth-century factory workers – and a very different picture emerges. There we read that although the three Factory Acts of 1833, 1844 and 1847 restricted the working hours of women and children in some circumstances, the liberal capitalists in the House of Commons had, with the passing of each act, clawed back some 'concession' in return. So, for example, when the 'relay system' was regulated in 1844 – making it impossible for factory-owners to work a child from 5 a.m. until noon and then again at 1 p.m. as if this second stint of work constituted a new 'shift' – the Lower House '*reduced* the minimum age at which the exploitation of children could begin from 9 to 8, this being done to ensure that capital could have "the additional supply of children" which capitalists are by human and divine laws entitled to demand'.[3] The various factory acts never changed the basic notion that males over the age of eighteen should work a fifteen-hour day from 5.30 a.m. to 8.30 p.m. Marx, reading through the small print of the 1844 act, was also able to remind his readers that though the law now forbade the employment of children after 1 p.m. who had been employed before noon, a child of eight, beginning now at noon, might be worked from 12 to 1 – one hour; from 2 to 4 – two hours; and from 5 to 8.30 in the evening – in all the legal six and a half hours – in order to make their work simultaneous with the adult workers. So the spirit of the act which desired the protection of children being kept at factories all afternoon and all evening was defied by its letter.[4]

The accumulation of evidence from factory inspectors adduced in Marx's chapter makes the protestations of Martineau and her readers seem as ridiculous as they are offensive. We read the testimony of doctors and factory inspectors who have examined potters, manufacturers of lucifer matches, railwaymen, brick-makers . . . Whatever the category of worker examined, the same story is told: the exploitation of workers to the point where the urban proletariat of Victorian England have become stunted in growth and subject to a whole range of debilitating illnesses, all of which are a direct consequence of their being overworked. The doctor in the North Staffordshire Infirmary, having enumerated the pneumonia, phthisis, bronchitis and asthma, as well as disorders of kidney and stomach, to which his 'ill-shaped and frequently ill-formed' patients were subject, summed up the causes of these complaints in two words – 'long hours'. The match-manufacturers of Manchester, Birmingham, Liverpool, Bristol, Norwich, Newcastle and Glasgow all suffer from 'phossy jaw' – half the workers are under thirteen.[5] Wallpaper manufacturers suffered from comparable chemical poisonings. The hours worked by a London baker must have made the (usually adulterated) bread roll dry in anyone's mouth if he had read *Capital* over his breakfast. Taking his information from the reports delivered to Parliament – the 'Blue Books' – Marx reminds Londoners of what someone else endured to put bread on their table.

The London journeyman baker's work began at 11 p.m., when he made the dough, a laborious task lasting half to three-quarters of an hour. Then he lay down on

THE CHEAP TAILOR AND HIS WORKMEN.

A cartoon satirising the cheap sweatshops of the clothing industry. Henry Mayhew in London Labour and the London Poor *noted that as the wages of a trade went down, so the labourers extended their hours of work to the utmost possible limits. 'My employer' I was told by a journeyman tailor working for a large West-end show shop, 'reduces my wages by one-third, and the consequence is, I put in two stitches where I used to give three.'*

the kneading board, with a sack for a mattress, and slept for a couple of hours. Then followed five hours of hard, rapid work, kneading, moulding and preparing loaves and rolls. Temperatures in the bakehouse were as high as 90°. When the bread was baked it had to be delivered, and a high proportion of journeymen bakers undertook this work as well, wheeling handcarts or carrying baskets of bread to shops and houses – work which lasted until 1 or 6 p.m. depending on demand. During the London 'season', when bread was required in larger quantities in the evenings, the work of the bakeries was continuous. London bakers, statistics showed, seldom lived beyond the age of forty-two.

And simplest and most life-threatening of all the hazards facing the urban Victorians was the sheer squalor resultant from their failure to understand that cholera, typhoid and typhus fever were water-borne.

The stench of London and its waters was remarked by all writers of the period. When the Queen and Prince Albert attempted a short pleasure cruise on the Thames in 1858 they were forced to turn back to land after a few minutes, the odours were so terrible. (That year of drought, Parliament had to rise early because of the smell becoming unendurable on the terraces outside the Palace of Westminster.)[6]

The chief propagandist for proper drainage in Victorian cities was Edwin Chadwick, who drew public attention to the filthy conditions in the large manufacturing towns. But the great scientific demonstration of the fact that disease was water-borne was made (against the fiercest opposition) by Dr John Snow. (He was also the genius who improved the use of chloroform during childbirth pioneered by James Young Simpson, and acted as a merciful anaesthetist to the Queen.)

Throughout the nineteenth century, as epidemic followed epidemic, there was heated debate about whether cholera was contagious.[7] Generally speaking, the contagionists were viewed by contemporaries as archaic, even antisocial. The anti-contagionists – modern, bourgeois, mercantile – were reluctant to admit the possibility – as we observed in the last chapter – that trade and traffic could spread pollution, disease, death.

The majority of the medical profession refused to accept Snow's findings. It was not until the cholera microbe was isolated and identified by Koch in 1883 that Snow's brilliant hunch – turning to circumstantial deduction – was proved.[8] Snow tried – and Chadwick too – to spread the gospel of cleanliness as a guard against waterborne disease: the creation of good drains; lodging houses for vagrants; public washhouses; quarantine for local visitors. The coal miners were the group who suffered more from cholera than any other – Snow urged that their work conditions be divided into four-hour shifts so that they did not need to use the coal pits as privies. In parts of London where the classes washed their hands – Belgravia – the rate of death by cholera was 28 in 10,000, compared with 186 per 10,000 in poorer districts. But, of course, such measures could not be introduced without control, and – as in the case of the Irish famine – the true laissez-faire liberal would, quite literally, prefer death to state interference.

Sewage and drainage provided the inspiration for one of Victorian art's most self-conscious efforts to make a social comment in paint: *Work* by Ford Madox Brown, a canvas begun in 1852 to celebrate the Public Health Acts inspired by Chadwick's campaigns, was not completed until 1863 – and not exhibited until 1865.[9] The idea came to the artist when he saw men digging in Heath Street,

Christ knocks at the door of the soul. Holman Hunt's
The Light of the World. *In 1905–7 the copy now hanging in Keble College, Oxford, toured the colonies and was viewed by hundreds of thousands who flocked to see it as a sacred object.*

Mayhew, scrabble in the dirt in the foreground; behind them loll the rich, their superfluity of wealth depicted by the groaning tray of the pastry-cook. To the left, posters on the wall suggest means of improvement for the working classes – 'The Working Men's College', the inspiration of F.D. Maurice, who stands to the extreme right of the picture, his gentle intelligent face curiously reposeful compared with the contemptuous tormented figure at his side, his teeth orange with tobacco smoke, his Diogenes-contempt for Benthamite society apparent in his grin. This is Thomas Carlyle. In the background of the picture are men carrying election posters for Bobus, the imaginary Benthamite parliamentary candidate lampooned in Carlyle's *Past and Present*. Carlyle's pessimism about Parliament and democratic processes had now become absolute. 'What can the incorruptiblest *Bobuses* elect if it be not some *Bobissimus*, should they find such?' – by which he means that the Victorian concept of an 'aristocracy of Talent', if guided solely by 'Midas-eared philosophies' of money-love, will only result in a society which is spiritually rotten and dead.[11]

Carlyle's belief that the human race – and the British in particular – had gone astray at the time of the Industrial Revolution was widely shared.

Much of this pattern of thought finds its echo in the Pre-Raphaelite Brotherhood – who were young enough to be Carlyle's sons. The 'brotherhood' began in 1848 at 83 Gower Street, when a group of art students vowed 'to produce thoroughly good pictures and statues'. Of the original seven, three members of the PRB – Dante Gabriel Rossetti, aged twenty, John Everett Millais, aged nineteen, and William Holman Hunt, aged twenty-one – went on to be famous artists. Other painters whom we think of as 'Pre-Raphaelite' – such as Ford Madox Brown himself – never in fact joined the Brotherhood, which was never a very tightly knit guild, and which dissolved with the years.

One sees the way in which these young painters set out to criticize the spirit of the age if one considers two of the most celebrated paintings of William Holman Hunt, companion pieces executed within two or three years of one another. *The Light of the World* was the most popular of all Victorian paintings. Engraved by W.H. Simmons and W. Ridgway, copied three times by Hunt himself, and photographically reproduced, it was an icon of faith in a time of doubt, the image of Christ which has hung in a thousand churches and chapels, and on millions of bedroom walls.

The original models for the figure of Jesus were Christina Rossetti, pious poetess, sister of Dante Gabriel

halfway up the Mount in Hampstead.[10] He painted it under the mistaken impression that they were con-structing a fresh water supply, whereas they were in fact constructing new sewage pipes. The picture, a punctiliously executed and still recognizable London view in a blaze of summer sunshine, is heavy with symbolism. Poor ragged children, characters from

Rossetti, and a whey-faced young woman, herself a painter of some ability, called Elizabeth Siddal.[12] Her family had an ironmongering business in Southwark and, like her sister, she originally worked in dressmaking and millinery. She probably began to work as an artist's model because she herself aspired to be a painter. She both modelled and studied in Newman Street, just north of Oxford Street, where there were drawing schools and where both Ford Madox Brown and Rossetti had studios. To say that there were few opportunities of self-improvement for young female milliners in nineteenth-century London is an understatement. Possibly the first time we see her in a painting of note is in Hunt's *British Family succouring a Christian from the persecution of Druids*. In 1852 she posed in a bath for John Everett Millais as Ophelia, her father taking strong exception, since she might have died of hypothermia. Her face is one of the most haunting of nineteenth-century England. She was a tall woman, in an age which praised the petite. Her lower lip tucked beneath the upper 'as if it strove to kiss itself' – the words are Rossetti's, destined to fall in love with her and, years later when love had faded, to marry her. She had translucent skin, freckles, and abundant red hair.

It is not entirely inappropriate that behind the bearded gentle figure of Hunt's *Light of the World*, standing with his lantern, and knocking to be let into our hearts, there should lurk those golden-brown eyes. If suffering could redeem, then poor Elizabeth Siddal would have redeemed us all.

It was widely assumed for years, on no evidence, that Gabriel Rossetti and Elizabeth Siddal were lovers in the modern way between 1851 – the year of their so-called 'engagement' – and their marriage in 1860. Rossetti's most learned biographer, Jan Marsh, has cast doubt on this and plausibly argues that Elizabeth's misery and frustration during these years, and her subsequent decline into drug addiction, were related to Rossetti's coyness, later neglect. Two years before he married, Rossetti probably lost his virginity, aged thirty, with a young woman who was cracking nuts in a bar in the Royal Surrey pleasure gardens, and who flicked a shell in his direction. This was Fanny Cornforth, another of the great icons of nineteenth-century painters, a large girl with abundant golden hair, pouting lips, a strong Cockney accent and a sensual laugh.

Lizzie was an image to be adored with the heart and the eye. Sick worship can kill its object, as the lives and deaths of modern icons, pop or royalty, demonstrate. Siddal sickened and died of being worshipped as a dead Ophelia, an ethereal Beatrice. Her husband's most loving image of her was of *Beata Beatrix*, the soul of Dante's beloved, painted from memory after her drug-overdose death.

Vulgar, pouting, sensual and strong, Fanny was destined to be housekeeper and muse to Rossetti and his

friends for years.[13] She was not, as it happens, the model for what I have called the companion-piece to Hunt's *Light of the World* – *The Awakening Conscience*. This was another 'stunner'; a teenage barmaid at the Cross Keys public house in Chelsea called Annie Miller.[14] Hunt first saw her when she was swabbing beer and spit off the pub floor – she was bare-foot and her red-gold hair fell over her shoulders in flaming ropes. She was soon part of the Pre-Raphaelite circle, affecting to be shocked by Rossetti's claim that 'women are so much nicer when they have lost their virtue', while loving the attention. She was one of the most successful artist's models of her day – much disapproved of by the would-be genteel Lizzie Siddal; she was the mistress of Rossetti and was for a time Hunt's fiancée.[15] In Hunt's view of Annie, communicated in his granddaughter's memoir *My Grandfather, His Wives and Loves*, Annie is represented as a spirited girl who could be 'trouble': her attempts to get Hunt to educate her, marry her, find her a position are seen as potential blackmail – but how else was a girl who had grown up in a warren of rooms used as a brothel supposed to make a life for herself?

The icon of the Victorian Christ – who was in fact a 'wronged woman' with a beard – represented that side of the Christian religion which was most under threat as the Sea of Faith ebbed away in the nineteenth century: namely a belief in the Divine Saviour, the Man-God. This was the 'falsehood' in which Carlyle and so many Victorian intellectuals refused to believe.

To discard Christian morality, however, was altogether more difficult, and this is one of the reasons for the fascinating double standards which we find in so many individual Victorian lives, particularly where sex and money were in question. Christ had taught that you cannot serve God and Mammon. A state which modelled itself on the socio-economic ideas of Malthus, Ricardo and Bentham had enthroned Money, so it was not

1 From 1864 to 1870 Rossetti was at work on his masterpiece, one of the great morbid statements of all nineteenth-century art, the Beata Beatrix *in which he depicted his wife, Elizabeth, as the Beatrice of Dante's* Vita Nuova. *Though he began painting it in her lifetime it seems unmistakably the face of a dead woman who has outsoared the shadows of earthly existence – a quite sublime combination of the spiritual and the merely morbid. Created in the first decade when Doubt had become not merely a coterie-secret but the norm for millions of people, it gently speaks both of religion's glory and its tragic impossibility.*

surprising they lost their sense of God. Chastity was no easier for Victorians than for anyone else, but their guilt-feelings about sex, combined with their attitudes to economics, could lead to those presumptions of possession, ownership, purchase of women by men against which feminism formed its inevitable Hegelian antithesis. (Hunt was in love with Annie Miller, wanted to marry her; but his very act of 'educating' her, treating her as a Pygmalion creation of his own, was in itself a form of purchase.)

Hunt's nickname among his friends was 'Mad' and his granddaughter tells us that he was a manic depressive – 'when in despair about his future or his work he would shut himself up in a poky bedroom above the studio and shiver with fear. He felt as if icy water were trickling down his spine. Alone in the dark, he raved, holding long noisy conversations with the Devil . . . He frequently lost faith in humanity and in his confused idea of God, but for him the Devil was always real.'[16]

The word 'Pre-Raphaelite' in popular modern parlance does not refer to particular painting techniques or attitudes to the Middle Ages. It means young women with pale faces, pouting lips and abundant hair. The hair was important; so important that hairdressing, for the first time in English history, came out of the private domain of the home. Women who could afford to now went to hair-stylists – the styles varying much from year to year. No respectable woman wore her hair loose – which is what gives these loose-haired Pre-Raphaelite maidens so much of their erotic charm for the men who painted them and the men who bought the pictures. And in an age where everything was up for sale, the exporters and importers did not stop at hair itself. Great quantities of hair were imported into Britain from the European continent. The 'hair harvest' in Italy was an annual feature in poorer villages and 200,000 lb of hair were sold annually in the Paris markets, at a price of 10*s*. or 12*s*. per ounce – 20*s*. for really long hair.

In *The Awakening Conscience* Annie Miller's hair tumbles down her shoulders and back, as she rises from the lap of her roué lover. Just as Carlyle saw at once that *The Light of the World* was not so much an expression of faith as – something radically different – a seeking after false consolation, so *The Awakening Conscience* disturbs us with its jingle-jangle of confused imagery and – more – confused sexual feeling on the part of the artist. The picture is meant to depict the 'awakening conscience' of a kept woman who rises from her lover's knee listening to the promptings of morality. It is in fact soaked, like so many Pre-Raphaelite canvases, in *male* feelings about

The Awakening Conscience *by Holman Hunt.*

novels such as Mrs Gaskell's *Ruth*, they probably felt that Hunt's picture had lifted too many veils. Hunt, while painting it, had lectured Annie on the dangers of going down such a path herself. While she posed for him in an expensive gown, fine linen trimmed with hand-embroidered lace, Annie was supposed to be staring into the pits of hell as her whiskery admirer tries to hold on to her bottom. Many observers of her face must have seen, rather, a young woman with an eye to fun and prosperity ahead if she continues in her 'degrading temptation' – Hunt's words.

The young Pre-Raphaelite Brotherhood found themselves to their good fortune with an eminent defender, none other than the greatest art critic of the age (or any age). Ruskin saw at once that the sexual aspect (confused as we may find it) of *The Awakening Conscience* is only part of the story. In his letter to *The Times* of 25 May 1854 expounding the picture's meaning, he sees that the hideous mid-Victorian furnishings speak of the moral destructiveness of new wealth brought in by the 'success' of industrial capitalism:

> There is not a single object in all that room – common, modern, vulgar (in the vulgar sense, as it may be), but it becomes tragical, if rightly read, that furniture so carefully painted, even to the last vein of the rosewood – is there nothing to learn from that terrible lustre of it, from its fatal newness; nothing there that has the old thoughts of home upon it, or that is ever to become a part of home . . .

In the coming decades, William Morris was to wage war on the factory-made ugliness of Victorian domestic interiors, and to expand, even more trenchantly than Ruskin himself, on the intimate connections between morality, as socially and privately understood, and design.

Ruskin in *Modern Painters* had been the great defender of Turner against production-line Academy painting rules. At first sight it might seem surprising that the man who could see Turner's smudgy seascapes as the highest painterly form would be able, at the same time, and so instantaneously, to form a generous judgement of the crystalline Pre-Raphaelite innovation. In both cases, what Ruskin recognized was that the fledgling Brotherhood, like the great old sun-worshipper, were devotees of truth, believers that painting must be true in two senses, both faithfully reproducing nature, and punctilious in its emotional integrity. When Ruskin first impulsively leapt to the defence of the PRB – against those who suspected them of being crypto-Catholics, or worse – he did not do so because they were

sex – purely mechanical lust clashing noisily with school-boy masturbation – guilt masquerading as serious moral feeling. This, apart from their sheer technical skill, must explain the enduring popularity of the Pre-Raphaelite painters.

Yet however sheepish a man, and satirical a woman, must feel when standing in front of one of these paintings today, and whatever the final analysis of their aesthetic worth, how pleasing it is that these faces, these images, survive. Lizzie Siddal, Fanny Cornforth and Annie Miller's are among the best-known faces of the nineteenth century – far better known to us than the faces of most of the prime ministers or novelists or civil servants. Next to the Queen herself, theirs are the faces which survive.

The Awakening Conscience, depicting the world of the 'kept woman', awoke some raw nerves among the critics. Carlyle liked it as much as he'd despised *The Light of the World*. *The Morning Chronicle* denounced it as 'an absolutely disgraceful picture'. Although the middle classes liked tut-tutting over the moral dangers of fallen women and lapped up depictions of their decline in

his friends: 'Let me state, in the first place, that I have no acquaintance with any of these artists, and very imperfect sympathy with them. No one who has met any of my writings will suspect me of desiring to encourage them in their Romanist and Tractarian tendencies.'

As the 1850s unfolded, however, Ruskin's social contact with these much younger men was to have momentous effects in his personal history. In Rossetti's raffish ménage, Ruskin was to find the very opposite of the prim, well-ordered, rich suburban household of his sherry-merchant father – both so stifling and so inescapable. In Holman Hunt, Ruskin was destined to discover a deep and important artistic friendship. But it was Ruskin's acquaintanceship with John Everett Millais which had the first and explosive effect.

Millais, ten years Ruskin's junior and a year younger than Ruskin's wife Effie, had been a child prodigy, admitted to the Royal Academy Schools at the age of eleven. He was twenty-two years old when Ruskin first called on him, and tried to convert him to Turner. 'He believes,' Millais wrote, 'that I shall be converted on further acquaintance with his works, and that he will gradually slacken in his admiration.'[17] Neither thing happened, but the two men had soon become friends, constantly visiting one another, and travelling together. Millais, the painter of Romantic Scottish history, had never been north of the border; Ruskin, ethnically a Scot and devotee of Sir Walter, put right the difference by arranging a Highland tour. In July 1853 they arrived at Glenfinlas, Brig o' Turk, near Stirling. Here, by the falls, Millais set to work to paint a portrait of his hero.

The picture did get painted, in spite of a very wet summer and a persistent cold suffered by Millais and by Ruskin's wife. Ruskin himself, and his friend Dr Acland, who was for a while of the party, and Millais's brother were all blind to what took place during that wet summer: Millais and Effie Ruskin fell in love. As they did so, Millais discovered that Ruskin, great art historian, was a man who 'appears to delight in selfish solitude. Why he ever had the audacity of marrying with no better intentions is a mystery to me. I must confess that it appears to me that he cares for nothing beyond his Mother and Father, which makes the insolence of his finding fault with his wife (to whom he has acted from the beginning most disgustingly) more apparent . . .'[18]

These words were written to Effie's mother. The Gray family discovered that summer not only that for five years their daughter had suffered neglect and reproach, but that her marriage was unconsummated. On her wedding night, Ruskin (who was completely ignorant of sexual matters) had been unable to consummate – 'he had imagined women were quite different to what he saw I was,'[19] Effie afterwards recalled. Later he was to suggest other reasons – religion, a lack of desire for children – why the marriage should not be consummated, at least until she was twenty-five.

Gladstone said that if one had known all three parties as well as he had done – Ruskin, Millais, Effie – one would be unable to blame any of them. Let this be our line. Ruskin was one of the great men of the nineteenth century, Millais a prodigiously accomplished (if ultimately uninspired) painter, Effie an affectionate, intelligent woman who married Millais – when the Ruskin marriage had been set aside – and bore him eight children. Peace to them all! Vulgarians claim to know precisely what it was about the female anatomy that Ruskin had found so shocking. The truth is actually unclear.

Far more important than the details of Ruskin's private life were the areas to which his 'vision' and his 'suffering' took him. Having begun as a pioneer student of art history, he had come to see that aesthetic theory cannot be detached from social theory. Increasingly a follower of Carlyle, Ruskin came to see the nineteenth century as a nightmare era, and the core of this horror – the corollary of its materialism – was its loss of faith.

The weathercock mind of Harriet Martineau is a good guide here to the movement of middle-class opinion in the 1850s. Carlyle himself was impressed by her – 'far beyond expectation. She is very intelligent-looking, really of pleasant countenance . . . full of talk though unhappily deaf as a post, so that you have to speak to her through an ear trumpet.'[20]

By the early 1850s the *Punch* wag Douglas Jerrold was quipping, 'There is no God, and Harriet Martineau is his prophet.' Marian Evans could not dispel the impression of Harriet's *vulgarity* when she first met her, but after a few encounters they had become intimate friends.[21]

Miss Evans, known later to the world as George Eliot, was, from 1851 to 1855 (i.e. from the age of thirty-two to thirty-five), living in the household of the radical bookseller John Chapman, 142 The Strand. She had translated in 1844 the revolutionary Hegelian version of Christ's life, *Das Leben Jesu* of David Friedrich Strauss, and in 1854 she was to translate Feuerbach's *Das Wesen des Christenthums* (Essence of Christianity). Both books saw religion as a purely human construct and the Christian religion as an exercise in mythology.

Nowadays, such views are commonplace, even among

the clergy. In the nineteenth century they were as revolutionary as George Eliot's unorthodox approach to sexual relations. (Escaping her love affair with Chapman, she lived for many years, even though he had a wife still living, with George Henry Lewes, journalist and German scholar, biographer of Goethe.)

Unbelief had been taken for granted among the sophisticated Whiggish upper crust which Lord Ashley knew well and which he found so detestable. The Queen herself had been given in marriage to Prince Albert by the most Whiggish of her uncles, the Duke of Sussex, a bibliophile with a huge collection of bibles. In the margin of his *The Book of Common Prayer*, this royal duke had drawn a fatal hand, pointing at the Athanasian Creed, with the comment, 'I don't believe a word of it.'[22]

The cynicism of an educated or upper-class coterie threatened to become endemic among the middle class, thanks partly to the efforts of unbelievers such as Harriet Martineau and Marian Evans in *The Westminster Review*. It would be misleading to suggest that in the 1850s 'atheism was the religion of the suburbs', as G.K. Chesterton claimed was the case for the next generation. But unbelief was widespread. What is perhaps most striking to the eyes of hindsight about the responses to Evans's translations of Strauss and Feuerbach is not the hostile reactions of the few but the silent acquiescence of the many. Yet, enough people shared Marx's view that religion was the opium of the people for conventional believers to be worried. Doubt had been the unspoken secret of sophisticates in the 1820s and 30s, the modish belief of the periodical-reading middle classes in the 1850s. What if it spread to the working classes too? Was not the concept of deference, based on religion, the social glue which held society together? In Catholic France, maybe: in Orthodox Russia, perhaps. The agonized middle-class minds who thought like this (Darwin did – it was one of his chief motives for keeping his evolutionary theories secret so long) had not, as Mayhew had done, gone out and confronted working-class people in England. Had they done so, they would have found religious practice (except among Irish immigrants) all but unknown, and indifference to religious ideas all but total.

Yet, on the surface of things, at least among the middle classes, Victorian England still looked as though it was a Christian culture. Churches were built, Christian books printed, in abundance. But there were signs of edginess. A self-confident religion, such as Judaism in the great Rabbinic age, or Catholicism at the time of the schoolmen, enjoys vigorous debate with itself. It is not

timorous. It might take sides, and argue with trenchancy, but it does not need to bully. The Victorian heresy-hunts should have warned those who conducted them that the ground they defended so loudly was sinking sand. Unable to face the arguments of Strauss or Feuerbach head-on, the hardline Orthodox chose to persecute the faithful innovators and original thinkers within their own midst. Two obvious examples spring to mind – those of George MacDonald and F.D. Maurice. Both, interestingly, came unstuck for the same sort of reasons – a refusal to gratify their more vindictive co-religionists by pretending to believe in Hell – and both at about the same period – in the years just before the outbreak of the Crimean War – a war which itself was entangled from the outset with religious fundamentalisms.

*

Western preoccupation with Jerusalem and the Promised Land showed a mingling of political, religious and colonial interest which in part seems a bizarre reflection of the medieval Crusades, in part a dire harbinger of the still unresolved conflicts of the Middle East.

Throughout four centuries, it had been the task of the Ottoman sultans to impose, for the sake of civil order, a culture of mutual tolerance on the inhabitants of their empire. In cities as various as Constantinople itself, Alexandria and Sarajevo, Christians, Jews and Muslims had been taught by their Turkish rulers that where religious difference was in question there really was only one political option: live and let live. Muslims and Jews were nearly always able to accept this, in relation to one another and to the Christians. The followers of Christ, however, while finding it possible to live at peace with their fellow monotheists of the Islamic or Judaic persuasion, could not always resist outbursts of violence against their co-religionists, and the inter-denominational hatred grew hotter, the closer they came to their most sacred shrines.

An agreement with the Porte (as the Imperial court at Constantinople was known) between the French government and the sultans, signed in 1740, gave the French 'sovereign authority' over the Holy Land. For this reason a silver star, adorned with the royal arms of France, was placed over the very spot where Christ had supposedly been born in Bethlehem. This precedent, of Western Roman Catholics, in the person of Franciscan friars, seeing themselves as the natural guardians of the holiest sites in Christendom, was a throwback to the disputes at the time of the Crusades. It did not alter the fact that apart from the shrine-guardians themselves in their humble brown habits, knotted with rope in imitation of Francis of Assisi, almost no Christians in the actual region were Roman Catholic, or even in communion with Rome. The huge majority were members of one or another of the autocephalous Orthodox churches – mainly Greek Orthodox, some Russian, Bulgarian, Romanian and others – or they belonged to one of the other Eastern churches such as the Armenian or Coptic traditions. To all these, the claim of French friars to look after buildings where nearly all the worshippers came from the Christian East was an outrage which mingled political with religious arrogance.

In 1852, Napoleon III wooed conservative opinion at home by asking for the keys of the church at Bethlehem to be returned to the French clergy. For a quiet life, the Sultan agreed, only to be greeted by protests from the Tsar. It gave Nicholas I the excuse to ask the Porte for certain guarantees, including the assignment to Russia of the general protectorate over Christians in the Turkish Empire.

There certainly seems a strong element of paradox, if not gross humbug, in an increasingly secular Protestant Britain choosing to involve itself in this dispute. Somehow, however, the British managed to persuade themselves that Russian expansionist ambitions were a direct threat to their interests. It was thought that the passage to India and the other trade routes would be in Russian hands if the Tsar continued to bully the Sultan.

'The state of *tension* is undoubtedly great, and scarcely to be long endured; but I persist in thinking that it cannot end in actual war,' Aberdeen had written, only in November 1853. Yet by Christmas, France and Britain had tied themselves into an alliance with Turkey which made war an inevitability. The Turks had been at war against Russia since October 1853. By the time the Russians sank the Turkish fleet at Sinope – it has been called the Pearl Harbor of the war – British public opinion saw it as a massacre, and the rest – the landing of a huge Anglo-French expeditionary force, headed for the Balkans and the Black Sea – looks like an inevitability.

Carts and cattle leaving Balaklava harbour.

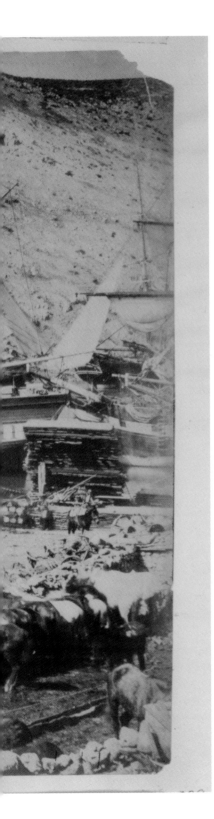

Chapter Eleven

The Crimean War

M. Alexis Soyer, *chef de cuisine* at the Reform Club in Pall Mall, was far from home. To be precise, he was riding by a new-built road and becoming spattered with mud as he descended from the 'Genoese heights', as they were called, to the harbour of the small Crimean port of Balaclava. At the bottom of the ravine, he found his way blocked by French and Sardinian wagons, unloading wine and shipping stores. It was a long while before M. Soyer got through the traffic jam to the Commissariat.

The reports of the Crimean campaign in *The Times* by William Howard Russell had been an historical innovation. Never before had the public heard such candid, or such immediate, descriptions of the reality of war, the bungling as well as the heroism, the horrible deaths by disease, as well as the bloody consequences of battle. Russell's reports of the complete inadequacy of hospital facilities, and the contrast between the woeful British treatment of the sick and wounded and the French military hospitals run by Sisters of Mercy, had prompted Florence Nightingale to pester the Secretary-at-War into allowing young women of good families to go as nurses to Scutari, on the shores of the Bosporus. Russell's legendary dispatches had also alerted Soyer to the knowledge that allied troops could do with some advice about food and provisions. The daily allowance for each English soldier was 1 lb of meat, 1 lb of bread, coffee, salt and sugar. Each man had to prepare this food himself, usually in difficult and – once the Crimean winter had set in – often in impossible conditions.

Soyer, as well as being a cook to the famous, and to the greatest of the new Liberal clubs, was also a man who cared for the unfortunate. He had taken soup kitchens to Ireland, where he had pioneered a practical stove – two steam boilers with a removable container on top. At the outbreak of the Crimean War, he saw that his stove would be invaluable as a way of providing hot food for large numbers of men encamped or entrenched in the field. He adapted many of his recipes from a book he had lately prepared to promote cheap and nutritious eating – *Shilling Cookery* (published 1854).

As he galloped off towards headquarters, Soyer noted a group of officers gathered about a sort of gypsy tent by the side of the road. Many of these officers, as London clubmen, recognized the celebrated Frenchman and called out to him. From inside the tent, a stentorian female voice asked, 'Who is my new son?'

'Monsieur Soyer, to be sure,' said one of the officers. 'Don't you know him?'

A plump Jamaican woman, past her first youth, emerged from the tent.

'God bless me; my son, are you Monsieur Soyer of whom I heard so much in Jamaica? Well, to be sure! I have sold many and many a score of your Relish and sauces – God knows how many . . . I had a gross about ten days ago . . .'[1]

The great French cook alighted from his horse and the Jamaican lady invited

him to drink a glass of champagne with her friend Sir John Campbell, the senior brigadier-general in the army, who after the battle of Inkerman was temporarily in charge of the 4th Division – destined to be killed in the assault upon the Great Redan.

The ample Jamaican lady was Mary Seacole, and she too, like M. Soyer, was in the Crimea because she had read Russell's newspaper reports. Sitting in Jamaica, she read of the battle of the Alma and the sufferings of the British soldiers, and realized that many of her army and navy friends, who had been stationed in the West Indies at some point in their careers, were now enduring the winter's cold in the Crimean peninsula. Since she was both a self-trained nurse and a boarding-house keeper, she knew that she could be of use.

Mary Seacole was one of the many extraordinary characters thrown into relief by the Crimean War. Born

in 1807, she was the child of a Scottish army officer and a free – not liberated, but born free – black woman who herself ran a boarding house in Kingston, Jamaica. By her late forties, Mary Seacole had travelled all over the Caribbean: Nassau, Haiti, Cuba and Panama. It was a momentous decision, however, to cross the world to Russia as a freelance nurse-hotelier. When Seacole reached London, Florence Nightingale had already left for the Turkish capital. She went to the organization in London which was recruiting nurses for Miss Nightingale's hospital at Scutari (present-day Üsküdar) and was turned down flat, despite her obviously useful qualifications. She then applied to the managers of the Crimean Fund and was also turned down. It was a shattering moment. In Jamaica, where she had always been popular with British visitors and where her own father had been a white soldier, she had allowed herself

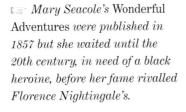

As the Lady of the Lamp at Scutari, Florence Nightingale became an instant icon.

Mary Seacole's Wonderful Adventures *were published in 1857 but she waited until the 20th century, in need of a black heroine, before her fame rivalled Florence Nightingale's.*

to associate racial prejudice with the slave-owning citizens of the United States.

'Was it possible that American prejudices against colour had some root here? Did these ladies shrink from accepting my aid because my blood flowed beneath a somewhat duskier skin than theirs? Tears flowed down my foolish cheeks as I stood in the fast-thinning streets.'

This overweight woman of forty-eight years and of boundless energy and spirit did not allow rejection to dash her spirits. She made her own way to Constantinople, and presented herself in person at the famous hospital at Scutari. Many of the wounded soldiers recognized her, and called out cheery greetings to 'Mother Seacole'. Once again, however, she met with rejection. The nursing officer rebuked her with: '"Miss Nightingale has the entire management of our hospital staff, but I do not think that any vacancy . . ." "Excuse

me, ma'am," I interrupted her with, "but I am bound for the front in a few days," and my questioner leaves me, more surprised than ever.' Undeterred, she engaged a Greek guide to escort her to the front. She called him Johnny – 'wishing however, to distinguish my Johnny from the legions of other Johnnies, I prefixed the term Jew to his other name and addressed him as Jew Johnnie'.[2]

Florence Nightingale's admirable hospital was several hundred miles from the Crimean peninsula. Mary Seacole did not pretend to Nightingale's formidable gifts of organization, but she was in the very front line. Her 'British hotel' in Balaclava was an important refuge. She served sponge cake and lemonade. 'They all liked the cake, poor fellows, better than anything else: perhaps because it tasted of "home".[3] The 'ranks' who had a fear of hospitals felt more at ease with 'Mother Seacole' than in the Turkish field hospitals. She treated patients suffering from cholera and dysentery. She was attentive to their practical needs. Officers and men had permanent colds throughout the Crimean winters. There were no pocket handkerchiefs until Mary Seacole established her 'stores'.

Many Crimean veterans had cause to remember Mary Seacole gratefully. (She came back to live in London after the war, and prospered; during the 1870s she was a friend, and masseuse, of the Princess of Wales; she died in 1881.) Miss Nightingale's hospital was where you were taken if you were wounded or fell sick. Mary Seacole was on hand for the troops in the long months when nothing much appeared to be happening and, unlike some of the officers, she showed courage under fire. She saw the fighting on the Redan and witnessed the horrors left behind when they finally lifted the siege of Sebastopol.

Florence Nightingale's was a somewhat different story. Two-thirds of the total casualties in the Crimean War were from disease and hardship, not from battle – the French lost nearly 100,000 by the end, the British some 60,000, the Russians over 300,000.[4] Russell's dispatches had told a truly horrible story. Wellington's first concern for an army on the march – the physical well-being of the common soldier – might have been shared by his former comrade-in-arms, now British commander-in-chief, Lord Raglan, but the poor organization of his expedition led from the beginning to unnecessary hardships. Britain declared war on Russia on 28 March 1854. By 8 April expeditionary forces were landing at Gallipoli, that strip of Turkish coast which in a later war was to see so much suffering and slaughter. The British troops watched the French troops being supplied by a flotilla of steamers – bakeries, hospital tents, stores. All their supplies were rushed on shore by a well-organized baggage train. The British, suffering badly from the cold, had no beds to lie on and waited several days for blankets or food to arrive. Disease had already broken out in Malta on the way down. By the time the officer class arrived in their comfortable transport ships and steamers the Sea of Marmara resembled a regatta and disease was rampant. The allied armies were transported through the Bosphorus, many of them decamping on the eastern shore to the makeshift field hospitals at Scutari.[5] The healthy made for the coast at Bulgaria; it was at Varna, on this coast, that the allied command – Marshal St Arnaud, Lord Raglan and Admirals Hamelin (commander of French naval forces), Dundas, Lyons and Bruat considered the orders of the English Cabinet that they should make a descent in the Crimea and besiege Sebastopol. By now cholera had killed 7,000 French. In the villages surrounding Varna, Turks and Greeks perished 'like flies'. The hospitals were full before a single shot had been fired in battle. On 10 August a further calamity was a fire in the stores at Varna, destroying weapons, provisions and 19,000 pairs of shoes.[6]

'The conduct of many of the men, French and English, seemed characterized by a recklessness verging on insanity,' Russell wrote.[7] 'They might be seen lying drunk in the kennels, or in the ditches by the road-sides, under the blazing rays of the sun, covered with swarms of flies.' Those who survived cholera and the fire were severely weakened by 'fever, ague, dysentery and pestilence'. Apart from minor skirmishes (in which a young Russian officer called Lev Nikolayevich Tolstoy took part) in Silistria, there was not much to show for the first six months of the war.

Russell's dispatches had revealed a miserable, unheroic, ramshackle campaign presided over by old men. Lord Raglan, fluent in French as he was, and genial, had a distressing habit – born of his youthful years of serving under Wellington – of referring to the French as 'the enemy'. The inspector-general of fortifications, Sir John Burgoyne, was seventy-one years old. Four of Raglan's aides-de-camp were relations – Major Lord Burghersh, Captain Lord Poullet Somerset, Captain Nigel Kingscole and Lieutenant Somerset Calthorpe. The cavalry was commanded by some truly grotesque specimens of aristocratic eccentricity. The commander of the cavalry division, Lord Lucan, had purchased the command of the 17th Lancers for £25,000, but had left the army in 1837 – since when he had been on half-pay. The closest he had come to seeing military action had been skirmishes with the Irish peasants on his estates in County Mayo. He was fifty-four when the war broke out. His brother-in-law, the 7th Earl of Cardigan, was pushing sixty. The noisy, lecherous life of this upper-class hooligan had been punctuated by scandals. He had been acquitted (by his peers) for fighting a duel in 1841; his command of the 11th Hussars (for which he had paid £40,000) had made him many enemies both among his officers, with whom he quarrelled regularly in the mess, and his men, who suffered merciless floggings.[8]

These were the men who joined the survivors (10,000 Englishmen died of cholera at Varna) for the invasion of the Crimea in September 1854, one of the most extraordinary armadas to set sail in the whole history of warfare. They were pursued by a flotilla of sightseers, well-wishers and busybodies, but none were more

Lord Raglan

The Times, *with its newly invented Applegarth presses, rolling out 200 copies per minute of W.T. Russell's reports, was able to make this the first war in history which could be treated by a large public as a spectator sport.*

important than William Howard Russell, since he revealed to the world the vulnerability and the sheer crass inefficiency of the supposedly great powers. The newspaper reports which prompted the charitable impulses of Alexis Soyer and Mary Seacole to rush to the aid of the British were also capable of revealing, for example, to disgruntled sepoy officers of the native Indian regiments, reading flyblown, yellowed copies of *The Times* in Kanpur and Lucknow, that the British Lion was not necessarily invincible.

But journalism is a curious art. Russell wanted to tell the truth, but he also wanted to tell a story, and a story, if it contains fighting, must have heroes. The public demanded it. Since European literature began, setbacks and defeats were capable of acquiring heroic status just as much as victories. Britain had not been involved in a European war for forty years, and in the pages of *The Times* each morning they found the opportunity for a modern *Iliad* to be played out for them. Unlike the Napoleonic Wars, this one was happening a safe distance away. Everybody was gripped by it. If a plague-ridden army commanded by whiskery, bottle-nosed old roués made unlikely material for heroic literature, the public

was perfectly prepared to hear and see what it chose. The invasion of Russian soil was followed avidly week by week.

The Silistrian skirmishes of the summer did not have the stuff of which good stories are made. For one thing, it could not be disguised from anyone that, while the English and French troops languished from heatstroke, alcohol and disease, it was largely through the skill of the Turkish army that the Russians had been kept at bay in their Balkan incursions. Russell's narrative pace quickens once the troops had disembarked in the autumn of '54.

The Russian commander, Prince Menshikov, had about 80,000 men deployed in the peninsula. The allied troops numbered 26,000 British (with 66 guns), 30,000 French (with 70 guns) and 5,000 Turks. The first major engagement was when Menshikov established himself with some 40,000 men and 100 guns on the rising ground to the south of the river Alma. The Russians failed to stop the allied advance. After the battle of the Alma,

Russell notes, 'there was a sickening, sour foetid smell everywhere, and the grass was slippy with blood'. About 5,000 died, though Raglan listed only 326 casualties, the French 60 and the Russians 1,755. *The Times* had never sold so many copies, and prophesied an early victory and the fall of Sebastopol long before Christmas.

Within the three weeks that followed, the British 'lost as many of cholera as perished on the Alma'.[9] It was on 25 October that they fought the most celebrated battle of the campaign, that of Balaclava. While the Alma had been an allied victory, and Balaclava a Russian one, there was no doubt which made the greater appeal – just as, in a much later war, the British retreat at Dunkirk in 1940 went on being celebrated for decades.

The battle of Balaclava fell into two distinct phases. At first, an unequal artillery duel between Russian and Turkish guns (18-pounders vs. 12-pounders) flew across the valleys above Balaclava. Overlooking the South valley were Lucan's cavalry division and Campbell's 93rd Highlanders. 'Remember there is no escape from here. You must die where you stand.' The Highlanders accordingly opened fire. 'The ground flies beneath their [the Russians'] horses feet: gathering speed at every stride, they dash on towards that thin red streak topped with a line of steel,' as Russell wrote. The Heavy Brigade moved westwards to help the Turkish guns. (Tennyson's own recording of his poem on the charge of the Heavy Brigade is in its way as impressive as his more famous lines on the Light Brigade and

Dahn the hill, dahn the hill, thahsunds uv Rooshians

nicely demonstrates his Lincolnshire vowels.) It was an extraordinary piece of gallantry, 300 mounted men of the 6th Inniskilling Dragoons, the Royal Scots Greys and the 5th Dragoon Guards and the 4th Royal Irish Dragoon Guards, charging with swords at heavy field guns. 'Some of the Russians seemed to be rather astonished at the way our men used their swords. It was rather hot work,' one officer recollected.[10] The charge of the Heavy Brigade was a moderate success, leading to a withdrawal of the Russians into the North valley to regroup behind a battery of eight artillery pieces.

The first phase of the battle was over and had ended in stalemate. The Russians could still threaten Balaclava. Raglan wished the cavalry to advance and reclaim the heights. He sent orders to Lucan to this

The battle of Balaklava, in which English cavalry meet Russian and Turkish heavy artillery, 25 October 1854.

effect, promising infantry support. Raglan wanted Lucan to move forward at once. Lucan thought he should await the arrival of the infantry before beginning a two-pronged assault. The infantry were slow in coming. Through his telescope Raglan could see the Light Brigade dismounting and idling in the mid-morning sun. He told the nattily dressed Airey (who had caused a sensation in Varna by sporting a red flannel suit) to repeat the orders to advance. Airey scribbled on a piece of paper: 'Lord Raglan wishes the cavalry to advance rapidly to the front – follow the enemy and try to prevent the enemy carrying away the guns. Troop Horse Artillery may accompany. French cavalry is on your left. – Immediate.'

The note was given to the ADC, Captain Nolan, who was a hothead who had been 'talking very loud against the cavalry . . . and especially Lucan'. Nolan rode to Lucan and told him to attack at once. No infantry support had arrived, and it was not clear in which precise direction Raglan wished the cavalry to ride. As Nolan arrived with his ambiguous order – to be greeted with Lucan's 'Attack, sir! Attack, what? What guns, sir?' – Lord Cardigan sent his ADC, Lieutenant Henry Fitzhardinge Maxse, to point out that 'the heights which flanked the valley leading to the Russian battery of heavy guns were covered with artillery men and riflemen'.

Nolan had not completely finished his unintentionally disastrous work. He asked permission to ride in the charge with the 17th Lancers. As the Light Brigade trotted forward, he suddenly galloped ahead, yelling and waving his sword. He was the first of 107 men and 397 horses who would be mown down by Russian guns in the next twenty-five minutes. The Light Brigade rode down into the valley, engaged the waiting Russian cavalry, and – there being no way out of the valley on the other side – they were obliged to turn round and once more run the gauntlet of deadly gunfire. A Russian cavalry officer remarked, 'It is difficult, if not impossible, to do justice to the feat of these mad cavalry, for, having lost a quarter of their number and being apparently impervious to new dangers and further losses, they quickly reformed their squadrons to return over the same ground littered with their dead and dying. With such desperate courage these valiant lunatics set off again, and not one of the living – even the wounded – surrendered.'

When Prince Albert was being 'broken in' by the landed classes, he surprised them all by his preparedness to make daring jumps when hunting with the Pytchley and the Quorn. Cardigan had been his host at Deene Park in Northamptonshire, magnificent hunting country. The celebrated reaction of the French Marshal Bosquet to the Charge – '*C'est magnifique, mais ce n'est pas la guerre*' – was totally accurate. Cardigan was showing himself more a master of foxhounds than a soldier in this magnificent display of bravado.[11] Raglan was furious with him. Lucan has generally been held responsible for the blunder. 'You have lost the Light Brigade,' Raglan curtly told him that evening. He was sacked a few months later. Cardigan had invalided himself out of the war by then – he returned to England to the strains of 'See, the conquering hero comes'. He was painted demonstrating the Charge of the Light Brigade on a plan of the battlefield to the royal family. (When she heard of the extent of Cardigan's depravities – Deene Park little different in atmosphere from a bordello – the Queen had herself painted out of this canvas.) But both men remained in the army – Lucan to become a field marshal and Cardigan the inspector-general of cavalry.

If this had been a serious war – that is, had there been any need for British and French troops to be in the Crimean peninsula (defending, for instance, their own national security) – then the Charge of the Light Brigade would have been a catastrophe. Raglan now could not risk his two infantry divisions in an attempt to move the Russian forces from Causeway Heights; he dared not risk losing possession of the port of Balaclava and being cut off from the sea. The siege of Sebastopol could not get going until the brisk infantry victory at Inkerman had brought about the worst battle casualties of the war, on 5 November. ('*Quel abattoir!* – What a slaughterhouse! – as one French officer observed.[12])

By then the winter had set in, and many seriously wondered whether the allied troops, with totally inadequate summer clothes and provisions, could survive the months of dark, wet and cold on those bleak uplands. But Russell had written one of his great journalistic set-pieces – 'A more fearful spectacle was never witnessed than by those who, without the power to aid, beheld their heroic countrymen rushing to the arms of death . . .'[13] And, reading it over his breakfast porridge at Farringford, Freshwater Bay, Isle of Wight, the poet laureate could be moved to write lines about 'the noble six hundred', one of those rare poems known by those who do not read or know poetry. He had penned it within 'a few minutes' of reading *The Times*.[14] Though Tennyson, in the Epilogue to his poem about the Heavy Brigade, was to assert that

Who loves war for war's own sake
Is fool, or crazed or worse;

ENTHUSIASM OF PATERFAMILIAS,
On Reading the Report of the Grand Charge of British Cavalry on the 25th.

A satire on the varying reactions to the newspaper accounts of the Charge of the Light Brigade at Balaklava. The Victorians love of the Crimean War is reflected in almost every town in England to this day, where old men in 'cardigans' or young men in balaclava helmets can still be found in Alma Villas and Inkerman Crescents. Some of us still possess Raglan over-coats. No British generals or admirals of the Hitler war were invested with the Homeric status which the Victorians gave to the quarrelsome and incompetent old men who led the Crimean invasion.

the public appetite for this war could not be explained by any simple political or religious 'cause'.[15]

An earlier generation of historians was able to read the history of the nineteenth and twentieth centuries as a diplomatic carve-up, organized by the chief ministers and ambassadors of the European powers. One of the most stylish of such accounts was A.J.P. Taylor's *The Struggle for Mastery in Europe 1848–1918*, a work published half a century ago. By this view of events, the Crimean War had nothing to do with the possession or administration of the Holy Places, and not much to do with the administration of the crumbling Ottoman Empire. It was entirely a struggle between the European superpowers, and could be seen as the ominous first stage in a tragedy which would reach a climax on the battlefields of Flanders and Northern France in 1914–18, a fiery denouement thirty years beyond that as the Russians pounded and bombed their way into the smouldering ruins of Berlin. This view of history sees the aims of Russia as opportunistic, wishing to establish its influence in the Christian East, clashing with the revived opportunism of Napoleon III and 'the gang of Bonapartist adventurers who ran France'.[16] Napoleon III had no wish to overwhelm the Russians, merely to check their power, in order to bring them into an alliance with France against the emergent powers of Prussia.

The rivalry between France and Germany, erupting into the Franco-Prussian war and all its cataclysmic consequences, is not something which hindsight can ignore. The defeat of Russia in the Crimean War, if seen in this light, is the crucial event of mid-nineteenth-century European history. Had Russia won, and established a claim on the Ottoman Empire: had she, in effect, taken over the running of the Eastern Empire: had Napoleon III been chucked out, and Palmerston's foreign policy, based on a breezy assumption that Britain allied itself with 'liberal' régimes, been discredited . . . From such unfinished and fruitless speculations, historians can play a parlour-game of what-ifs and might-have-beens. No Napoleon III, no power games in Europe, but a developing recognition of the economic and political strengths of the Prussian Empire . . . Might this have led to the sort of federalism and spirit of European reconciliation which made the closing decades of the twentieth century so much more peaceful than those of the nineteenth? A Europe in which there was no First World War, no Russian Revolution, is tragically unimaginable for us.

Once it was clear that the 'victory' of Inkerman notwithstanding, the Russians and their oldest ally, the winter, would insist on a long struggle, there was an overwhelming case for a negotiated settlement to the war. Such a flat outcome to the story was inevitably going to come, but not until the Peace of Paris in 1856, and many lives were to be lost before then. Tsar Nicholas himself died on 2 March 1855, and perhaps if his successor Alexander II had not been bound to appease patriotic fervour at home, many of the miseries of 1855 could have been avoided – the dreadful sufferings during the siege of Sebastopol, the 'forgotten war' afterwards, the fighting in Armenia (Kars and Erzerum) during that grim year. *The Times* by its repeated exposures of British inefficiency and weakness was the classic example of exercising 'power without responsibility'. Russell's dispatches could work up public rage, most notably during the terrible winter of 1855, about the absence of provisions and supplies. It could find no shortage, moreover, of Guilty Men – sometimes suggesting that The System itself was to blame, sometimes finding a scapegoat – Raglan and his staff officers, Lord John Russell, Aberdeen. At the same time, the newspaper created a public hunger for a satisfactory end to the story, and that end could only be outright military victory. Perhaps this is why the war created such peculiar alliances. Christian socialist F.D. Maurice believed that *The Times* was horribly wicked, that the press was killing the nation's mystic unity. Extremists of left and right, however, could unite in Russophobia.[17]

Aberdeen's coalition had collapsed at the beginning of 1855 and the Queen had made heroic struggles against the inevitable – a Liberal government with Palmerston as prime minister. She asked Lord Derby to form another administration with a Conservative minority in the Commons; Derby offered Palmerston the post of secretary for war and Pam's reply was that he could only serve if Clarendon – Derby's deadliest political foe – were made foreign secretary. When the idea of a Derby government instantly collapsed, the Queen summoned Lord Lansdowne, but he told her he was too old. (Four years older than Palmerston – the two were rival candidates as MP for the University of Cambridge as long ago as *1806* – when Byron, another Harrovian, in 'Hours of Idleness' had mocked them.)

Then Victoria asked Lord John Russell, who had regarded Palmerston as a political rival for decades, but he found on consulting colleagues that they would not serve under him again – though he was destined to become prime minister one last time when Palmerston died in the office in October 1865. The Queen begged Clarendon to serve under Russell – 'Lord John Russell may resign, and Lord Aberdeen may resign, but I *can't* resign. I sometimes wish I could,' she complained.[18]

There was nothing for it. On 4 February 1855 Palmerston was summoned to Buckingham Palace and invited to form a government. The Queen's objections to him were based partly on deep personal revulsion.

Palmerston's wife, when Lady Cowper, had been a much-trusted lady-in-waiting in the dear days of Lord M., but Lord Palmerston had disgraced himself, when staying at Windsor Castle, by a 'brutal attack on one of the ladies' – in effect, a rape. The Queen and Prince Albert had also fallen out with Pilgerstein, as Albert called him, in 1846–7 when they discovered that he had been sending dispatches to Portugal and taking sides in the civil war without consulting his sovereign.

For others, however, Palmerston's arrival in the premiership was what the middle classes had been longing for, during the previous year of drift and muddle. Peter Bayne, a journalist writing thirteen years later, described the feelings of 'the ordinary Englishman' when he heard that Palmerston had become prime minister: 'When we were at war with Russia and when the nation, after trying statesman after statesman, continued in the distressing consciousness that the administration lacked vigour, the man who, for a quarter of a century, had been checkmating the policy of Russia was naturally called for.' The importance here was the perception of the Palmerston 'myth', since as Urquhart and others would wish to say, Pam had been if anything pro-Russian in the years leading up to the war. But – as Bayne told the readers of *St Paul's Magazine* – Palmerston was the man to whom the business of war could be committed, and in whose hands the name of England was safe.[19]

Palmerston was adept at self-promotion. The peace-loving free-trader John Bright could complain that 50,000 men died to make Palmerston prime minister, but with his eye to the populace, the war prime minister could make even this objection seem unpatriotic. Bright, he replied, reduces everything to pounds, shillings and pence. If confronted with the threat of imminent invasion, Bright would 'sit down, take a bit of paper, and would put on one side of the account the contributions which his Government would require from him for the defence of liberty and independence of the country, and he would put on the other the probable contributions which the General of the invading army might levy upon Manchester'.[20]

Sir Henry Layard was a radical MP with a fervent anti-Russian view who had been in the Foreign Office (like Urquhart he had been attached to the British embassy in Constantinople and was regarded by Palmerston as a clever middle-class upstart). His speeches about the inefficiency of the British aristocracy, and their bungles in the Crimea, made a great impression and were cheered on by *The Times*. Palmerston's instinct

Piling Arms

Zouaves

George de Lacy Evans

John Campbell

was to silence Layard by giving him a post in the government, but the Queen was so horrified by his attacks on the aristocracy that she refused. Layard proposed sending MPs to the Crimea who should have the power to overrule and dismiss incompetent com-manders. 'I have no doubt that a Cavendish in the Cabinet is a very important thing, but the public think more of 20,000 lives than they do of a Cavendish.' However true this seems in retrospect, the popular mood at the time was against Layard and behind Palmerston.

Mounted French Infantry Officer

James Scarlett

John Lysaght Pennefather

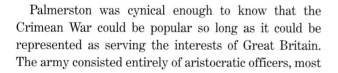

☞ *Omar Pasha*

Palmerston was cynical enough to know that the Crimean War could be popular so long as it could be represented as serving the interests of Great Britain. The army consisted entirely of aristocratic officers, most of them buffoons, and working-class men driven to the dire expedient of soldiering by poverty. Many, therefore, were Irish or Scots. The battles took place far away. No English town was reduced to rubble, as was Balaclava.

It was an armchair war, fought, as far as the English bourgeoisie was concerned, by classes as remote from their own lives as the Sultan and his entourage in the Topkapi palace. Yet war is a Pandora's box, even when fought at a distance of over a thousand miles. Palmerston's complacent belief in the love affair between the English and the aristocracy was, like most things in England, only half true.

For most Englishmen, hatred of the enemy was not really enough to fuel war fever. It would have been absurd to suppose that the subjects of Queen Victoria in 1854, whether mill operatives or farmers, clergymen or railway engineers, felt so natural a kinship with the Turk that when the Sultan declared war against Russia, they longed, to a man, to fight the Tsar. What happened was more muddled and, from the point of view of the collective consciousness – that mystic unity beloved of Maurice – more complex. A war puts a society on its mettle. While fighting Hitler's war, the British – through the experience of coalition government, rationing and the like – were also working through the dreadful social legacy of the 1930s and determining to refashion a welfare system and their whole attitude to the state. Many on both sides of the political spectrum saw the Crimean War as a comparable test for the British. As fast as the chancellor of the Exchequer throughout the war – through two administrations – William Ewart Gladstone – was trying to pay for it by temporary impositions of income tax, events were challenging even his laissez-faire economic certainties. A modern state, and this was what post-Crimean England was becoming, could not without calamity allow the untrammelled market free rein. Fiscal controls – and a taxation system – arose willy-nilly.

The very lack of political definition at home, and the lack of distinction of the two war Cabinets, in fact points up the questions which Victorian Britain was asking itself *of itself* during this war. 'We working-class and professional men are only listeners in the trial going on between merchants, manufacturers and tradesmen and aristocracy,' F.D. Maurice complained to an audience at the Working Men's College on 31 May 1855. This was to be one of the political conundrums which would preoccupy the British for a hundred years – how to find political representation *both* for intelligent non-commercial middle-class opinion and for the working classes. The result would be that fascinating political hybrid, the Labour Party.

Until that hybrid had grown, however, society was to pass through many transformations, some directly political – to do with parliamentary reforms, extension of the franchise, and so on – others more nebulous, but no less interwoven with the fabric of life.

The war as theatre, as spectator-sport, as tragic absurdity, came to a close. Having reduced Balaclava to rubble, with great loss of life, the British invited the Russian commanders to dinner *en plein air*. M. Soyer describes the scene:

> At ten to the minute, the Russians arrived. After the introduction, the guests sat down, and every jaw was soon doing its best; for in less than twenty minutes there were only the names of the various dishes to be seen, and they were upon the bill of fare – which was not eaten. The Russian general, who has only one arm, ate as much as two men with the use of both. A servant waited upon him, and carved his meat. Better-looking men I have seen, but not more military. He seemed as hard and as round as a cannon-ball . . .
>
> The general was a man of very agreeable manners – spoke French rather fluently – had a very quick eye – was no sooner seated than he took a survey of the company. The lunch was much relished – the speeches were short and to the point, and all went on to everybody's satisfaction. The Russian general was particularly pleased, and highly complimented his host upon the dainty repast, which he could not conceive was to be had in the Crimea.

Two things to emerge from the Pandora's box of war were the importance of photography, and a change in the Western world's smoking habits.

We do not know why a Scotsman called Robert Peacock Gloag was in the Crimea, but while he was there he saw Turks and Russians smoking cigarettes. 'In them, he found an idea and an ideal. From the war a purposeful man emerged.'

The first Gloag cigarettes on sale in London were cylinders of straw-coloured paper into which a cane tip was inserted and the tobacco filled in through a funnel. These are what Russians call little scorchers, *papirosi*. You can still buy them in Russia. Gloag filled them with strong Latakia tobacco.

By 1860–1, a Greek captain in the Russian army, John Theodoridi, had set up a shop in London – Leicester Square – selling Turkish cigarettes. Four other cigarette-makers followed. Theodoriki Avramanchi, another Greek, opened a shop in Regent Street in 1865, Caranjaki in Great Winchester Buildings, D. Mazzini in Union Court and A. Zicaliotti in Bloomfield Street. Gloag settled in Peckham, a south-eastern suburb of London. He made cigarettes called 'Moscows' for Theodoridi (these had a piece of wool in the end to act as a filter) and 'Tom Thumbs' – 'penny lines to be smoked to the bitter end'. From one room, he expanded to his whole house, then to another. Then he had six houses. He sold his 'Don Alfonso' in bundles of 25 for 1 shilling. This 'Whiff' was introduced in 1871. In 1870 he had founded the church of St Stephen, Peckham, in gratitude for his profits. By now, he had a factory, 40 Boyson Road, Walworth. The text over the door of his 'tobacco church' was – 'But when the blade was sprung up, And brought forth fruit, then appeared the tares also.'

This seemed an intelligent recognition of the fact that, from the first, the habit of cigarette-smoking was seen as both a blessing and a curse. Arthur E.J. Longhurst, assistant surgeon to HM (Prince Albert's) Light Infantry, attributed the decline of the Ottoman Empire itself specifically to the Turkish fondness for cigarettes. Having noted the 'imbecile progeny' of native American tobacco-addicts, Dr Longhurst adds, 'We may also take warning from the history of another nation, who some few centuries ago, while following the banners of Solyman the Magnificent, were the terror of Christendom, but who since then having become more addicted to tobacco-smoking than any of the European nations, are now the lazy and lethargic Turks, held in contempt by all civilized communities.' An American contemporary of Dr Longhurst's, William A. Alcott, noted that 'the slave of tobacco is seldom found reclaimable'. He added that smoking damaged teeth, lungs and stomach, as well as the morals of the addict.

What Gloag had introduced to the West, however, was a narcotic so addictive that social attitudes were forced to change, in order to accommodate the cigarette compulsion. In the pre-cigarette age, smoking was chiefly regarded as a 'low' activity. In 1861 a notice was pinned on the board at the Travellers' Club 'respectfully requesting' members to refrain from smoking, except in one specified area – this was because someone had lit a cigar in the hall.[21] It was not until the 1880s that smoking was generally permitted in the public rooms of London clubs. In respectable households men either had to smoke out of doors or else 'sneak away into the kitchen when the servants had gone to bed and puff up the chimney'.[22] Smoking was first allowed in railway carriages in 1860.

The real smoking revolution happened in the generation after Gloag's, when the Bristol tobacco firm of W.D. and H.O. Wills pioneered the first Bonsack cigarette-making machine, bought from America in 1883.*[23] It enabled them to manufacture approximately 200 cigarettes per minute. Between 1860 and 1900, Britain became a smoking nation, its consumption of tobacco rising 2.4 per cent in 1862, 4.7 per cent in 1863 and an average of around 5 per cent per annum for the rest of the century.

By 1886, the adoption of the Bonsack machinery by Wills had been followed by firms such as Lambert and Butler (London), John Player and Sons (Nottingham) and the Liverpool firms Hignett Bros and Cope Bros. These Liverpool factories competed for the franchise to display and sell cheap cigarettes in the Railway Refreshment Rooms. Spiers and Pond, the company who ran all the refreshment rooms for the Midland Railways, sold the right to Cope Brothers for £800 p.a.

A price war in the 1880s led to the 'penny cigarettes'. In 1888, Wild Woodbine made its appearance, the most famous cheap smoke in the Western world, forever associated with the men fighting in the trenches a quarter of a century later. It was during this price war that Wills watched their profits rocket – £6.5 million in 1884, £13,961,000 in 1886, shooting to nearly £127 million in 1891. The working classes had become hooked. This was the true opium of the people, and Gloag's legacy of the cigarette habit could be said to be the most lasting and notable consequence of the Crimean War. When the Turkish, Russian and British empires are now as obsolete as the Bonapartist dynasty, the British working class, 146 years after the treaty of Paris, are still addicts of what Gloag brought home – though in other classes the custom, like its adherents, is dying.

One man who was quick to adopt the cigarette habit was Emperor Napoleon III. When Prince Albert and Queen Victoria visited Paris in 1855 they found him chain-smoking.* They brought with them three hundred and sixty photographs of the Crimean campaign taken by Roger Fenton – one of the more successful photographers in that war. Probably the Romanian court painter Carol Popp de Szathmari took more dramatic shots, including scenes of battle, but only one of his photographs has survived.[24] This is a splendid old Turkish irregular soldier, a Bashi-Bazouk, lolling beside a bare-chested female companion. Szathmari's albums

*Prince Albert, who abominated the habit, did not join him. As his verse biographer, the Rev. Paul Johnson, aged 94, recalled,
    The Prince a singular example set
    And smoked not e'en a fragrant cigarette,
    Nor feared to give his royal host offence
    As deemed unsocial in this abstinence.

*The invention of James A. Bonsack of Salem, Va.

belonging to Napoleon III were probably consumed by fire when Communards burnt the Tuileries in 1871. The army photographer Richard Nicklin and two assistants in the Royal Engineers drowned, with sixteen cases of equipment, in Balaclava harbour when their ship, the *Rip Van Winkle*, was sunk on 14 November 1854.[25]

Fenton was a commercial photographer who saw the war as a chance to practise his (comparatively) new hobby. We exclaim at his prints, as at those of James Robertson (an Englishman based at Constantinople): but they are nearly all portraits, and only a very few, if the truth is told, actually convey much of the atmosphere of the war.

Action photographs were barely a technical possibility. All these photographers used the wet-plate solution which had been developed in 1852 by Scott Archer, an Englishman. A glass plate was immersed in collodion, a solution of ether, guncotton and alcohol, which was blended with silver iodide and iodide of iron. Then the plate was sensitized by means of a coating of silver nitrate solution. The wet plate was then placed inside the camera. Exposure took between three and twenty seconds, which accounts for the air of frozen stillness in most of these frames. The plate then had to be removed at once to a dark room, which is why photographers in the Crimea were encumbered with, in Szathmari's case, a carriage, in Fenton's with a specially covered van. Whereas wet collodion plates in England would probably be usable for up to ten minutes, in the heat of a Crimean summer they dried almost instantaneously.

So, the wonder is that we have any plates at all of the

Roger Fenton's camera van. This was the first photographed war.

Crimean War. We do, however. Wherever his van (overpoweringly hot in that sweltering summer) turned up, the soldiers clustered round, wanting to be immortalized. They stare at us, or so it seems, just as much as we stare at them. Clearly, Fenton has managed to freeze certain moments in the past, but what strikes us more forcibly is their wistfulness as they look at us, and the future.

A group of Gurkha soldiers with their British officer during the Indian Mutiny, c. 1858. Viscount Canning, who took over the governor-generalship of the East India Company in 1856, thought the sepoys 'curious creatures . . . just like children. *Ombrageux* is the word for them I think. Shadows and their own fancies seem to frighten them much more than realities.'

Chapter Twelve

India 1857–9

On 9 May 1857, in the parade-ground at Meerut, some forty miles north-east of Delhi, a melancholy scene was enacted beneath the rolling stormclouds and the sunless sky. Eighty-five sepoy troops were being stripped of their uniforms – for which they had themselves paid – and handed over to blacksmiths who riveted fetters on their arms and legs. These were no common criminals. How did it come about that these proud soldiers, who had fought so bravely for the East India Company in the Sikh wars in the Punjab less than a decade before, found themselves humiliated and paraded before their comrades like common criminals? What was their offence?

The new Enfield rifle with which they had been issued could not be loaded unless each and every cartridge had its end bitten off before insertion into the gun. These sepoys had refused, fearing that the grease used on the cartridge came from the fat of an animal forbidden in the dietary laws of their religion. Their commanding officer, Colonel Carmichael Smyth of the 3rd Native Cavalry, was a choleric, unpopular figure. On 23 April he had ordered a parade to demonstrate the use of the new cartridges and a method by which they could be used without biting. It was not in itself an ill-intentioned idea, but as many of the colonel's fellow officers observed, it was crashingly tactless and almost bound to have a disastrous consequence. Ever since the new rifle, with its notoriously greased cartridges, had been introduced to the subcontinent, there had been rumours flying. In January, at Dum-Dum, a low-caste lascar was said to have approached a Brahmin sepoy who worked in the musketry department and told him that the grease used for these cartridges – which had to be put in the soldier's mouth before he loaded his rifle – was made from the fats of forbidden beasts – beef dripping would have most alarmed the Hindus, pork fat the Muslims.

Incredibly – given the sensitivity of dietary matters in religion – it seems as though forbidden fats had, in some instances, been used to grease the cartridges, though as soon as the mistake was noticed the East India Company gave strict orders that the cartridges should be greased with a mixture of tallow (sheep fat) and beeswax.[1] But the rumours were now ablaze. It was widely reported among the sepoy regiments that the British had deliberately engineered a situation in which Hindus would eat beef fat in order to make Christians of them. Although this was not true, it was not so preposterous a suggestion in 1857 as it might have been in the time of Warren Hastings. Lord Dalhousie in his time as governor-general (1848–56) had been a modernizer, an improver, a moral policeman. The Evangelical desire to improve met the Benthamite ambition to organize the lives of others and together they found a perfect object for their busybodydom: Indian religion. William Wilberforce said he really put the conversion of India to Christianity 'before Abolition' (of slavery) as a task for God and His Englishmen. What were the Hindu divinities after all but 'absolute monsters of lust, injustice, wickedness and cruelty. In short, their religious system is one grand abomination.'[2]

As well as fears, in the late 1850s the sepoys had cause for discontent. As the great Indian scholar S.B. Chaudhuri noted, it was not so much the fear for their religion that provoked the rural classes and their landed chiefs to revolt: 'It was the question of their rights and interests in the soil and hereditary holdings which excited them to a dangerous degree.'[3] The British under Dalhousie had taken over the property of many of the Indian landowners. The rents were now fixed by the East India Company.

The sepoy armies were of use to the Company not merely to police the territories already occupied by the British but also to conquer and subdue more – for example the garrisons of Lower Burma. For Indian troops to be moved efficiently and speedily to Burma it had been deemed necessary by the British to insist on the abolition, or ignoring, of the caste system in such areas as military transport. These 'common-sense' reforms were much resented, especially by Brahmin sepoys who objected for example to having to travel alongside Sikhs.

Who were the sepoys? Many were 'distressed gentlefolk' whose families could no longer make a living from the land, or perhaps had been impoverished by British land reform. The Bengal army was largely recruited from a limited number of districts in Southern Oudh, the eastern regions of the North-Western provinces and Western Bihar, where Brahmins and Rajputs (who claimed descent from the ancient Kshatriya soldier caste) belonged to proprietary brotherhoods of small landowners. Military service was a dignified option for these men. Out of their 7 to 9 rupees per month, they had to pay for food, uniform, and transport of baggage. After the wars of conquest and expansion in the Punjab were over, the British cut the allowances to their sepoy troops and hinted that 'foreign' troops, for example the Gurkhas, could be recruited more cheaply if the Brahmins and Rajputs did not want the work. The sepoy was therefore torn, at this period, between a need to make a living and a profound resentment at the high-handed reforms of the British, especially when these reforms were made in the name of Western progress. If 1857 was something more than a disturbance among the troops, if it was a rising against the *angreezi raj*, or English rule, then it was very much a revolt against the Modern. The aggrieved sepoys had more than a little in common with the hand-loom weavers of Lancashire put out of work by machines; with the dispossessed working classes of England who found themselves forced into Benthamite workhouses; with the Irish whose right to their own religion, and even life itself, was questioned in some English quarters; with Canadians and Jamaicans whose livelihood was wrecked by Free Trade; and with those many Radicals and Chartists who demonstrated and petitioned not so much for the creation of a brave new future as for a share of the freedoms they had enjoyed in the past and which the March of the Modern had taken away from them.

So here are the eighty-five sepoys standing in the parade-ground in Meerut in the sweltering, thunderous, sunless heat while the stormclouds gather: eighty-five brave, old-fashioned fighting men manacled like disgraced slaves and marched to the prison house before the shocked gaze of their comrades. Rather fewer than 2,000 sepoys witnessed the spectacle. That evening one of the native officers went to Hugh Gough, who was sitting on the veranda of his bungalow, to warn him that there would be a mutiny of the native troops at Meerut the next day. Gough was an intelligent man who knew that since the discontents at Dum-Dum in January there had been minor mutinies at Barrackpur and Berhampur, and a serious uprising of the 48th Native Cavalry at Lucknow.[4] He went at once to Colonel Carmichael Smyth, who reproved him for listening 'to such idle words'. Later in the evening Gough tried to persuade some of the other senior British officers at Meerut – Brigadier Archdale Wilson and Major-General W.H. Hewitt, commander of the Meerut Division – but they too dismissed the suggestion.

The mutiny began the next day, a swelteringly hot day, so hot that the evening church parade was postponed from half-past six to seven o'clock. Before the padre had time to implore the Deity to deliver the Christians from all the perils and dangers of that night, billows of smoke were rising into the torrid air from the bungalows which had been set alight. The sowars of the 3rd Cavalry rode to the prison to release their eighty-five humiliated comrades. Young Gough – subsequently to win a VC* – and Major Tombs rallied the European troops. Many of the Native troops were on the European side. The colonel of the 11th Native Infantry galloped across to see what 'all the noise was about' and was shot on the parade ground. Mayhem broke out, with Colonel Carmichael Smyth conspicuous by his Duke of Plaza Toro-like skill in

*With great prescience the monarch had instituted the Victoria Cross for gallantry on 29 January 1856.

The 'Mutiny' as seen through the eyes of an Indian artist.

taking cover and spending the night in the safety of the cantonment under the protection of the Artillery.[5]

During a night of fires and violence the rabble from the bazaars of Meerut swarmed over the military quarters, looting and killing. Wajir Ali Khan, deputy collector, afterwards gave evidence that though plunder was going on all night the sepoys did not touch a thing.[6] Gough later said that none of the sepoys in the 11th or the 3rd murdered their own officers. By morning, however, some fifty Europeans, men, women and children, had been killed. Gough had ridden through the baying lines of the 20th Native Infantry as they called out *Maro! Maro!* – Kill! Kill! – but, though he survived, he could see that they were out of control.

Moreover, it was obvious that the mutineering sepoys were now in the reckless position of having nothing to lose. Whether they surrendered or pleaded for clemency, they knew that the gallows or the firing squad inevitably awaited them. They might as well fight on.

The Europeans listened to the shouting of slogans, the crackling of flames, the cry of '*Yah! Ali! Ali! e nara Haidari!*'[7] The Indians were crying out that they had 'broken the Electric Telegraph and overturned the British Rule, and boasting they had committed these atrocities in the name of religion'.

By morning, the mutineers had escaped Meerut and had ridden off to Delhi. The Meerut outbreak, however unpleasant in itself, might have been seen as no more than a summer heat-storm had the fire of discontent not spread. 'Oh why did you have a parade?' wailed General Hewitt to the colonel. By then the rebels had proclaimed the last Moghul emperor, eighty-two-year-old Bahadur Shah II, the king of Delhi. The sepoy mutineers also issued the following proclamation:

To all Hindoos and Mussulmans, Citizens and Servants of Hindostan, the officers of the Army now at Delhi and Meerut send greeting:

It is well known that in these days all the English have entertained these evil designs – first, to destroy the religion of the whole Hindostani army, and then to make the people by compulsion Christians. Therefore we, solely on account of our religion, have combined with the people, and have not spared alive one infidel, and have re-established the Delhi dynasty on these terms. Hundreds of guns and a large amount of treasure have fallen into our hands; therefore it is fitting that whoever of the soldiers and people dislike turning Christians should unite with one heart, and, acting courageously, not leave the seed of these infidels remaining . . . It is . . . necessary that all Hindoos and Mussulmans unite in this struggle and, following the instructions of some respectable people, keep themselves secure so that good order may be maintained.

For ninety years after 1857, the British liked to represent the terrible events of that summer as 'the Indian Mutiny'. It was necessary for the British self-image that the outbreaks of incendiarism and violence should have been of a purely military character, an aberration by a few fanatics who (mistakenly, of course) believed that they were being asked to put the fat of forbidden meats in their mouths. These maniacs – so the British historians saw things – were prepared to reverse all the benefits of civilization which had been brought to them by the East India Company for the sake of returning to the most superstitious adherence to a backward-looking religion. They were a few diehards discontented with army life. The huge majority of Indians, it is averred in this notion of events, recognized that the British administered their land and their institutions far more fairly than the corrupt princelings of the decayed Indian dynasties, whether Moghul or Mahratta.

At the other extreme are to be found the Indian nationalist historians who liked to see 1857 as the first serious attempt at a united Independence Movement for the subcontinent. For these historians, the Delhi Declaration is of the utmost significance, giving the lie to the British supposition that Hindu and Muslim could never coexist without a European administration keeping the peace. They would link the Delhi declaration to the momentous Calcutta Congress of 1886 whose spirit was captured by the Nawab Reza Ali-Khan, Bahadur of Lucknow, who said – in Urdu – 'Hindus or Mahomedans, Parsees or Sikhs, we are one people now, whatever our ancestors six or eight hundred years ago may have been, and our public interests are indivisible and identical . . . we Mahomedans (at least such of us as can think at all) think just as all thinking Hindus do on these public questions.'

Most Indian historians today view with some scepticism the notion that 1857 was Act One of the Independence Drama. But its memory undoubtedly fuelled later supporters of the Freedom Movement, just as the memories of the Famine shaped the development of Irish Republicanism. Had the events of 1857 been no more than a mutiny, then there would not have been places, such as Banda and Hamirpur, where civilian mobs rose against the British without military assistance.[8] If, however, one tries to see these uprisings as part of a concerted Independence movement, it is difficult to explain why the greater part of the subcontinent was unaffected. The conflict was a phenomenon of the North-West of India, and central North-West at that. It never spread up as far as Lahore in the Punjab, nor – by a mixture of good luck and clever tactics by the British – did it ever reach the administrative capital, Calcutta. Bombay, Hyderabad, Mysore, the Carnatic, Ceylon remained all but unaffected by the bloody events.

Nor should one forget the chief reason for the successful suppression of the uprisings: namely that the Indian majority fought alongside the British in the various battles and siege-reliefs and – it must be supposed – that the majority of Indian citizens, for whatever reason, did not wish to take part in a violent war either against the Europeans or against their local Indian landlords. In *Narratives of Events at Cawnpore*,*[9] the Indian author Nanak Chand witnesses the murders, the burnings and the sheer chaos brought about by the uprising. On one terrifying, broiling hot day he found himself cowering in a garden hut for all the hours of daylight without food or water while the mob, who had refreshed themselves by plundering a British wine-cellar, rampaged around the plantations of Madarpoor. These were not aggrieved sepoy officers but peasants on the razzle, completely out of control. At midnight under the cover of dark, Nanak Chand crept to the banks of the Ganges, tiptoeing over untold numbers of corpses. 'These drunken boatmen were armed; some with clubs, others with weapons, and they were running about the woods like wild men. I cannot describe the terror that seized me at that moment. How I sighed for the British rule.'

It is only fair to record this Indian impression of things before recognizing that 'British rule' was not restored without very great cost to the Indian population. The ruthlessness of British reprisals, the preparedness to

*Modern Indians spell this Kanpur, the spelling followed here except when quoting Victorian sources.

'punish' Indians of any age or sex, regardless of whether they had any part in the rebellion, is a perpetual moral stain on 'the Raj', and it is no wonder that in most popular British histories these atrocities are suppressed altogether or glossed over with such a distasteful anodyne phrase as 'dark deeds were done on both sides'.[10] It is not to defend the murders of European women and children that one points out that such remarks suggest an equivalence where none can properly exist. Even if 1857 was not quite an independence war, it was much, much more than a 'mutiny' – a word which not merely, inaccurately, suggests that violence was restricted to the military, but also begs every moral question by assuming the legitimacy of British 'rule'. The sepoy, for reasons of economic necessity, had accepted his 7 or 9 rupees a month from the East India Company for four generations. Did that give a British historian sitting in London, who had never set foot in India, or a Whiggish president of the Board of Control – also in London – or a local 'collector' the right to tell the Indian how much rent he should pay, what he should eat, how he should treat his wife or his neighbours? 'The people of this country do not require our aid to furnish them with a rule for their conduct or a standard for their property,' Warren Hastings had wisely remarked in 1773 when Lord North's Regulating Act set up a Supreme Court in Calcutta.[11] The Victorians rode roughshod. There can be no moral equivalence between a people, by whatever means of atrocity, trying to fight for their freedom to live as they choose, without the interference of an invading power, and that power itself using the utmost brutality to enforce not merely a physical but a political dominance over the people.

The terrible story has three phases. It started in the summer of 1857, when the Europeans suffered massacres at Meerut, Delhi and Kanpur – and when the last-named town and Lucknow underwent sieges which, for the heroism and suffering displayed, fast became legendary. Next came the relief of Lucknow and the demonstration that the British were regaining control of the situation. Third came the war of reprisal of 1858–9 in which the brilliant guerrilla leader Ramchandra Pandenanga, known as Tatya Tope, fought a series of heroic rearguard actions and gave the hardened campaigners Sir Colin Campbell and Sir Hugh Rose a 'run for their money'. By then, though, there was no doubt about the inevitable outcome of the war. Nearly all the British accounts dwell, for reasons which do not need to be explained, on the first two of those phases, and turn a blind eye to the third.[12]

When the rebels reached Delhi on the night of 10/11 May 1857, probably no one was more surprised than the eighty-two-year-old king, whose days were largely devoted to composing poetry, illuminating manuscripts and listening to the cooing of his pet doves and nightingales. The city was garrisoned, but largely with sepoy troops – there were no European regiments there – and the cry to massacre the infidels was obeyed in a way that most Indians appear to have deplored. The European women who were lucky enough to escape the cantonments – Mrs Wood, the doctor's wife in the 38th Native Infantry, and her friend Mrs Peile – recorded many acts of kindness from natives who assisted their getaway.[13] Many were not so lucky. James Morley, a merchant from the Kashmir bazaar, was typical in finding his whole family massacred. He escaped disguised as a woman, but that would not have saved him in many quarters where the shootings of women and children were indiscriminate. In the aftermath of the violence, careful inquiries were unable to reveal a single instance of rape or torture being a prelude to the death of European women in any of the atrocities of that summer. One official noted that this information was of some comfort to those who had lost wives, sisters and daughters, but there were many in Britain who simply refused to believe it.[14] So shocking were the Delhi murders of British women that, paradoxically, the British wanted to make them even more shocking, with the automatic assumption that the 'angels of Albion' had been ravished as well as shot. The Reverend John Rotton, British chaplain during the Meerut and Delhi atrocities, reveals the double standards which had crept into British attitudes to the Indian. This clergyman witnessed some terrible things, and buried many of his massacred fellow countrymen, so one does not in any sense wish to patronize him. To say that his partisan attitude is understandable is not, however, to find it especially elevating. He had rushed out his *Chaplain's Narrative of the Siege of Delhi* within a year of the event itself, one of the hundreds of books published in the next thirty years demonstrating comparable habits of mind, steeped in a certainty of racial superiority to the Indians. This is something new since the era of Clive, or even of Wellesley, and it was to shape the pattern of 'British India' for the next century.[15]

Besieged in Delhi, the few remaining Europeans had to wait through the hottest months of the year, until August, before Brigadier-General John Nicholson, a tormented homosexual soldier in his mid-thirties who had been in India since 1839, appeared on the ridge above Delhi to relieve the siege. A huge figure, with a long black beard and a deep voice, Nicholson was destined to die in the fighting. Soon after there was a cholera outbreak in the 8th and 61st regiments, which killed hundreds, including General Sir Harry Barnard, in command of the force, and severely weakened his successor General Reed, the provisional commander-in-chief.

Meanwhile, as cholera swept through the camp in Delhi, they heard the news of the disasters at Kanpur. These were perhaps the most shocking losses suffered by the Europeans during the whole summer. The killings were disgusting; the treachery of the local princeling, Nana Sahib, was demonstrable; no one can deny or minimize these facts. From the first, however, Kanpur acquired a mythic significance. The aged poet of Delhi, Bahadur Shah II, or the obese king of Oudh could hardly be represented, even to a furious British newspaper-reading public, as demon-kings. In the local princeling at Kanpur, Nana Sahib, was found an ideal candidate.

Dhondu Pant (Nana Sahib's actual name) was archetypically one of the Indian bigwigs who stood to lose by the modernizing reforms of Lord Dalhousie. Under Dalhousie the East India Company had dethroned the last Peshwa of Bithur, Baji Rao II, and given him a pension worth £80,000 per annum – 8 lakhs of rupees. The Company took his revenues from rents. When he died, however, his adopted son Dhondu Pant/Nana Sahib was not considered by Dalhousie to be entitled to such lavish treatment.[16] No one visiting Nana Sahib in his palatial residence five miles from Kanpur, no one who saw his luxurious carpets, crystal chandeliers, soft Cashmere shawls, his menageries and aviaries, would have believed him to be on the breadline, but the Company had deprived him of vast revenues, which he believed to be his, in 1851. In 1857 he would demonstrate the truth of the proverb that revenge was a dish best served cold.[17]

A glance at the map shows the strategic importance of Kanpur. This town – at the time, numbering 60,000 – on the banks of the sacred Ganges was an important post on the Great Road, the trunk road connecting Delhi and Benares. It is fascinating, from the point of view of military history, that Tatya Tope, the 'Napoleon' of the uprising, Nana Sahib's general, never grasped the importance of this road. Had he but managed to block it at one, preferably at two points, he might have inflicted real damage on the British – perhaps, who knows, broken their nerve.

The massacre of European women at Cawnpore deeply inflamed British public opinion.

THE TREACHEROUS MAS

UPON THE ADVANCE OF GENERAL HAVELOCKS VICTORIOUS COL
OF THE DEAD AND DYING WERE THROWN DOWN THE WELL IN THE GA

OF ENGLISH WOMEN & CHILDREN AT CAWNPORE BY NENA SAHIB.

F OF CAWNPORE, NENA SAHIB (PREVIOUS TO HIS RETREAT), ORDERED ALL THE CHRISTIANS REMAINING IN HIS POWER, TO BE BARBAROUSLY MASSACRED, AND THE MANGLED BODIES
E, THE REMAINING PORTION OF THE GARRISON WERE DESTROYED BY A MASKED BATTERY IN THEIR BOATS, OR SABRED ON THE SHORES OF THE RIVER"

Kanpur was, however, ripe for his picking in summer 1857.[18] The British reorganization of the sepoy regiments had weakened morale. When the 2nd Cavalry mutinied at Kanpur on 2 June, the native regiments were in disarray. All the native officers of the 56th at Kanpur, for example – all – were on furlough, and seconded to mercenary soldiering in districts miles from home, at the time of the rising.[19]

Tatya Tope had the guerrilla leader's knack of seizing a chance, but lacked the weapons or manpower to hold on to Kanpur indefinitely. Useful as it might be to occupy this point of the trunk road for a few weeks (or, if he was lucky, months), he knew that he would not be able to hold out against a fully armed British contingent of trained men when they came marching westwards up the Great Road.

It is in these circumstances that we must envisage the unfortunate Europeans' plight in Kanpur. It would appear that after the outbreak of Mutiny, Nana Sahib offered protection and hospitality to the European women and children, and safe-conduct to those who wished to escape by boat down the Ganges. Conditions within the cantonment quickly became intolerable. Dysentery and heatstroke were rife, and morale was weakened by an apparently accidental fire which destroyed all the medical supplies in the Europeans' possession. The double atrocities with which the name of Kanpur is always associated in British minds concerned the treatment of the British women and children. First – help for Lucknow not appearing – General Wheeler, the British commander, oversaw the European refugees being put on the forty or so boats provided by Nana Sahib. As soon as they were all afloat, their Indian escorts leapt ashore, many of them able to set the thatched roofs of the boats alight before jumping into the water. As the convoy drifted downstream, they were met by an organized firing party of insurgents, who bombarded the boats with musket fire, burning arrows and heavier artillery. They were afloat for two days in these circumstances, the semi-clad survivors being dragged from the river at Satichaura Ghat. Then on 10 July, the women and children were taken to a house known as the Bibighar. It was a large bungalow with a courtyard, formerly the residence of a British officer and his Indian mistress. To the survivors of the boats were added those officers' wives who had escaped the cantonment and been rounded up by Tatya Tope.

He knew that Brigadier-General Henry Havelock was on his way to relieve Kanpur – which he did, successfully, on 16 July. The British troops who went into the court-yard, and peered into the dried-up well at the Bibighar, were too late to save the women. The newly appointed magistrate, J.W. Sherer, wrote to a senior civil servant, Sir Cecil Beadon:

May God in his mercy, my dear Beadon, preserve me from ever witnessing again such a sight as I have seen this day. The house they were kept in was close to the hotel – opposite the theatre – it was a native house – with a court in the middle, and an open room with pillars opposite the principal entrance. The whole of the court and this room was literally soaked with blood and strewn with bonnets and those large hats now worn by ladies – and there were long tresses of hair glued with clotted blood to the ground – all the bodies were thrown into a dry well and on looking down – a map of naked arms, legs and gashed trunks was visible. My nerves are so deadened with horror that I write this quite calmly. It is better you should know the worst – I am going this very moment to fill the well up and crown its mouth with a mount. Let us mention the subject no more – silence and prayer alone seem fitting.[20]

It remains uncertain whether Nana Sahib had any prior knowledge that the massacres would take place.[21] They were committed in his name, but he always denied having any part in the murders. This did not stop the British press demonizing him as the very type of oriental duplicity and callousness.[22] Sherer, the magistrate just quoted, recalled that Nana was an *excessively uninteresting person*; rather overweight, boring. Nevertheless, *The Spectator* suggested that Nana should be 'caged and exhibited as Macduff intended to do with Macbeth. He should be caged as a matter of study and after exhibition in India should be brought to England and carefully guarded to live out the term of his natural, or unnatural life, a monster without sympathy.'[23] For some years after the Massacres,[24] a well-known 'portrait' of Nana Sahib circulated, comparable to the Wild West 'WANTED' posters of criminals. The same picture was also used to hunt for Rajah Kunwar Singh. It was in fact a picture of a blameless banker from Meerut who had given his portrait to a London barrister named John Lang, who successfully prosecuted a case on his behalf. Lang lent it to the *Illustrated London News*, where it became a serviceable icon 'against which the public could direct their hatred'.

The revenges exacted by the British for the massacres at Delhi and Kanpur were far from being purely emblematic in India itself. From the very first, the British decided to meet cruelty with redoubled cruelty, terror with terror, blood with blood. At Delhi, Nicholson

Reprisals against innocent Indians were gleefully welcomed by the British public.

had urged, 'Let us propose a Bill for the flaying alive, impalement, or burning of the murderers of the women and children at Delhi. The idea of simply hanging the perpetrators of such atrocities is maddening.'

Sir Henry Cotton was summoned from his tent by a Sikh orderly. 'I think, sir, you would like to see what we have done to the prisoners.'[25] Muslims had been stripped, tied to the ground and 'branded over every part of their bodies with red-hot coppers'. With his own hand, Cotton put an end to their agony by blowing out their brains, but no action was taken against the torturers. Russell, the *Times* journalist who had covered the Crimean War, saw Sikhs and Englishmen calmly looking on while a bayoneted prisoner was slowly roasted over a fire.[26] Sewing Muslims into pigskins, or smearing them with pork fat before execution, was another torture favoured by the British. When 'Clemency Canning' – the sobriquet was intended to insult the governor-general – implored army officers not to countenance the burning of villages, his words were met with contempt. Long before the Kanpur massacres, whole villages had been sacked by

the British. Rape and pillage were encouraged by the British officers before old women and children were burnt alive in their villages. Officers boasted that they had 'spared no one', or that 'peppering away at niggers' was a pastime which they 'enjoyed amazingly'.[27] The troops who 'relieved' Delhi were drunk, killed hundreds quite indiscriminately, and sent thousands of homeless refugees into the surrounding countryside.

Many Indians had the experience of being lashed, standing, to the mouth of a cannon and blown apart by grapeshot. 'One gun,' recalled a clergyman's wife who had come out to watch the executions, 'was overcharged and the poor wretch was literally blown to atoms, the lookers-on being covered with blood, and fragments of flesh: the head of one poor wretch fell on a bystander and hurt him.'[28]

Colonel James Neill was one of the many British officers who fought in India at this time with a religious sense of duty. (He was to rise to the rank of brigadier-general.) Like Nicholson in Delhi, Neill at Kanpur felt that hanging was too gentle a fate for the murderers. In fact, no sepoy would take part in the massacres in the Bibighar and the disgusting slaughter had been the work of five local butchers. This did not stop Neill embarking on a system of wholesale torture and butchery himself when he and his men retook possession of the station. Prisoners were made to lick the blood from the floor of the Bibighar while a European soldier lashed their backs with a whip. Every means was taken to offend the religious sensibilities of prisoners, whether they had any proven part in the uprising or not. Brahmins, therefore, would be made to lick parts of the floor previously moistened with water by 'untouchables'. 'We broke his caste,' wrote one Major Bingham. 'We stuffed pork, beef and everything which would possibly break his caste down his throat, tied him as tight as we could by the arms and told the guard to be *gentle* with him . . . The guard treated him *gently*. I only wonder he lived to be hung, which I had the pleasure of witnessing.'

Neill killed as many Indians in Allahabad alone as were killed on his own side in the entire two years of fighting. Yet the British continued to feed their self-esteem by representing themselves as the underdogs, heavily outnumbered, never more so than during the legendary siege of Lucknow.

This great feudal court-city, the capital of the nawabs of Oudh, was much the most prosperous precolonial city in India.[29] An Englishwoman who married a Lucknow nobleman (Mrs Meer Hasan Ali) was reminded by the city of the visionary castles of the Arabian Nights. Russell, the war correspondent, saw

> A vision of palaces, mirrors, domes azure and golden, cupolas, colonnades, long façades of fair perspective in pillar and column, terraced roofs – all rising up amid a calm still ocean of the brightest verdure. Look for miles and miles away and still the ocean spreads, and the towers of the fairy-city gleam in its midst.

Russell also observed the appalling squalor and poverty of the slums for which the British, like the nawabs before them, had done nothing.[30]

Dalhousie's reforms were especially resented in Lucknow, not least because of Lucknow's religious significance in the Muslim consciousness, site of many holy mosques, and because of the blatant greed with which the governor-general regarded the ancient Muslim kingdom.

When the uprising had engulfed the city it was something much more than a mutiny of the sepoy regiments. On the first Sunday of the outbreak, in April 1857, thousands of Muslims marched through the streets under the banners of their faith, while less thoughtful rioters ransacked and burnt houses, looted the shops, and indicated their contempt for the Europeans by staging mock decapitations of life-size dolls dressed in British army uniform.[31]

The British retreated into the Residency of Sir Henry Lawrence, chief commissioner of Oudh, and the financial commissioner, Martin Gubbins, fortified his own substantial house, using seventy-five native servants to build bastions and dig ditches. The siege itself lasted 143 days, and the courage and endurance of the British men, women and children who held out in the entrenchment inspired a mass of literature. Cholera and dysentery carried off as many as did enemy bullets. Food supplies were limited, and morale was undermined by bickerings and resentments. Gubbins and Lawrence were perpetually at odds. The civilian volunteers resented very deeply the lack of gratitude displayed to them by the military. Twenty volunteers, civilians not in the government employ, stood guard at various key positions around the entrenchment.

> One half of the soldiers were thus on duty every day, and the other half off duty at the Residency; not so with the volunteers, for *every day and night of the whole five months* [his italics], did they stand sentry and do their duty, yet so unjust were the military authorities, that, while the soldiers got sugar and tea (as long as it lasted) the volunteers got none, while the soldiers drew rum and porter rations *daily*, until Havelock's force came in, the volunteers were refused it – while the soldiers received meat *daily* the volunteers were only allowed it every second day, and while the soldiers got otta, the volunteers were served out with wheat and told to grind it into flour themselves!

When at last, after several botched attempts, General Havelock relieved the siege, the conquering heroes themselves – Havelock himself and Neill – were exchanging such notes as this – 'I wrote to you confidentially on the state of affairs. You send me back a letter of censure of my measures, reproof and advice for the future. I do not and will not receive any of them from an officer under my command be his experience what it may.'[32]

Havelock contracted dysentery at Lucknow, from which he died[33] – 'Harry,' he said to his son, 'see how a Christian can die.' Henry Lawrence died of wounds during the siege – every one of the soldiers who carried him to his grave kissed him on the forehead. This was not a war when the senior officers escaped. General Barnard died of cholera. At the funeral of General John Nicholson, aged thirty-six, the men of the Multani Horse threw themselves on the ground and wept. 'Probably not one of these men had ever shed a tear before; but for them Nicholson was everything.'[34] It was not only the suffering, and deaths, of women and children which excited passionate British emotion during this tragic period. The Mutiny, as they called it, had caught them all by surprise. The possibility that Indians could, for whatever motives, expose their vulnerability summoned forth in the collective psyche violent and passionate emotions.

The fluttering, torn Union Jack was never removed from the flagpole of the Residency at Lucknow through all the hellish nine months. It was not a moment for national self-questioning about what right they had to be in India in the first place. The uprisings and wars of 1857–8 were seen as the assault of barbarism against Christian civilization.

In something like fifty years, the British had radically changed the rules and terms by which the East India Company had operated in India. From being a trading monopoly which worked, where successful, to the mutual advantage of greedy English merchants and greedy, or timorous, Indian princes, it became an administration, claiming the right to the revenues and rents of those princes, and the rents of the peasant-farmers. It had taken upon itself the role of educator, civil servant and improver, making no secret not merely of its disapproval of Indian religions, but, more, of its right to disapprove. The sharp reactions these events in India had produced were seen by the English public at large (apart from the inevitable croakers) as 'treason' – though how you can 'betray' an interloping authority which you do not regard as legitimate, these English imperialists did not trouble to ask themselves. By the next year, when the Act of Parliament abolished the EIC, it was 'provided that the splendid empire raised by the East India Company during the last and present century should be transferred to Queen Victoria'.[35] The nation of shopkeepers had become the nation of imperialists. The late Victorian historian of *Punch*, M.H. Spielmann, saw as the 'masterpieces of Sir John Tenniel his Cawnpore cartoons depicting "The British Lion's Vengeance on the Bengal Tiger." . . . Once this fine drawing is seen, of the royal beast springing on its snarling foe, whose victims lie mangled under its paw, it can never be forgotten.' Spielmann tells us that Tenniel's cartoon served as 'a banner when they raised the cry of vengeance, it alarmed the authorities, who feared that they would thereby be forced on a road which both policy and the gentler dictates of civilisation forbade'.

It is with relief that one turns to the exchanges between the governor-general and his monarch.

> One of the greatest difficulties which lie ahead, and Lord Canning grieves to say so to Your Majesty, will be the violent rancour of a very large proportion of the English Community against every native Indian of every class. There is rabid and indiscriminate vindictiveness abroad, even amongst many who ought to set a better example, which it is impossible to contemplate without something like a feeling of shame of one's fellow-countrymen.[36]

The vehemence of the Queen's response does her great credit. She entirely shared Canning's 'feelings of sorrow and indignation at the unchristian spirit shown – alas! also to a great extent here – by the public towards Indians in general and towards *Sepoys without discrimination!* [her italics]'. She emphasized that the Indians should know 'that there is no hatred to a brown skin'.

These words were totally sincere, and borne out in her unfeigned delight in the company of Indians, an aspect of the Queen's character which would lead to minor troubles later in the reign. Apart from being shaming, the British vindictiveness towards all Indians in general, in the aftermath of what they called the Mutiny, blinded them to the most extraordinary aspect of the period 1857–9 in Indian history: namely that sepoy regiments on the whole remained loyal to the East India Company. Even those which did not conspicuously refused to take part in the worst atrocities upon Europeans.

Historians from Indian and British backgrounds both tend to write as if the defeat of the 'Mutiny' were an inevitability. Certainly, by the end of 1857 the British had largely gained control of the situation: Lucknow and Delhi had been relieved. Tatya Tope, however, and other Indian resistance-fighters, kept up fairly vigorous guerrilla warfare for the whole of the next year. The king of Delhi, who was put on trial in March 1859 for having aided and abetted the 'mutineers', was exiled for life to Rangoon. Sir Colin Campbell, the veteran Crimean hero, pursued Tatya Tope in some exciting campaigns and the defeat of the Mutiny at Jhansi by Sir Hugh Rose really signalled the end of the war.[37] Tatya Tope was hanged at dawn on 18 April 1859.

Undoubtedly a factor in the Indian defeat was the tendency for rebel groups to disintegrate. At the outbreak, the 17th Native Infantry had marched out of Azamgarh for Faizabad 'with all the pomp of war: elephants, carriages, buggies and horses accompanied Bhundu Singh Rajah their leader'. They fought in the action there – the 200 troops having swollen to 500 non-uniformed rabble. After August 1857 there were no organized sepoy resistance-fighters in the entire Doab district. By contrast the British, who had their share of setbacks, always regrouped, closed ranks. Much has been made of the importance of the telegraph and the railway, which the British had at their disposal and the rebels did not.

Such would be the common-sense or occidental version of events. Perhaps it would be truer to say that India, and the Indians, did not yet have an alternative vision of themselves to put up against the European bullies in their midst. The notion of 'enlightened' politics was itself a Western import which, having taken root, would require nurture before achieving the desired result of British withdrawal. Viewed in this light, it is hard to see who was the victor of 1857–9. The British ground the Indians down, but what followed – ninety years of 'The Raj' – was in fact an odd sort of coalition. The British could not 'govern' India without Indian consent. The subsequent occasions of violence, such as the notorious massacre at Amritsar of 1919, were in fact signs of British weakness, a losing of grip, rather than the reverse. The Raj worked only for so long as the Indians themselves, fearful of the divisions within their own ranks, between castes, religions and cultures, got along as best they could with their European visitors.

Sikh soldiers helped the British to put down the Mutiny in the Indian Army.

THE LONDON SKETCH BOOK.

PROF. DARWIN.

This is the ape of form.
Love's Labor Lost, act 5, scene 2.

Some four or five descents since.
All's Well that Ends Well, act 3, sc. 7.

Chapter Thirteen

Clinging to Life

In February 1858, lying sick of a fever at Ternate in the Moluccas, Alfred Russel Wallace, an amateur naturalist, began to think of Malthus's *Essay on Population*. Unlike Charles Darwin, who was always rich, thanks to the Wedgwood inheritance, Wallace had had to work his way through the world – as a schoolmaster, self-taught railway architect, and explorer. Like Darwin he had made a trip to South America, and been awestruck by the equatorial forests, the beauty and strangeness of the flora and fauna, and by the native population. Financing his travels by the sale of specimens, he had also spent eight years exploring the Malay Archipelago. Like Darwin, Lyell, Chambers, and indeed most scientists of the day, Wallace was preoccupied by the problem of the origins of life on Earth, what Goethe called 'The mystery of mysteries'. Since the time of Darwin's grandfather, Erasmus Darwin, who wrote *Zoonomia* (1794–6), a work which anticipated the opinions of Lamarck, scientists had believed in the evolution of species. It was Jean-Baptiste Pierre Antoine de Monet, Chevalier de Lamarck (1744–1829), who finally put paid to the notion of the immutability of species, but the question remained – *how* did such changes take place? The caricature of the question is, how did the giraffe acquire a neck long enough to reach the tree? The secondary question is, what happened in the meanwhile to all the generations of short-necked giraffes whose mouths never came near the foliage?

Lamarck's answer to the first question is that species inherited acquired characteristics. The parent acquires some useful survival technique and is enabled thereby to pass this on to the offspring. Lamarckian evolution was popularized in England by Herbert Spencer – a self-taught philosopher, pioneer sociologist and universal wiseacre – and later in the century by Samuel Butler, grandson of Darwin's headmaster at Shrewsbury School. Although it can now be demonstrated that Lamarck was

1 *Darwin and his cousin the ape, a cartoon of 1874.*

wrong about acquired characteristics being inheritable, it was in fact the metaphor in which most Victorians believed. Darwin, interestingly, adapted his own theories after the publication of his most famous book, adding mistakes to subsequent printings of *The Origin of Species* in order to conform more nearly to the Lamarckian theory he actually set out to disprove. This alerts us to the truth that two things are always going on during scientific research, even in the case of scrupulous scientists such as Wallace and Darwin: on the one hand there is a painstaking search for objective reality, on the other there is the medium in which this search is conducted – language, a metaphor-encrusted tool which dates as easily as clothes. Thus, while we can see the Victorian evolutionary biologists as making truly world-changing 'discoveries' of verifiable (in Popper's terms) phenomena, likewise we can see their ideas as shaped by their times: the 'origin of species' question being to this extent as much a phenomenon of the 1850s as stovepipe hats, steam railways and Pre-Raphaelite art.

But – back to Wallace in 1858, sweating through his fever and thinking of Malthus. Within two hours, he suddenly thought out the whole theory of natural selection. Three days later he had finished his essay.

It is very typical of the difference between the two men that Wallace worked out in a couple of hours what it took Darwin twenty years to decide to publish. Like Wallace, Darwin had been inspired by Malthus – only in 1838. He had sat on his theory, mulled it over, concealed it from himself and his wife, agonized about it. Then, when Wallace sent him his own essay on natural selection, he decided to act. The Wallace–Darwin theory was duly read out at the Linnaean Society in London on 1 July 1858, and the first person to apply it, and to publish it, was Canon H.B. Tristram, a clergyman–ornithologist who, in an article in *Ibis*, October 1859, used it to explain the colours of desert birds. Charles Darwin, who had written and rewritten several drafts of his essay, expanded it to *On the Origin of Species by Means of Natural Selection, or the Preservation of Favoured Races in the Struggle for Life*. It was published by John Murray, himself an amateur geologist. Murray was in fact unconvinced by the theory, but when the whole edition of 1,250 copies sold out in one day he saw its commercial potential. It was to be one of the bestsellers of the age. The number of pamphlets, debates, books, speeches, sermons, quarrels it generated is numberless. It was a book which grew out of pure observation of Nature, but which on another level seemed to define the age to itself. Its primary discovery, that an impersonal process of selection is at work in nature, comparable to the process by which pedigree dogs or hybrid roses are 'improved' by breeders, was seen by the Victorians themselves as a picture of a competitive world. Perhaps it was only in the late twentieth century that some of its other implications – the need to be a Friend of the Earth, since we are all descended from the same roots and sources – were worked out.

Wallace and Darwin had been working on the same material for twenty years quite independently. It was twenty years since a rough version of the theory had been penned by Wallace. Graciously, however, Wallace allowed Darwin to publish. Since he was still in Malaya when Darwin's *Origin of Species* appeared, Wallace did not read the book until 1860. He read it five or six times, 'each time with increasing admiration'. He later said he was glad that it had been Darwin, fourteen years his senior, and not himself who had been called upon to set forward the theory in detail. Later he did publish his own *Contributions to the Theory of Natural Selection* (1870), which confirmed that his mind and Darwin's had been working towards the same conclusions by completely independent means.[1]

Darwin and his beloved cousin-wife Emma moved quite early in their married life to the village of Downe,* near Sevenoaks, Kent. Here he battled with his lifelong mystery illness, which left him breathless and exhausted for half of every day. Here he basked in the love of his wife and children and cousins, here he fulfilled his duties as a local citizen, sitting on the parish council, befriending the vicar, even sitting as a magistrate. Darwin, in his diffidence and self-doubt, is one of the most attractive of all men of genius. Wholly typical is the story told of some quite unimportant discussion at the parish council. Much later that night, the vicar of Downe, the Rev. John Innes, was surprised by a knock at his front door. The tall, bald, troubled figure of Charles Darwin stood there. 'He came to say that, thinking over the debate, though what he had said was quite accurate, he thought, I might have drawn an erroneous conclusion, and he would not sleep till he had explained it.'[2]

Given that this was the nature of the man, it is not surprising that he was so unwilling to test the waters by publishing *The Origin of Species*. Darwin was acutely aware of the intellectual objections to his theory, and this was his primary reason for anxiety; *was it true?* In 1844, when Chambers had anonymously published *Vestiges of the Natural History of Creation*, there had been an

*In those days, Down.

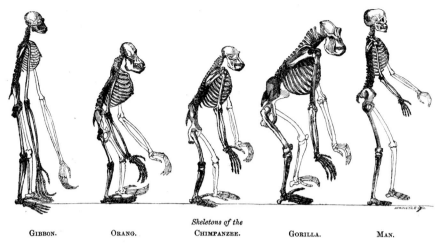

From Thomas Huxley's
Evidence as to man's place in
nature, *1863, a progress of*
skeletons from Gibbon to man.

GIBBON.   ORANG.   Skeletons of the CHIMPANZEE.   GORILLA.   MAN.

Photographically reduced from Diagrams of the natural size (except that of the Gibbon ,which was twice as large as nature),
drawn by Mr. Waterhouse Hawkins from specimens in the Museum of the Royal College of Surgeons.

outcry. 'Mr Vestiges' or 'The Vestigarian' was seen as a 'practical Atheist'.[3] The Church had seen, even in Chambers's generalized transmutationist tract, that such a view disposed of the need for any kind of interventionist God. Scientists had trod very warily since the furore. Figures such as Sir Richard Owen (1804–92), the finest anatomist of his day, first Hunterian professor of anatomy at the Royal College of Surgeons, Gold Medallist in the Geological Society, and in his latter days in charge of the natural history departments at the British Museum, provided a good example of the difficulty faced by any Victorian scientist who wished to get on in the world. In private he freely discussed evolutionary theory. In public he offered simple-minded defences of the literal truth of the Old Testament.[4] He denounced *Vestiges* and in time he would denounce Darwin.

Today we live in an age of scientific triumphalism. It is difficult to recapture the spirit of Victorian England before Darwin published his famous theory. The Church and the clergy still had tremendous power. Not only did they control nearly all university posts, but the convention remained (whatever was said in private) that Parliament and the Press all supported Orthodoxy. For so retiring and shy a man as Darwin to stand up against them all was a formidable challenge. Added to these was the religious distress caused to his wife Emma. Darwin knew that there would be those, including himself, who felt that his theory of natural selection did away with the necessity of believing in a Creator.

Yet if, from the beginning, the Theory of Natural Selection was seen as incompatible with religious belief, much of the blame for this must rest with the churchmen who were too timorous to study the scientific, too lazy to work out the theological implications in sufficient depth. No wonder the perception took root that a choice must be made, *aut Darwin, aut Christus*, Darwin or Christ.

In his highly readable book *Darwin for Beginners* (1982), for example, Dr Jonathan Miller stated that 'for pious Christians, it was an article of faith that the living world was an unaltered replica of the one which God had created at the outset. No species had been lost and none had been altered.' It would seem as though some Christians made this curious notion into an article of their faith, but if so it was not an idea of very ancient or creditable vintage. St Augustine of Hippo (354–430), who was the first great philosopher-theologian of the Latin West, had taught that the original germ of living things came in two forms, one placed by God in animals and plants, the other scattered through the environment, only destined to become active in the right conditions. It wasn't necessary for God to create each living species. The Creator provided the seeds of life and allowed them to develop in their own time.[5]

The Renaissance was the period during which the doctrine of Special Creation emerged. This was an idea of nature which saw all species as the direct, unchanging creation of God. Milton depicts the Creation in this manner in *Paradise Lost.*

Against this is the Wallace–Darwin view that species all emerge, ultimately, from a single life-form. The theory does not suggest that we are descended from monkeys, but that the higher primates, human beings among them, share a common ancestry. The monkeys are cousins, not grandmothers.

If one had to isolate a single all-consuming idea which has taken hold of the human race in the post-political era in which we now live, it is the interrelatedness of natural forms – the fact that we are all on this planet together – human beings, mammals, fish, insects, trees – all dependent upon one another, all very unlikely to have a second chance of life either beyond the grave or through reincarnation, and therefore aware of the responsibilities incumbent upon custodians of the Earth. 'Let it be borne in mind,' Darwin writes in *The Origin*, 'how infinitely complex and close-fitting are the mutual relations of all organic beings to each other and to their physical conditions of life.'[6] This surely explains why, in our generation, Darwin has grown in importance and stature, whereas almost all his contemporary thinkers and sages are half-forgotten. Herbert Spencer is all but unread. With the demise of European communism, it seems to many – especially to the majority who have not read much Marx – as if *The Communist Manifesto* and *Das Kapital* are dead. Freud, in many schools of psychology, is discredited; Hegel is of more interest to historians of philosophy than as a living inspiration to many of our contemporary philosophers. Carlyle and Ruskin are unknown to general readers; Mill is read selectively by students, but is no household name. But neo-Darwinians – Richard Dawkins, Daniel C. Dennett and the rest – can still write bestsellers.

The literature on Darwin and his impact is almost limitless. The truth remains that the majority of Victorian scientists went on being Christian, or at least holding on to some form of religious belief.[7]

Natural selection, it need hardly be explained, means not selection by the conscious will of men or of gods, but by successful procreation. The 1858 Matrimonial Causes (or Divorce) Bill became law in England, but not in Ireland, enabling men and women to obtain divorces through a special court, at a cost of around £100. Prime Minister Palmerston, the old roué, told Parliament, 'we shall return here and sit day by day, and night by night, until this Bill be concluded'.[8] His chancellor of the Exchequer – Gladstone – was horrified by the measure, intervening in the debate seventy-three times, and devoting long speeches to the horror of bringing divorce to the doors of all classes. (Hitherto, divorce had only been possible in England by introducing a special Act of Parliament for each marital breakdown. By 1872, with the new law, some 200 decrees were granted annually.)

The existence of the new divorce law formalized the recognition that Victorian men and women committed adultery – thus, it defined them not merely as property-owning, but as sexual beings. Predictably the law remained biased against women; whereas husbands could sue for divorce on the simple ground of adultery, a wife could do so only if she could prove that her husband was guilty of bestiality, bigamy, incest, rape or cruelty in addition. Though Darwin very consciously and conspicuously omitted a discussion of human behaviour from *The Origin of Species*, its first readers brought to it, and extracted from it, a new sense of the human place in nature, and this sense in part was inevitably something which found its expression in the many novels and poems which touched on relations between the sexes.

The art-form, however, which was most blatantly concerned with adultery and sexual feeling was the music drama of Richard Wagner. The year which saw the publication of *The Origin of Species* in November had also been that in which Wagner completed *Tristan und Isolde*[9] – though the music drama was not performed until June 1865. Already in the midst of his great *Ring* dramas, Wagner paused to return to the medieval romance of Gottfried von Strassburg's *Tristan*. In so doing, he wrote an erotically charged manifesto; the hero's preparedness to betray his liege-lord King Mark is an act of magnificent anarchy.

Wagner's dreams of the uses to which human beings put their powers – now the slaves and now the masters of greed and passion – are, like Darwin's, with us still. *Tristan und Isolde* is perennially 'modern'. Its Second Act is a sustained musical evocation not merely of erotic feeling but of the sexual act itself. Had such a thing ever been attempted in European art – and has it ever been bettered? And yet it speaks not merely of the ecstatic joys of coition, but also of the impossibility of two human beings ever fully getting beyond sex to union of mind or soul. Its reason is the tragic and realistic one that Western humanity could no longer energetically believe in an afterlife. This great theme of *Tristan*, its *Liebestod*, therefore transcends sex just as Dante had done when he wrote the *Paradiso*. But whereas the great medieval poet could synthesize the personal and the erotic into a grand political and religious vision, culminating in Paradise, Wagner – a genius of comparable power – sees all human aspirations, their hope of political progress, of philosophical enlightenment, of religious comfort or of sexual ecstasy, interwoven with their consciousness of mortality. As he would expound in his extended mythical *Ring* dramas, the gods themselves cannot escape the extinction which awaits each one of the species being swept down the evolutionary river; whereas the dream of

Marx is one of ultimate triumph for the poor, and the fascination of Darwin's theory for Darwinian optimists was in the concept of progress through struggle, Wagner, with a realism which perhaps only comes to artists, saw the progress of his century – and ultimately of the human race – as one towards destruction.

In England, the *Liebestod* is transposed into a minor key when we turn to the home life of Queen Victoria, doomed for most of her reign to be a grief-stricken widow, her emotional life a blend of yearning and morbidity, which if not Wagnerian in tone at least matched Wagner's dramas in intensity. So aware are we of her last forty years as a half-life, an epilogue to the *Morte d'Albert*, that we must sometimes suppose there was an inevitability about the Prince's death, aged forty-two, or that he had already begun to decline into melancholy and inactivity before he was struck down by typhoid fever. This fiction began with Lytton Strachey's life of *Queen Victoria* which asserted that Prince Albert 'believed that he was a failure and he began to despair'. But he wasn't a failure, he had not begun to despair, and despite a premature baldness and paunchiness (he wore a wig indoors during his latter days because the Queen kept their rooms so cold)[10] and despite his very bad teeth, there was no reason to think that, had he escaped the typhoid fever, he would not have continued to lift himself from gloom and lead a full, happy life. In the very closing months of his life he thanked God 'that he has vouchsafed so much happiness to us', and this was heartfelt, even if life with his temperamental wife had its tribulations, and life among the unserious and ungrateful English its trials. (When the Queen was finally allowed to dub him Prince Consort in 1857 *The Times* cattily imagined that this would lead to increased respect for Albert, 'on the banks of the Spree and the Danube'.)[11] In fact, this is one of those feeble jokes which rebound on the teller, for hindsight makes us see what a valuable European dimension Albert brought to the political scene in England, and forces upon us the wistful game of wondering what might have been, had, for example, Albert (whose international, and in particular whose pan-German, stature grew by the year) lived into the era of Bismarck and beyond . . . No man single-handedly could have prevented the disastrous growth of rival nationalisms which came to catastrophe in 1914, but one can say that, had Albert's policies, rather than those of Lord Palmerston and those of subsequent prime ministers, been pursued, world war would have been less likely.

In the marriage of his firstborn – Vicky – to Prince Frederick William (Fritz) of Prussia, there occurred the first of those dynastic alliances by which Albert, had he been spared, might have exercised an influence on a European scale. The marriage took place in the Chapel Royal at St James's Palace on 25 January 1858. The bride was just seventeen, the bridegroom twenty-six.[12] Disraeli, attending the bridal ball at Buckingham Palace, thought there were as many European princes as at the Congress of Vienna – here were the King of the Belgians, the Duke of Brabant, the Count of Flanders, the Prince and Princess Frederick William of Prussia, the Prince and Princess of Prussia, Prince Albert of Prussia, Prince Frederick Charles of Prussia, Prince Frederick Albert of Prussia, Prince Adalbert of Prussia, the Prince of Hohenzollern Sigmaringen, the Duke of Saxe-Coburg-Gotha, the Duchess of Orleans, the Comte de Paris, the Duc de Chartres, the Princess of Salerno, the Duke and Duchess d'Aumale, Prince Edward of Saxe-Weimar, the Prince of Leiningen, Prince Victor of Hohenlohe Langenburg and Prince Julius of Holstein Glücksburg.[13]

This was Britain 'at the heart of Europe' at a period of crucial European change. Prince Albert wanted this dynastic marriage because he saw that the future of Europe was to be shaped by the future of Germany. From his earliest years, under the tutelage of Baron Stockmar, and later as a student of Bonn University, Albert had come to want the unification of Germany.[14] Ever since his arrival in England, partly through his friendship with the German ambassador the Baron Bunsen, Albert had formed the view that a strong Anglo-German alliance could influence the direction this unification took. For as long as the German duchies and states were divided, the forces of reaction – in the states themselves, in Russia and in Austria – could go unchecked, save by the dangerous forces of revolution. Albert's view was that a Germany united by Prussia – but a Prussia which had adopted constitutional government – could be the safest bulwark Europe could have against tyranny on the one hand, anarchy on the other. Many within his own family disagreed with his view – old uncle Leopold, king of the Belgians, was afraid of a 'Prussian super-nation' if German unity took place.[15] Albert, persuaded partly by Stockmar, partly by his own observation, thought that the little duchies, such as Coburg, were going to be swept aside anyway. The only question was not *whether* there would be a united Germany, but what kind of nation it would be – a Peelite (as it were) well-balanced Germany, with parliaments and representative government, living at peace with itself and its neighbours and allowing learned men like

Baron Bunsen to continue educating the world (Germany's destiny), or a more tragic, belligerent Germany, economically and politically unstable, falling back on militarism as a poor substitute 'quick fix' to achieve national unity.[16]

It is possible to disagree with the drift of Albert's hopes for Europe; it is not possible to be blind to the fact, however, that he was a very well-informed, intelligent and moderate-minded German who knew whereof he spoke. Palmerston, who liked crossing swords with the Prince over European policy, was an old man, a very old man, who never saw that the rise of modern Germany was going to change Europe forever. One sees this in his well-known joke about the Schleswig-Holstein question. Palmerston made the remark when prime minister in 1863 – namely that there were only three people who had ever understood the Schleswig-Holstein question. One was a German professor, and he had gone mad. One was the Prince Consort, and he was dead. The third was himself, and he had forgotten all about it.[17] This 'forget-fulness' was a handy cloak for diplomatic ineptitude and political-cum-military impotence.

But if the intricacies of the question were of proverbial complexity, its broad historical implications – in terms of what it meant for the political balance of Europe – were very simple. Throughout the late 1840s and particularly after the revolutions of 1848, Albert was urging Pilgerstein to accept the claims of the overwhelmingly German duchy of Holstein to belong to the German Federation. The position of the predominantly Danish Schleswig was rather different.[18] Palmerston's diplomacy held the pass in 1852, when the London Protocol put both duchies under Danish suzerainty. But ten years later the problems had not gone away. The German-speakers of Holstein wanted to be part of Germany. Bismarck could win popularity at home by invading the duchies – in 1864. 'God forgive you for it,' the Queen wrote to Vicky, by then Crown Princess of Prussia. Then – seeing that events would be no different whether God forgave them or not – Victoria urged, 'only make peace – give the Duchies to good Fritz H[olstein] and have done with it'.[19] By the time she wrote this letter Albert was dead, and the Schleswig-Holstein question had become a family row – the Prince of Wales (Bertie) being married to Princess Alexandra of Denmark, and the Princess Royal to the Crown Prince of Prussia. Pilgerstein was prime minister, and he was in the humiliating position of realizing, after the Crimean War, that Britain was militarily powerless against Prussia.

After the war over the Danish duchies it was left to the Austrians and Prussians to pick over the pieces. Britain had lost any real European influence. For the next thirty years the British could conceal this fact from themselves by greater and greater imperial expansion and concerns with Empire. This is the true legacy, not merely of the Crimean War, but of the aristocratic principle, which enabled an old man of Palmerston's very limited qualities to remain in positions of power for the best part of half a century.

Would any of it have been different had Prince Albert lived? It is hard to believe his influence would have been absolutely negligible. The Queen's grief-stricken language about him after he died is so hyperbolic that we are apt to dismiss Albert as a figure of some absurdity, overlooking how enormously he was respected by scientists, diplomats, academics, politicians – and by his own children. The traditional patterns of a 'Victorian' family were largely reversed at Osborne and Windsor. It was very much the Queen who was the stern one. Prince Albert once confided in Lord Clarendon that the disagreeable task of punishing the children had always fallen on him, and he regretted not resisting the harshness of the Queen towards her children for fear of exciting her if she were thwarted.[20] Lady Lyttelton became superintendent of the Royal Nursery. She was amazed by how severely the children were punished. At four, Princess Alice received 'a real punishment by whipping' for telling a lie. The young children were often admonished with their hands tied together, and the Prince of Wales and his brother received even harsher treatment.[21] The children did not however seem to respond to Albert either with fear or resentment. At a Royal Academy banquet some years after Albert's death the Prince of Wales tried to speak of his father and broke down sobbing. After her marriage to Fritz, Vicky wrote – on board HMY *Victoria and Albert* on the Scheldt – 'The pain of parting from you yesterday was greater than I can describe; I thought my heart was going to break when you shut the cabin door and were gone – that cruel moment which I had been dreading even to think of for 2 years and a half was past – it was more painful than I had ever pictured it to myself' – and so on for pages. 'All your love, etc. I shall most earnestly endeavour to deserve. To you, dear Papa, I owe most in this world.'

The Princess Royal had comparably intense feelings about her mother. Their frequent correspondence she was to describe as 'so natural and like thinking aloud'. Certainly these remarkable letters, spanning forty years, give an insight into the Queen's character and psyche which is like no other. The candour of Queen

Victoria's dislike of her eldest son, the Prince of Wales, is shocking. 'Poor Bertie! He vexes us much. There is not a particle of reflection, or even attention to anything but dress! Not the slightest desire to learn, on the contrary, il se bouche les oreilles, the moment anything of interest is being talked of! I only hope he will meet with some severe lesson to shame him out of his ignorance and dullness' (17 November 1858).[22] Bertie 'is not at all in good looks; his nose and mouth are too enormous and as he pastes his hair down to his head, and wears his clothes frightfully – he really is anything but good looking. That coiffure is really too hideous with his small head and enormous features' (7 April 1860).[23]

Her imperiousness and her attention to detail were, on occasion, provoking. Poor Vicky was given advice by her mother about every conceivable area of life – the temperature to keep her rooms, the desirability of installing water closets not only in her palaces but 'throughout Germany',[24] as well as every aspect of political life. Sometimes the stream of opinions – the Queen's dislike of the Anglican Communion Service, her love of the novels of George Eliot, her distaste for babies – might have been entertaining.

The Queen's temperament, ever volatile, became actually unhinged on the death of her own mother, the Duchess of Kent, on 16 March 1861. Like many egomaniacs – and was not the whole success of Dr Freud to be based on the universality of the condition? – Queen Victoria had sustained her leap from adolescence to young womanhood by the inner belief that her parent was her enemy. When she became Queen, her rejection of her mother had been total, though with the passing years there had been some rapprochement, not least because her twenty-year marriage to Albert had strengthened her sense of belonging to Coburg. After her mother died, however, the Queen went through the Duchess's belongings and found the incontrovertible evidence that her mother had always loved her, saving and treasuring every scrap of childhood memorabilia. For a month, Victoria became a morbid solitary, refusing to see her own children, eating her meals alone, and leaving Albert 'well nigh undone' with managing the Queen's business as well as his own.

There is no doubt that Albert was weakened by living with the full blast of his wife's hysteria. As the summer of 1861 wore on he drove himself to work harder and harder, partly, one suspects, because her behaviour had become insufferable. He took her to Ireland to inspect the troops – the Prince of Wales was serving ten weeks in the army there. She complained constantly – of feeling 'very weak and nervous'. The chief reason for his, and the court's, insistence that she went was to *show* her in public, since rumours were now flying all over Europe that she had been incarcerated in a padded cell. They saw Bertie – not deemed real officer material by his seniors in the Grenadiers. His coevals had played him the trick – no doubt very welcome to that young sensualist – of insinuating Nellie Clifden, a young 'actress', into his bed.

By the autumn, rumours of this silly escapade had reached the London clubs and the royal family was looking more than usually absurd. On 24 November, in drenching rain – *entsetzlicher Regen* – and with a heavy head cold, Albert inspected the troops at Sandhurst. The next day he went to Cambridge, where Bertie was supposedly a student, to upbraid him, and there followed a painful reconciliation between father and son. The general feeling of overwork and of being 'run down' had turned into something more serious. For some time Albert had been depressed, and suffered from stomach pains, toothache and exhaustion.

Something had died in him. *Ich hange gar nicht am Leben; du hängst sehr daran* . . . he had said to the Queen when he was at a low ebb – 'I do not cling to life; you do; but I set no store by it. I am sure that if I had a severe illness I should give up at once; I should not struggle for life. I have no tenacity for life.'[25]

By the beginning of December 1861, it was clear that the Prince Consort was gravely ill: the likeliest explanation for this is that he had succumbed to typhoid fever. When Princess Alice told him on 7 December that she'd written to Vicky to say he was ill he replied, 'You did wrong. You should have told her I am dying.'[26]

The doctors, as so often, were worse than useless, but perhaps it was a hopeless case. On 14 December, the Queen knelt by his bed and said *Es ist kleines Fräuchen* (It is your little wife). He signalled his consent when she offered him *ein Kuss*, but he was slipping away into the only condition which guaranteed a respite from her moods, tantrums and noise.

As the Princess Royal knew from her mother's letters on the subject, Queen Victoria was insistent on the installation of 'very necessary conveniences' near the bedrooms in royal residences.[27] Such was her need to avail herself of this modern provision that it was left to the ladies in waiting, the equerries and the Prince Consort's children to witness his actual demise.

By the time she returned, she exclaimed, 'Oh, this is death, I know it. I have seen this before' . . . 'I took his dear left hand which was already cold and knelt down by him. All, *all* was over.'

A charmingly natural picture of Queen Victoria and her children.

When she withdrew to the Red Room the equerries and her children, all 'deeply affected but quiet', gathered round her. She clutched the hand of Prince Arthur's governor, Sir Howard Elphinstone, and pleaded, 'You will not desert me? You will all help me.'[28]

In an instant, everything had changed, not merely in the Queen's life, and in that of the court and the royal family, but in England and Europe generally. Put bluntly, there was no longer an intelligent member of the royal family. British constitutional monarchy had been a very limited power, but now there was no serious check on the oligarchy of politicians who could flatter, cajole or sidestep the royal ego entirely. Whereas, in Albert's day, an intelligent influence was brought to bear, as it were, downwards from the throne, on social questions in particular but to a smaller degree on foreign policy, the relationship between politicians and the Crown now became merely a camp joke. Over the next half-century, the progeny of Victoria and Albert would marry and be given in marriage to all the important royal houses of Europe except the Austrian. Within seventy years of Albert's death nearly all these dynasties would be swept away – in Russia, Prussia, Austria, Spain and the Balkans. The fact that the monarchy survived in England was not a token of its strength but of its triviality. Had Albert lived, Britain, too, might have paid its monarchy the compliment of wishing to check, or even to abolish, its influence. As it was, the Widow of Windsor, living as a virtual recluse for years and performing almost no constitutional function, helped to lead the monarchy into a position where it was not worth abolishing. The claim that Britain was a monarchy in any but the most titular sense was now a fantasy.

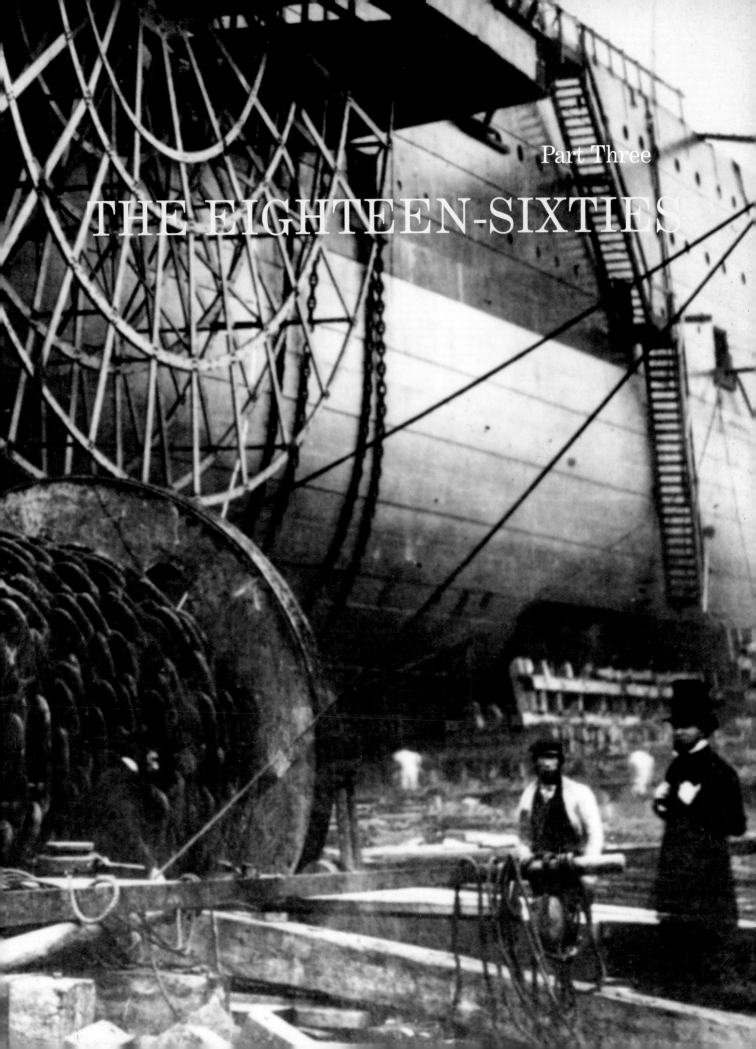

Part Three

THE EIGHTEEN-SIXTIES

Chapter Fourteen

The Beloved – Uncle Tom – and Governor Eyre

The little boy holding up a small golden bucket of roses in Rossetti's canvas *The Beloved* wears a doleful expression, not altogether suitable for this supposed celebration of connubial bliss. The melancholy of the child, whose name is not remembered, is understandable when we know that he was suffering from a cold. Rossetti had spotted him on the steps of a London hotel and realized that he would make an exotic adjunct to this work, which had been commissioned as a Christmas present for the wife of a wealthy Birkenhead banker called Rae. The child, a black boy, was a slave, travelling with his American master. Finding himself whisked off to Rossetti's studio in Chelsea, the boy had wept copiously, an object of fascination to the painter, who noticed that the moisture on his cheeks made his dark skin even darker. While Dante Gabriel Rossetti patiently sketched and painted, the destiny of the boy's fellow African-Americans was being forged in the bloodiest war of the century. While the child wept, and Rossetti begged him to keep still, Sherman's army was advancing through Georgia to Atlanta, burning and pillaging, while in an opposite direction on ox-drawn carts and makeshift wagons black refugees fled from slavery, some to a new life which was an improvement on the old, many or most to poverty and ill-treatment every bit as horrible as their lives under the old dispensation.

Few, if any, who looked at *The Beloved* today in a gallery would be able to find a glimmering of political significance in the child's presence. He has, surely, been added for purely aesthetic reasons to this crowded and not entirely successful composition for which Mr Rae paid £300 – about a third as much money as he would have had to pay for the boy himself.

It is this, the concept of actual ownership by one person of another, which makes slavery not merely an abhorrent concept but to almost all modern sensibilities an unimaginable one.

Yet even from the remote perspective of Dante Gabriel Rossetti's studio, the question of American slavery was not one which could be seen in morally simple terms. The Englishman, particularly the English liberal, might deplore the notion of purchasing 'blood, bones, sinew, flesh and brains', but what else was the nineteenth-century factory-owner doing to his workforce? What – come to that – was the status of English women, of whatever class, in relation to their father or husband? (Not until 1882 did the Married Women's Property Act grant to married women the full right of separate ownership of property.)

Then again, there was the intimate economic connection between the English capacity to mass-produce cotton goods, and hence increase their national wealth

Isambard Kingdom Brunel (on the left) with Scottish naval architect and civil engineer John Scott Russell (wearing top hat) standing next to the Great Eastern, *1857. The* Great Eastern *was the largest ship of its time and her maiden voyage to New York on 17 June 1860 heralded the beginning of a new technological age.*

immeasurably, and the American capacity to grow and harvest cotton in ever greater, ever cheaper quantities. If James Hargreaves, the poor weaver of Blackburn, had never pioneered the spinning-jenny in 1764, and if Richard Arkwright had never invented the water-frame spinning machine a little later, or Cartwright invented the power-loom, the quiet home-weavers of Lancashire, rustic characters who belonged in the pages of Wordsworth, might still have been pursuing their calm, untroubled lives deep into the third decade of Queen Victoria's reign. But they weren't.[1] The population-explosion had occurred; the Malthusian struggle was conjoined; the masses had thronged into the mills and factories of Northern England – Lancashire by now contained 12 per cent of the population. Between 1821 and 1831 17,000 persons per annum had flocked to Lancashire. By 1860 there were some 2,650 cotton factories, worked by a population of 440,000, their wages amounting to £11,500,000 per annum. In order to employ this population at this rate it was necessary to import 1,051,623,380 lb of cotton: nearly all of this raw material came from America.[2]

If the population-explosion in England fed upon and needed the industrial genius set in motion by Arkwright, Cartwright, Hargreaves and others, cotton itself could not have supplied their need had it not been for comparable advance in American agriculture. In 1793 Eli Whitney had invented the cotton gin, which enabled the cotton seed to be easily separated from the lint. The declining agrarian economy of the South was immediately revitalized. Cotton was an easy crop to grow in the rich virgin lands of the Mississippi basin, and a cheap labour force was to hand – in the slaves. Article 1, Section 9 of the American Constitution had envisaged the ending of the *trade* in slaves, though not the institution of slavery, by 1808. To meet the demands of nineteenth-century trade, slavery in America actually increased, from 1 million slaves in 1800 to approximately 4½ million in 1860.

Those who profited from the overproduction of Southern cotton were not just planters. They were the Northern middlemen, the New York merchants who bled the Southerners dry by selling them manufactured goods at ever-increasing prices; and they were the English merchant class, liberals almost to a man, loud in their advocacy of the abolitionist cause, but only after they had made millions out of a system which had depended, for its initial profitability, on American slave labour to harvest, English child labour to manufacture, cheap cotton goods for the export market.

These uncomfortable truths were not lost on observant Englishmen and women in the 1860s, which is precisely why we find many English people turning a blind eye to America at this time, or almost wilfully missing the point of what was going on there; and also perhaps why we find some of the keenest abolitionists in the ranks of those who had defended capitalist industrialism.

We should expect that most paradoxical of political figures, Gladstone, to typify the many-stranded complexity of this matter. Prince of humbug, yet deeply the man of principle; guilt-ridden profiteer from his father's Demerara slave-plantations, yet defender of the old man's good intentions; stern, in youth an unbending Tory, yet in old age visionary radical; populist with an eye to the main chance, yet prepared throughout his long political life – from resignation over the Maynooth Grant to his destruction of the Liberal Party over Irish Home Rule – to stand on firmly rooted moral conviction; visionary prophet, but crashing bore: at the time of the outbreak of the American Civil War, Gladstone was, aged fifty-two, the chancellor of the Exchequer in Lord Palmerston's 'Liberal' government. Lord John Russell was foreign secretary. England was still being governed by the 'two dreadful old men' who had been around at the time of the 1832 Reform Bill, the Irish Famine and the Indian Mutiny. Victorian England was a gerontocracy, which made the life of the politically ambitious keenly frustrating. While his opposite number in the Commons, Disraeli, made a comparably agonizing ascent of 'the greasy pole', patiently awaiting the retirement or demise of Lord Derby, the Conservative leader, Gladstone was the Liberal leader in waiting, ever anxious to establish himself as the only possible successor to Palmerston.

At this date, the North-Eastern region of England was as prosperous – from exports to Europe, from shipbuilding, from coal – as the North-Western cotton-producing towns of Lancashire were distressed. As Liberal chancellor of the Exchequer Gladstone was widely credited with this prosperity, and he was invited to address a dinner at the town hall in Newcastle on 7 October 1862. He was given 'the reception of a king', in the words of his biographer and admirer Morley. A great procession of steamers followed him to the mouth of the Tyne, and workers from the forges, furnaces, coal staiths, chemical works, glass factories and shipyards lined the river bank to cheer: 'and all this not because he

Cotton pickers on a plantation in Georgia, c. 1870.

had tripled the exports to France, but because a sure instinct had revealed an accent in his eloquence that spoke of feeling for the common people'.[3] This is not, of course, a reference to the Liverpudlian timbre which is (just) detectable in the recorded voice of Etonian and Oxford-educated Gladstone but to his streak of populism, his feeling, amounting to genius, for public mood. At the grand dinner, no doubt carried away by the warmth of his reception in Newcastle, Gladstone moved into one of those oratorical flights for which he was long remembered. On this occasion, his words occasioned a diplomatic incident between Britain – in the person of the foreign secretary – and the American minister in London, Charles Francis Adams. Was it a gaffe as is generally supposed? Or did Gladstone, who was a most unusual combination of passionate impulsiveness and deviousness, *intend* his words to cause the discomfiture which they unquestionably did?

'We know quite well,' he said, 'that the people of the Northern States have not yet drunk of the cup – they are still trying to hold it far from their lips – which all the rest of the world see nevertheless they must drink of. We may have our own opinions about slavery; we may be for or against the South; but there is no doubt that Jefferson Davis and other leaders of the South have made an army; they are making, it appears, a navy; and they have made what is more than either, they have made a nation.' The words were greeted with loud cheers.

Adams – of the great dynasty – did not have an easy task. From the beginning of the Civil War, over the question of British neutrality, he had been forced to emphasize that Britain could not recognize the Confederacy without putting itself on terms of hostility with the Union. Russell smoothed things down, and forced Gladstone to withdraw his implication that the British government believed in the inevitability of a Confederate victory. Much later in life, Gladstone expressed dismay at his words. He had never, he said, desired a division of the American Union and indeed feared that such a thing would put a 'dangerous pressure on Canada'. The 'tokens of goodwill' which, over the last twenty-five years of his career, he received from the American people made him all the more anxious to dissociate himself from his earlier position. This was because it suited Gladstone the octogenarian democrat to believe that he had always been a fervent believer in government of the people, for the people and by the people. The new orthodoxy of a shared political vision, linking Britain and America, enabled early twentieth-century historians to see the 1860s as the great turning point for both countries, the era when both put the old world, and with it old hostilities, behind them. 'The Reform Bill of 1867 brought a new British nation into existence, the nation decrying American institutions was dead, and a "sister democracy" holding out hands to the United States had replaced it' was one genial American view, published six years after Woodrow Wilson had imposed his disastrous conclusions on the Versailles Peace Agreement.[4] This is still very much the way some people, on both sides of the Atlantic, see the 1860s.

At the time, things looked very different. Many would have shared Disraeli's view that the 'immense revolution' taking place in the United States would 'tell immensely in favour of aristocracy'.[5]

The neutrality of the British government was certainly not based on any form of natural common feeling with Lincoln or the Federal government. Adams noted that when it became clear that the North would fight on to victory the attitude of Palmerston and Russell became favourable to the Union, but this was 'no special sympathy, but merely a cool calculation of benefits to Great Britain in maintaining that policy of friendship determined upon in the fifties'.[6] (In the early stage of the war, they had taken no chances, though, and dispatched 11,000 troops to Canada to protect the border.)[7] Lincoln's secretary of state, Seward, the man who had himself hoped for the Republican nomination for the presidency, described Britain, perhaps understandably, as 'the greatest, most grasping, and most rapacious power in the world'.

That power depended on trade, on manufacturing, on exports; and a crucial part of that trade was concentrated upon the cotton-mills and factories of Lancashire. Jefferson Davis's decision to impose a cotton embargo, rather than attempting to defy Federal blockades of the ports, was a major political blunder. In the first year of the war it was ineffectual. Canny British merchants had seen the danger of raw materials running out and had bulk-bought cotton in a year when its price was in any event low. By the following year, however, in May 1862, the situation in formerly prosperous Lancashire was desperate. In a cotton town such as Blackburn 'of 84 mills, 23 were silent and smokeless';[8] 9,414 persons had applied for poor relief; the pawnshops were crammed with furniture and clothing; starvation beckoned.

The British press, on the whole, took the view that the commercial and human calamity which had now befallen Lancashire mattered far more than the issue of slavery. *The Times* reminded its readers that abolitionists had been persecuted in the North, as well as in the South, before the war; and that even at the outset of the conflict,

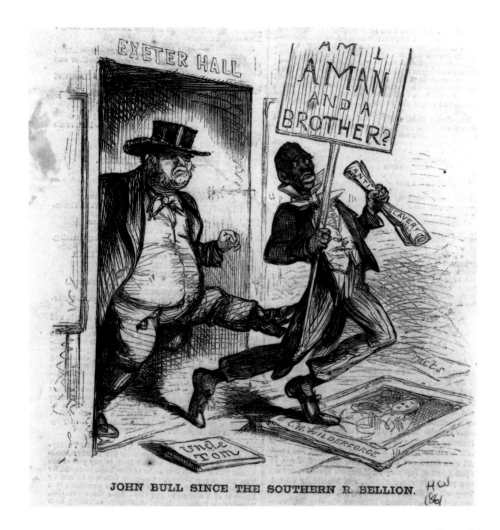

JOHN BULL SINCE THE SOUTHERN R. BELLION.

The widespread support for the Confederates in the American Civil War suggests to the cartoonist that John Bull has forgotten his hostility to slavery.

Lincoln and his allies had not come out unambiguously against slavery. The more populist *Reynolds' News* urged, if necessary, force to break the blockades.[9] 'England must break the Blockade or her millions will starve.' 'Better to fight the Yankees than starve our operatives.'[10] The American consul in Manchester reported that public opinion among the working classes was 'almost unanimously adverse to the Northern cause'.

Urged on by the English abolitionists and the economic radicals, Lincoln himself wrote to the people of Lancashire recognizing their plight, and trying to imply that the English working classes would prefer to starve rather than tolerate the existence of slavery on the other side of the Atlantic. The truth is that in years of prosperity the working classes, as well as the factory-owners themselves, had been content to make profits out of cheap imported cotton which, without slaves to harvest it, would have been twice the price. Equally true was that most workers would have preferred an early end to the war in exchange for regular paid work in the mills and factories. The factory operatives of Lancashire did not have any influence, one

way or another, either on the conduct of the war in America, or on the decisions by Palmerston and Russell about their policy of neutrality.

But while this is undoubtedly the case, and while from month to month of the crisis the import of the American Civil War, its monumental significance as a turning point in the tide of world history, was very largely lost on English politicians and the English public, on another level the issue of slavery was perfectly clear.* Gladstone's biographer, Lord Morley, explains the superficial

*Compare Carlyle's squib 'Ilias (Americana in Nuce) [America in a Nutshell]'.
PETER *of the North* (to PAUL *of the South*) 'Paul, you unaccountable scoundrel, I find you hire your servants for life, not by the month or year as I do! You are going to Hell you _____!'
PAUL 'Good words, Peter! The risk is my own ... Hire you your servants by the month or the day, and get straight to Heaven; leave me to my own method.'
PETER 'No, I won't. I will beat your brains out first!' (*And is trying dreadfully ever since but cannot yet manage it.*)
Macmillan's Magazine, August 1863, p.301

English myopia over the matter by saying, 'we applied ordinary political maxims to what was not merely a political contest, but a social revolution. Without scrutiny of the cardinal realities beneath, we discussed it like some superficial conflict in our old world about boundaries, successions, territorial partitions, dynastic preponderance. The significance of the American war was its relation to slavery.'[11]

Another way of putting it if one were not, as Morley was, a paid-up Liberal, was that the English at this date took an ambivalent view of the disturbance of 'the aristocratic settlement', to use Disraeli's phrase.[12] The English preserved in large measure their 'aristocratic settlement' while advancing towards modern democracy. They were not confronted, as the Americans were, with a stark choice, because they did not have slaves, or indeed large numbers of black people, living in their towns and villages. Rossetti's little black model was an exotic who stood out in a London street, which is how the artist came to spot him.

Black people were people, on the whole, who were abroad. Many Victorians would have shared the kindly minded and in all respects Liberal Thackeray's view – 'Sambo is not my man & my brother; the very aspect of his face is grotesque and inferior'. Many, too, if they had visited Virginia as Thackeray did in 1852–3, would have concluded, 'they are not suffering as you are impassioning yourself for their wrongs as you read Mrs Stowe: they are grinning & joking in the sun'. He wondered how they would survive after abolition, believing that the need to compete with whites in the labour market would lead to 'the most awful curse and ruin . . . which fate ever yet sent' the black man.

By the cruellest of ironies, these views, which seem so unenlightened to us, were borne out by events in America. The Northern victory which landed Jefferson Davis in jail and in irons led to the destruction of those rich estates and plantations where benign slave-ownership was at least possible. The existence of the Ku Klux Klan would have been unimaginable in the old South. It sprang up, like National Socialism in Germany, in reaction against the sheer lack of magnanimity of the supposedly liberal victor: and as a result of economic hardship. The plight of the poor, white and black, in the Southern states over the next hundred years was unimaginably horrible.

There were indeed changes in the 1860s. The 'social revolution' seen by Morley in America drove the labour force in the same direction in which the British and European labour force had been driven in the earlier decades of industrialization, but with fewer protections and much less willingness on the part of the big capitalists or the governing class to appease its proletariat. The 'aristocratic settlement', though as Ashley had seen, totally opposed to the selfish cut and thrust of capitalism, nevertheless provided checks, in England, to an unbridled market economy. If it is true that Christianity and communism provided the only real opposition in dialectical terms to the Market, the existence of an aristocracy provided a background against which pure Darwinian competition was tempered by a notion of *noblesse* or *nouvelle richesse oblige*. Not only did many aristocrats remain in positions of real power and influence in the nineteenth century but, with their new-found wealth, many of the new rich chose to live their own versions of an aristocratic life. Of course this involved a system of hierarchy which to modern eyes appears arcane; also, we moderns might bridle at the concept of patronage. But it is no accident that when the British chose formally to dismantle their aristocratic system after the Second World War, they modelled the state, with its system of welfare and patronage, less on the Soviet monolith than on the old-fashioned Christian aristocrat who looked after the poor on his estate from cradle to grave, built them schools and cottages, and provided them with specially created work projects when economic crisis dried up the demand for work in mills, factories or mines. Attlee and Sir Stafford Cripps were more the heirs of the 7th Earl of Shaftesbury than they were of Karl Marx.

A major crisis in capitalism occurred during the Cotton Famine when many Northern landlords, Gladstone included, devised schemes of work. At a rally in Manchester on 2 December 1862 Derby praised the 'noble manner, a manner beyond all praise in which this destitution has been borne by the population of this great country'. He gave £5,000 at one time to the relief fund, the largest single subscription, it was said, made by a single Englishman to a public fund for a single purpose or a single time.[13] It inspired others to give – altogether Derby was to raise £130,000, and donate £12,000.[14] The numbers of those seeking relief rose from half a million in January 1813 to 1,260,000 in 1865. There was, no doubt, practical self-preservation instinct at work here. Derby feared the mob. As the greatest landowner in Lancashire he was always careful to keep quiet about his personal sympathies for the Confederacy, knowing that some of the working classes had sympathies with the 'democratic' Northern states.

Thus – to return for a moment to the little black boy in

Rossetti's *The Beloved* – we can legitimately find, in the work of this least political of painters, echoes of the socio-political world in which the artist took so little interest. There is, for a start, the object itself, the gilded, framed icon: an erotic or semi-pagan altarpiece intended not for a church but for the house of a financier, a banker, Mr Rae of Merseyside. The picture supposedly illustrates a biblical text – 'My beloved is mine and I am his: let him kiss me with the kisses of his mouth': but it is designed as a Christmas present for a Victorian capitalist's wife: it is not merely an exploration through symbol of erotic and spiritual desire, it is also a social status symbol and an expensive object of domestic furniture. Rossetti's very detachment from the contemporary political debate lends the little black boy, by paradox, a greater eloquence for us than he would have if he had been made to carry a burden of symbolism – such as Wedgwood's famous ceramic medallion 'man and a brother' in chains. Rossetti's sister Christina and his brother William as well as Burne-Jones, Holman Hunt, Browning – to name a few in his circle – were keen abolitionists. Whistler on the other hand had a brother in the Confederate army, and Ruskin would have followed Carlyle's line – of which more later. Rossetti chose to remain aloof, laughing when his friends quarrelled about the issue.[15]

What the distance of a century and a half suggests is that the British could afford to shed tears over *Uncle Tom's Cabin* as a nursery-book, but perhaps not to inquire too deeply into their own highly ambivalent attitude to the peoples and races of the world whom, by commerce or empire, they had subdued without the means of overt slavery. We have observed how British self-congratulation at having escaped an 1848 revolution needs to be tempered by a recognition of the many areas of conflict in different parts of the globe. Moreover, post 1857–8 in India, we noted that a change had come over the British attitude. Those who saw the Indians, with their ancient dynasties and principalities, their culture, languages and religions, as independent beings, to be won over in commercial arrangements by the East India Company, were now heavily outnumbered by those who believed that the Indians were savages who must be subdued – either on Benthamite principles of social economy or for reasons of Christian evangelicalism or through an amalgam of the two. The culture of British imperialism had evolved, and with it, the need for the British to persuade themselves that the white man was superior to the black man.

*

Will the eager glance of the young woman in Arthur Hughes's painting be justified by 'The Long Engagement' to the sexless-looking clergyman?

By the standards of a later generation, European childhood, up to the 1860s, was like human life itself, nasty, brutish and short. Not only was infant mortality high. Childhood itself, if we define childhood in modern terms as a time of play, of learning, of innocent idleness and amusement, was virtually non-existent for the majority. Millions of children in the nineteenth century had the experience of working in a grown-up world when aged

A middle class family tea party, c. 1865. Everyone who could do so in the 1860s was settling down into domestic life. The Marxes abandoned their cramped flat in Soho and moved to a variety of new-built family-houses in Kentish Town. At the same point in time, Philip Webb was designing the Red House, Abbey Wood, for William Morris, that young idealist-aesthete, destined to become a revolutionary socialist, but not before he had founded his firm, Morris and Co., on the back of the domestic bourgeoisie, hungry for his wallpapers, carpets, curtains and cushion-covers.

ten. Thousands of middle-class boys like Mill would have been expected to conform in manner and even in dress to the *mores* of middle-aged parents.

Childhood as Americans or Europeans of the twenty-first century understand the term is really quite a new phenomenon in human history and began – roughly speaking – in the 1860s. It was the privilege of the ever-expanding middle classes and of the upper classes. The working classes continued to go to labour in factories from an early age – though they might receive some rudimentary study in the afternoons. As soon as may be, they left the parental roof and began themselves to breed.

By contrast, between the dates 1840 and 1870 the average age of gentlemen, aspirant gentlemen and aristocrats for getting married was twenty-nine.[16] Arthur Hughes's painting *The Long Engagement* depicts an emotional predicament stemming directly from an economic situation. The prosperity which had created the vast bourgeoisie with its gradations from lower to upper middle class had also created a code. You could not

marry, and maintain the position in society to which you aspired, until you had a certain amount of money in the bank. This was the age of savings, of investment incomes, of unearned income. Marx was wrong to consider the proletariat to be the equivalent of a slave class. Everyone who could do so aspired to rise from a condition of dependency. In 1861 there were 645 banks and the value of the ordinary deposits was £41,546,475.[17] Many of these deposits were extremely modest. The Savings Bank movement initiated in Ruthwell, Dumfries, by the Rev. Henry Duncan in 1810 had blossomed, via Penny Banks, Friendly Societies and such, to the larger Trustee Savings banks; these had been regulated by Act of Parliament in 1863, and in 1861 the Post Office Savings bank had protected the small saver after a number of swindles. The whole system of society began to revolve not simply on how much you earned but on how much you could squirrel away.[18]

This was the great era of 'carriage folk'. At the beginning of the century, elliptic springs had made this soon-to-be-obsolete mode of transport enjoy a magnificent flowering.[19] The berlin, barouche, calèche, coupé, clarence, daumont, landau and phaeton all crowded the streets of London in that supposedly prosaic railway age. In 1814, there were 23,000 four-wheeled vehicles in the capital; by 1834, 49,000; by 1864, 102,000, with a further 170,000 two-wheelers.[20] This represents a huge social class, as well as huge congestion in the streets; and it is this class, this immensely privileged class, probably more comfortable than any human class who had ever existed on the planet, whose offspring were the first with the leisure and time to have a childhood.

Capitalism was not just the relentless machine, crushing the wage-slaves at the bottom: it had also created a fantasy-world of rapid social change, leisure, fairy-tale. It is not accidental that the decade of the consolidation of the rentier class, the decade of carriage-folk, of the expansion of the suburbs, the growth of the savings banks, the era of the nouveau-riche business man and the stockbroker, should also have been the golden age of children's literature. In the Victorian day nursery a picture of the world could emerge, simply from reading the books on offer to a child of that time, which would not differ materially from turning the less interesting pages of Hansard or *The Times*.

There is an apocryphal story that when tiny Harriet Beecher Stowe, less than five feet in height, was presented to the tall lanky president at the White House in 1862, Abraham Lincoln said, 'So, you're the little woman who wrote the book that started this great war.' Even if this exchange did not take place, Lincoln certainly did entertain the author of *Uncle Tom's Cabin*. Moreover it is from this book, now classifiable as children's literature but not especially meant as such, that many people in the Western world formed their impressions of the United States, and of the convulsions which would engulf them during the momentous 1860s. More than a million copies of the book sold in England on its first publication there in 1852, ten times as many as had previously been sold of any work except the Bible.

Yet, as we have seen, the American Civil War and its aftermath by no means inspired the English to support or even much to sympathize with the Union. It is possible to generalize and say that many English people, particularly those who had admired *Uncle Tom's Cabin*, took a pride in the part their country had played in the abolition of slavery, but would defend the right of the Southern states to determine their own affairs. But this generalization might provide too sweet an interpretation of public mood. One wonders whether *Uncle Tom's*

Cane-cutters in Jamaica, c. 1880.

Cabin, so popular in the England of 1852, would have gone down so well in the England of, say, 1868. The Sixties were a decade, after all, in which the English were compelled to confront their own attitudes to the issues raised by the liberation of slaves. But the theatre in which the drama was played out was not Alabama or Mississippi but the colony of Jamaica.

In 1865, when the war between the Confederacy and the Northern states was concluded in the supposed liberation of African Americans, Jamaica had a population of something over 440,000. Thirteen thousand were white, the remainder were the descendants of the former slave population (320,000 Jamaican slaves had been liberated in 1807). The island was ruled by a governor, flanked by a council, and an elective assembly of forty-seven members. Two thousand Jamaicans, by virtue of being property-owners, were entitled to vote. As a 'settled' colony, Jamaica was under the law of England – a crucially important fact in the story, since technically exactly the same laws should have applied there as in Britain. There were very strong feelings of discontent among the blacks, especially those who, through the medium of the Baptist Church, had acquired a modicum of political education. They resented their political destiny being determined by an assembly overwhelmingly supported by the planters, the former slave-owners, and the triumphs of the anti-slavery armies, marching through Georgia, had fired them with dreams of liberty: government of, for and by the people.

Edward John Eyre became the governor of Jamaica, aged forty-nine, in 1864. Of English birth, the son and grandson of clergymen, his colonial career in Australia and New Zealand had been conspicuous for its fairness. He defended the aborigines against white Australians. It was his enlightened experience with aborigines and the Maoris which led to his appointment first as captain-general, then governor, of the Caribbean sugar-island.

Eyre tried to broker peace between the planters and the political malcontents, and in so doing excited the scorn of George William Gordon, the illegitimate son of a wealthy white planter and a slave woman. Gordon was elected to the assembly in 1863 and made the new governor's life as difficult as possible. Gordon predicted 'anarchy and bloodshed' if the franchise were not extended.

In October 1865 there was an uprising of black peasants in the planting district of Morant Bay. The courthouse was burned to the ground and at least twenty whites were killed. A riot spread. There was talk of the slaughter of Frenchmen when the natives of Haiti proclaimed a republic. The governor received reports that 'the most fearful atrocities were perpetrated . . . The Island curate of Bath, the Rev. V. Herschell, is said to have had his tongue cut out whilst still alive, and an attempt is said to have been made to skin him. One person (Mr Charles Price, a black gentleman, formerly a Member of the Assembly) was ripped open and his entrails taken out.'

Eyre had to act and the possibility of total anarchy, of the British being driven from the island altogether, made him act with great severity. First he declared a state of martial law in Morant Bay. Then he had Gordon arrested in Kingston, but rather than allowing him a civil trial there, Eyre had him moved to Morant Bay, where he was tried by court martial and summarily hanged. Over the next month, 608 people were killed or executed, 34 were wounded, 600, including some women, were flogged and about 1,000 leaf-hut dwellings were destroyed. Eyre was regarded by the whites on the island as their saviour. The Council was abolished and Jamaica became a Crown colony.

But on his return to England in 1866, Eyre found a country divided around the issue. At Southampton where he docked, a huge dinner was given in his honour. Some dubbed the dinner 'the Banquet of Death', and a mob collected in Southampton High Street. In London, there was more mob violence, denouncing 'the Monster, ex-Governor Eyre' – for the poor fellow, entirely dependent on his salary, had been deprived of his governorship. The Jamaica Committee was formed, with such worthies as Thomas Hughes, lately elected MP for Lambeth, and John Stuart Mill, believing that Eyre had no more right to declare martial law in Jamaica than he would in England. The fact that he deliberately moved Gordon from a civil legislature to a place where he could be condemned without a proper trial was seen by Eyre's critics as murder. When he had retreated to Market Drayton in Shropshire, Eyre was indeed forced to stand before local magistrates and face charges of murder. They were rejected by the justice and the bells of Market Drayton rang out in consequence.

The liberals then tried to assign on murder charges Colonel Alexander Abercromby Nelson – he it was who had confirmed the capital sentence which hanged Gordon – and Colonel Brand, who had presided at that court martial. Once more, magistrates rejected the lengthy legal arguments in favour of prosecution. For Mill and the Liberals, the question was, 'Who are to be our masters: the Queen's Judges and a jury of our countrymen, administering the laws of England, or three military or naval officers, two of them boys, administering as the Chancellor of the Exchequer tells us, no law at all?'

For Eyre's supporters – Tennyson, Ruskin and, most eloquent of them all, Carlyle – it was clear that the governor had been justified in restoring order, even if his justice had been rough:

> The English nation never loved anarchy, nor was wont to spend its sympathy on miserable mad seditions, especially of this inhuman and half-British type; but have always loved order and the prompt suppression of seditions, and reserved its tears for something worthier than promoters of such delirious and fatal enterprises who had got their wages from their sad industry. Has the English nation changed then altogether?

It was largely through the influence of Carlyle that Parliament voted the ex-governor a pension. But the answer to the question was, yes, England had changed, and the Eyre controversy was but a symptom of it. The mobs who called Eyre a murderer were concerned less with the fate of a few seditious Jamaicans than they were with what Eyre represented – the suppression of fair government. Old Palmerston had died days after the

The uprising of Jamaican planters in Morant Bay, 1865, was punished with the utmost severity by Governor Edward John Eyre.

Jamaican rebellion. The successive governments of Russell, who took over as prime minister, and Derby, who became Tory prime minister in 1866, had to face the question of how to extend the franchise without losing the aristocratic balance. (That they very largely did so was one of the triumphs of the Conservatives, and of Derby himself.)

Meanwhile, the attitude displayed at this time by the British towards blacks, and towards the subject peoples of the Empire in general, showed that there had been a perceptible change. The 'burden' of Empire coarsened public sympathy. The nation which at the beginning of the century had prided itself on the moral beauty of the anti-slavery cause had the greatest sympathy with a man who had flogged, tortured, burned and hanged the descendants of slaves whose rebellion Dr Johnson himself would have applauded. Was this because they wanted such rough justice applied in England? Or was it

that, in imperial times, they had come to believe that there was one law for the white man, and another for the black? Eyre himself, who had defended the Australian aborigine, had come to the view that Caribbean aspirations to freedom were illegitimate, based on 'the indolence, apathy, improvidence, profligacy and crime which characterize the mass of the people'.[21] This view of black people, so widespread among the white Europeans of the coming decades, was believed to justify, even to necessitate, the subjugation and conquest of Africa itself.

'We are too tender to our savages,' Tennyson protested to Gladstone when they quarrelled over Governor Eyre. 'We are more tender to blacks than to ourselves . . . niggers are tigers, niggers are tigers.'[22]

Is it entirely accidental that the European 'Scramble for Africa' began only after such views had become entrenched, in the decades which followed the supposed 'emancipation' of the friends and family of Uncle Tom?

Chapter Fifteen

The World of School

Arthur Penrhyn Stanley (1815–81) has sunk into obscurity in the minds of many twenty-first-century readers. Indeed, if he is remembered at all he is, for many people, best known as a character in fiction – the delicate young Arthur in *Tom Brown's Schooldays* who dares to risk the sneering laughter and hurled bedroom-slippers of the bullies by kneeling down in a dormitory and saying his prayers – 'a snivelling young shaver' – before getting into bed. 'It was no light act of courage, in those days, my dear boys, for a little fellow to say his prayers publicly, even at Rugby. A few years later, when Arnold's manly piety had begun to leaven the school, the tables turned; before he died, in the school-house at least, and I believe in the other houses, the rule was the other way.'[1]

In this, the most celebrated of many Victorian school stories (published in 1857), Arthur expounds the scriptures to Tom Brown and his madcap friend East. 'The first night they happened to fall on the chapters about the famine in Egypt, and Arthur began talking about Joseph as if he were a living statesman; just as he might have talked about Lord Grey and the Reform Bill; only that they were much more living realities to him.'[2] There were clearly only the smallest of differences between young Arthur the schoolboy and Arthur Penrhyn Stanley who, in 1864 became dean of Westminster, appointed by Queen Victoria herself. Like the Queen, and like his hero, Dr Thomas Arnold of Rugby, Stanley was Broad Church, a variety of Christian which has all but died out, which is a puzzle, since in many respects it seems the most obvious sort of Christian to be. He sat light to doctrines. Many of his contemporaries doubted whether he was worthy to be counted a Christian at all.

It was, presumably, the high reputation of Thomas Arnold (1795–1842), who became headmaster of Rugby in 1828, which persuaded Bishop Stanley to educate his delicate little son at the famously rough Midland boarding school.[3] 'Unfortunately,' Arthur wrote home to his sister in his first term there, 'the writing master here is called Stanley, and so I think I shall get the nickname of Bob Stanley's son.' It showed a charming optimism. When they saw the tiny lad, in his blue many-buttoned jacket and grey trousers adorned by a pink watch-ribbon, the boys devised a somewhat better nickname. They called him Nancy.

Arnold's achievement, perhaps, historically, was to see the public school as the ideal social expedient by which the liberal–conservative ideals of the early nineteenth-century reformers could be put into practice. Rather than the bourgeoisie, as on the continent, displacing the aristocracy as the governing class, they could themselves acquire some of the attitudes, and speech inflexions, of the upper class by having the education of 'gentlemen'. From a comparatively small pool of privately educated boys, the colonial governors, senior ecclesiastics, politicians, statesmen, lawyers and other professionals could be drawn. An easily

Social reformer the Reverend Thomas Guthrie at the blackboard of his Ragged School in a church hall in Princes Street, Edinburgh, 1857.

expandable governing class could quietly be created in which aristocrats did not lose their place, but in which there was room for those clever enough to push for, or rich enough to buy themselves, a position. Of course, this cynical Benthamite explanation of Arnold's campaign to make the boys of Rugby into 'Christian gentlemen' misses out the personal and religious sincerity of Arnold's ideals: but it is a fair description if not of Arnold's aims, then of the effects of his reforming zeal at Rugby. (The numbers of which we are speaking remain proportionately tiny – only 7,500 boys were at boarding school in England during the 1860s.)[4]

Tom Brown's Schooldays, unconsciously perhaps, mirrors the feelings of the Victorian middle classes towards the public schools. Although a sunny book, devoted to celebrating the manly joys of pure comradeship, games, Bible-reading and hero-worship of Dr Arnold, the bits we all remember are about bullies tossing the little boys in blankets and roasting them before the fire.

Those 'first-generation' families who sent their sons off to public school were not necessarily appreciative of what they found. Arnold had high academic standards. The cleverer boy, taught by his principles, would certainly have been very good at Greek; and the more receptive might have imbibed muscular Christianity. But after Arnold's premature death, aged forty-seven, the major public schools remained insanitary nests of bullying, sexual depravity and – as far as a general knowledge of the natural or social world was in question – ignorance. Gladstone was just such a middle-class product of a public-school education bought by parents who had learned to see these places as the training-grounds of a new aristocracy. Eton made him, and he remained obsessed by the place to his dying day. But the Liberal in him was forced to recognize that public schools, like everything else in the world, would benefit from Reform. For this reason Gladstone, when chancellor of the Exchequer in Palmerston's second Cabinet, was largely instrumental in the setting up of a parliamentary commission under Lord Clarendon to investigate the condition of the public schools.[5]

Yet throughout its deliberations, and the discussions in both Houses of Parliament of its final report – leading eventually to the Public Schools Act of 1868 – it is hard to avoid the feeling that the main thing under discussion was class. Even when it came to the anodyne question of whether science was a suitable subject to which to draw a young gentleman's (or would-be gentleman's) attention, you have the sense that they are not really discussing

whether boys ought to know chemistry. Speaker after speaker in Parliament, including Gladstone, emphasized the undesirability of science as a school subject. Lords Derby, Stanhope and Carnarvon all argued that it would lead to 'cramming' and overwork, and cut into time needed for games, and the Earl of Ellenborough was able to spell out exactly where this could lead: examinations in which tradesmen's sons could succeed against, for example, the sons of army widows 'who had learned truth and honour at home'.[6]

So popular was the idea of public-school education that even as the Clarendon Commission sat, new 'public schools' were founded – Beaumont in 1861, Clifton and Malvern in 1862, Cranleigh and St Edward's, Oxford, in 1863. For the clearer it became in everybody's mind that the schools were to be the reinforcement of the new class system – indeed its seedbed – the more necessary it was to have a hierarchy of schools.

An extension and elaboration of this hierarchy was indeed the life's work to which the Reverend Nathaniel Woodard (1811–91) was devoted. From the first he recognized that 'middle class' was now a term which applied both to 'gentlemen with small incomes, solicitors and surgeons with limited practice, unbeneficed clergymen, naval and military officers' and to a second class of 'respectable trades folk'. There was also a third category who could afford his fees but who were not, strictly, respectable – the keepers of 'second-rate retail shops, publicans, gin-palace keepers', etc.[7]

Woodard established three sorts of school: the first were mini-Etons, which would educate boys until they were eighteen and then send them to university or into the army; the second class would keep them until sixteen; the third until fourteen. All would have the architecture of an 'old school' – a chapel, a quadrangle, masters and headmasters in academical caps and gowns, all the bogus appurtenances of 'public school'. Such is the eagerness of the socially mobile that the publicans were only too happy to send their sons to the third-class Woodard schools, such as St Saviours, Ardingly, knowing that these boys might so better themselves in later life that they could aspire to send their own sons to grander Woodard establishments, such as Lancing. Who knows? Within three generations they could even have escaped the Woodard group altogether, and be rubbing shoulders with the upper middle classes at Charterhouse or Shrewsbury.[8] Woodard was clever enough to see that such arcane transformations would be hindered by too much of the stabilizing influence of home, which is why from the first he insisted on the need for boarding schools.

1 2 *A group of Eton schoolboys c. 1870. All the public schools had been founded to teach poor scholars; but it was centuries since a poor person had been to Eton; and those public schools which retained places for poorer pupils found them in a distinct minority. Other schools found it less embarrassing actually to found new establishments for the worthy townsfolk, lest the 'young gentlemen' boarders in Eton collars from richer homes should have to mix with the children of local tradesfolk or even of artisans.*

The non-hierarchical or anti-hierarchical spirit of our age is so much at variance with Canon Woodard's ideals that we are in danger of ignoring the obvious fact that they were ideals. The children of gin-palace keepers deserved educational opportunities just as much as the children of the ducal palace, the vicarage, the suburb or the slum. The Victorians invented the concept of education as we now understand it; even if we believe ourselves to be more egalitarian than they, it is from them that we derive our axiomatic assumption that learning should be formalized learning, education institutionalized, the imparting of knowledge the duty of society and the state to every citizen. The 1860s, which began with the Clarendon Report on Public Schools and ended with the parliamentary Act guaranteeing elementary education for all, was the decade in which this culmination of Benthamite control was accomplished. Bishop Stanley, choosing to send the delicate Arthur Penrhyn Stanley, his son, to Rugby School, was emblematic of the change which had come upon England with the coming of the age of Reform. Having exercised their sway over the poor, the criminals, the agricultural and industrial classes, the civil service and – this was next – the military, the controllers had turned to the last free spirits left, the last potential anarchists: the children.

As Woodard had realized from the first, in creating his hierarchy of boarding-schools with their bogus traditions, faked-up slang, and imitations of the older public schools, education was a necessary part of the new class system which capitalism had brought into being. To be truly effective, it was necessary not merely to set up new middle-class schools, but to deprive the poor of the education which had been provided them for generations. The original founders of the public schools had all meant them to educate the poor. In 1442, Henry VI had instructed that 'no one having a yearly income of more than five marks' was eligible to attend his foundation at Eton. In the early nineteenth century, however, the public schools had begun the process of social segregation on which Victorian England very largely depended. Thomas Arnold, for example, closed the free lower school at Rugby so that, without hiring a tutor to teach their children, the poor could not reach the standard necessary to pass into the upper school. Winchester in 1818 claimed that its pupils were the 'poor and needy' specified by the founder William of Wykeham: it was only their parents who were rich. The Public Schools Act of 1868 took over any remaining endowments dedicated to poor pupils and gave them to the rich schools. In Sutton Coldfield, for example, whose poor were educated free by virtue of an endowment, £15,000 was plundered from the old charitable foundation in order to provide a 'high school for well to do children'.

The independence which education provided was thus removed from the poor, as was the element of choice. After 1870, and W.E. Forster's Education Act, it was to become compulsory for everyone to attend schools, but to do so in places strictly assigned to them according to income and social status.[9]

For the first time in Protestant history, even females were not exempt. Here is in fact the central, the classic example of the rule that, in order to find liberty in the Benthamite controlled world, you had to submit to its slavery. Education, first at schools, a little later in the century at university colleges, was the key means by which women were to enter upon a professional world on terms with men. Florence Nightingale founded a school of nursing in 1857 and provided others with a template of how women might, independently of men, establish a professional identity – hence, eventually, a political one. But in order to compete with boys, girls had, from the very first, to fight for such dubious privileges as the right to sit for public examinations.

'*Preparatory School for Young Ladies*'. *A cartoon lampooning the growing fashion for cookery schools.*

F.D. Maurice had been the chief inspiration behind the setting-up of Queen's College, Harley Street, as an adjunct to the University of London, and from that institution emerged two of the most important educationalists of the nineteenth century:[10]

Miss Buss and Miss Beale
Cupid's darts do not feel.
How different from us,
Miss Beale and Miss Buss.

The lines, invented by a Clifton schoolmaster when Miss Buss insisted on attending a Headmasters' Conference to discuss public examinations, rebound upon their own masculine limitations. The glory of Miss Beale and Miss Buss is that they established, for educational purposes, that women are *not* 'different from us'.

Frances Mary Buss opened the North London Collegiate School for Ladies on 4 April 1850 at No. 46 Camden Street. Her great triumph, apart from the establishment of the school – and with it an inspiration to other 'Girls' Public Day Schools' – was to battle for the right to sit public examinations. The Cambridge Syndicate in 1863 was at first fiercely opposed to girls

sitting exams. Through the influences of her friends Elizabeth Garrett and Emily Davies she was able to win this vital concession. (In 1869 Miss Davies opened, at Hitchin, the college eventually known as Girton – it moved to Cambridge in 1873.) Miss Buss was a tiny woman with an extraordinary flair for teaching and an intelligent fervour for the rights of women. In a long career, and a violent century, she never raised her hand against a child, though pupils, like the men who attempted to check her reforms, quailed in her presence.[11]

Her friend Dorothea Beale had witnessed, as a teacher, the rough end of school life. While Buss left Queen's College, Harley Street, to establish the North London Collegiate, Beale was appointed, at the age of twenty-six, head teacher of the Clergy Daughters' School, Casterton, Westmorland. This establishment, which had been founded in 1823 by the Reverend Cairns Wilson at Cowan Bridge, was destined, by the hand of its most famous pupil, to become the most notorious girls' school in European history: for it is none other than the Lowood of *Jane Eyre* (1847).

The Victorians invented school as a social instrument which moved forward the potentiality of the bourgeois revolution while it retained old hierarchies, and invented new ones. The public school ethos both enshrined and evangelized the combination of individualism with the crushing of self by institutionalism which is so distinctive and paradoxical a feature of the Victorian experience.

Tom Brown arrives at Rugby a free spirit, a child of the pre-industrialized English countryside. He could, for all the difference it makes, be an Elizabethan or an eighteenth-century child. He is confronted by the rough world of school – both the admirable 'hearty' Brooke and the bullies, Flashman and Speedicut. It is often supposed that the morality of the novel derives from the pure athleticism of these earlier chapters, and that Hughes was advocating a philistine pursuit of games and hero-worship. The book is deeper than that.

It has been skilfully pointed out that many of the jolly boyish reminiscences in the first part of the story – the football game, the bullying, the birds-nesting and so on – were in fact derived by Hughes from the written recollections of other old Rugbeians; the apparently unrealistic second half in which Tom experiences a

The cricket team of Tonbridge School, Kent, c. 1865.

spiritual renewal through his friendship with little Arthur (and Arthur's near-death experience) is all purely autobiographical. The crucial thing is that Tom has become institutionalized. He has become a team player. This is of vital significance to Hughes the socialist.

'The world of school' in other words – to use the subtitle of another famous story (*St Winifred's, or, the World of School*, by Dean Farrar) – was seen as a microcosm of the political world and as a preparation for it. That is why failure to conform to the conventions of school is seen as so anarchic; and why expressions of individualism are seen as so potentially damaging. This socio-political attitude colours what might be considered a prudish Victorian attitude to masturbation. *Eric, or, Little by Little* has been described as 'the kind of book Dr Arnold might have written had he taken to drink'.[12]

The 'little by little' is the gradual slither of Farrar's eponymous hero from small sins to great. He begins by laughing when a grasshopper gets into a lady's hat in church – for which he receives a flogging from the headmaster, Dr Rowlands. Before long, he is indulging in far worse sins than laughing in church. At first, the filthy talk in dormitory No. 7 shocked Eric 'beyond bound or measure'. Dark though it was, he felt himself blushing scarlet to the roots of his hair, and then growing pale again, while a hot dew was left upon his forehead. Ball was the speaker . . . Farrar himself apostrophizes: 'Now, Eric, now or never! Life and death, ruin and salvation, corruption and purity, are perhaps in the balance together, and the scale of your destiny may hang on a single word of yours. Speak out, boy!'

But Eric is silent, and after half an hour 'in an agony of struggle with himself' he falls. Farrar never spells out the precise nature of Eric's sin but a sermon by Dr Rowlands on Kibroth-Hathaavah (in the book of Numbers) makes it abundantly clear what is meant. Kibroth-Hathaavah is the burial ground of those who have lusted. Masturbation, in Farrar's story, leads inexorably to death.

The school story was one of the most distinctive of Victorian contributions to literature. There are no Elizabethan or Jacobean tragedies about school. Novels about school did not come from the pens of Richardson or Fielding. Yet Jane Eyre's experiences at Lowood, Nicholas Nickleby's at Dotheboys Hall, remain some of the most vivid experiences in our reading of nineteenth-century fiction. School, as well as being for Dr Arnold and his followers an archetype of society, becomes too a paradigm of the inner life, the waking nightmare that we will be snatched from the emotional comforts of home and thrust into the hardship, the psychological and physical torture, of a single-sex institutionalized existence. No wonder, for pupils and teachers alike, this should prove so endlessly addictive a theme. *Tom Brown's Schooldays* was published in April 1857, and by November of that year it had gone through five editions, selling 11,000 copies.[13] Twenty-eight thousand copies had sold by the end of 1862. Altogether fifty-two editions were printed by Macmillan before 1892.

The popularity of school stories shows how potent the boarding-school experience was for generations of English boys. You see how firmly it was embedded in the consciousness of the next generation in Henry Newbolt's (1862–1938) anthology piece 'Vitaï Lampada', in which memories of the breathless hush in the Close at Clifton are carried into the Imperial Wars.

The sand of the desert is sodden red –
Red with the wreck of a square that broke; –
The Gatling's jammed and the Colonel dead,
And the regiment blind with dust and smoke.
The river of death has brimmed his banks,
And England's far, and Honour a name,
But the voice of a schoolboy rallies the ranks:
'Play up! play up! and play the game!'

Newbolt, like Hughes, was a man of the left, who saw in the team-spirit of public schoolboys on the cricket pitch a useful paradigm of the cooperative unselfishness of an ideal society.

The games ethos affected not merely the men, but their wives. Arthur Stanley showed no aptitude for cricket when he was a boy; indeed, when at Rugby, he rather disliked the game. Yet when he was installed as the dean of Westminster, all this was forgotten. The boys of the Abbey choir-school were entertained to a cricket-tea by Dean Stanley and Lady Augusta and politely wrote to thank for it. Clearly neither Stanley nor his wife had stayed to watch the close of play, but this did not prevent Lady Augusta from seeing the games afternoon as an admirable excuse for a sermon. 'My dear Boys,' she wrote:

I am sure that you will all strive, down to the youngest among you, to make the Dean happy by shewing that not only in the Cricket field but in Church – in yr Houses – in School & at play – the 'score' may be such as to gladden the hearts of those who desire your good.[14]

It is so easy to mock this, so hard to recapture a world where grown-ups took children and childhood so passionately seriously that they could see in an afternoon of cricket, interrupted by lemonade and buns, an occasion for recalling the essentially moral texture of existence itself.

The illogic of the 'Broad Church' position would infuriate, on the one hand theological bigots, on the other those heirs of Enlightenment thought who believed the human race had left behind the need for a religious framework to life. But viewed differently, the intellectual 'inheritance' of Dean Stanley and friends was precisely a source of strength. They accepted the rigours of the scientific principle when it applied to science; they went on reading Plato, convinced that a religious attitude to the universe was allowable even when the mind had recognized the implausibility of many, perhaps most, perhaps all, Christian dogmas. In rather comparable ways, the alliances and rivalries of the changing political scene allowed an aristocracy to survive in England while a bourgeois democracy was forged: the two were not, as on the continent, deemed incompatibles. This ability to live with contrarieties which are not necessarily contradictions was one of the foremost strengths of Victorian England, seen in many aspects of life, not least – a theme for later in the century – in the writings of those British Hegelian philosophers who in large degree grew out of, though many would come to despise, the Broad Church theology of which Arthur Penrhyn Stanley was so charming and delicate an exponent.

Chapter Sixteen

Goblin Market and the Cause

Returning to the nineteenth century in a time-machine, the twenty-first-century traveller would notice immediately dozens of differences between our world and theirs: the smells of horse-dung and straw in the streets, and, even in the grander houses, the sweaty smell of the servants who had no baths – just the kitchen tap, very often; the darkness at night without electricity; the gas-flares against sooty skies; the fatty food and 'smell of steaks in passageways'; the beautifully made hats, worn by all social classes, and the properly tailored clothes, even on window-cleaners or factory-hands; the continued acceptance of social hierarchy and, with the obvious perky exception, the underlying deference; the racial coherence – Dante Gabriel Rossetti, we recall, found the sight of a slave boy in London exotic – no one in today's London would find anything odd about seeing a little black boy in the street; the superiority to ours of the postal service – four or five swift deliveries per day – and the splendour – red coats and gold or blue piping – of the postman's uniform; the excellence of the rail services; the truly terrifying inadequacy of dentistry and medicine – and with these, the toothache, the halitosis; the generalized acceptance of infant mortality, the familiarity of children's coffins being trundled in glass-sided hearses down cobbled streets; the poverty of the children who survived, the ragamuffins who swept crossings and still, in spite of Lord Shaftesbury's reforms, continued to work, and run about at large, in the alarming, overcrowded cities – all these things and more would assail the eye, heart and nostril and make us know that the Victorian world was utterly different from our own. But the greatest, and the most extraordinary, difference is the difference between women then and now.

We can seek all manner of reasons for the existence in the past of 'patriarchal attitudes', for the fact that the world was male-dominated and phallocentric. The 1860s were the decade in which these things seriously began to change. One of the things which paradoxically occasioned the change was a step backwards, a further diminution of women's rights in English law. It is an episode in history which occupies about twenty years, from the 1860s to the 1880s, when there came into effect, and then were abolished, the Contagious Diseases Acts.*

Among the surgical outpatients at Bartholomew's Hospital in London, one half had venereal disease, mostly the deadly syphilis – at Guy's it was 43 per cent. At Moorfields Eye Hospital and at the Throat Hospital in Golden Square, one fifth of patients admitted were suffering from venereal or contagious diseases, VD or CD, as they were called.[1] That there was a crisis of the greatest magnitude no one could doubt. How the repeal of the CD Acts became enmeshed with the growth of

A beautifully-dressed domestic servant takes a bottle and a lit candle to her master, c. 1860.

*The first was passed in 1864, amendments in 1866, 1868 and 1869. The Acts were repealed in 1886.

feminism will belong to a later chapter. What is so revealing – and to our eye so extraordinary – is the manner in which these parliamentary acts came into being in the first instance. The Acts were an attempt to apply the continental system of regulated prostitution to British garrison towns, in order to control the spread of disease. It was taken for granted that British soldiers and sailors needed prostitutes. It now became enshrined in British law that women were a source of contamination. No attempt was made to regulate the spread of disease by, for example, penalizing the men who tried to pay for sex. The working-class women whom economic circumstances moved in this direction were, by the standards of their contemporaries, 'fallen' women. Their sin was much greater than the man's.

The CD Acts meant that any woman found by the police within a certain radius of the garrison areas could be arrested. Quite inevitably, from the first, there were dreadful mistakes made – 'innocent' mothers and daughters were rounded up together with prostitutes themselves. Any woman so arrested was deemed by the law *ipso facto* a common prostitute. The law of habeas corpus had been suspended. If she refused to comply, and to undergo a medical examination, she could be imprisoned indefinitely. The medical examinations were horrific and, literally, intrusive. Josephine Butler, the great opponent of the CD Acts, and the woman who would eventually succeed in her campaign to have them repealed, wrote, 'By this law, a crime has been *created* in order that it may be severely punished, but observe, that has been ruled to be a crime in women, which is not to be a crime in men.'[2]

In the context of the 1860s the CD Acts were not, by most, seen as an issue of sexual politics so much as of public health. The war on cholera in the earlier decades of the century, and Edwin Chadwick's attempts to sanitize the towns and clean up the water supplies, were all part of a great Benthamite programme of state-fuelled improvement and control of the expanding populace. As well as the CD Acts the British Parliament brought in the Sanitary Act of 1866, tightening up the 1848 Act on sanitation; and in 1867 the Vaccination Act greatly enlarged the penalties for failure to vaccinate infants and children against smallpox.[3] It is easy to see why the British Medical Association was overwhelmingly in favour of the CD Acts. The increase in social status of the doctor, from village sawbones – often the very same person as the barber – to lofty professional, exactly follows the growth of Benthamism from private fad of the Philosophic Radicals in the Regency period to the underlying ideology of the whole Victorian state machine. Doctors were essential officers of control.

At the same time, the spread of sexually transmitted diseases in an age which knew no effective cure for syphilis, with all its debilitating and deadly consequences to the second and third generation, was a cause for desperate concern. If we criticize the government of Lord John Russell in the 1840s for failing to do enough to fight hunger in Ireland, we should try, perhaps, to understand why the government of Lord Derby twenty years later felt it had a duty to control the spread of a disease which affected – obviously – not merely soldiers, sailors and the women they sought out in garrison towns, but their children; and nor was anyone blind to the fact that middle- and upper-class families were also likely to be infected.*

So monstrous was the phallocentric ideology which so unthinkingly framed the CD Acts in their particular form that the abuses caused by the Acts, and the debates which led to their repeal, worked as a powerful stimulus to the Women's Movement. The fact remained, however, that a huge population, no more or less chaste than any other generation in human history, was capable, every time nature prompted one of them to sexual intimacy with another, of passing on a condition which would lead first to painful lesions, rashes and enlargement of the lymph nodes; later, in the one third of cases who were unlucky enough, to major disorders of the cardiovascular and central nervous systems – paralysis and insanity.[4]

That is why, when the feminists turned to the only woman in England practising as a doctor, Elizabeth Garrett (1836–1917), and asked her to attack the Contagious Diseases Acts, she refused. 'Degradation cannot be taken by storm and the animal side of nature will outlive crusades,' she believed. Some members of the women's movement never forgave her support for the CD Acts. She saw them as 'very limited in scope' and an 'attempt to diminish the injury to public health which arises from prostitution'. As an experienced hospital doctor, Elizabeth Garrett saw it largely as a class matter – 'Every member of the medical profession knows only too well how terrible are the sufferings of this class, and how difficult it is for them to get out of their life of vice, or even to discontinue in it for a time when in a state of urgent bodily suffering . . . Hospitals do not as a rule admit them, dispensaries cannot cure them; even soup kitchens for the sick will not help to feed them.'[5] Garrett

*Though statistically less likely than the working classes. *Vide infra.*

INTERIOR OF A WEST-END BROTHEL.

saw no alternative for these women than that they be compelled to undergo treatment in accordance with the Acts.

Incidentally, all modern research confirms Garrett's contention that this was a problem overwhelmingly affecting the lives of the poor. Analysis of court and poor law records, hospital and penitentiary reports following the CD Acts in York shows that 73 per cent of men associating with prostitutes were working class.[6] In many working-class districts women were prepared to take the risk of catching venereal diseases since, unlike their 'respectable' sisters, they were able to afford rooms of their own, new clothes, heat, cooked food, and above all alcohol; unlike the dressmakers and laundresses working fourteen hours a day, the prostitutes tended to avoid consumption.[7] The very concept of prostitution was a vague one in such classes.

One should remember these women if one tries to form too neat a picture of middle-class men corrupting or seducing working-class women. When we read of Elizabeth Garrett, pioneer medic and keen supporter of women's suffrage, it is almost as if there are two issues at stake in the 1860s – the Subjection of Women and the Improvement of the Working Classes. It is clear from her support of the CD Acts that she did not wish them muddled.

The resistance put up to a woman studying medicine by the entirely male medical establishment was huge.

The Lancet, champion of liberty for the poor, for the teaching hospitals, for scientific research against obscurantists and for the independence of coroners' courts against whitewashing politicians, had a disgraceful record in opposing Elizabeth Garrett's very presence at lectures and demonstrations. Its objections were based on the supposed 'refinement' of women which we began by noting, or quoting. There are few clearer examples of how the idea of female delicacy was invented as a way of keeping women down. *The Lancet* dismissed Elizabeth Garrett, the sensible daughter of a merchant from Aldeburgh, as an hysteric. It congratulated the students of the Middlesex Hospital for trying to get rid of her. Against all the odds, and with the help of Elizabeth Blackwell, who obtained an MD in the United States and was then admitted to the British Medical Register, Elizabeth Garrett became a doctor. (She studied in London but only got a *degree* in Paris, partly through the support of the British ambassador, Lord Lyons, partly through that of Napoleon III himself.) Thereafter came the foundation of the London School of Medicine for Women by Dr Sophia Jex-Blake (in 1874), and though for many years Dr Garrett Anderson (she married George Skelton Anderson in 1871) was the only female member of the BMA, the barricades had been broken.

The nineteenth-century women's movement was largely, if not essentially, a bourgeois movement. It certainly grew out of the prosperity of the early capitalist

MILL'S LOGIC; OR, FRANCHISE FOR FEMALES.

"PRAY CLEAR THE WAY, THERE, FOR THESE—A—PERSONS."

John Stuart Mill, logician, politician and social reformer, was one of the first men seriously to address Women's Rights in Britain; Punch *therefore mocked him.*

decades. The women who changed the lives of their sisters and daughters by campaigning for equal educational rights, equal, or at any rate just, parental rights, or for political suffrage were overwhelmingly either from the rich merchant class like Dr Garrett Anderson or daughters of the parsonage, the rentier class or the minor aristocracy. Dr Garrett's friend Emily Davies was typical in being the daughter of a clergyman. Bessie Parkes was the daughter of a rich Birmingham businessman. Barbara Leigh-Smith – in marriage Mme Bodichon – was a cousin of Florence Nightingale, the daughter of the Radical MP for Norwich. Mme Bodichon helped Emily Davies found Girton College, Cambridge, in 1873,

though it was not until after the Second World War that that university permitted women to take degrees.

Just as the Broad Church appeared to demolish Christianity but actually helped it to survive;* just as the Reform Bill appeared to undermine aristocracy but actually enabled it to remain politically powerful; so the incipient women's movement grew out of rentier and bourgeois money, seemed at odds with (some) new bourgeois values, but actually preserved and underpinned

*Elizabeth Garrett was typical of those who nearly abandoned religion but recovered a version of it under the influence of F.D. Maurice – see Manton, p.97.

the strength of the class system. These women were all asking for preferments – professional qualifications and university degrees – which were denied to all but a handful of the *male* populace. Except for the heady days of Chartism, and for certain unusual moments since – in the days of Lloyd George, for instance, or during the election immediately following the Second World War – the English working classes have not been politically engaged, any more than they aspired to be barristers or surgeons. The Women's Suffrage Movement could be seen as the final confirmation of the triumph of the *haute bourgeoisie*, not the first blast on the trumpet of revolution.

The Kensington Ladies Discussion Society met four times a year; under the chairmanship of Dr Garrett it rounded up the usual suspects – Mme Bodichon, Miss Beale, Miss Buss and Miss Helen Taylor, stepdaughter of the newly elected MP for Westminster, John Stuart Mill. In 1866 they presented to him a petition signed by 1,498 women asking for – demanding – women's suffrage. Mill believed that bringing about the first parliamentary debate on the subject was 'by far the most important public service' which he was able to perform in the Commons.[8] When one considers the size of the opposition both in Parliament and in the country at large, it is remarkable that eighty MPs voted with Mill.

*

Since *Goblin Market* was published at the beginning of a time of stupendous change in the lives of women in Britain, it is not surprising that modern literary criticism should have tried to tease out gender-politics and references to overt sexuality in the poem which its author insisted was 'just a fairy story' but others perceive as 'a Victorian nursery classic, like many works, somehow considered appropriate for children . . . actually full of sinister, subterranean echoes fortunately too sophisticated for their understanding'.[9] Many critics in the late 1960–2000 period went further than this and imagined that this poem, one of the undoubted masterpieces of the mid-nineteenth century, was too sophisticated for its author to understand either.

Having refused various marriage proposals, Christina Rossetti lived much under the shadow of a pious mother and of Maria, her elder sister who was a member of the Anglican sisterhood of All Saints. Much has been made of the harsh pieties of the Anglo-Catholics of the period and of Christina's morbid feelings of guilt and depression which this religion supposedly fed. To

discourage her from moping, Christina worked in the Highgate penitentiary, a House of Mercy for 'fallen women'. The volunteers – Christina was known as Sister Christina in the House – undertook the work of reclaiming the fallen.

Christina conceived *Goblin Market* as a moral tale to be read aloud in the penitentiary.[10] Just as Milton's *Masque at Ludlow Castle* (i.e. *Comus*) was first performed for a noble family rocked by the grossest sexual scandal – an audience which would have responded with particular eagerness to the moral: 'Love Virtue, she alone is free' – so the girls and young women in the Highgate penitentiary had probably learnt early that excess could bring wretchedness as well as ecstasy. This is the simple theme of *Goblin Market*, a theme as old as the story of the Garden of Eden.

The poem tells of two sisters, Laura and Lizzie, who are tempted by the tiny goblin merchants who haunt the woods and glens offering ripe fruit for a penny. Laura succumbs, and when she has run out of money, like a true addict she pays with anything to hand – in her case a lock of her golden hair. Then she really lets rip – 'She sucked and sucked and sucked the more/Fruits which that unknown orchard bore./She sucked until her lips were sore.' Lizzie goes to the wood to obtain an antidote for her sister's sickness. The goblins try to force her to eat their fruit but she 'laughed in heart to feel the drip/of juice that syrupped all her face'. She remains virginal, runs back to her sister, knowing she has it in her power to save – 'Did you miss me?/Come and kiss me./ Never mind my bruises,/Hug me, kiss me, suck my juices/Squeezed from goblin fruits for you.'

One does not need to bring a blush to the reader's cheek by spelling out some of the 'explanations' which critics have brought to these vivid lines. They are faced with a ludicrous dilemma. Either they have to imagine that Christina was so emotionally stupid that she did not know what she was writing. Or they have to suppose that the nun-like Christina was a pornographer. Neither is true. Christina's relationship with her nun sister Maria is reflected in this poem – as, no doubt, is her observation of the excesses which led her brother Dante Gabriel into alcoholism, and the 'fallen women' with whom she worked in Highgate into ruin. The poem is about the dangers of excess – of an unbridled appetite. To say it is 'really' about rape, incest, lesbianism is to miss the point. It is about the human tendency, which could no doubt be shown by incestuous lesbians but is actually more general, to self-destruction by means of self-indulgence. A child who had been sick after eating too much

Dante Gabriel Rossetti's frontispiece illustration for his sister Christina's masterpiece Goblin Market.

chocolate would understand *Goblin Market* better than many of the academic commentators.

The inability of some modern critics to grasp the surface meaning of *Goblin Market*, their insistence that its author could not have known the *kind of things* going on beneath that surface, is suggestive of the gulf between the women of the twentieth and of the nineteenth century respectively.

Elizabeth and Gabriel Rossetti's marriage, never perhaps very happy, entered a dark phase with the birth of a stillborn child on 2 May 1861. When Ned and Georgie Burne-Jones called on them they found Lizzie, dosed to the eyeballs with laudanum, rocking an empty cradle.[11] From now on, other visitors noticed Gabriel wincing and shrinking when his wife spoke sharply to him. Her behaviour has been described as disruptive, ill-tempered, jealous.[12] When Gabriel came home one evening he found that his wife had taken a huge overdose of laudanum: she died at 7.20 in the morning on Thursday 11 February 1862. Impulsively he buried with her, in the family plot in Highgate Cemetery, the manuscript of his poems which, as the years of his widowhood passed, he came to miss.

By the end of the decade Rossetti wanted his poems back, and in one of the most macabre scenes in the history of literature, on 5 October 1869 the coffin was opened. Lizzie was holding her Bible and Rossetti's poems. Some believe – the lawyers entrusted with the gruesome task found all 'quite perfect' in the casket – that the opium had preserved her as if in formaldehyde, and that her hair was still red-gold, but this is mere speculation, a good example of the iconic status which Elizabeth achieved in death.[13]

Modelling and drawing were, for a woman of her socio-economic background, a means of escape. If, for the less economically advantaged feminists of the Beale, Buss, Bodichon school of thought, the Cause – college, education, professional life – was an escape from the fate of being a governess, then for the Elizabeth Siddals art was the means of not being a domestic servant or a seamstress. The higher feminists wanted to save their sisters from becoming Jane Eyre: practically speaking, far more had to choose between becoming Dickens's Marchioness or the Doll's Dressmaker.

A concentration on the exotic life and death of Elizabeth Siddal should not make us forget those who did not end up either as painters or paintings. The largest occupational group among nineteenth-century women in England was, overwhelmingly, the servant class. In 1851 there were 751,540 domestic servants in the census; forty years later the number had swollen to 1,386,167.[14] In London one person in every fifteen was in service. It was a simple matter of supply and demand. As the rentier class grew more prosperous, more and more servants were required, and figures lower and lower in the social scale not merely employed servants but considered any menial activity – such as putting coal on their own fires – as demeaning. If this seems to a modern mind like exploitation, one has to remember from the other point of view the comparative restfulness of the servant life. The master was expected to provide food, housing and a modest cash wage; and for those working in larger households, there was the camaraderie of the servants' hall. Many found such a life in every way preferable to the long hours and daily grind of factory work. Only in the 1930s in England did the number of domestic servants sink below one million.[15]

Chapter Seventeen

Wonderland

The changes which had come upon the world – and upon industrialized Britain in particular – during the first quarter-century of Queen Victoria's reign were without historical parallel. The population explosion; the revolutions, industrial, social and political; the changes of world-view; the collapses and revivals of belief-systems were all prodigious. Historians can still play the game of cause and effect and ask which of these disruptive events was the origin, which the consequence of the other.

The age which had begun to fear that materialism was the only truth built railway stations in the manner of Gothic cathedrals. The Pre-Raphaelites were not alone in choosing for theme, not the changing industrial townscapes and ever-varying modern fashions in clothes and houses, but historical tableaux. David Wilkie Winfield, who changed his name to Wynfield, was a characteristic creature of his age.[1] Having trained at the studio in Newman Street of 'Dagger' Leigh (the model for Barker in Thackeray's *The Newcomes*), he painted such subjects as Oliver Cromwell in the night before his death and – his most acclaimed work – *The Death of Buckingham*, which depicted the murdered body of Charles I's favourite. Wynfield and his friends constituted the 'St John's Wood Clique', self-consciously Bohemian young men whom he photographed in a variety of fancy dress – Elizabethan ruffs, skullcaps redolent of Colet and Erasmus, breastplates and turbans. Wynfield's photographic portrait of Frederic Leighton, whose own early canvases included *Dante in Exile*, shows a figure who is every inch a young man of the 1860s with his slightly wispy moustache and bushy beard, but whose costume – medieval? ancient Roman? – suggests the child's dressing-up box. The 'Clique' were of course going out of their way to stand apart from their bourgeois origins; but as is so often the case, rebels seem as much characteristic of their age as conformists – in some ways more so, the retreat into fantasy being an urgent, even a central compulsion of the mid-Victorians, their literature, architecture, religion or lack of it.

It was typical of them to use the modern invention of photography for the furtherance of fantasy. Just as Newman did not want to be a clergyman of the nineteenth, as much as of the fourth century, so Wynfield could use the means of collodion (a gummy solution of gun-cotton) spread over glass plates to immortalize his friends as if they were figures in Ainsworth's *Tower of London* or Bulwer-Lytton's *The Caxtons*. Meanwhile, Julia Margaret Cameron had persuaded her much older husband to go and live at Freshwater on the Isle of Wight to be near the poet laureate. Her villa, Dimbola, became a centre of photographic activity, social voraciousness, affection, noise.

Mrs Cameron's lens, eye, imagination, transformed the great men of the age, and anyone else she could persuade to sit for her – parlour-maids, children, friends

Julia Margaret Cameron's photographic tableaux transformed friends and neighbours into figures of myth – here, 'The passing of King Arthur'. The King, far from being dead, looks impatiently at Mrs Cameron's lens.

and relations – into creatures of fantasy. Her Benthamite old husband with his long white beard became King Lear. The American artist/model Marie Spartali, who sat for Burne-Jones and Rossetti, becomes Mnemosyne the Goddess of Memory and mother of the Nine Muses.[2] Lady Elcho posed beside a tree as a spectre in Dante . . . Tennyson was perhaps never better depicted than in the Cameron portrait known as The Dirty Monk. And who is this – looking half away from the camera in 1872, a full-bosomed twenty-year-old woman, her hair loose against the shrubbery? Cameron entitled the picture *Alethea*, truth, and the model was Alice Liddell.

Very different she seems in one of the most celebrated of all nineteenth-century child-images, 'Beggar Child', as photographed by the Rev. Charles Dodgson, leaning against a rough stone wall in the Deanery Wall at Christ Church, Oxford, and lifting her ragged slip to reveal a slender knee and a hint of thigh. Dodgson must have taken dozens of pictures of Alice and her sisters Lorina and Edith. The dons' wives seemed content to allow this stammering clergyman to photograph their daughters completely nude, though only when they were very young. More than one friendship came to a sudden end when he asked to photograph a girl of eleven or older.[3]

No one knows why Dodgson so abruptly ceased to be friends with Alice's parents. When Liddell arrived at Christ Church as dean, in 1856, Dodgson (1832–98) was already installed as the young mathematics lecturer and sub-librarian. (He was ordained deacon, aged twenty-nine, in 1861, but never became a priest.) Alice was his most devoted little 'child friend' during her ninth and tenth years, and it was during a picnic in July 1862, when she was ten, that the first version of *Alice's Adventures Underground* were told to her as an oral narrative. The written version was finished the following year, with Dodgson's own illustrations. The next year – 1863 – Tenniel agreed to illustrate the much-expanded *Alice's Adventures in Wonderland*. By the time *Through the Looking-Glass* was published (1872) Alice had grown into the wistful young figure photographed by Mrs Cameron.

☞ *The Mad Hatter's Tea Party – Tenniel's illustration coloured.*

It was no less a figure than Lord Salisbury, no fanciful observer, who wrote to a friend six years later, 'They say that Dodgson has half gone out of his mind in consequence of having been refused by the real Alice. It looks like it.'[4] If true, then the rift with the Liddells, occurring in 1863, would have been caused by the thirty-one-year-old Dodgson proposing to Alice when she was eleven. This probably seems more shocking to a twenty-first-century sensibility than it might have done to the Victorians. Edward White Benson, future archbishop, proposed to Mary Sidgwick when she was twelve and he twenty-four – though they waited six years before marrying. The 1861 census shows that in Bolton 175 women married at fifteen or under, 179 in Burnley.[5]

Alice Liddell, however, was evidently capable of exciting affection from older admirers. Dodgson's photographs, which might produce queasiness in the eyes of some, conform to that most horrible cliché of paedophile fantasy – the little child who 'wants it' is leading on the voyeur. (Voyeurism, we may be sure, is all that was at work with Dodgson, and he was probably so much in denial about the erotic nature of his photographic pursuits that he believed the asexual nature of the naked poses he set up for his child models made them 'innocent'.)

The author of the *Alice* books has been the subject of innumerable biographical studies, quack psychiatric examinations, and bogus in-depth analyses. He has been shown to be crypto-homosexual, crypto-atheist, crypto-more or less anything. The evidence for these speculations is usually sought – and being sought, conveniently discovered – not in his letters or diaries but in the pages of a whimsical story about Alice. Since the first publication of *Alice's Adventures in Wonderland* Lewis Carroll (as Dodgson styled himself) has been much the most celebrated 'children's author' in the English language. The stories have never been out of print, and they have been translated into almost as many languages as the Bible.

The secondary literature on Carroll and the *Alice* books – vast, and mostly more nonsensical than the stories themselves – tells us much about the commentators from generation to generation. Some try to enter into the Carroll whimsy. Others offer joke 'explanations' of the tales – such as Sir Shane Leslie's brilliant spoof, purporting to have made the discovery that Carroll was writing about the religious controversies of the day: the Cheshire Cat is Cardinal Wiseman, the Blue Caterpillar Benjamin Jowett, the battle between the Red and White Knights the controversy between Thomas Huxley and Samuel Wilberforce. Others have taken such jokes seriously and attempted different interpretations – political, philosophical, psychoanalytical and so on. Or there have been the attempts to link the events in the book to actual events in the course of its composition. The royal visit to Christ Church – Queen Victoria coming to visit the Prince of Wales when he was an undergraduate – has as much absurdity as anything in the pages of Carroll's fantasy: 'I had never seen her so near before,' noted Dodgson, 'nor on her feet, and was shocked to find how short, not to say dumpy and (with all loyalty be it spoken) how *plain* she is.'[6]

Likewise, commentators have found real-life, or rather real dead, hatters, who died as Victorian hatters tended to, of mercury poisoning – symptoms of which included rushing manically about stuffing bits of bread and butter in their mouths. Others, not all medics, have joined sides and tried to prove that Alice's Hatter does not demonstrate the symptoms of mercury poisoning.

When Carroll first showed the story to George MacDonald, however, we can safely assume that none of these qualities were what arrested the greater writer's attention. MacDonald will have seen that Carroll was in some ways borrowing the techniques of his own *Phantastes* of 1858. MacDonald was a master myth-maker, intuitively aware of the way that fantasy works precisely by not having specific allegorical or symbolical equivalence. Just as the 'originals' of the story were all 'recognized', so one can see, particularly in their published form with the Tenniel illustrations, that the tales bristle with contemporary allusion. The Reverend Robinson Duckworth, who was present at the picnic in July 1862, afterwards 'saw' himself as the Duck, the Lory as Lorina, the Eaglet as Edith Liddell and the Dodo as poor stammering Do-do-dodgson. But it would be mad to read the *Alice* books as autobiography, any more than the clear resemblance between Disraeli and the gentleman sitting opposite Alice in the train in Chapter 3 of *Looking-Glass* has any satirical significance. The liberating thing about reading *Alice* – both *Wonderland* and *Looking-Glass* – is that they are *games*: they are what Wittgenstein called language-games, playfully and brilliantly exposing the fact that signifiers such as words and numbers will not bear the weight or fixity which systems of language, theology, metaphysics or logic often wish to place on them. To this extent, they represent an intellectual holiday for the author, a teacher of mathematical logic who as a devout churchman did think that theology was important, and voted against giving a proper salary to Professor Jowett because of his supposed heresy.

Charles Dodgson (Lewis Carroll) lolls with the wife of another great story teller, George Macdonald, with four of her many children.

What many of the serious commentators miss about the Alice stories is their surface-obviousness. They do not work – if they do work for us, rather than embarrassing us by their archness – on a secret level but on a superficial level. The failure of language-games to do their work, the very simple failure of human beings of the same language-group to understand what one is saying to another, this is the essence of the Carroll comedy, found in the relentless puns, double-takes and double entendres of the dialogues. There is also the additional 'comedy' of children being kept out of the grown-up world by language-games. This is perhaps the least attractive feature of the books as far as real children are concerned.

Carroll's is a merciless eye, as cold as the collodion spread on the glass plates of his camera. Innocent of full paedophilia in the physical sense, he has the paedophile's habit of viewing children as objects: the suffering and bewilderment of Alice is preserved in the stories as

funny – just as funny as the antics of the grown-up creatures, and just as unreasonable. The Reverend Charles Dodgson jokes about the little girls' failures in comprehension in the same callous way in which Mr Murdstone and his friends joke about 'Brookes of Sheffield', laughing all the more merrily when David Copperfield, unaware that he himself is being guyed, tries to join in the joke. To compare Carroll with Dickens is to recognize the essentially callous quality of the mathematics don's humour. Far from empathizing with little children everywhere, as his various saccharine postscripts* to the books suggest (as the tales went into their endless bestselling reprintings), the evidence of his

*e.g. 'To all my little friends, known and unknown, I wish with all my heart, "A Merry Christmas": . . . May God bless you, dear children, and make each Christmas-tide, as it comes round to you, more bright and beautiful than the last – bright with the presence of that unseen Friend, who once on earth blessed little children,' etc. etc.

WARWICK GOBLE

letters, diaries and photographs suggests that he did not really have sympathy for children at all – still less the obsession with his own boyhood without which it would be difficult for the biographers to enflesh the essentially dull life of this shy, dry old stick of a man.

*

Most of us first read Charles Kingsley's *The Water-Babies* in some lavishly illustrated edition – though whether the illustrator was Heath Robinson, Mabel Lucie Attwell or Margaret Tarrant, they tended to over-look the fact that water-babies, having returned to a state of innocence and redemption, were naked. Kingsley explicitly states that the drowned chimney-sweep's boy Tom 'felt how comfortable it was to have nothing on but himself'.

This story, however, 'a Fairy Tale for a Land-Baby', first appeared not as a beautiful 'children's book' but serialized in two grey, unillustrated columns of *Macmillan's Magazine* from August 1862 to March 1863. Those who first wanted to follow the adventures of

When Charles Kingsley wrote The Water Babies *his Platonist mysticism found a perfect marriage with his Social Gospel. Within a year of the publication, Parliament had banned the use of little boys as chimney-sweeps. This 1909 illustration is by Warwick Goble.*

search for *The Water-Babies* among the periodical literature of the day, jostling with Kingsley's eminent contemporaries. Kingsley's energetic engagement with his times, his taste for controversy, his extraordinary range, can all be found reflected in *The Water-Babies*. His wife said it was 'perhaps the last book he wrote with any real ease'; he dashed it off, completing the first chapter exactly as published, and without alteration (5,000 words at least?), in an hour.[7]

He was forty-two when he wrote it: destined to die aged fifty-six, exhausted by an American lecture tour, by chain-smoking, and hyperactivity.

To read *The Water-Babies*, with its teasing denunciations in Chapter Two of scientific materialism, and its attacks on Professor Owen and Professor Huxley, you might think Kingsley was anti-scientific, in fact he enjoyed a friendly correspondence with Darwin. The dean of Chester once asked Kingsley how he reconciled science and Christianity. 'By believing that God is love' was the reply. And to one who objected that the explanation of the development of the Mollusca given by Darwin could not be orthodox, Kingsley answered, 'My friend, God's orthodoxy is truth; if Darwin speaks the truth, he is orthodox.'[8]

This did not prevent Kingsley, in *The Water-Babies*, developing one of his most successful satires on his selfish, hedonist, capitalistic contemporaries: the lazy Doasyoulikes who evolve backwards, moving from houses to caves, through savagery and ugliness ('when people live on poor vegetables instead of roast beef and plum-pudding, their jaws grow large, and their lips grow coarse, like the poor Paddies who eat potatoes'). Pass five hundred years and they have grown hairy and stupid and are forgetting the use of language; in subsequent generations they go back to being apes. The point of this parable, however, is not to mock Darwin, but to suggest that human individuals, and societies, can choose between 'a downhill and an uphill road'.[9] It is an almost unbelievable fact to us that children were still being sent up chimneys until the publication of *The Water-Babies* and that a year after its publication, Parliament abolished the abuse.

Tom, who works for the cruel Grimes the chimney-sweep, who is shoved up a chimney flue at Harthover Place, comes down into the bedroom of little Ellie and is accused of being a thief, had to do so by turning over prolix articles by Leslie Stephen on the economic-liberal case for supporting the Confederacy, lengthy reviews by Matthew Arnold on Stanley's *Jewish Church*, scientific disquisitions on oysters, on geology, or the antiquity of man; or a worthy consideration by Thomas Hare on the ideal form of local government in the Metropolis.

There is something apt about the fact that we must

Chapter Eighteen

Some Deaths

Using children's literature as a prism through which to view the Sixties of the nineteenth century has helped, perhaps, to focus the decade as one which was indeed an 'age of equipoise'. That the mid-Victorian era knew a special flowering of literature for children is itself, as we have seen, a fact of sociological reverberations and significances.[1] So, too, is the fact that books such as *Uncle Tom's Cabin* (1852), which were not meant for children in the first instance, could so easily and so soon have found a place on the shelf beside *The Children of the New Forest* (1847), *Tom Brown's Schooldays* (1857), *Eric, or, Little by Little* (1858), *Goblin Market* (1862) or *Alice's Adventures in Wonderland* (1865). This was also the period when Hans Christian Andersen's tales were first translated into English (1846 onwards) and began their prodigious world popularity. All these books differently reflect the ways in which the world was changing, and some reflect how it was not.

While the gerontocracy lasted, England resembled one of those arrested families where, the ancient parents still living, the grown-ups, even in middle age, continued to see themselves as 'the children'. Hence, perhaps, in large measure, the truth of Disraeli's view that the era was like a fairy-tale, and hence too the fittingness of so many of its great writers being the authors of books for children.

But in the 1860s the older generation at last began to die off. Palmerston died on 18 October 1865. 'Gladstone will soon have it all his own way,' he had said to Shaftesbury, 'whenever he gets my place, and then we shall have strange doings.' But he was succeeded as the Liberal prime minister, not by Gladstone, aged fifty-six, but by Russell, aged seventy-three. Russell (Earl Russell since 1861) was determined to deal with the matter of electoral reform. The author of the first Reform Act in 1832 was prime minister in 1865: no more potent symbol could be found of the gerontocratic nature of early to mid-Victorian England. The first Reform Act had done little enough to enfranchise the middle classes. Now, the bourgeoisie, both *haute* and *petite*, was huge. And five out of six adult males in the population were voteless.[2] How far this mattered, and how far the population as a whole really minded about the vote per se, may be an open question. At the time, the extension of the franchise was the great object of political debate. 'It was the flag and shibboleth of the new nation against the old.'[3]

At this historical distance, it seems extraordinary, if an electoral process was accepted at all, that the franchise should not be extended to all, regardless of income or gender; but this is not how it appeared to those in the thick of the debate, either inside or outside Parliament. The order of events was dramatic and exciting. In 1866, Russell's Liberal government brought in a very moderate Bill to extend the franchise to householders of a certain level of wealth. There was a right-wing revolt within the Liberal ranks at the notion of such a concession to Radicalism,

A comic photograph showing an elector being bribed surreptitiously. This is a reference to the Anti-Bribery Bill which became law as the Corrupt and Illegal Practices Prevention Act in 1883.

Thomas Carlyle by James McNeill Whistler. Carlyle in his seventies found the new age little to his taste: 'We are a people drowned in Hypocrisy, saturated with it to the bone – alas, it is even so, in spite of far other intentions at one time, and of a languid, dumb, ineradicable inward protest against it still . . . Certain it is, there is nothing but vulgarity in our People's expectations, resolutions or desires in this Epoch. It is all a peaceable mouldering or tumbling down from mere rottenness and decay . . .'

and the Bill was defeated. Russell resigned, to be defeated in the general election by Lord Derby. The (minority) Conservative government then surprised everyone by bringing in a more far-reaching Reform Bill. The diehards in Derby's Cabinet – General Peel, the Earl of Carnarvon and Viscount Cranbourne (the future prime minister, as the 3rd Marquess of Salisbury) – resigned in protest. This in itself helped the purposes of Derby and his political genius of a leader in the Commons – Disraeli. What Disraeli and Derby were able to do, by an *apparently* more radical extension of the franchise, was to have a much greater say over the distribution of constituencies and, without open gerrymandering, to make it likely in the future that they would have a good chance of forming majorities in the House of Commons. This is what was going to happen – Conservatism, of a sort, was the dominant political creed of the second half of

Victoria's reign. 'Disraeli was educating his party, and preparing it for the inevitable future.'[4]

Derby, his leader and prime minister, had seen that the Liberal Bill of 1866 – the one they defeated – was 'the extinction of the Conservative Party and of the real Whigs'. As a man who had actually been a member of the Whig government which brought in the 1832 Act, Derby knew whereof he spoke. What we are able to see more clearly was how remarkably successful the Conservatives were in preserving some element of aristocratic government down to, and even after the First World War. There was at least an alliance between the landed classes and the new bourgeoisie, and that large portion of the population, the working-class Tories. How much Disraeli foresaw all this, how much he was even its architect, there will always be room to debate. Though, in the short term, the Second Reform Act did not do the Tories any good – the Liberals won the election of 1868, bringing in Gladstone as prime minister for the first time – there is no question that without it the Conservative Party would have been annihilated. Gladstone would eventually have come in, come what may, and 'strange doings' would have been the ineluctable consequence.

Yet to diehards, the extension of the franchise by some 938,000 voters was all a disaster. Carlyle put it more trenchantly and gloomily than anyone in his pamphlet *Shooting Niagara: and After*, in which he imagined civilization plummeting over the rapids. 'That England would have to take the Niagara leap of completed Democracy one day' was now regarded as an inevitability. 'Swarmery', he called it, the swarming together, not even of mobs, but of Constitutionally Reformed Majorities. The notion that things could be changed or reformed by the holding of elections, by making speeches on the hustings, by the return to Parliament of Honourable Members for this borough and that, was palpably absurd to the author of *Heroes and Hero-Worship*:

Inexpressibly delirious seems to me, at present in my solitude, the puddle of Parliament and Public upon what it calls 'the Reform Measure'; that is to say, the calling in of new supplies of blockheadism, gullibility, bribeability, amenability to beer and balderdash, by way of amending the woes we have had from our previous supplies of that bad article. The intellect of man who believes in the possibility of 'improvement' by such a method is to me a finished-off and shut-up intellect, with which I would not argue.

Carlyle's is a voice which we can hardly understand now. The great novelists of the early to mid-nineteenth century, Dickens and Thackeray, remain freshly alive. They were destined to die before the old Chelsea curmudgeon, much younger as they were.

Thackeray's death at the very end of 1863 – he was aged fifty-two – brought an end to a career which in many respects never began. His finest achievements – *Vanity Fair*, *Henry Esmond*, the first half of *Pendennis* – are better than anything in Dickens, but it would be paradoxical to consider him, on the whole, the greater writer. He was worn out by journalism, by syphilis, by the need to maintain himself as a gentleman, his beloved daughters as ladies, in difficult domestic circumstances – his wife having for many years been humanely confined as a lunatic. His imagination was not at home in the Age of Equipoise – his best work all depicts the time of the Regency, or even the eighteenth century. Curiously

Charles Dickens two years before his death in 1870.

enough, he seems closest to his own age in the pantomime-burlesque written for children, *The Rose and the Ring* (1855): his old trick of puncturing snobberies and class-obsessions was never more deftly employed than in chronicling the fortunes of Rosalba, first seen as an urchin in the Park, to be condescended to by the odiously bourgeois Princess Angelica, but soon revealed as a princess. The physical unimpressiveness and general dinginess of the British royal family is never actually alluded to, but you feel it constantly hinted at in Thackeray's satire. Children still find it funny, but it remains one of those many mid-Victorian children's books which are ultimately written for the amusement of the adults who had to read them aloud.

Dickens, by contrast, wrote as a child, he understood as a child, he thought as a child: and when he became a man he never put away childish things. It is often suggested that Dickens was restrained by the conventions of his age from writing openly about sex, but this is to beg many questions. You could equally point out that he did not write as Balzac or Zola would have done about money: and there was no Victorian taboo about the open discussion of shillings and pence. He writes about the world as a highly intelligent, profoundly imaginative child would write about it. Balzac would be able to take us through every stage of Mr Dorrit's ruin, and when the rescue takes place, we should feel that we had had an interview with the Dorrit auditor, the Dorrit family solicitor and the Dorrit banker. But as Dickens tells the story it is a fairy-tale, a romance. Dorrit is in the Marshalsea, unable to clear his debts, and it is the world of the Marshalsea which matters to us more than the exact financial troubles which took him there. We see him through the eyes of Little Dorrit, who was born in the debtor's prison. Then – hey presto! – Pancks the rent collector exposes the wickedness of Mr Casby, and the lost inheritance of Mr Dorrit is found with the arbitrariness of a story in the Brothers Grimm.

The events and concerns which a grown-up might consider important – sexual feeling and finance, and politics – do not interest Dickens. Or they interest him only as they have an effect on the lives of children. That is why *Great Expectations* and *David Copperfield*, which tell the story of childhood with raw and unforgettable realism, are the finest things he ever wrote. Not to see the merits of Dickens is more than a literary myopia: such an absence of sensibility would suggest a failure to see something about life itself. That is why Dickens occupies a place of all but unique importance in the minds of the English. One of his acutest readers, G.K. Chesterton, was also able to see that in his cast of characters there was something archetypical, if not actually symbolic. 'The first and last word upon the English democracy is said in Joe Gargery and Trabb's boy. The actual English populace, as distinct from the French populace or the Scotch or the Irish populace, may be said to lie between those two types. The first is the poor man who does not assert himself at all, and the second is the poor man who asserts himself entirely with the weapon of sarcasm.'5

There is deep truth here. Marx did not see the truth it contained, which is why he waited in vain for an English revolution. The English rich have never understood the sarcasm of Trabb's boy and they have taken the silence of Joe Gargery for deference. The middle-class liberals, with their sanitation acts, education acts, board schools and churches, throughout the nineteenth century and beyond, wanted not merely to improve conditions for the poor but to improve the poor. From the beginning of his early *Sketches by Boz*, through his tales of workhouses, vagrants and petty criminals, Dickens always knew that this was a misguided, not to say odious, ambition. If all Dickens characters possess some of the qualities of pantomime, he allows to all an equal dignity. There was something apt in his dying – that he who had excoriated the early Benthamites and mocked the improving workhouses, and the parish-pump bossiness of early nineteenth-century liberalism, should have died as its second phase – of sanitation and an extended franchise – began.

He was fifty-eight when he died, at Gad's Hill in June 1870, worn out by overwork, and by the insanely energetic public readings from the novels with which he had entranced theatre audiences on both sides of the Atlantic.

The funeral was in Westminster Abbey, the national Valhalla. It could have been nowhere else. Dean Stanley read the funeral service from the book of Common Prayer. There was no singing, though the organist played the Dead March from *Saul*. When reporters arrived at half-past nine to inquire when the ceremonies were to begin, they were informed that they were over: but the dean left the grave open all day – on the edge of Poets' Corner. All day – Waterloo Day, 1870 – a crowd flowed past and looked down at the coffin. 'No other Englishman,' said Walter Bagehot, 'had attained such a hold on the vast populace.' They still trudged into the Abbey as the hour of midnight approached. The truth of Bagehot's words – the importance of Dickens – tells us as much about the English as it does about the novelist himself.

If you had to seize on one way in which Britain had changed during the 1860s, you could do worse than focus on the theme of public executions. 1868 saw the last of these ghoulish spectacles in England. Was this liberal progress? Or was it part of the mid-Victorian bourgeoisification of life, an indication of prudery, not compassion? What is so interesting is that liberals, who had been in favour of the abolition of capital punishment altogether in the 1840s, had, by and large, changed their minds in the Age of Equipoise. They had decided that for a heinous crime such as murder, execution was permissible so long as it did not happen in public.

It is an eloquent fact that the last man to be hanged publicly in England was an Irishman, Michael Barrett. Gladstone's mission, when he finally took over leadership of the Liberal Party, and became prime minister in December 1868, was to 'pacify Ireland'. The Fenian movement – the notion that Ireland could become independent of British rule by violent means – was

THE FENIAN OUTRAGE IN CLERKENWELL: THE GAP IN THE PRISON WALL, AND THE RUINS OF CORPORATION-LANE, AS SEEN ON THE NIGHT OF THE EXPLOSION.—SEE NEXT PAGE.

Fenian Irish Nationalists bombed their way out of Clerkenwell gaol in 1867 and provided a template for Irish resistance to English policing for the next hundred years. The Penny Illustrated Paper, *21 December 1867, records the 'outrage'.*

focused after the close of the American Civil War when many Irish soldiers in the Federal army, supplied with American money, decided to imitate the Polish or Italian nationalists and stage outrages – first in Canada, then in Britain. As many as 1,200 Fenians assembled at Chester in February 1867.

Gladstone, anxious to demonstrate that he had outgrown his wrong-headedness at the time of the Maynooth Grant (1845), brought in a Bill to disestablish the Irish Church. Meanwhile, Fenians had been arrested on a number of charges. A policeman in Manchester had been killed. An attempt was made to rescue two Fenian prisoners in Clerkenwell jail, less than a mile from St Paul's Cathedral, the Bank of England and the Guildhall. A barrel of gunpowder was placed against the outer wall of the prison and blown up. Twelve persons were killed,

120 others injured. Gladstone pressed on urgently with the Irish Land Act (1870), demonstrating a lesson which was eagerly learnt by the Fenian movement: that the English move slowly over Irish affairs when the Irish are at peace, but develop an astonishing capacity to expedite pro-Irish legislation when a few bombs have been exploded, particularly if they have been let off in London.

The English, for their part, could use the opportunity of the Clerkenwell bombing to demonstrate another sorry pattern of behaviour which, in the course of Anglo-Irish relations, would be repeated for a hundred years: namely the belief that draconian punishment of the bombers and gunmen would cow or silence Ireland rather than dignifying the murderous activities of buccaneers and turning them into political martyrs.

Part Four

THE EIGHTEEN-SEVENTIES

QUADRILLE

BY

CARL VOLTI.

Chapter Nineteen

Gladstone's First Premiership

In 1870–1, Europe was involved in wars and ideological conflicts of a cataclysmic dimension. Two pairs of immense irreconcilables clashed together: on the one hand, France and Germany; on the other, Catholicism and the new secularism – in particular, atheistic communism. As things played out, these two archetypical, monstrous struggles for power – ideological and territorial – were interwoven with the last vainglorious political posturings of Napoleon III. For he had guaranteed the safety of the pope and the temporal power of the Papacy with French troops which had to be withdrawn when he declared war on Prussia in the summer of 1870. In the space of one year, the ideological map of Europe was changed, and it was to be locked in a geopolitical rivalry, and a war of ideas, unresolved – if ever – until the late twentieth century.

1870–1 was in the truest sense a European catastrophe. The sheer slaughter was something without parallel – first in the war in which the well-disciplined Prussians inflicted such total defeat on the French at Metz, then in the Paris Commune. (During the Bloody Week of 21–28 May 1871, 25,000 French died at the hands of their own compatriots.) The ominous drama of it all makes almost intolerable reading, since we know what will happen forty, fifty, seventy years later. The victory of Prussia led directly to the creation of a united Germany. The treaty of Versailles of 1871 absorbed the kingdoms of Bavaria and Württemberg, and the grand-duchy of Baden, the grand-duchy of Hesse and many of the other German states were now incorporated in the Reich, centred on Berlin and recognizing the king of Prussia as their emperor. The king of Prussia – Wilhelm – was proclaimed the Kaiser. Bismarck his chancellor was triumphant. In the Hall of Mirrors, at the Palace of Versailles, the proclamation was made before the devastated government of France – a humiliation which would be revenged in 1919, repeated in 1940 . . .

A lens which is focused on Britain at this watershed of European history, the opening of the 1870s, depicts then a scene which is out of kilter with the rest of Europe, almost comically so. After his release from imprisonment in the palace of Wilhelmshöhe above Cassel, Napoleon III went into exile in England, living with Empress Eugénie at Chislehurst, Kent, for the last two painful years of his life. He merely crossed the English Channel, but in some ways he could have been crossing to a different universe.[1] He had left behind the bloodshed, passion and wretchedness depicted in Emile Zola's 1892 novel *La Débâcle* (which must be the best war novel ever written, set in 1870–1) and entered *Middlemarch* (published in 1872 the year *after* Marx's *The Civil War in France* but holding up a mirror to a world whose continental equivalent had been pounded, mortared, out of existence, but which would survive in England for another forty years).

Most English followers of events on the continent felt pity for France in its desolation, and above all for Paris, the hunger and despair of the siege, the internecine

▢▢ Gladstone took office for the first time as Prime Minister in 1868 when he was in his late fifties. In this cartoon he is seen as a band-master holding together the disparate elements of British politics from John Stuart Mill (Liberal) on the harp, to Disraeli on the Jew's Harp (Conservative); from John Bright, the old free trader (on the wind instrument, the ophicleide, here spelt ophecleide) to the Duke of Argyll (Secretary for India in Gladstone's first Cabinet). Carl Volti, a Glaswegian whose real name was Archibald Milligan, wrote 'popular melodies' – which is what the wily Gladstone tried to do in politics.

▢▢▢ A comic map of Europe depicting the countries as various personalities, 1871.

The Grand Old Man – Gladstone – in about 1875, a photograph which captures his keen intelligence and a vein of ruthlessness.

destructiveness of what followed. London alone sent £80,000 worth of provisions to the starving,[2] but here her kindly-minded subjects were not at one with the Queen, who was cock-a-hoop at the Prussian victory. 'How dreadful the state of Paris is! Surely that Sodom and Gomorrah as Papa called it deserves to be crushed,'[3] she wrote to her daughter the Crown Princess of Prussia. 'The joy of our army,' Vicky gushed back to her mother, 'around Paris is not to be described.'[4] (But Queen

Victoria changed her mind after the Prussian annexation of Alsace-Lorraine.)

The British government retained a neutral stance. Vicky was displeased by her mother's speech from the throne on 9 February 1871 which referred to the belligerents, in a war as yet unresolved, as 'two great and brave nations'. She must have known that the Queen's Speech at the State Opening of Parliament was simply an expression of the politics of her government; that,

French troops encircled by the Prussian Army at the Battle of Sedan, 31 August 1870. Britain was at best tangentially involved with the European conflicts which were to leave everything so changed: Germany united at last under Prussia; the Italians at last a nation, in occupation of the pope's temporal domains; the pope gamely fighting back with weapons of the Spirit by the declaration of his own infallibility; the Commune in Paris attempting the complete obliteration of the cathedral of Notre Dame – only themselves to be massacred by the thousand.

though the sovereign read out the words, they had been scripted by the prime minister – in this case Gladstone.

As had happened before in Gladstone's career, there was a tortuous moral and intellectual complexity in his attitude to the Franco-Prussian war, to the annexation of Alsace-Lorraine in particular, to Europe generally. He told the Queen 'in a very excited manner' that there would 'never be a cordial understanding with Germany if she took that million and a quarter people against their will'. But his sovereign, and his Cabinet, were against Gladstone, favouring the neutral stance adopted in the Queen's Speech. That wasn't the end of the matter, however. Although in public Gladstone was a neutral, he let off steam by writing, anonymously, in *The Edinburgh Review* an article entitled 'Germany, France and England' in which he deplored Bismarck's action, and denounced 'Bismarckism, militarism, and retrograde political morality'. The *Daily News* seized on the obvious identity of the author and 'leaked' it. It was a moment comparable to the Newcastle speech at the beginning of the American Civil War when Gladstone, as it were,

accidentally blabbed out his sympathy with the Confederacy. Consummate politician that he was, he knew how to use such supposed gaffes to play to the gallery, to signal to his supporters that he would like to take particular views, populist or otherwise, were he not restrained by party, or Cabinet, colleagues. He was 'the People's William'.

Setbacks – such as Disraeli trouncing him and introducing a more radical, and fairer, second Reform Bill than his own – could be represented by Gladstone to his huge and adoring audiences as triumphs of his own. 'God knows I have not courted them,' he recorded in his diary after a deliberately rabble-rousing tour of Lancashire.[5] His consummate political skills and his long run of political luck could, in his own mind, be very easily explained – 'The Almighty Seems to Sustain me.'[6] A.J.P. Taylor, in *The Struggle for Mastery in Europe*, maintained that Bismarck encouraged the idea of himself as a Machiavel, and revelled in the idea that he had tricked Napoleon III into declaring war on Prussia over the trivial question of the candidature for the Spanish

NEW GUY FAWKES; OR DIZZY'S
CHEF-D'ŒUVRE.

"*Under the guise of Liberalism—under the pretence of legislating in the spirit of the age—they are, as they think, about to seize upon the supreme estate of the realm.*"—See MR. DISRAELI'S Speech, April 3rd, 1868.

throne. The more people read the confusion of events as a subtle spider's web of Bismarck's invention, the stronger Bismarck's hand. Gladstone, in his prime, had some of these qualities, not of overt humbug, but of quite instinctual political genius, knowing when to surf with, when to swim against, each rolling wave.

As the 1870s unfolded, Gladstone's preoccupation with Christian Europe as a morally cohesive union was to develop alongside, paradoxically, the distrust of that Roman Catholicism which historically had been the guardian of all the things he held dear: Latin language and culture, theology, the spiritual ideals of the author. Next to Homer, he most idolized Dante. Like the trecento visionary, Gladstone looked for a Catholicism in which the temporal vanities and political ambitions of the Papacy had been crushed; he longed instead for a true Catholicism – i.e. universal Christianity – which would unite the people of Europe against the Muslim culture of the Ottoman Empire and the atheist encroachments of scientific materialism.

England, and the world, are still living with these polarities: on the one hand England, a European nation, culturally at one with Europe, is politically detached from it; on the other, while a portion of Britain will always by commerce or politics feel involvement with Europe as a primary interest, others will draw on the historic trading traditions of a seafaring race and look to a greater world. The great contrast between modern Britons and those of the 1870s – speaking now of the intellectual and social elite – is in their sense of German cousinhood.

A discovery of German philosophy, literature and culture was, for the mid-Victorian generation, the eye-opener into a larger world. It was in 1844 that Benjamin Jowett and Arthur Stanley set out for a walking holiday in Germany and met Erdmann, Hegel's chief disciple. Thereafter, not only was German philosophy to be the chief source of inspiration for British logicians, meta-physicians and political thinkers for half a century and more; but the whole German educational method – from universal state primary schools to the treatment of science as an essential academic discipline – was to be the envy and inspiration of British schools and universities.

As the nineteenth century drew to its close, the British love of all things German would widen from the intellectual to the middle classes. But it would go hand in hand with a growing awareness that there was now a power in Europe which was actually preparing to outstrip Britain not only in military power but also in economic prosperity. The aged Carlyle with his last gasp could point to the fact that England had fought a war against Napoleon with Prussia as its ally, and consistently feared and hated France: he could also point out – which a railway journey across the European land-mass could make clear to anyone – that the German states, and the German-speaking peoples of the Austrian Empire with whom they were in a perpetually uneasy relation, made up the huge proportion of the European peoples. Not since the Thirty Years War in the seventeenth century had the peoples of Europe learned to live at peace with one another. If they were ever able to do so it would probably be on the basis of some German federalism, of the kind favoured by Prince Albert, and which appears to be the basis of the modern European Union.

What can't be denied in terms of population and land-mass is the inevitability of some kind of German 'domination' of Europe. The only thing which held this in check was that very French nationalism and expansionism which the British most dreaded. Once, under Bismarck and the new Kaiser, 'noble, patient, deep, pious and solid Germany should at length be welded into a nation' the foundations of the Reich had been laid. The figures for the next forty years or so show the dramatic increase in German power vis-à-vis Britain. In 1871, Britain had a population of 32,000,000, Germany 41,000,000. These lived respectively in territories of 120,000 and 208,000 square miles. Their respective armies numbered 197,000 and 407,000. By 1914 the British army numbered 247,000, and the German a staggering 790,000. The British navy had 60,000 men in 1872, 146,000 in 1914: the German navy had expanded from a mere 6,500 men to 73,000. Prussian military expansion was being paid for by vast investment in the infrastructure, and by prodigious industrial growth, comparable to Britain's expansion in the first half of the century. In 1850 there were 10,000 miles of British railway and 6,000 miles of German. By 1910 there would be 38,000 miles of British railway and 61,000 miles of German. In 1880 Britain produced 980,000 tons of steel, to Germany's 1,550,000 tons. By 1913 this had increased to 6,900,000 tons in Britain and 18,600,000 tons in Germany. As European 'players' Britain, for decades easily the most modern, the most technologically efficient and the most industrially productive, now had a

Disraeli in his political propaganda tries to depict Gladstone as a Guy Fawkes undermining the British Church – a clever sleight of hand when we remember that Gladstone went to Church every day of his life.

The East Coast Railway Express, c. 1875. By now the Victorian growth in technology and industry was at its zenith.

major rival against whom competition, in purely European terms, was impossible.

The area where Britain bore up, and continued to dominate, was in exports and world trade: though Britain's *share* of world trade fell from 38 to 27 per cent between 1870 and 1913, Germany's rose only by 5 per cent. Britain's colossal wealth, and her world influence, would increase in the last half of Victoria's reign, but this increase would be dependent on her empire. Hence, for the purposes of a full picture, one must always remember that 'the Victorians' were not merely the British, but the Indians, the Egyptians, the Sudanese, the Zulus, and many other peoples of the globe caught up for commercial and political reasons into the drama, their destinies and futures irrevocably changed. To this extent, Disraeli's semi-serious definition of Britain as an Asiatic, not a European power is true. But the spectre of a mighty Conservative empire in Europe, ruthless enough not merely to annex Danish provinces but if necessary to starve the people of Paris and reduce their monuments to rubble, had a wonderful power to concentrate Liberal English minds.

In the event, however, increased population and increased international commerce went hand in hand with increased armaments in all the prosperous countries. Inevitably, the expertise which had been devoted to ingenious machinery in factories was turned to the development of weapons. If the human race could mass-produce it could also mass-destroy. The Russian shells at Sinope had annihilated the Turkish fleet, and the British warships, little changed since the days of Nelson – wooden ships with masts and sails – had suffered badly from the bombardment by Russian guns

at Sebastopol. Inevitably, new technology would be required in the event of another war. The French pioneered *La Gloire* in 1859, a wooden ship protected above the water-line with a corselet of iron behind which the guns were mounted. The British, not to be outdone, produced HMS *Warrior* in 1860, the first all-metal battleship with an iron hull, and a belt of iron armour thick enough to resist shells.

The fact that Britain did not fight a European war between the time of the Crimea and August 1914 should not abet the assumption that this era of plenty was achieved peacefully. The Empire and its spoils were preserved, and won, at the end of guns. There was scarcely a year, from the 1860s onward, when some British troops, somewhere in the world, were not fighting. From 1863 to 1872 there was the Third Maori War. In 1870 Canada saw the Red River expedition; in 1871–2 there was the Looshai expedition in Bengal; in 1873–4 the Second Ashanti War in West Africa; in 1874 the Duffla expedition. In 1875–6 there was the Perak campaign in Malaya, and race riots in Barbados. In

Britannia introduces the torpedo to the British navy in a cartoon by John Tenniel. During the next thirty years, iron replaced wood as the material for ships' hulls. Armour was incorporated; breech-loading, rifled ordnance firing explosive or armour-piercing shells replaced smooth-bore, muzzle-loading cannon. Gun turrets replaced broadside guns, and locomotive torpedoes, hydraulic machinery and electricity all eventually made their appearance on warships. These developments were the inevitable consequence of industrial expansion at home and colonial-cum-commercial expansion abroad.

"FIAT EXPERIMENTUM—!"

Britannia. "ALLOW ME TO INTRODUCE A YOUNG GENTLEMAN WHO HAS JUST MADE HIS DÉBUT ON THE DANUBE, AND TO WHOM YOU AND I WILL, I RATHER THINK, HAVE A GOOD DEAL TO SAY."

1877–8 there was the Jowakhi campaign and the Ninth Kaffir War. Indian troops were sent to Malta in 1878 in readiness for a showdown with Russia over the apparently insoluble Eastern Question. In 1879 came the Zulu War, coinciding with the Second Afghan War. In 1880, Britain fought its first war with the Boers. That is just one decade – and one could make a similar list for the 1880s and 1890s which would include major conflicts in the Sudan, Burma, Matabeleland and China, culminating in the Boer War and the Boxer Rebellions as the century drew to its close. But just as the British – who saw numberless troubles in their colonies or would-be colonies in 1848 – could claim they survived the Year of Revolutions without incident, so the free-trading Manchester Liberals could imagine that their imperial revenues came to them unstained with blood; or at least, to put it a little less melodramatically, without a strong navy and an adequate army on land to defend, where necessary, British interests.

Throughout the latter part of the nineteenth century, Britain was basically a sea-power, and the navy took priority over manpower. In terms, though, of political trouble for Gladstone's government, the army was more to the forefront of attention. While it came unstuck over the question of expenditure on the army and the navy – 'the critical factor in the decision to dissolve Parliament' in 1874 – much parliamentary time in the earlier sessions – which Gladstone and his Liberal backbenchers would like to have devoted to Ireland, to educational matters, to reform of the tax system – was taken up with army organisation.[7]

The impetus for many of these reforms came not in the first instance from the back benches of the House of Commons, but from the Press. It saw in the victorious Prussian army overrunning France a well-trained machine where officers were chosen on merit, rather than because they could afford to buy their positions. And how did the Prussian officer material achieve the necessary range of skills? Why, through an effectively organized system of education in which the government took an active interest. If any one thing in 1870 emphasized the moribund character of the aristocratic system in Britain, was it not the system of purchase? Abolish it, and Britain might become as efficiently meritocratic as the Germans!

What the newspapers really wanted was not to build up an escalation of arms, leading eventually to a European Armageddon in the trenches – though we can see this was the eventual consequence of making the army more 'efficient'. What the newspapers, and the

HATHERLEY E. CARDWELL R. LOWE CLARENDON

Radical backbenchers, wanted was to strike a blow against the aristocracy, who ran the army.

Gladstone on this as in many other areas of life was double-minded. This isn't the same as hypocrisy, but the

NE'S FIRST CABINET 1868

GRANVILLE   H.CHILDERS   C.J.GOSCHEN   J.BRIGHT   ARGYLL   KIMBERLEY HARTINGTON
C.FORTESCUE   H.A.BRUCE   W.E.GLADSTONE

Gladstone's first cabinet at the National Liberal Club in London. Gladstone's administration of 1868–74 is seen by us as his first. It is abundantly evident from his diaries, however, that he thought of it as his one and only chance of leading a government. It is only hindsight which enables us to see this as the first Liberal government – to be followed in 1874 by a Conservative government. The two-party system as understood by modern political historians was being born.

two can be confused. When Ruskin accused Gladstone of being a 'leveller', he elicited the reply, 'Oh, dear no! I am nothing of the sort. I am a firm believer in the aristocratic principle – the rule of the best. I am an out-and-out *inequalitarian*' – a confession, we read, 'which Ruskin treated with intense delight, clapping his hands triumphantly'.[8]

As the son of a Liverpool merchant who had been to Eton and married into the landed gentry – the Glynne family – Gladstone lived at Hawarden the life of an aristocrat: a huge house, and many acres, and the income from farm rents and coal mines. His brother likewise lived like a Highland laird at their great house, Fasque, in Aberdeenshire. His entire life, except when in the House of Commons, or wandering the streets of London to rescue prostitutes whom he engaged in interminable conversations about the state of their soul, was spent in a country-house world.

The man whom he placed in charge of reforming the army was Edward Cardwell, like himself a Peelite, like himself the son of a Liverpool merchant. There were a number of reasons why his reforms, embodied in the Army Enlistment Act (1870) and the Army Regulation Act (1871), were of very limited efficacy.[9] First he wanted to redress the balance of troops by reducing the colonial garrisons and basing the army in Britain. This measure, overwhelmingly popular with Northern grocers because of the money it saved, did not work out in practice. By February 1879 there were eighty-two battalions abroad and only fifty-nine at home, for the simple reason that, the Fenian threat in Ireland apart, there were few reasons for troops being in Britain and many – during an Ashanti or a Zulu war – for them being abroad.

Of all the aspects of military reform to capture Press attention, public interest and parliamentary time, it was the system of purchase which was the most contentious. And like so many reforms imposed by politicians on a non-political class, it actually had only partial effect, since officers went on selecting members of the 'officer class', regardless of whether their pips and coronets had been bought or awarded gratis. Cardwell was adamant that he was not attempting a class war. 'It is a libel upon the old aristocracy to say that they are ever behindhand in any race which is run in an open arena, and in which ability and industry are the only qualities which can insure success,' he told Parliament in March 1871. But after three months in which his diehard opponents had questioned every clause of his Bill, and after they had filibustered in committee, he complained to Gladstone,

'there sits below the gangway on our side a plutocracy – who have no real objection to Purchase – and are in truth more interested in its maintenance than the Gentlemen opposite'. He referred to the Whig aristocrats. 'They say in private that they want something *more* for the money involved; that something being the removal of the Duke of Cambridge: – while in truth they wish to purchase an aristocratic position for personal connections, who would never obtain it otherwise.'[10]

It is a strange fact, but the purchase of commissions had already been made illegal in 1809, except where regulated by royal warrant. When, after months of parliamentary time had been wasted, Cardwell's Bill had been rejected by the Lords, Gladstone cancelled the warrant. 'It was a brilliant manoeuvre,' says Lord Jenkins: but it wasn't very brilliant. The government had to pay out £8 million in compensation to officers who suffered from the measure.[11]

Although Gladstone was a devout monarchist, and a believer in the Church of England, he could not compete with Disraeli as a royal flatterer. The period of Gladstone's greatest triumph coincided with the Queen's decline in public esteem, and she would not have been unaware of this. In 1874, when Gladstone was so unexpectedly defeated, she was able to express relief that 'It shows that the country is not *Radical* . . . what a good sign this large Conservative majority is of the state of the country.'[12] 'How far the monarchy really was in danger in 1868–72 no one can say for certain,' said Lord Blake in his Romanes lecture, 'Gladstone, Disraeli and Queen Victoria'. 'But if it was, much of the credit for removing the danger goes to Disraeli.' Some of the credit, too, must go to the republicans. Although some of the working classes were Radicals or republicans, most were not. Those who attempted to stir up republican sympathy seemed a little too slick, a little too like metropolitan sophisticates or pushy, rising plutocrats.

The rich young Radical Sir Charles Dilke (1843–1911), now Liberal MP for Chelsea, was openly republican, as was his fellow Radical Joseph Chamberlain (1836–1914), not yet an MP, both destined to be bright stars in the late Victorian political sky. The Queen had been a virtual recluse since being widowed, and refused to perform even simple public duties such as the State Opening of Parliament. She did so in 1871 solely because they were about to debate royal allowances, and then only on four more occasions in the next thirty years. *What Does She Do With It?* was a popular pamphlet, anonymously published but written by G.O. Trevelyan, another young Radical. (It rightly opined that the Queen was squirrelling away money given to her from the Civil List, amassing a private fortune from public funds, the basis of the colossal personal wealth of the present British royal family.)

The young Radicals were representative of a widely held and modern view of life. They wanted to be rid of the Queen. They had no time for the Church. They were unlikely to be impressed either by the Queen or by her heir.

Bertie had been obliged to appear as a witness in the scandalous Mordaunt divorce case in 1870 – narrowly avoiding being cited as a co-respondent. The Queen asked Gladstone to 'speak to him'. 'I cannot help continually revolving the question of the Queen's invisibility,' Gladstone told his colonial secretary Lord Granville. Speaking 'in rude and general terms, the Queen is invisible and the Prince of Wales is not respected'.[13] Then in December 1871 Bertie went down with enteric fever. It was approaching the tenth anniversary of his father's death when he nearly died himself. The illness did something, temporarily, to restore the fortunes of the monarchy in the eyes of Press and public. The Duke of Cambridge approached Gladstone and they arranged for a Thanksgiving Service in St Paul's Cathedral on 27 February 1872 which made one of those royal spectacles which the British public enjoy.

Gladstone genuinely believed that the times were out of joint, and that he had been given a golden chance, with his triumphant election victory of 1868, to bring real changes to pass, changes which would be based on justice and which would make life fairer for more people. He had swallowed his Anglican pride and realized that Ireland would never be pacified so long as the law appeared not to recognize that the majority of the Irish were Catholics. The Irish Church Bill of 1869 disestablished the Anglican Church in Ireland, making it one Christian denomination among others. The Irish Land Act of the following year was a step towards giving Irish peasant farmers freedom and independence. The introduction of the Secret Ballot in 1872 was a protection of the independence and liberty of voters. The civil service was made more open, with the possibility of posts being advertised and competed for by likely candidates.

The 1870 Education Act provided for education to be available for everyone under thirteen – but of course it was years before enough schools were built, or teachers recruited, and secondary education was still limited to the middle and upper classes. The Act did not provide free education: everyone had to pay for a place at one of the 'board schools' which it created, unless they could establish their poverty.

By 1874 the radical programme of Gladstone's government had run out of energy, as had Gladstone himself. After a number of setbacks – a defeat in a Commons vote over the Irish universities, a government defeat in a by-election (Stroud) – he declared that he wanted a dissolution of Parliament. As one last fling at popularity, he went to the hustings with the promise to abolish income tax, but the Conservatives won the election with a majority of 83 seats, and Gladstone's first administration was over. Since he was sixty-five years old, it would have been reasonable to suppose that as well as being his first, it would also be his last. He was able to devote the first year of his retirement as prime minister to the subject which interested him most: religion.

Chapter Twenty

The Side of the Angels

On Low Sunday, 1873, a new curate arrived in Wapping, to serve at the mission church, St Peter's, London Docks. He was Lincoln Stanhope Wainwright, the son of an old military family (his father was ADC to Lt General Sir Willoughby Cotton), educated at Marlborough and Wadham College, Oxford, and now aged twenty-six. He was to spend the remaining fifty-six years of his life in this slum parish. He never took a holiday. He hardly ever thereafter slept a night out of Wapping. He led a life which, compared with the comfortable world into which he had been born, was one of extraordinary austerity. He slept on a straw mattress in an uncarpeted room.

Drink was an obvious narcotic to numb the hell of Wapping life. Children grew up with drunken parents, 'with brothers and sisters already deep in sin, and abroad thieves and prostitutes a little older than themselves'.[1] The pubs of the parish doubled as brothels for the sailors – Greeks, Malays, Lascars, Dutch, Portuguese, Spanish, French, Austrians – who crowded the cobbled streets, and 'there were frequent fights between foreign and English sailors about the girls with whom they were keeping company'.

No one who came to this exotic part of London could fail to be impressed by the fact that this squalid, wicked and poverty-stricken square mile yet 'contains one of the main supplies of London's wealth and commerce, as well as one of its most curious sights, the London Docks. The extensive basins, in which may be seen the largest ships in the world; the immense warehouses which contain the treasures of every quarter of the globe – wool, cotton, tea, coffee, tobacco, skins, ivory; the miles of vaults filled with wines and spirits; the thousands of persons employed – clerks, customs officers, artisans, labourers, lightermen, and sailors – make the Docks a world of itself, as well as a cosmopolitan rendezvous and emporium.'[2]

When Wainwright arrived as Charles Lowder's curate, he was shown into St Peter's church and 'it was far beyond what, ritualist as I was, I had been accustomed to'.[3] The first generation of the Oxford Movement or High Church revival – Newman, Pusey, Keble – had been concerned primarily with doctrine: much of that doctrine, such as the impossibility of reducing the number of Anglican bishoprics in Ireland since Anglicanism was the one true Church, now seems esoteric to us. These founding fathers of the Movement would have seemed, to all outward appearances, indistinguishable from Low Churchmen or Broad Churchmen when conducting the liturgy. In the next generation, however, High Churchmen were, very gradually, to adopt customs which came to be known as Ritualist. Instead of standing at the north end of the Communion table, they stood facing east, as a symbol of the fact that the Eucharist was Christ's banquet to be celebrated in the (New) Jerusalem. They lit candles on the Holy Table. Some wore coloured stoles over their surplices. Others wore full Eucharistic vestments.

Gustav Dore's depiction of the Bluegate Fields in the East End of London in 1874 has a surreal quality but the poverty of the slums was shockingly real.

"He makes religion a tragedy, and the movements of his muscles a solemn ceremony."

☞ *Caricature of the great 'ritualist' priest, Father Alexander Heriot Mackonochie. The Ritualist movement was, as Canon Scott Holland was later to remark, 'the recovery in the slums by the Oxford movement of what it had lost in the university . . . It wore poverty as a cloak, and lived the life of the suffering and the destitute. It was irresistible in its élan, in its pluck, in its thoroughness, in its buoyancy, in its self-abandonment, in its laughter, in its devotion. Nothing could hold it. It won, in spite of all that could be done by authorities in high places, or by rabid Protestant mobs to drive it under.' Customs which before the 1874 Public Worship Regulation Act had been the esoteric preserve of a handful of exotic slumshrines had become, within a generation, the normal practice of Anglicans.*

Whether these customs were permissible to the clergy of the Church of England was a matter of dispute, depending on how you interpreted the rubric in the Book of Common Prayer.

Some would maintain, accurately, that vestments, incense, altar-lights and other elaborations of ritual *were* practised in the reign of Edward VI. What could not be denied is that in the middle years of Queen Victoria these observances became popular. The churches where these rituals were practised tended to be the poorer parishes.

Queen Victoria hated the High Church ritualists and continued to practice her own distinctive blend of Presbyterianism and semi-Shinto cult of the dead. She is seen here at Whippingham Church, Isle of Wight.

The clergy who laid on the incense-drowned, candle-lit ceremonials brought colour, mystery, a sense of the numinous, into the lives of people who had nothing. But moreover, they were visibly men, like Lowder, like Wainwright, like Alexander Heriot Mackonochie at St Alban's, Holborn, who were themselves prepared to embrace poverty and to fight the poor's battles for them. They had absorbed the Catholicism of F.D. Maurice, which saw that in order to worship Christ, who became man – and a poor man at that – it was necessary for the Church not merely to preach orthodoxy from its pulpits but to engage with the lives of those most victimized and oppressed by the capitalist experiment: the urban poor.

No doubt it was this fact which, combined with gut anti-Catholic prejudice, made the 'Ritualists' so disturbing a presence for the Victorians. As early as the 1850s at St Barnabas, Pimlico, mobs had burst into the church to protest at the allegedly Romish goings-on, hissing in the aisles and rattling at the chancel gates.[4]

You would have thought that an attempt by Anglican clergy to engage with the lives of the poor in an imaginative and unselfish way might have received support, even from those who found the 'smells and bells' bizarre. Archibald Campbell Tait (1811–82), a Rugbeian Liberal, was certainly inclined to reach accommodation with the Ritualists when he was bishop of London. He yearned to bring Christianity to the poor – he it was who insisted on services at Westminster Abbey being free and open to the public. He built churches. He preached in omnibus yards, in Covent Garden Market and in ragged schools. Had the Ritualists been prepared to tone down some of

their departures from the liturgical norm, Tait's inclination was to sympathize with their pastoral devotion.[5] Nine hundred people came to hear Tait preach when he and his wife visited the survivors of the cholera epidemic of 1866 and to speak at the newly consecrated St Peter's, London Docks.[6] But during Disraeli's brief tenure of the prime ministership (1868) Tait had succeeded Longley as archbishop of Canterbury, and on Disraeli's return in 1874 Tait found himself as primate while a Parliament now composed of a handful of Jews and atheists as well as many Nonconformists brought on to the statute-book the Public Worship Regulation Act, forbidding certain ritual acts – the mixing of wine and water in the chalice, the wearing of Eucharistic vestments – which emphasized the Catholic nature of the Church of England and seemed to some Protestants to be letting in Popery by the back door.

Unlike Gladstone, Disraeli was not an ecclesiastical obsessive: indeed he felt somewhat out of his depth when Church was being discussed.[7] Quite why Disraeli should have chosen to spend much of his first session introducing this Bill remains something of a mystery, but perhaps he saw it as a comparatively easy way of bringing cheer to his monarch. Queen Victoria was obsessed by the Ritualists.

Needless to say it was Church ritual to which she objected. She had an instinctual fear that the Church of England was becoming too high for her – 'I am very nearly a Dissenter – or rather more a Presbyterian – in my feelings, so very Catholic do I feel we are.'[8] And though she believed Bismarck had gone too far in his

The Village Choir by Thomas Webster depicts the Church of England as the young Thomas Hardy knew it, and which would be changed utterly by urban innovations such as Ritualism or Evangelicalism.

persecution of the Catholics, 'they are dreadfully aggressive people who must be put down – just as our Ritualists'.[9]

The sovereign was not alone in her detestation of the Ritualists. Pamphlets and sermons by the score rolled from the presses denouncing them for their crypto-Romanism, their 'mass in masquerade', their advocacy of auricular confession ('the enemy of domestic peace'), their links with 'the bondage of Judaism' (this from the dean of Carlisle, who believed their sacerdotalism to derive from the Jews); there were even those who saw Father Lowder and Father Wainwright and their friends as 'the enemy of national independence'.

Some Ritualists, a minority, were aspirant Roman Catholics or in two minds about the question. For most of them, it was not an issue. For such as Mackonochie or Lowder, the point was, first, to bring Christ to the poor, next – in reaction to the intrusive parliamentary interference – to preserve the 'doctrines, rights, and liberties of the Church'.[10] The 1874 Act provided the Ritualist movement with its 'martyrs'. Five clergymen were imprisoned for refusing to comply with the requirements of the Act, Arthur Tooth of Hatcham, 22 January 1877 to 17 February 1877; Thomas Pelham Dale of St Vedast's, Foster Lane, in the city of London, 30 October 1880 to 24 December 1880; R.W. Enraght of Bordesley, Birmingham, 27 November 1880 to 17 January 1881; S.F. Green of St John's, Miles Platting, Manchester, who had much the longest imprisonment – 19 March 1881 to 4 November 1882; and Bell Cox of St Margaret's, Liverpool, 5 to 21 May 1887. The British, in their persecution of Ritualists, had found their own version of the Prussian *Kulturkampf*. Nor can one forget that these laws were brought into effect when the Contagious Diseases Act defined any woman detained by the police in garrison towns as a common prostitute; when many forms of sexual 'deviancy' were outlawed; when the 'rights' of married women were on a par with those of children and horses; when most adults still had no vote.

For those, perhaps, who actually knew the Ritualist heroes, these political points counted for less than the witness of their lives and deaths. Charles Lowder was the first secular priest known by his people as 'Father' – a custom subsequently imitated by Roman Catholics. The people of Docklands called him 'the Father', 'Father' or just 'Dad': he had quite simply made the island parish feel like a family. The funerals of these priests tell us so much. When Lowder died, exhausted, in September 1880, Wainwright preached at his Requiem from the text 'Weep not!' No one, the preacher included, could keep the injunction.

Of course, if this had simply been a matter of the aesthetic and liturgical preferences of a few churchgoers a century ago, it would not have been worth the space we have devoted to it. But it was more than that. Disraeli's government introduced these anti-Ritualistic measures in part, surely, as a consequence of something which had nothing to do with a few High Churchmen in the slums.

It was a self-defining gesture, in response to what had been happening in Europe over the previous five years. No one was more conscious of this than Gladstone himself.

As a High Churchman who went to church every day of his life, Gladstone was dismayed by the Public Worship Regulation Act, partly because he sympathized with the religion of the Ritualists – though it was not quite his type of Anglicanism – chiefly because he distrusted the Erastian thinking behind the legislation. All his adult life he had been considering the relationship between Church and state. His change of heart over Ireland, his wish to liberate the Irish Catholics from the implication that they *ought* to be Anglicans, had lost him many friends among the Irish Protestant Ascendancy, but he had done what he deemed to be right. There were those Anglicans who saw the 1874 Act as an interference by the Secular Power in what should be a sacred sphere. They began to talk of not merely the Irish but also the whole English Church cutting its ties with the state – disestablishing itself.

Gladstone did not want this, but, keen student of Dante that he was, he knew that this conflict between Church and state, pope and emperor, ran through European history like a fault-line. Dante, who believed all power came from God, consigned to hell those popes and ecclesiastics who seized for themselves powers which should be exercised by the emperors. Gladstone really did believe, with the majority of thinking Anglicans, that his Church, for all its faults, was closer to the ideal Catholicism of Dante than was the Church of Pope Pius IX. That is, he thought you could be a Catholic without owing obedience to a pope who, in the theological sphere, peddled the blasphemous notion of his own infallibility, and in the political sphere had so far left behind him the liberalism of his youth as to support such dreadful tyrannies as the kingdom of Naples, whose prisons and police-cruelty had so shocked Gladstone when he saw them.

When writing his pamphlet, *The Vatican Decrees in their Bearing on Civil Allegiance*, Gladstone would have found himself thinking of the wreckage of broken friendships with which his circle was littered as a result of the many English conversions to Rome. It is a curious work for a man who regarded it as his prime political mission to pacify Ireland. For if disestablishing the Irish Church was calculated to alienate the Protestants of that island, the *Vatican Decrees* pamphlet was calculated to offend the Catholics. It questions whether, after the First Vatican Council and the doctrine of Papal Infallibility, the Catholic could be a completely loyal citizen of a non-Catholic state. It ends with a peroration whose meaning in intellectual terms is opaque, but whose patriotic music is unmistakable. It is frankly rabble-rousing, and Gladstone can only have been pleased that his pamphlet sold 145,000 copies, with a large number also buying its sequel, *Vaticanism*, in the following year of 1875.

Gladstone's wild pamphlets finally brought his friendship with Manning to a close, and drew from Newman the graceful rebuke in his *A Letter Addressed to his Grace the Duke of Norfolk on Occasion of Mr Gladstone's Recent Expostulation*: 'If I am obliged to bring religion into after-dinner toasts . . . I shall drink – to the Pope, if you please – still, to Conscience first, and to the Pope afterwards.'[11]

Yet the gracefulness does not really get round the difficulty. If Gladstone was impugning the political loyalty of Catholics, then his pamphlets were unpardonable. But very many Catholics knew what Pius IX and his more extreme supporters would make of Newman's after-dinner toast; and many knew that though they chose to remain in the Church for reasons of spiritual solidarity, Catholics of Newman's colouring were, to put it mildly, dismayed by the infallible pretensions and political posturings of the Papacy. After all, this bizarre debate stirred up by Gladstone was taking place at a period of history when many Europeans, far from worrying about the claims of infallible popes, Presbyterian monarchs or ritualist saints, were asking the more searching question, whether religion itself was true.

In the year that the pope declared his own infallibility Darwin published *The Descent of Man, and Selection in Relation to Sex*, with its humbling conclusion: 'Man still bears in his bodily frame the indelible stamp of his lowly origin.'[12] There are certain passages in this book which make disturbing reading for us in the twenty-first century. One of the core beliefs of the Western world, post-National Socialism and its *Götterdämmerung*, is in the equality of all the races of humankind. The easy way in which Darwin assumes the superiority of Northern and Western and white human beings to those of other climates and hemispheres will bring a blush, or an embarrassed smile, to many readers today. There is something, for us, chilling in Darwin's meditations on the contrast between those 'Eastern barbarians' who overran the Roman Empire, and the 'savages' who wasted away at the prospect of British colonization. He cheerfully speaks of the 'inferior vitality of mulattoes'.[13] Savages have 'low morality', insufficient powers of reasoning to recognize many virtues, and 'weak power of self command'.[14] Darwin accepts Malthus's view that barbarous races reproduced at a lower rate than civilized ones and he appears (he who so abominated the cruelty of Brazilian slave-owners in *The Voyage of a Naturalist*) to believe that acts of genocide, if perpetrated by the British, were somehow part of the Natural Process:

When Tasmania was first colonised the natives were roughly estimated by some at 7,000 and by others at 20,000. Their number was soon greatly reduced, chiefly by fighting with the English and with each other. After the famous hunt by all the colonists, when the remaining natives delivered themselves up to the government, they consisted of 120 individuals who were in 1832 transported to Flinders Island ... The grade of civilisation seems to be a most important element in the success of competing nations.[15]

This is the element which the twenty-first-century reader would find most shocking in Darwin. Most Victorian readers would be untroubled by the notion that European races were superior to those in other parts of the world. Had not Tennyson spoken for all of them by stating, 'Even the black Australian, dying, dreams he will return a white'?[16]

What upset Darwin's contemporaries was the possibility that evolutionary theory eliminated the need for God as an hypothesis. 'The declining sense of the miraculous,' as Lecky called it in 1863, 'was pushed further into decline by Darwin and the public acceptance of evolution. By removing special creation of species, Darwin removed the need for very numerous interferences with physical laws.'[17] Those words are by a Church historian. We should now see, as the late Victorians in general began to see, that even to talk about 'laws' of nature – if by that is implied any external agency or mind behind matter or grand Designer of the universe – is to talk in metaphor. Things happen in certain ways. Darwin's patience in assembling evidence for why he believed evolution worked by a process of sexual selection is untainted by rhetoric or noise. His is a quietly reasonable tone of voice. The metaphysical implications of what he so slowly and so gently worked out caused him grief. His disciple Huxley and others could shout these implications through a megaphone, but not Darwin. It makes him all the more deadly as a voice to undermine traditional theism.

Many Christians absorbed Darwinism, or other versions of evolutionary theory. Perhaps theologians were, in the decades after Darwin, more inclined to stress God's indwelling in the creation than his part in its origin, but men and women continued to go to church. Nonconformism, with its heavy reliance upon a literal interpretation of Scripture, might have been more vulnerable to the assaults of scepticism if it had numbered among its adherents more Herbert Spencers, George Eliots or Edmund Gosses. It is unlikely, however, that

the American evangelists Dwight L. Moody or Ira D. Sankey, who visited Britain in 1874–5, found many in their large audiences whose evening lamp shed its rays on the pages of Feuerbach or Darwin. Their meetings took the form familiar in our own day to those who have watched such American revivalists as Dr Billy Graham.

Of course there will always be mockers. 'A London Physician' wrote a pamphlet claiming that 'The People Go Mad Through Religious Revivals.' 'Alas! judged by the low standard of an American ranter, Mr Moody is a third-rate star,' wrote this acerbic, anonymous medical gentleman. 'As for Mr Sankey, the friend who can sing, his voice is decidedly bad, and, like all worn-out singers, he endeavours to conceal this by startling alternations of high and low notes.'

Similar sneering was no doubt directed to the activities of William Booth (1829–1912), who started as an Anglican layman, became a Methodist lay preacher, and then adopted the uniform and style of a musical army – 'The Salvation Army'. 'Its impact upon slums can easily be exaggerated,' says a modern historian of this well-meaning movement, established in 1878.[18] We need not be so dismissive, even though William Booth's most famous rhetorical question – 'Why should the Devil have all the best tunes?' – must puzzle anyone with an ear. To compare the hurdy-gurdy noises made by the Sally Army with Haydn's masses, or even with the conventional Anglican psalm-settings, would suggest that the Devil was in fact comparatively lacking in musical advantage. The Salvation Army particularized a general tendency among the many movements to improve the lot of the Victorian poor, whether these worthy efforts were sacred or secular. In general, there was no evidence of the populace at large taking kindly to schemes of human improvement. Improve their houses, their conditions of work, their drains and, if you must, their doctors – this seemed to be the mood: but hold back from the rather less attractive wish to improve *them*. This surely is what distinguishes the liberal from the conservative temperament throughout the ages and helps to explain, in a time when there was such continuing inequality and such evident hardship in some quarters, why electors chose to return Conservative governments.

There was also the fact that in Disraeli the Conservatives had a leader of consummate charm, wit and lightness of touch. This by no means suggests, because his surface shone, that he was a man of no depths. Over the religious questions of the day, for example, Disraeli was in his way as keen to preserve the orthodoxies as Gladstone, though less anxious to be seen

"CRITICS."

(*Who* have not exactly "*failed in literature and art.*")—See Mr. D.'s New Work.

Mr. G-Ð-s-t-ne. "*Hm!—Flippant!*"   Mr. D-s-r-li. "*Ha!—Prosy!*"

Gladstone and Disraeli depicted as rival authors by John Tenniel. To savour the spiritual distance between the two men, you have only to turn from Gladstone's speeches on Ireland, quoted in Hansard, or his pamphlets on Ritualism and the Vatican decrees, to Disraeli's novel Lothair *(1870). Gladstone wrote and spoke like a mad clergyman – earnest, excitable, unstoppably prolix. Disraeli's novel covers much the same ground. Its themes are the predatory character of modern Catholicism, with a sub-plot involving Italian radical nationalists and Fenian terrorists. Its settings are just those grand London dinnertables and country houses with which Gladstone and Disraeli were both familiar. But* Lothair *has fizz, and like the best satire it delights in what it mocks.*

like the Pharisees praying in the marketplace. Though he quipped, 'I am the blank page between the Old and the New Testament'[19] he was in fact a simple Church of England man, as far as observance was in question. As to belief – when he addressed the dons and undergraduates of Oxford in 1863, who were agonizing about whether humanity was of the apes or the angels – 'My Lord, I am on the side of the Angels.'[20] Disraeli's wit, in such marked contrast with the prolixity and the intense seriousness with which Gladstone wished to be seen to take not only the world, but himself, opened up a fascinating gulf in the politics of the 1870s. If Gladstone's first administration was the first really Liberal government, Disraeli's second – of 1874 – was the first clear Conservative government in the modern understanding of the term. The electorate were choosing not simply between two great coalitions, new-formed into political machines; nor yet alone between two of the giants of British political history; but, as it were, between two visions of life itself.

Chapter Twenty-One

The End of Lord Beaconsfield

Disraeli was sixty-nine years old when he formed his second Cabinet, and he was destined to die a year after leaving office. He was never in the best of health as prime minister, especially in the winter months when he was subject to severe bronchitis. His premiership, then, was inevitably a series of inspired energetic bursts rather than a sustained marathon or a carefully considered programme. In so far as this government of 1874–80 did have a long-lasting consequence, it was to confirm Britain as 'an Asiatic power' rather than a European one. The phrase is typical of Disraeli's playfulness but it was meant. He would no doubt have liked to make Britain more influential in Europe, but after the triumph of Prussia in 1870, and the establishment of the *Dreikaiserbund* – the alliance of the three emperors of Austria-Hungary, Russia and Germany – Britain was condemned to a marginal role in Europe.

In the first major foreign policy decision of his administration, however, Disraeli showed a decisiveness, and a flair, which were all his own – and which it is difficult to imagine any other statesman of the time achieving with such expedition and style.

The Suez Canal had been opened in 1869. It cut the journey from Britain to India by several weeks and thousands of miles, and by 1875 four-fifths of its traffic was British. In the event of an invasion of India by Russia through Afghanistan (an ever-present possibility in British paranoia if not always in Russian foreign policy), or if there were another Mutiny, the Suez Canal could carry troops from England far more quickly than the old route round the Cape.

In 1870, when Lord Granville was foreign secretary, there was a chance of the British government buying either the Egyptian khedive's interest in the Canal Company, or the whole concern. The French engineer, Ferdinand de Lesseps, who had constructed the canal and founded the Suez Canal Company, was happy to negotiate either arrangement but, incredibly, the British could not see what advantage would be gained. In 1875 Khedive Ismail was again very short of money and was looking to dispose of the 176,602 ordinary shares (out of a total of 400,000 in the Suez Canal Company as a whole). Frederick Greenwood, editor of the *Pall Mall Gazette*, was told by the financier Henry Oppenheimer that the khedive was negotiating with two French groups. Greenwood told the foreign secretary, the young 15th Earl of Derby, who did not at all like the idea of the purchase.[1]

Disraeli himself now intervened. The Cabinet opposed him, but he overruled them. Undoubtedly his friendship with the Rothschilds helped. Disraeli's secretary, Monty Corry, went to see Lord (Lionel) Rothschild in his office at New Court, Lincoln's Inn, and the banker advanced the British government £4 million. He charged a commission of $2\frac{1}{2}$ per cent and made £100,000 for his firm out of the deal. Those were the days before 'insider trading' was made a sin. Henry

21 Disraeli photographed at Osbourne House, Isle of Wight, two years before he was decisively thrown out of office by the election of 1880. Late in his second term Disraeli was heard to say 'Power! It has come to me too late . . . There were days when, on waking, I felt I could move dynasties and governments; but that has passed away.'

Cartoon by Tenniel showing the British Lion having secured the safety of 'the key to India' by Disraeli's acquisition of Egypt's shares in the Suez Canal, 1876.

THE LION'S SHARE.

"GARE À QUI LA TOUCHE!"

Oppenheimer with his syndicate 'was the speculator who made most out of the deal', buying shares before the government purchase was public knowledge. The Rothschilds themselves however did not speculate on the Stock Exchange with their secret knowledge.[2] Nor, as was suggested, did Natty Rothschild – a member of Parliament – directly profit from the deal negotiated by his family's bank.[3] (A Mr Bigger alleged that Nathaniel Rothschild was in breach of the Act on Privilege, 22 Geo. III, c. 45, but he was neither a partner in the firm, nor privy to the deal.)

It was paid for by the chancellor of the Exchequer, Sir Stafford Northcote, passing an Exchequer Bonds Bill, raising £4,080,000 from the Post Office Savings Bank at $3^1/_2$ per cent; and by raising income tax to 4d. in the £ – a 'penal' level, as has been said by a later member of the Rothschild family.[4] It was, however, one of the best investments ever made by a British government. In purely financial terms, the profits were huge. The shares were bought for £22 10s. 4d. per share and had risen, by January 1876, to £34 12s. 6d. By 31 March 1935 they were worth approximately £528 per share.

Even more important than the paper valuation of the shares, however, was the symbolic importance of Disraeli having secured British control of the Canal Company. As Cairns, lord chancellor, put it to Disraeli, 'It is now the *Canal and India*; there is no such thing now to us as

India alone. India is any number of cyphers; but the Canal is the unit that makes these cyphers valuable.'[5] The Canal was a symbol of British imperial dominance of the world. It is apt that the end of that dominion should have been signalled by Colonel Nasser, in 1956, nationalizing the Canal. British impotence to reclaim it made unambiguous her reduced power and status among the nations. It had become in any case meaningless since the loss of India in 1948 and the gradual dismantling of the Empire. But Disraeli's purchase was the beginning of that period – which extended perhaps until the Second World War – when British political power could be defined in terms of overseas dominion.

Discarding (as she coquettishly allowed him to do) the convention by which the prime minister and his Sovereign conversed in the third person, Disraeli wrote to the Fairy (his special nickname for her), 'It is just settled; you have it, Madam!'

The next spectacle, which did not even require the painful expedient of putting up the income tax, was to make the diminutive, pudgy little Fairy into an empress. Without so much as consulting the Liberals, let alone debating the matter in Parliament, Disraeli slipped into the Queen's Speech in 1876 that the Prince and Princess of Wales would be visiting India – and by the way, from now on the Queen would be known as the Empress of India: Victoria R.I.[6] At a time when the monarch had

Edward, Prince of Wales, enters the Suez Canal at Port Said on the royal ship Victoria & Albert, *en route to India, 1875.*

never exercised smaller actual power, she invested herself with a title which would have embarrassed her despotic predecessors. If, to some, the phrase 'Empress of India' was more suggestive of a pig or a railway engine than a constitutional monarch, it made her happy, and it helped to define her country's self-image during that uncharacteristic period – again, lasting until the Second World War – when it thought of itself in terms of Imperial pomp.

How does one define an empire, or imperialism? Empires of the past – Persian, Roman, Byzantine – tended to be continuous land-masses, taking in differing lands, language and racial groups, all administered with some ultimate reference to a centralized autocracy. Clearly the 'British Empire' could not conform to this pattern, scattered as it was all over the globe. What astonishes posterity, considering the comparatively primitive state of communications in the nineteenth century, was how cohesive this 'empire' managed to be. Germany, France and Belgium continued in rivalry with the British to lay claim to various parts of Africa and Asia as part of their colonial dominion.

This is all rather different from the old empires which, like dozing dragons nested too close together, alarmingly gave off signals of discontent with one another throughout the period – namely the Austro-Hungarian, the Russian and the Ottoman empires.

This is not the place to attempt a full analysis of the history or extent of the Ottoman Empire, but its decline – the decline of the power of Turkey – is the dominant political fact in the last quarter of the nineteenth century. We live today with its consequences. For

Gladstone and the Liberals, it was axiomatic that rebellion against the Ottoman Empire was a legitimate 'nationalist' aspiration. They thought that any group that wanted to declare its 'independence' of the sultan was like the Irish Home Rulers, and should be supported. Disraeli and the Conservatives took a more cautious approach, but they – together with the senior statesmen and diplomats of Russia, Germany and Austria-Hungary – saw it as their business to decide the future of the Ottoman Empire. They all accepted the Russian emperor's contemptuous definition of Turkey as 'the sick man of Europe'. They took it as axiomatic that the Ottoman Empire should be broken up, and if they did not have the Liberal belief in nationalism (for Bulgarians, Albanians, Bosnians, Egyptians *et al.*) they nonetheless believed that they could use the weakness of the Turks to seize these territories, or influence them.

Life in all these places was more poverty-stricken under the sultans; differing religions and racial traditions tended to live together more peaceably – *faute de mieux* – when Turkey was a Sick Man than when the Russians, the British and the Germans decided to effect a cure for the sickness. The 'cure' was administered from a position of complete ignorance of the actual conditions of life in the sultan's dominions, and, it need hardly be said, without consulting either the Turkish authorities or their subjects. The individual outbursts of fighting and discontent were seen entirely against a background of rivalry and fear between Russia and Austria-Hungary, with Count Andrássy, the Hungarian prime minister and Austro-Hungarian foreign minister (from December 1871 onwards), looking to Britain as his ally to shore up

The Power of the Demon *by Mihaly Zichy, 1878. This painting is an allegory on the war between Christian Europe and the Ottoman Empire; amongst the depicted are Emperor Alexander II, Emperor William I and Pope Pius IX, who died in the year it was painted.*

the Ottoman Empire and prevent the Russians fulfilling their dream – the occupation of Constantinople, the annexation of the empire. Russia was not merely looking for advantage of this kind. It was gripped by a quasi-religious Pan-Slavic fervour, so that the plight of the Serbs harassed by their Muslim neighbours became a matter of anxiety for the Great Russian Soul.

Perhaps if the Powers had not persisted in believing that there was an 'Eastern Question', a phrase which suggests that there might have been an Eastern answer, the consequences of collective failure would not have been so catastrophic. Count Andrássy, prime minister of Hungary, was right to foresee that 'if Bosnia-

Hercegovina should go to Serbia or Montenegro, or if a new state should be formed that we [i.e. Austria-Hungary] cannot prevent, then we should be ruined and should ourselves assume the role of the "Sick Man"'. The Magyar determination for separate nation states for Hungary would follow, and the collapse of the Habsburg Empire. No one can forget that the participants in these international discussions would all be plunged into world war by the assassination of Archduke Francis Ferdinand in Sarajevo by a Serbian terrorist in 1914, a conflagration which would destroy in turn the aspirations of Bismarck, the House of Hohenzollern, the Romanov dynasty in Russia and with it all that the Russian emperors believed

by civilization and religion. Hindsight can sometimes provide historians with a parlour-game: in this case it is difficult to see what could have turned the tides, given the ambitions and composition of the countries and statesmen concerned. We can see clearly enough what went wrong: but what might have prevented the disaster?

Money might be one answer. Probably there would have been no 'Eastern Question' had Turkey in the 1870s not been financially ruined, actually bankrupt. Foreign trade had suffered badly since the Crimean War. Turkey was largely non-industrialized. Eighteen and a half million people in the Ottoman Empire were employed during the 1870s in manufacturing cotton textiles, and their incomes gradually declined in competition with the industrialized nations.[7] Agriculture, though, fared better. Between 1840 and 1913, despite substantial declines in population and losses of land, exports increased fivefold.[8]

Britain increased her trade with the Ottoman Empire by 400 per cent in the decades after the Crimean War.[9] The Turks imported almost all their machinery, iron, coal and kerosene, and the sale of cotton, cereals, dyestuffs, silk, opium, dried fruit and nuts did not balance the books. The extravagance and fiscal incompetence of the sultans at this period is staggering.[10] Abd-ul-Aziz had 5,500 courtiers and servants, 600 horses, 200 carriages and a harem of 1,000 to 1,500 women. He built two palaces on the Bosphorus, Ciragan and Beylerbey. In 1874 over half of government expenditure was devoted to servicing external debt, and in 1875 the Ottoman government issued a declaration of bankruptcy.[11]

When the Balkan crisis – which we are about to describe – arose, Abd-ul-Aziz faced a profound discontent at home, demonstrations in the mosques and squares of Istanbul, and eventually deposition by a military coup. The army appointed Murat V as sultan. Abd-ul-Aziz, under house arrest in the Feriye Palace, was found dead on Sunday 4 June 1876 with his veins cut and one artery slashed, having committed suicide with a pair of nail-scissors.

The reign of Sultan Murat V lasted only a few months. His early manhood had been marked by intelligence and political acumen. He was seen as a potentially enlightened reformer, but the situation was such that he suffered an emotional collapse. It was given out that he was dead, though he actually lived until 29 August 1904, making several attempts to regain his throne.

The Cabinet next appointed Abd-ul-Hamit II, a thirty-four-year-old destined to be sultan for the next thirty-three years, until 1909.[12] He it was who had to face, in the first few years of his reign, the formidable task of coping with a war with Russia, a collapsed economy, unrest all over the Balkans, and international outrage in consequence of the Turkish treatment of these uprisings.

In the summer of 1875 a revolt by a few peasants in several small villages in Hercegovina began one of those waves of violence which have periodically disrupted the Balkans for the last thousand years. The cause of the riots was economic. The peasants had set upon collectors who demanded full payment of a sheep tax in spite of a failed harvest the previous year. The military were brought in. The deaths of Muslim peasants were ignored; those of the Christians were trumpeted as religious martyrdoms.[13]

Refugees started to flood into Serbia, Montenegro and Austria, many with exaggerated stories to tell, and the Porte was issued with an ultimatum from Count Andrássy – broadly supported by Britain: namely that tax-farming would be suppressed, and religious liberty guaranteed by the setting-up of a special commission composed of equal numbers of Christians and Muslims. This was followed by the Berlin Memorandum of the Dreikaiserbund, insisting on the inflammatory condition that Christian subjects of the sultan should be allowed to bear arms.

In July 1876 Montenegro – under the leadership of the swashbuckling adventurer Prince Nicholas – joined Serbia in declaring war on the Turks. (Sultan Murat with his incipient nervous breakdown had just been installed.) The Ottoman government, and the world, knew what this meant. Serbia was seen by the Russians, and by many Slavs in the Austro-Hungarian Empire, as the plucky little Christian country standing up against the infidel tyrant.

Disraeli's position, as British premier, differed from that of his foreign secretary Lord Derby and, to a lesser extent, that of his secretary for India, the increasingly influential Lord Salisbury. 'If the Russians had Constantinople' – this is Disraeli's view – 'they could at any time march their Army through Syria to the mouth of the Nile, and then what would be the use of our holding Egypt. Not even the command of the sea could help us under such circumstances . . . Our strength is on the sea. Constantinople is the Key of India, and not Egypt and the Suez Canal.'

Salisbury as the younger man felt Disraeli was fighting old battles and imagining, twenty years after the event, a re-enactment of the Crimean War. Derby – described by A.J.P. Taylor as 'the most isolationist

Caricature of Abd-ul-Hamit II, the Ottoman sultan responsible for the Bulgarian atrocities. The incident had all the ingredients of a story calculated to thrill and excite the British. 'If you want to drive John Bull mad,' said Fitzjames Stephen, 'the plan is to tickle (rather delicately – yet not too delicately) his prurience with good circumstantial accounts of "insults worse than death" inflicted on women, then throw in a good dose of Cross and Crescent, plus Civilization v Barbarism, plus a little "Civil and Religious liberty all over the world", & then you have him, as the Yankees say, "raging around like a bob-tailed bull in fly-time".'

Foreign Secretary that Great Britain has known',[14] wanted non-involvement at any cost. Events were to spiral, however, in such a way that British isolationism was no longer really possible.

The nationalist mood in the Balkans had spread across the Maritsa to Mount Rhodope, where the Christians fought against the Pomaks or Muslim Bulgars, fanatical devotees of Turkish rule. The village of Batak on the northern spurs of Rhodope was preparing to join forces against the Muslims when a force of Bashi-Bazouks (tribal irregulars) arrived there under the command of Achmet Aga of Dospat and his colleague Mohammed Aga of Dorkoro. In the course of the summer of 1876, the Christians had probably killed some 4,000 Muslims. Achmet Aga's forces of volunteers undoubtedly visited a merciless reprisal on the Christian villagers of Batak, though whether it was 'the most heinous crime that has

stained the history of the present century' (the words of the British commissioner) will probably depend on what you think of the massacres of tens of thousands in Napoleonic battles such as Austerlitz or Borodino; the deaths of 1 million Irish in the famine; the reprisals against 'innocent' Indians after the troubles of 1857–8 or the murder of thousands of Muslims in the previous years of Balkan conflict. A thousand Christians perished in the village church at Batak, the Bashi-Bazouks first firing through the windows, then tearing off the roof tiles and setting fire to the building with burning rags dipped in petroleum. Possibly 4,000 Bulgarian Christians died that summer, though the figure was soon multiplied to 15,000, 30,000 or even 100,000.[15]

This was one of those instances where British political life was fanned into a state of frenzy by a newspaper article: in this case in the *Daily News*, which first told an excited but morally disgusted British public of the 'Bulgarian atrocities'. In British political terms, there were two immediate consequences, one of tangential import to the surviving Bulgarian hill-villagers, the other a more purely British and local drama. First, then, it became all but impossible for Disraeli to maintain an openly Turcophile foreign policy without appearing to side with the rapists and pillagers in Achmet Aga's brutal army. Second, the arrival of the *Daily News* in the Temple of Peace at Hawarden convinced Gladstone that he must lay aside his theological researches into 'Future Retribution' – the uplifting task he had set himself in his retirement – and re-enter the political fray. Dizzy, after two years as a giant facing comparative pygmies in the Opposition, was once more to confront his old sparring partner: but a new Gladstone, a Gladstone even by the milder standards of later years transformed into something between an old-fashioned revivalist preacher and an entirely modern campaigning politician, taking the issue of the Bulgarian Atrocities to the people, and reaping mighty political advantage.

The Bulgarian news had come to him as a call from God to return to public life. He had been seized with one of his periodic fits of manic energy combined with psychosomatic illness. During his frenzy over the Vatican Decrees in 1874 he had suffered from diarrhoea. Now it was lumbago which afflicted him; but like other 'driven' persons, William Ewart Gladstone used periods of physical illness as a time of preparation for immense outpourings of energy. As soon as back-pain allowed, the old man – sixty-six – made his way to the Reading Room of the British Museum (did his eyes meet those of Karl Marx, engaged on the second volume of *Das Kapital*?) to check references and quotations. His spell of lumbago the previous week, which he had spent in bed at Hawarden, had been passed scribbling his pamphlet *The Bulgarian Horrors and the Question of the East*. On his completion of this inflammatory text he had shown it to Granville and Hartington. Though Granville persuaded him to delete some of the wilder passages, both he and Hartington must have realized that Gladstone was back in the political fray, intent – though out of Parliament and with no seat in the Commons – on seizing back the leadership and taking the party in the direction of radicalism, demagoguery and something akin to, if not actually related to, religious revivalism.

John Murray ordered a print-run of 2,000 copies of the pamphlet, and increased that to 24,000 by 7 September. By the end of September 200,000 copies of Murray's printing had been sold, with innumerable pirated and cut

versions in the newspapers. Anthony Trollope read it aloud to his family.[16] The pamphlet caught that mood of public indignation to which Disraeli in his cynicism had been deaf.

On the Saturday after his pamphlet appeared Gladstone spoke for an hour at Blackheath to a crowd of 10,000 people. 'When have I seen so strongly the relation between my public duties and the primary purposes for which God made and Christ redeemed the world?' he asked his diary. It was undoubtedly the religious inspiration of Gladstone's feelings which urged him on and which gave such electrifying power to his moral message.

Even Gladstone himself, however, could not have known quite how successful he was going to become as an orator and a populist. As he went round the country, speaking to huge crowds, the Queen could dismiss 'that half madman' as 'most reprehensible and mischievous ... shameful . . .' Meanwhile, events in the Balkans moved on.

The Sick Man of Europe was not so sick after all. The Bulgarian agitation was put down. The Montenegrin 'war' against the Turks resulted in defeat. The new young sultan might be short of cash, but he still administered a potentially powerful government and he had well-trained armies at his disposal. The British had been happy to believe this during the Crimean War. The Russians reawakened memories of that era by declaring war on Turkey on 24 April 1877. Cossack troops were soon visiting on Muslim villagers reprisals no less horrible than the massacre of Christians by Turkish irregulars the previous year. No English newspaper bothered to mention these new 'Bulgarian atrocities',[17] and the 'barbarity' of these Orthodox Christian soldiers did not prevent Gladstone escorting Madame Novikov from the platform at an anti-Turkish rally.

Disraeli's attitude to the Russian war was that, by showing military strength at once, Britain could force Russia into peace and hold her back from occupation of Constantinople. He sent Lord Salisbury – increasingly, his closest ally in the Cabinet – on a tour of European capitals to ensure support for the armed resistance to Russia if she could not be brought to the conference table. In November he addressed the Lord Mayor's banquet and said that Britain's resources for a righteous war were 'inexhaustible'.

Undoubtedly this bullish stance was popular with a large proportion of the British populace. If one section enjoyed working themselves into a frenzy about the Bulgarian horrors, another derived equal pleasure from the prospect of a war. Many, of course, would have enjoyed both prospects. Mass hysteria does not always follow logic. The term 'jingoism' was coined, based on 'The Great Macdermott's song':

> We don't want to fight, but, by Jingo if we do
> We've got the ships, we've got the men, we've got
> the money too.
> We've fought the Bear before, and while Britons
> shall be true,
> The Russians shall not have Constantinople.[18]*

Both Disraeli and Macdermott were wrong, as it happened. Britain didn't have 'the men' to mount an all-out war against Russia. Immediately after the speech at the Lord Mayor's Banquet, Disraeli tried to extract from the War Office the numbers needed to hold Gallipoli and the lines north of Constantinople. Having said 46,000 they upped their estimate to 75,000 men. 'The Intelligence Dept. must change its name,' wrote Disraeli to Monty Corry. 'It is the Department of Ignorance.'[19] It was just as well that the Russians were not as belligerent as Disraeli supposed. After the treaty of San Stefano, signed with the Turks in a small village near Constantinople on 3 March 1878, ratified and emended at the Congress of Berlin in the summer, peace was secured: for a while.

Disraeli, however, had identified himself and his party with the policy of jingoism. Lord Derby, for thirty years his friend and colleague, resigned as foreign secretary when Disraeli insisted on the British fleet sailing through the Dardanelles. Indian troops were dispatched to occupy Cyprus, since it was deemed necessary for Britain to have a Mediterranean base to strengthen her negotiating position with Russia. By the time the sepoys had warmed up their first billycan of curry on Cypriot soil, the Russo-Turkish crisis was over. Rather than withdraw from the island Britain held on to Cyprus – a real rod for its own back in the twentieth century. This was Salisbury's acquisition, but Gladstone did nothing to hand it back to Turkey when the obvious chance presented itself in his later premiership, at the time of his withdrawing the military consuls from Asia Minor. The partition of the island between Greek- and Turkish-speakers and the farcical humiliations of the British at the hands of a buccaneer archbishop in the 1950s were all the consequence of Salisbury's nifty (as it must have seemed at the time) annexation of territory which was, for all its difficulties, much better off under the loose suzerainty of Constantinople than under the Union Jack.

*The song was written by G.W. Hunt (1829–1904) but performed and popularized by Gilbert Hastings Macdermott (1845–1901).

If the prospect of Indian troops occupying Turkish Cyprus to show what Britain thought of Russia seems bizarre to our perspective, the agitation of the Second Afghan War seems little more than a footnote to the proceedings in Turkey. Lord Lytton, the erratic viceroy of India, decided that the Russian approaches to Afghanistan represented a threat to British interests. This would probably have been true if, by the time he decided on this show of strength, Salisbury and Disraeli had not been cosying up to the Russians in Berlin.[20] The invasion of Afghanistan was temporarily successful. Thanks to the diplomatic interventions of Sir Louis Cavagnari, a good old English name, an Afghan band was playing its own extraordinary rendition of 'God Save the Queen' in Kabul on 24 July 1879. The line, for the time being, had been held.

But jingoistic imperialism was not without cost, either in human life or in the self-disgust which from its beginning it was likely to engender. While the Russo-Turkish War was being fought, ended and negotiated, and while the Afghans under Ayub Khan were engaging disastrously with the forces of Roberts – an immensely skilful general – a very different story was being played out in Southern Africa. Sir Bartle Frere, a convinced imperialist who had lately been appointed high commissioner at the Cape, decided that the power of the Zulu people must be broken. He had not reckoned on the courage and military skill of Chief Cetewayo, one of the most charismatic and ruthless of nineteenth-century Africans. Not only did he enjoy keeping Europeans on their toes by periodic massacre of missionaries, but he also had a way with prime ministers which would on occasion have been the envy of Queen Victoria: having murdered Masipula, his father's prime minister, he exclaimed to Sir Theophilus Shepstone (secretary for Native Affairs in Natal), 'Did I ever tell Mr Shepstone I would not kill? I do kill!'[21]

On 20 January 1879, four invading columns of African troops, led by British officers, entered Zululand. One, under Lt Col. Durnford, encamped at Rorke's Drift ready to act in concert with General Lord Chelmsford. They marched ten miles and camped under the southern face of a steep hill called Isandhlwana, 'The Little Hand'.

Four days later two men, speechless with panic, exhaustion and hunger, staggered to Sir Bartle Frere's bedside at Pietermaritzburg with the news that 800 white and 500 native soldiers had been killed, their camp routed. Meanwhile 3,000 to 4,000 Zulus led by Cetewayo's brother had marched on Rorke's Drift and been beaten off by a much smaller force of British. The

Zulus – 'A very remarkable people; they defeat our generals; they convert our bishops; they have settled the fate of a great European dynasty.' (Disraeli)

defence of Rorke's Drift by the British inflicted heavy casualties on the Zulus and they lost over 3,000 of their bravest warriors.

Chiefly for reasons of honour, Cetewayo now held back from further killing. Partly persuaded by Bishop Colenso of Natal (who had been tried in London for heresy by his fellow ecclesiastics for doubting the literal truth of the Pentateuch), Cetewayo believed the British were his friends. His was the morality of Achilles or Beowulf; Lord Chelmsford seized the advantage. After his defeat at Ulundi (4 July 1879) Cetewayo was captured and the Zulus defeated. They had given the British a run for their money, and in the course of the fighting Prince Louis Napoleon, only child of Emperor Napoleon III and Empress Eugénie, educated at Woolwich, was killed. 'A very remarkable people the Zulus,' observed Disraeli, 'they defeat our generals; they convert our bishops; they have settled the fate of a great European dynasty.'[22]

In fact, the Zulu War was a calamitous mistake. Disraeli did not really approve of Frere's disastrous policy, and by alienating the great Zulu people he had merely lost valuable potential allies against the Boers.

Disraeli had always been brilliant at seizing political advantage from a situation – improvising opinions and positions, and then, in the aftermath of triumph, consolidating his position and making something of it which was truly statesmanlike. He had used the Corn Laws – about which he did not care very passionately – as an occasion to ridicule Peel and destroy him. He had subsequently rebuilt the Conservative Party over long painstaking years and become the effectual architect of modern Conservatism. In the international crises of the late 1870s he had taken a bold Russophobic view and beaten the patriotic drum. It brought him momentary popularity in the country – though not enough to win him another election – and it crowned his career with a place of apparent importance at the Congress of Berlin, summoned in the summer of 1878.

At home, the opposition which Gladstone was

preparing against Disraeli was fuelled by an unedifying arsenal of anti-semitism, a flaw which has historically been *more* a feature of the Left and Centre-Left in England than it has of the Right. When Gladstone was roundly beaten in the 1868 election, his wife took it not only as an almost personal affront, but as a defeat for the Church by unbelieving Jewry – even though Disraeli was as much a baptized member of the Established Church as herself. 'Is it not disgusting after all Papa's labour and patriotism and years of work to think of handing over his nest-egg to that Jew?'[23] Gladstone himself, after the success of the prime minister's Guildhall speech – the Jingo one – threatened to obscure his own rabble-rousing, blood-curdling evocations of massacres in Bulgaria, mused, 'the provocation offered by Disraeli is almost incredible. Some new lights about his Judaic feeling in which he is both consistent and conscientious have come in upon me.' The historian E.A. Freeman referred in print[24] to 'the Jew in his drunken insolence' as his measured view of Disraeli's Guildhall speech; and when the Queen lunched at Hughenden he described her as 'going ostentatiously to eat with Disraeli in his ghetto'.

Bismarck, who disliked Gladstone as cordially as did Queen Victoria and Disraeli,[25] got the measure of the man at the Congress of Berlin, at which the Great Powers, France, Austria-Hungary, Britain and Russia, gathered in the Prussian capital to discuss the future of the Ottoman Empire, and to unpick the somewhat draconian Russian conditions of the treaty of San Stefano. It is characteristic of the way diplomacy was conducted in those days that no representative of the Porte, no ambassador from the sultan, not a single Turk, was invited to Berlin.

Disraeli, in poor health, attended in the company of Salisbury. He was the 'lion of the Congress'[26] and his incisiveness, intransigence and charm all deeply impressed Prince Bismarck. Britain deprived Russia of almost all the Turkish territories seized in the war and returned them to the Ottomans. The sultan retained military rights in southern Bulgaria. Disraeli had indeed won 'peace with honour'.

Der alte Jude, das ist der Mann! (The old Jew, he's the man!) Bismarck's judgement is that of posterity. When Disraeli came back to London, the Queen offered him a dukedom. He turned down all the honours she wished to shower upon him, except the Garter, which he accepted only on the condition that it was also given to Salisbury. 'High and low are delighted,' crowed the Fairy, 'excepting Mr Gladstone, who is frantic.'[27]

She had created Disraeli Earl of Beaconsfield in the

very summer of the Bulgarian atrocities. When he made his final speech in the House of Commons in August 1876 he let on to no one that it was his last appearance on that stage where he had been such a scintillating presence for forty years. Someone noticed – that was all – that there were tears in his eyes that night.[28]

As the time approached for a general election, Disraeli badly miscalculated the Conservative Party's chances. He hoped that the diplomatic triumphs of the Congress of Berlin would give him another victory. Two by-elections, one in Liverpool, another in Southwark, were

Disraeli at the Congress of Berlin, 1878, which met to discuss the reorganization of the Balkans. Such instinctive territorial interference was not carefully considered. Opinions might differ about the quality of administrative efficiency, or its degree of justice, in those places administered by the Turks and their dependency. It is a different question, whether any plausible alternative, agreeable to all peoples in any given region, would provide the utilitarian ideal of the greater happiness to the greater number.

won by Conservatives where the Liberals might have been expected to win. So he asked the Queen for an early election, and Parliament was dissolved on 24 March 1880. Disraeli retreated to Hatfield as the guest of Lord Salisbury to imbibe copious quantities of Grand Château

Margaux 1870 and wait for voting to start on 31 March. He had ignored all manner of factors which would have been apparent to a more humdrum politician. Harvests had been bad for two years running and the rural economy had collapsed. The Conservatives lost 27 county seats. A slump in trade and the continuation of the hated income tax led to catastrophic results for them in the boroughs. In fact they did badly everywhere. The seats in the Commons when counted were as follows, with the figures at the dissolution in brackets: Liberals 353 (250), Conservatives 238 (351), Home Rulers 61 (51). 'The downfall of Beaconsfieldism,' wrote Gladstone gleefully, 'is like the vanishing of some vast magnificent castle in an Italian Romance.'[29]

Gladstone himself had spent the previous two years campaigning, not for an English seat – though he was offered, and won, the seat for Leeds* – but for Midlothian, or Edinburghshire as it was sometimes called in Scotland. It was a comparatively unpopulous seat to win – only 3,260 registered electors, as against the 49,000 in Leeds – but since he won *both* it would not be fair to say he feared failure in either. Perhaps he liked the notion of returning to his Scottish roots for this remarkable transformation of himself in his late sixties into a modern-style campaigning politician.

The campaign-manager, Lord Rosebery, had attended Democratic rallies in the United States and modelled the meetings partly on American political conventions, partly on the evangelical rallies of Moody and Sankey. Of the thousands who attended, very few were eligible to vote in an election and over half were women. Proceedings began with a selection of Liberal songs, set to familiar hymn-tunes, to 'warm up' the audience. Then the Grand Old Man would arrive, often in a carriage pulled by cheering Liberals. Then the speechifying would start – often with a theatrical admission that he had mislaid his eyeglass. The old Pro was capable of speaking for hours and hours and hours on any of his pet subjects, and he and his team could build up a formidable list of the crimes and blunders of the Conservative government. The purchase of the shares in the Suez Canal could be seen as a profligate waste of taxpayers' money; the acquisition of Cyprus as a major blunder. (Once in office the Liberals would not reverse either.) The bloodshed of the Zulu and Afghan wars could be represented *both* as a shaming loss of British dignity and as an immoral exploitation of a people weaker than the Europeans. He insisted that we should ever 'remember the rights of the savage, as we call him'. There would follow the set pieces which were soon to be famous – 'Remember that the sanctity of life in the hill villages of Afghanistan, among the winter snows, is as inviolable in the eye of Almighty

*He passed it to his son Herbert. In those days you could contest as many seats as you liked.

God as can be your own. Remember that He who has united you as human beings in the same flesh and blood, has bound you by the law of mutual love . . .'[30]

F.D. Maurice had emphasized the obligation on Christians to believe that the law of Christ is 'applicable to all persons and all cases . . . he must believe that it lies at the root of all politics'. The cynicism which kept Christianity for Sundays or believed that politics was a necessarily dirty business was one of Maurice's most persistent targets. Though Gladstone's Midlothian campaign speeches seem hammy to modern tastes, it would be unfair not to understand how deeply he meant what he said, and how wide was his appeal to some sections of the electorate. Disraeli's management of the economy was as easy to lambaste as his moral record, particularly since the election coincided with an economic slump. So Gladstone came back from his retirement – not just to restart his political career at the age of seventy-one, but to put to his wider public – who read his speeches in the newspapers – a fundamental choice. The election was a chance to throw out the cynical Utilitarianism of the early nineteenth century, in favour of the applied social Christianity – if not quite Christian socialism – of Maurice. Did we say not *quite* socialism? Not *at all* socialist. Gladstone offered the Northern Nonconformists and Scottish Presbyterian businessmen who were his natural constituents the chance to vote for a specifically moralistic, indeed religious, political programme without having to do anything so disturbing as to dig into their pockets. They could huff and puff about the sanctity of life in the hill villages of Afghanistan without feeling an immediate need for state-funded (i.e. tax-funded) aid to the poverty-stricken families of the big British cities.

Disraeli died – in a house he had acquired since leaving office – in Curzon Street on 19 April 1881, aged seventy-five. The grief-stricken Queen ('The loss is so *overwhelming*')[31] was in favour of a public funeral and burial in the Abbey: but Disraeli's will was specific:

I DESIRE and DIRECT that I may be buried in the same vault in the Churchyard of Hughenden in which the remains of my late dear Wife Mary Anne Disraeli created in her own right Viscountess Beaconsfield were placed and that my Funeral may be conducted with the same simplicity as hers was.

There is an obvious sincerity and quiet dignity in this which seems to suggest that with all his love of show, and all his overweening political ambition, Disraeli was with a large part of himself a detached observer of the public scene. Archbishop Tait had been appalled by Disraeli's last completed novel *Endymion*. He read it 'with a painful feeling that the writer considers all political life as mere play and gambling'. Those who admire, indeed love, Disraeli find the hint of this spilling into his political performance highly sympathetic. When the time came for election defeat, though, he took the news with immense dignity. He remained Lord Beaconsfield, leader of the Conservative Party, and made regular visits to the Lords. But the novels, and the instructions for a private funeral, bespeak an admirable detachment.

He was a unique being – one of the very few English prime ministers who could be described as a lovable human being, and one of the few with any claim to be thought of as a writer. Disraeli has a greater claim than that. He is a singular novelistic wit, only now perhaps, after an interval, being appreciated again. It is hard to think of many other Victorian novelists being a safe pair of hands as prime minister for so much as a week, let alone stage-managing the Congress of Berlin. George Eliot (assuming a change in the law to allow women MPs) is the only Victorian novelist one can imagine having the gravitas or staying power, but only on condition that she were merely placed in office, like one of the Platonic Guardians. One can't see her loving, as Dizzy did, all the intrigue and calculation of the political life.

George Eliot, as it happens, was one of those who saw the great merits of Disraeli. She would also, as one who in *Daniel Deronda* (1876) had written so intelligently and sympathetically about the Jews, have seen the importance for England of having so brilliant a prime minister of Jewish birth and parentage. (She was an accomplished amateur Hebraist as well as philosemite.)[32] When the question first arose in 1848 of whether to admit Jews to Parliament. Disraeli was brave enough to vote against his party over the question, consistently siding with the Liberals and bravely scandalizing the House by suggesting, in effect, that Judaism was a religion with at least as good a pedigree as Christianity. The Jews were admitted in 1858. It was in no small measure owing to Disraeli. His own career (baptized Anglican though he was) exemplified the willingness of the English political class to make a sensible compromise. Seeing his qualities, the Tory grandees were quite happy to convert Disraeli into a Conservative country gentleman and to treat him accordingly. But though his father had left the synagogue – on the grounds of insufficient belief and a wish to assimilate his children into Anglican culture – Disraeli was always loyal to his roots. His career, ambivalent and exotic, utterly sui generis, was among other things a signal that although anti-semitism existed in England, it was something from a *political* viewpoint above which the British determinedly and deliberately rose.

Race goers stand on their carriages to get a better view at the Punchestown races, one of Ireland's premier race meetings, 1859.

Chapter Twenty-Two

Wagner – Gilbert and Sullivan

With money came time; with time, leisure, even for those classes who in former ages toiled and struggled all week long. The professional and commercial classes were the first to obtain a Saturday half holiday. By the 1850s, the textile mills in the North tended to close at 2 p.m. on Saturday. (Wordsells, the Birmingham engineering works, seems to have been the first factory to give its workers Saturday afternoon off – in 1853.) The combination of time, leisure and money led to the increase of leisured activity, and the invention of popular pastimes to fill the newfound vacant hours. There was an enormous growth in the popularity of the turf – with 62 new racing events added to the calendar in the 1850s, 99 in the 1860s, 54 in the 1870s. The growth of railways, combined with the growth of free time, made this possible.[1]

Football, whose rules became formalized by 1859, became the British national game, linking undergraduates and public schoolboys to the chapels and trade unions and working men's associations who formed many of the early clubs. The Football Association began in 1863. Thirty clubs had joined by 1868, this largely southern phenomenon echoed by a northern equivalent in Sheffield.[2] A Birmingham FA was formed in 1875, and a Lancashire one in 1878. Aston Villa Wesleyan Chapel was typical as an example of the religious origin of many of these clubs, as was Christ Church, Bolton, which became Bolton Wanderers in 1877.[3] There was big money to be made by those with the wit to build stadia, charge at the turnstiles and to link home and away matches by arrangement with the railway companies. Bramhall Lane, Sheffield, was drawing crowds of 10,000 by the late 1870s.[4] (It was also used for cricket matches.) Very many clubs could draw crowds of seven or eight hundred, and more than thirty clubs in this decade could draw two to five thousand on a Saturday.[5]

For those with a taste for crowds of a different kind, shopping had become an activity in itself, not just a means of acquiring goods and groceries. William Whiteley started as a draper's assistant in Wakefield, and first came to London to see the Great Exhibition in 1851. He started his own haberdashery; by 1867 he was selling silks, linens, drapery, costume jewellery, furs, umbrellas, artificial flowers. The 1870s were the great era of his expansion, with his huge emporium in Westbourne Grove catering for that expanding part of London. His assistant John Barker asked to be taken into a partnership. Whiteley instead offered Barker £1,000 per annum – an enormous sum for a drapery employee. Barker refused, setting up on his own in Kensington High Street with prodigious success. These big stores, still in existence though differently owned and managed, owed much of their success to being on the doorstep of newish suburbs. Many other big shops cashed in on this principle, some such as James Marshall (of Marshall and Snelgrove) and William Edgar (founder of Swan and Edgar) moving in to the centre of London having made fortunes in the suburbs. The vast Marshall and Snelgrove building on the corner of Oxford Street and Vere Street replaced an attractive row of miscellaneous Georgian houses and shops in 1879. It is built in a pseudo-Parisian manner, trying to suggest that the middle-class clientele who went there to sample the newfangled ready-made costumes were as sophisticated as their richer sisters who patronized the great houses of the French capital.[6]

If shopping and games and race-meetings flourished with the arrival of ready-made leisure, so too did the arts. The 1870s witnessed a remarkable musical revival in Britain, with a flowering of concerts and operas. This in turn led to the founding of the Guildhall School of Music in 1880 and the Royal College of Music in 1883, with Hubert Parry and Charles Villiers Stanford as professors.

Parry (1848–1918) and Stanford (1852–1924) are the best British composers to appear before Elgar (1857–1934). It seems unfair to them to draw attention to the fact that while they were writing their apprentice-work, Verdi (1813–1901) was writing *Don Carlos* (1867), or Brahms (1833–97) his *German Requiem* (1868) and his four symphonies in 1876, 1877, 1883 and 1885 – works which were contemporary with Tchaikovsky's *Evgeny Onegin* (1879) and the Hungarian Rhapsodies (1846–85) of the Abbé Liszt. One cannot blame the few heroic souls who kept orchestral and choral music alive in Britain for the general philistinism of churches, colleges and schools which led to the near-death of music in Britain in the generations after the Industrial Revolution.

Parry and George Eliot both played their part in the visit of the most distinguished musical visitor to London in the 1870s. Of all the unlikely customers in Whiteley's new department store in Bayswater, few could have been more incongruous among the genteel suburban folk than Richard Wagner, who went there in May 1877 with Chariclea Dannreuther. She helped him choose frocks for his daughters and he bought a rocking-horse for his sons which he called Grane, after Brünnhilde's horse in *The Ring*. Edward Dannreuther was an American-born German living in London; he was a virtuoso pianist who introduced English audiences to Grieg, Liszt and Tchaikovsky and hosted the London Wagner Festival.

Wagner's visits to London were made when he was strapped for cash. In 1855, concert versions of his early and more accessible operas had good receptions, though he can't always have been pleased by the manner in which this praise was expressed. The author of the 1850

Caricature of Richard Wagner from Figaro, 1876. *On their visit to London the Wagners found that the industrial landscape of the Thames docklands 'made a tremendous impression'. Wagner said, 'This is Alberich's dream come true – Nibelheim, world dominion, activity, work, everywhere the oppressive feeling of steam and fog.'*

polemic *Das Judentum in der Musik* (Judaism in Music) was depressed by the English fondness for Meyerbeer and Mendelssohn. So when the leading music critic of the day, George Hogarth, still going strong at seventy-three – he lived until eighty-seven – thought to pay Wagner a compliment, he said that a concert rendition of 'highlights' from *Lohengrin*, 'with scenic action and adjuncts of the opera house . . . would be as effective as the music of Meyerbeer himself'.

Wagner left twenty-two years before visiting London again. By then his tempestuous artistic and personal career had stamped itself on the European imagination. His revolutionary status, and his uncompromising consciousness of his own genius, received the predictable philistine mockery from *Punch* – 'Having been a considerable time accustomed to play the trilogy [*sic*: i.e. the Ring cycle] with one finger on the accordion, I was naturally anxious to hear the same work of art performed by a band of two hundred, at the Albert Hall' etc. etc. *The Daily Telegraph*, being edited by a Jew, could hardly take kindly to Wagner the man. 'In the midst of whatever honours are paid to Herr Wagner – and the deserts of his genius are great – there should be no false sentiment about the master's personality.'

The Prince of Wales, famously philosemitic, attended the concerts, and the Wagners were received at court – at Windsor – by Queen Victoria. The concerts conducted by Wagner himself were conspicuously less successful than those under the baton of his great interpreter Hans Richter. Wagner's beat was completely lost during an extract from *Tannhäuser*, and when Richter resumed the podium the audience greeted him 'almost uproariously'.

His London concerts complete, Wagner had returned to Germany long before November 1877, when the curtain went up at the Opera Comique Theatre, just off the Strand, which had been leased by the theatrical impresario, Richard D'Oyly Carte. The German musical dramatist was therefore not in a position to see the Gilbert and Sullivan opera, *The Sorcerer*.[7]

The first hit,* *Trial by Jury*, had played at the Royalty

---

*There had been a flop in 1871 with an imitation of Offenbach entitled *Thespis, or The Gods Grown Old*.

Theatre from 25 March to 18 December 1875 with prodigious success. 'It seems, as in the great Wagnerian operas, as though poem and music had proceeded simultaneously from one and the same brain' – as *The Times* critic put it. The music was sublime. The play absurd. Yet in a bizarre way, it was a recognizable picture of the audience's actual world. Those who saw the operas as they first appeared went out into the street with words and music in their heads which – love them or loathe them – are ineradicable. But more than that, for the fans, of whom there are millions to this day, the world itself is transformed by the Gilbert and Sullivan experience.

There is a pathos, not to say tragi-comedy, about the fact that the operas did, and do, indeed seem as if they had proceeded simultaneously from one and the same brain. Arthur Sullivan (1842–1900), the son of a sergeant bandmaster from the Royal Military College, Sandhurst (formerly a clarinettist and music teacher), rose through the route of choirboy at the Chapel Royal and star pupil at the Royal Academy of Music to being a serious aspirant musician and composer. He had studied at Leipzig, and if it had not been for his frivolous association with Richard D'Oyly Carte and William Schwenck Gilbert (1836–1911) he might have had an illustrious career as a minor nineteenth-century musician, known only to the devotees of kitsch as the composer of 'The Lost Chord' – one of the most popular of all English songs – and to churchgoers as the composer of the most rousing tune to 'Onward Christian Soldiers' ('St Gertrude', 1871).[8] As it was, this dignified biography was denied him. He was fated to be prodigiously rich and famous – and to be 'and Sullivan' for as long as the English language endures.

Gilbert, a failed barrister with a grotesque penchant for rather cruel burlesque, was a most unlikely collaborator for Sullivan. For parallels you have to imagine what it might have been like had Mendelssohn gone into partnership with Dickens.

However much a modern prude might abhor Gilbert, or a musical snob be foolish enough to despise Sullivan, they are essential objects of study if we want to catch the flavour of the late Victorian world. 'Mere entertainment' is all they are; but they share with great art the capacity to make us see their world in a particular way.

Now, as the example of Gilbert's ungallantry about women makes clear, this is not a way of viewing the world of which we would necessarily approve. I could imagine a Marxist critique of *The Savoy Operas* – as the works came to be known when D'Oyly Carte built the Savoy Theatre in 1881 on the south side of the Strand (the first theatre in Britain to be lit by electric light). Perhaps the Marxist might argue that the audiences who streamed into that brightly lit world, who were beguiled by Sullivan's tunes and who laughed at Gilbert's burlesques and puns, were being numbed with a real opiate, something much more potent than religion. The institutions of the Law, Parliament, the Armed Forces, the Class System are all held up to ridicule in *The Savoy Operas*: but it is an essentially undisturbing ridicule, on the whole inspiring affection not loathing for its objects. No one coming out of *Trial by Jury* – which represents the judiciary as ludicrous and corrupt – stands on the pavement wanting the destruction, or even the overhaul, of the legal system.

This was one of the great eras of education for women, with the foundation of colleges of higher education for them. The prospectus for 'Vassar Female College' – Poughkeepsie, NY – was published in 1865, 'to accomplish for young women what our colleges are accomplishing for young men'.[9] British equivalents included the opening of the London Medical School for Women in 1875, against tremendous opposition; the foundation of the Royal Holloway College in Egham, Surrey, in 1879; and the admission of women to Oxford and Cambridge. Newnham College became part of Cambridge University in 1871, though women had to take separate exams, and were not considered capable of studying Latin and Greek. In 1880 the British-American Charlotte Scott (1858–1931) studied at Girton College, Cambridge, and was allowed to take the same mathematics examination as the men. She came eighth, which, had she been of a different gender, would have allowed her the title 'eighth wrangler'. Since women were not allowed degrees, she was not allowed. When the name of the eighth *male* wrangler was read out in the Senate House, a party of doughty feminists chanted, 'Scott of Girton! Scott of Girton!'[10]

It is hard to recall these things without being moved. For Gilbert and Sullivan fans of course the very notion of females in higher education is inherently ludicrous, as their version of Tennyson's *The Princess – Princess Ida* (1884) – confirms.

In Mathematics, Woman leads the way:
The narrow-minded pedant still believes
That two and two make four! Why, we can prove,
We women, household drudges as we are –
That two and two make five – or three or seven;
Or five-and-twenty, if the case demands![11]

A respectful operatic perversion of Tennyson's "PRINCESS" in Three Acts.
ENTITLED
PRINCESS IDA
WRITTEN BY
W. S. GILBERT.
OR, CASTLE ADAMANT.
MUSIC BY
ARTHUR SULLIVAN.
ACT I.—Pavilion in King Hildebrand's Palace——EMDEN.
ACT II.—Gardens of Castle Adamant.—HAWES CRAVEN—ACT III.—Courtyard of Castle Adamant.——EMDEN.
AN INTERVAL OF 12 MINUTES BETWEEN ACT I AND ACT II.
AN INTERVAL OF 12 MINUTES BETWEEN ACT II AND ACT III.
The Opera produced under the personal direction of the Author and Composer.

21 *A programme for the Savoy Theatre showing* Princess Ida *by Gilbert and Sullivan, 1884.*

The downside of Gilbert and Sullivan mania – as an expression of the English character and attitude to life generally – is that it can make large sections of the populace who ought to think a bit harder snigger instead. There is no doubt that the progress of feminism – both the education of women and the extension of the franchise – was held back by decades simply because so many people, women as well as men, could dismiss it as a joke.

And, in England, events did so attempt to force themselves into Gilbertian, farcical mode. What could be more satisfying to the philistine public than the legal spat between James McNeill Whistler, American aesthete, painter and author of *The Gentle Art of Making Enemies* (1890), and John Ruskin, who by 1877 was beginning to exhibit symptoms of the insanity which would at length enclose forever that lovable and wonderful prophet? Ruskin went to the Grosvenor Gallery to see the Whistlers on show there, and in the next instalment of his highly distinctive *Fors Clavigera*, a sort of open letter to the labouring classes and others – a stream of consciousness which contains some of his finest writing – he was to observe fatefully, 'I have seen, and heard, much of Cockney impudence before now; but never expected to hear a coxcomb ask two hundred guineas for flinging a pot of paint in the public's face.' Whistler sued. The trial was heard by Sir John Huddleston, famous for 'the tiniest feet, the best kept hands and the most popular wife in London'[12] (i.e. Lady Diana Beauclerk, daughter of the

Duke of St Albans). The trial was a farce. Poor Burne-Jones was asked as a witness on Ruskin's behalf and lost Whistler's friendship. The jury found Ruskin guilty of libel and awarded Whistler a farthing's damages. W.S. Gilbert on a particularly whimsical day could not have dreamed up anything more absurd. But the opera about the aesthetes, *Patience* – which in an earlier draft was to have been a spoof of the Ritualist clergy – has about it that whiff of cruel satire which in England has the occasional tendency to turn into mere bullyism. In 1881 they were laughing at an aesthete who walks down Piccadilly with a poppy or a lily in his medieval hand, and has 'an attachment à la Plato for a bashful young potato, or a not-too-French French bean'. Fourteen years later, the spectator-sports were the Wilde trials.

Likewise, in the most popular of the Savoy Operas, *H.M.S. Pinafore* (1878), it would be a po-faced member of the audience who had not laughed at the 'ruler of the Queen's Navee', Sir Joseph Porter KCB, First Lord of the Admiralty.

SIR JOSEPH   Now landsmen all, whoever you may be,
      If you want to rise to the top of the tree,
      If your soul isn't fettered to an office stool,
      Be careful to be guided by this golden rule –
      Stick close to your desks and never go to sea,
      And you all may be Rulers of the Queen's
                Navee![13]

Any observer of the English scene over the last two hundred years knows that this is archetypical – that the political history of Britain is one of chancellors of the Exchequer who know nothing about money, education ministers who can't spell, bishops with little or no religious faith. The original audiences for *Pinafore* would have roared their recognition at the first lord of the Admiralty played by George Grossmith, who had made so many of the 'patter songs' his own. For here *was* Disraeli's first lord of the Admiralty in person, that land-lubber son of the Methodist chain of newsagents, W.H. Smith. In fact, this Wesleyan grammar-school boy of philanthropic mien who had probably never stepped aboard a paddle-steamer, let alone a battleship, was destined, first as first lord of the Admiralty, then – in Lord Salisbury's second administration – as secretary

The armour-clad ship HMS Devastation at Spithead on the occasion of the Naval Review in honour of the Shah of Persia's visit, 23rd June 1873.

second, governments – there was agitation by the jingoists for an ever-bigger and more devastating navy. Both Smith as a Tory, Gladstone as an old Peelite, were more anxious by instinct to save money than to increase military or naval expenditure. But events, and the large political fact that Britain had an economy which was bound up with an ever-expanding empire, made so judicious a hold on the purse-strings only a partial possibility. During the war scare of 1878–9 Smith was obliged to think of a greatly expanded navy. And in 1884, when Gladstone was in power, a series of scaremongering articles by W.T. Stead – 'The Truth About the Navy by One Who Knows the Facts' – jumped the government into programmes of rearmament. A supplementary vote of £5,525,000 was given by the Exchequer in 1885 – '£3,100,000 of it to be devoted to building one ironclad, five protected cruisers, ten protected scout vehicles and thirty torpedo boats'.[15]

Since no weapon or ship in the history of warfare has been invented without being used, these belligerent developments could only lead to the inevitable *Götterdämmerung* of war – not in the lifetime of W.H. Smith, but in the lifetime of many who attended the first night of *Pinafore*. Only a lunatic would blame Gilbert and Sullivan for the build-up of armaments and the sparring of the Great Powers. But it is fair to observe that a culture which threw up, and feasted upon, *H.M.S. Pinafore* (and the operas of Gilbert and Sullivan are effectively the *only* memorable music produced by the English in the 1870s and 1880s) was also the culture that failed to ask itself any serious questions about the desirability of a country which was still *au fond* a small trading island – albeit a prodigiously rich and energetic one – playing the role of world-dominator, superpower and 'Empire'. Its lifetime of so doing was short and on the whole disastrous; which is why, though Gilbert and Sullivan can still delight us with their zany jokes and whistleable tunes, the operas themselves in the context of their times seem like Neronic fiddling against a fiery sky.

of state for war, to oversee an extraordinary transformation in British naval policy.

HMS *Devastation*, 285 feet long by 62 feet, was built in 1873, four years before Smith became first lord. It has been described as 'a floating armoured castle, invulnerable to any foreign guns'.[14] The name alone sends a chill into the spine. Throughout the late Seventies and early Eighties – the time of Disraeli's last, Gladstone's

Chapter Twenty-Three

Country Parishes – Hardy

The abolition of the Corn Laws in the 1840s had been for the radical economic liberals the means of bringing about a glorious era of meritocracy and plenty. Cobden, the chief agitator for Corn Law repeal, has his statue in many an English town. Working men's clubs are called the Cobden Club. Meaner terraces of houses in industrial conurbations are named Cobden Crescent and Cobden Terrace.

Twenty years later, the agricultural poor of Britain were, on the whole, more wretched than ever, though the big landlords continued to own most of the agricultural land. Though land values and rents fell in the course of the century, half the entire country was owned by 4,217 persons in 1873.[1]

In the 1860s Cobden exclaimed, 'If I were five and twenty . . . I would have a League for free trade in Land just as we had a League for free trade in Corn.' He and his economic liberal allies could not see what effects were visited upon the land by treating farming as just another 'industry'.

In 1860 the United States had some 30,800 miles of railway; by 1870 this had reached 53,200 miles and by 1880 some 94,200. It was now possible for the grain-producers in the great prairies to send their grain to market fast and cheaply. Transatlantic steamer-transport also reduced transportation costs. In 1873 the cost of sending a ton of grain from Chicago to Liverpool was £3 7s.; by 1884 it had fallen to £1 4s. – a cheapening equal to 9s. 9d. on every quarter of corn *for water-freight alone.*[2]

Almost every country in Europe responded to this threat by introducing tariffs on imported corn – i.e. by introducing Corn Laws very similar to the ones so enthusiastically abolished by Sir Robert Peel and his Liberal friends in 1846. Russia – itself a big corn exporter now, much of its cheap grain coming into Britain along with the American – slapped on import tariffs, as did France and Germany. Only industrialized Britain and Belgium chose to believe Cobden's discredited dogma that commercial intercourse between nations inevitably spells progress. Wheat – the largest arable product of English farms – fell in price from 56s. 9d. per quarter in 1877 to 46s. 5d. in 1878. By 1885, the British area under wheat had shrunk by a million acres. By the 1880s the British were importing an absurd 65 per cent of their wheat, and nearly a million workers had left the land, most of them by emigration, though others had swarmed into the industrial towns.[3]

In addition to the devastating ravages of capitalism, rural England in late Victorian times suffered a series of terrible natural calamities. In 1865–6 and 1877 outbreaks of cattle plague (rinderpest) and pleuro-pneumonia were so severe that the government had to restrict the movement of cattle and pay compensation to the owners of slaughtered beasts to check the spread of infection.[4] A run of wet seasons from 1878 to 1882 produced an epidemic of liver-rot in sheep in Somerset,

Rural labourers taking a break from the barley harvest. Life for the rural poor became much bleaker in the closing decades of the Victorian era.

William Barnes, the parson-poet, at Winterbourne Came Rectory, Dorset, surrounded by his womenfolk and his son in the autumn of 1882. One knows this is a world where extreme hardship and poverty are the norm, but in his verses there is an elegiac note, a regret for a way of life which will never come again.

north Dorset and the Lincolnshire marshes – 4 million sheep were lost in the period.[5] The floods caused wipe-out for many arable farmers. Foot-and-mouth disease raged, out of control, through British livestock from 1881 to 1883.

Wheat and wool – the two staples of English and Welsh prosperity since the Middle Ages – fell into the hands of overseas markets.[6] One must not exaggerate the agricultural depression of the closing decades of the nineteenth century, nor simplify its causes. Farmers who did stay in business during these bad years managed not merely to survive, but to increase their profits.[7] There was an increase in meat-production, dairy produce and vegetables, and the introduction of machinery improved economic efficiency, so the period saw the grubbing up of

many hedges. Wiltshire at this period acquired the bleak leafless look which it retains today.[8]

But – overall – the cost to the rural poor, to the agricultural labourer, was terrible. Life had always been tough for them, but in the glossily wealthy new world of the 1870s onwards, rural poverty must have seemed even bleaker. When the Earl of Yarborough died in 1875, his stock of cigars was sold for £850, and this has been calculated as more than eighteen years' income for the agricultural labourers on his estate.[9] Child labour is an inevitable part of agricultural life for the poor. Lord Shaftesbury's reforms, which began to better the lives of factory children, did little to help those in the country. The Gangs Act of 1869 aimed to remedy the abuses brought on the children by gangmasters, who dragooned their gangs – sometimes as young as six years old, numbering anything from ten to a hundred persons – as itinerant cheap labour, offering stone-picking, weeding, turnip-singling, potato-setting, hoeing. Life in these gangs was brutal. The children were knocked about a lot, the women forced to drug their babies with opium and leave them in the hedgerows while they worked.[10] The new Act laid down that no child could work in such a gang under the age of eight, but this did not stop small farmers who needed cheap or free labour from setting children to work as young as six. One such, named George Edwards – who rose to become a Member of Parliament – recalled that he started work aged six, and was paid 1*s*. per week.[11] Poor families in the Celtic fringes could live at incredibly low levels of subsistence: crofters in the Highlands of Scotland were living on as little as £8 a year.[12] In the south, where there simply was no work, and where the farms were not broken up into peasant smallholdings, there was no option. The labourers had to leave the land or starve.

Canon Girdlestone, vicar of Halberton in north Devon, organized single-handedly the migration of between 400 and 500 men with families over six years from areas where they were trying to survive on as little as 7*s*. or 8*s*. a week for a 10½-hour working day to towns, factories or parts of the country which were more prosperous and could afford to pay a living wage. In a letter to *The Times* to publicize their plight this good country parson described how 'almost everything had to be done for them, their luggage addressed, their railway tickets taken, and full plain directions given to the simple travellers written on a piece of paper in a large and legible hand'. Though their destination was Kent or the north of England, they often timorously inquired if they were going 'over water'.[13] By 1881, 92,250 fewer labourers were at work than in 1871.[14]

By 1901, males employed in agriculture in England and Wales had diminished by one third, and British farming which had led the world had been reduced by doctrinaire Free Trade to a state of ruin. Only in the two world wars of the twentieth century, when isolationism and protectionism came about perforce and when governments were forced once again to consider the primary importance of a nation husbanding its own land and feeding its own population, did British agriculture revive. Even so – as recent unhappy decades have shown – this revival was but an 'episode in a general drama of pain'. Short of another world war, or a British political party with the imagination to repeal the repeal of the Corn Laws, the decline will continue. Much as we have

praised Disraeli in these pages, one cannot leave this painful subject without pointing out that he rose to prominence, and splintered the Tory Party, by his eloquent defence of the Corn Laws and his attacks upon Sir Robert Peel. When he was prime minister and the men and women whose livelihood depended on wheat were being destroyed by the grain-giants of the American prairies, Disraeli did nothing to help them.

Thomas Hardy (1840–1928) is one of those great writers – Carlyle was one, in the late twentieth century Solzhenitsyn was another – who do not merely produce great artworks, but who seem to embody in their life-pilgrimage deep truths about the nature of their own times. None were 'typical' – whatever that may mean – as Scot, Russian or Englishman. All were in fact outsiders. But in their lives and writings they were instinctively attuned to *what was going on* in their society. Dostoyevsky, half-crazy as he was, had this quality where Tolstoy for example, though obsessed by the state of Russia and the world, did not. I'm talking here less of the writers' *views* per se – though these are clearly affected by the phenomenon – and more of the sense of inevitability about what they wrote and what they were. Whereas lesser writers imitate, pose, strike attitudes, these unfailingly truthful men have something in them of Luther's *Hier stehe ich, ich kann nicht anders*. Carlyle and Dostoyevsky with their despondent fury saw through the lie of nineteenth-century Liberalism: Solzhenitsyn saw through the much bigger and much uglier lie of Soviet communism. Hardy in his oblique, gentle, provincial English way had a bigger target in his ever-bright blue countryman's eyes. 'I have been looking for God for 50 years, and I think that if he had existed I should have discovered him.'[15]

It does not matter that many of Hardy's novels have creaking plots, any more than it matters that he can write on occasion with immense clumsiness – tears are 'an access of eye-moisture'; early morning or suspense do not chill a man, they 'cause a sensation of chilliness to pervade his frame'.[16] There is a greatness of scheme, a truthfulness about Hardy which makes his faults seem trivial.

A master mason's son born in an obscure Dorset parish, he knew poverty from birth, both in his own family and that of his neighbour. As a little boy he dipped his toy wooden sword into the blood of a freshly killed pig and danced about the garden crying, 'Free trade or blood!'[17] Like the majority, the Hardys believed that the repeal of the Corn Laws (it happened when Hardy was six) would bring down the mighty from their seats and

JUDE AT THE MILE-STONE.

Engraving by W. Hatherell in the first serialisation of Thomas Hardy's Jude the Obscure, *published in* Harper's Monthly *in 1895.*

exalt the humble and meek; but from an early age he had a sense that life was not to be explained politically. This was the little boy who dressed up as the vicar and preached sermons to his cousin and grandmother. By the time the depression in British agriculture had begun to show itself, Hardy was grown up, a trainee architect in London – his Church interest transferred to the stones and glass in which the Almighty was worshipped rather than to the Holy Orders he supposedly instituted. It was while 'restoring' – wrecking, we should say – the church of St Juliot in North Cornwall that Hardy met his first wife, Emma Gifford – the niece of an archdeacon, as he proudly informed readers of *Who's Who*.

His most successful early novel, *Under the Greenwood Tree*, is a Shakespearean comedy about his parents, who met when members of the same church choir: it lovingly evokes the pre-Tractarian Church of England, the world of box pews, wheezing parish clerks, and the music

played not by an organ but by string instruments. The many twists of irony in the plot, however, and the whole *tone* of the thing, can leave the reader in no doubt where Hardy stood, even at this early stage of his writing life (the book was published in June 1872).[18] In his notebook for 30 October 1870 Hardy had written, 'Mother's notion, & also mine: that a figure stands in our van with arm uplifted, to knock us back from any permanent prospect we indulge in as profitable.'

In the great novels – *Far From the Madding Crowd, The Return of the Native, The Mayor of Casterbridge, Tess of the d'Urbervilles, Jude the Obscure* – we encounter human beings against whom all the odds are stacked. One reviewer said that *Tess*, the most popular of all Hardy's works, 'except during a few hours spent with cows, has not a gleam of sunshine anywhere'.[19] *Jude the Obscure* (1895) was burnt by a bishop, which provided Hardy with an excuse to give up writing novels and concentrate on the poetry. Not that the novel did not cost him dear, both in domestic peace (his pious wife gave him hell for the supposed 'immorality' of Jude and Sue) and in reputation. He valued his membership of the Athenaeum Club, where gaitered bishops were found behind their newspapers in the library. (He was elected in 1878.)[20]

Hardy is certainly the most religious of all great English novelists, the most spiritually engaged of all great Victorian writers. He went on regarding himself, after a fashion, as a churchman. 'The struggle between an intellect subdued to determinism and an imagination nourished upon the Christian assertion of spiritual and moral order wrought Hardy to poetry'[21] – that is well said by J.I.M. Stewart, and perhaps is most apparent in the obliquer shots in the poetry than in the doctrinal statements, powerful as 'God's Funeral' and 'God's Education' are. I am thinking of such matchless poems as 'The Impercipient', 'I Look into my Glass', 'A Wet Night', 'Drawing Details in an Old Church', 'A Church Romance',

'Where the Picnic Was', 'A Wife in London', 'We Sat at the Window (Bournemouth, 1875)', 'Afternoon Service at Mellstock' and dozens more. 'Much confusion has arisen and much nonsense has been talked latterly in connection with the word "atheist". I believe I have been called one by a journalist who has never read a word of my writings,' he stated during the First World War. (The journalist was G.K. Chesterton.) 'Fifty meanings attach to the word "God" nowadays, the only reasonable meaning being *the cause of Things*, whatever that cause may be . . .'

Hardy's was a dignified witness, not merely for a cultural nostalgia for churchy things, much as he loved all that – and as *Jude* shows, he had a taste for the new urban ritualist churches as well as for the old country ways – but for the shared spiritual life which a national Church could uniquely supply. He went on hoping all his days for intellectual candour from the Church, and was bitterly disappointed by its failure to speak seriously to modern thinking minds.[22]

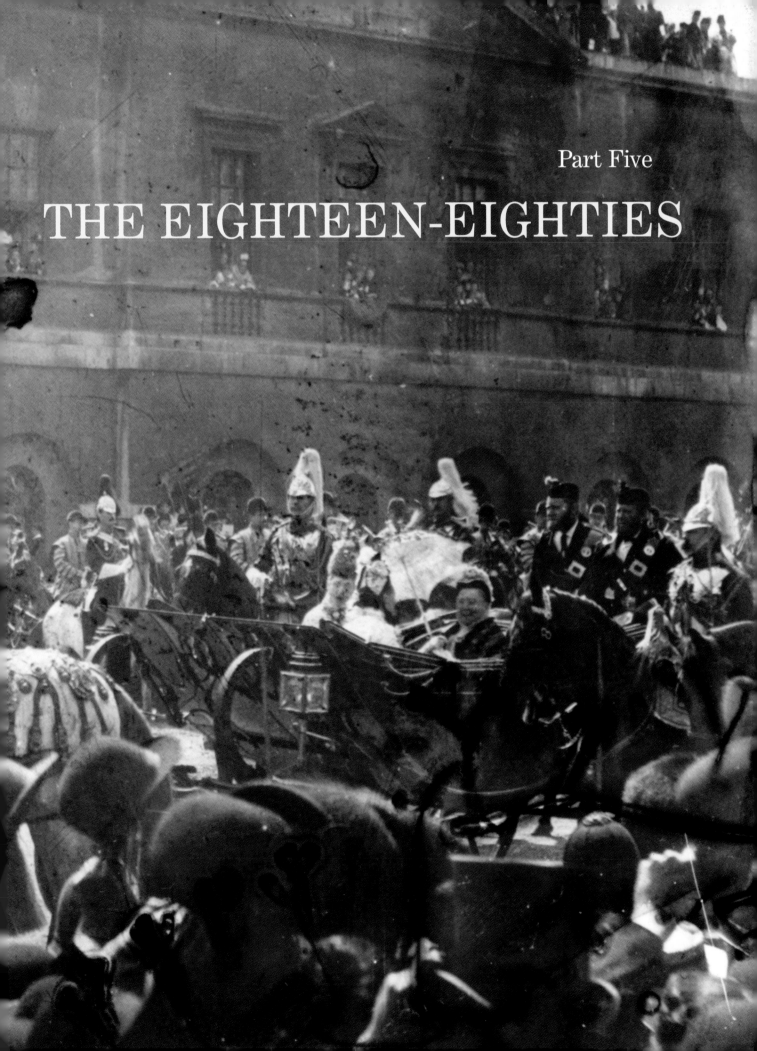

Part Five

THE EIGHTEEN-EIGHTIES

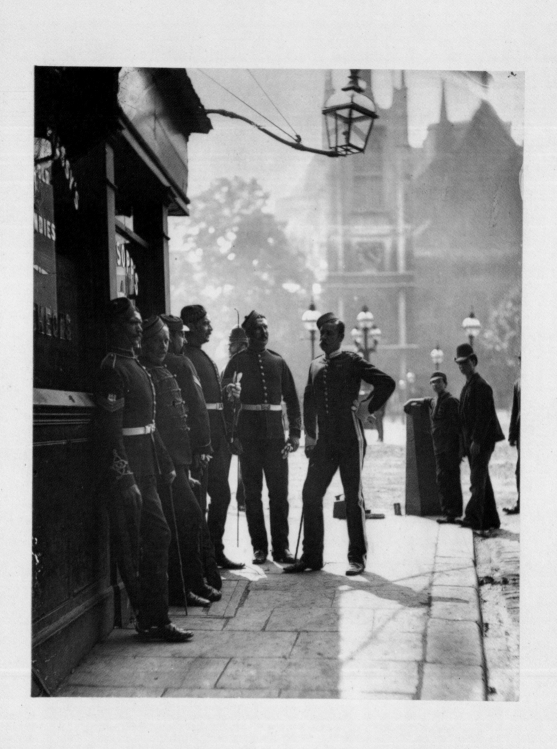

Chapter Twenty-Four

A Crazy Decade

Photography made rapid advances in the 1880s, chiefly in consequence of the invention of the dry plate. It was pioneered by various British researchers. By the end of the 1870s, Sir Joseph Swan's company was selling them, and the famous 'Ilford' plate was introduced in 1879. With smaller, more portable cameras increasingly available, and exposure time reduced to a matter of seconds, it began to be possible to capture moments which earlier photographers could never immortalize. Eadweard Muybridge (his name was originally Muggeridge), working in Paris, invented his photographic gun – *fusil photographique* – in which he mounted tiny glass plates in a disc to facilitate quick changing. Muybridge was able to establish the pattern of birds' wings in flight, and to show that a galloping horse lifts all four feet off the ground simultaneously. His zoopraxiscope was to be the pioneer motion-camera – a mere step away from moving pictures. Meanwhile his, and others', pioneering work could be applied and commercially marketed by Eastman in the form of a portable box-camera, Eastman Number One – slogan 'You press the button – we do the rest!'[1]

The 1880s therefore come to life to us in a way that earlier decades do not: for here have been captured unposed moments. Queen Victoria's smile during her Golden Jubilee in 1887, caught by Charles Knight, would have evaporated by the time Julia Margaret Cameron or Étienne Carjat or David Octavius Hill had anointed their glass plates with collodion and set up their laborious contraptions of an earlier vintage. The 1880s therefore are the first decade we can see unfrozen, and turning the pages of its photographic achievements is *both* like watching the modern world beginning to rouse and like intruding into a world which is about to evaporate: as cadavers preserved for centuries in their lead coffins are said to turn to dust when exposed to sunlight.

The very fact that we look at these photographic images at all and take them as emblems of reality, or imagine their reality to possess a new authenticity denied for example to the author of an Icelandic saga or to the canvas and brush of Sir Joshua Reynolds, is a symptom of how deeply we collude in the Victorian love-affair with science, the confused empiricism which supposes that the distinctions between Appearance and Reality can be made by some organ independent of a human mind. The camera is then elevated into an arbiter. The belief that it can never lie becomes itself not merely an invitation to hoaxers but the source of a tremendous confusion about the very nature of truth.

In January 1882 a group of intelligent and scientifically-minded scholars, public figures, clergymen and university graduates founded the Society for Psychical Research. The founders were Sir William Barrett, professor of physics at the Royal College of Science in Dublin, Henry Sidgwick, the Cambridge philosopher, Frederic W.H. Myers, Edmund Gurney and Frank Podmore – representing the

'Recruiting Sergeants at Westminster' by John Thomson, 1877. Taken from Street Life in London *(1877) written by Adolphe Smith. The aim of the book was stated as being: 'to bring the public some account of the present condition of the London Street folk, and to supply a series of faithful pictures of the people themselves'. It is one of the first examples of photography used as social documentary.*

Queen Victoria's Jubilee Procession, Whitehall, 1887. Victoria, smiling broadly, looks delighted by the occasion.

scientific, or at least sceptical, spirit: the spiritualist founder-members were the Reverend W. Staintin Moses, Morell Theobald, Dr George Wild and Dawson Rogers. In time, the Society would include two prime ministers – Gladstone and Arthur Balfour – Alfred Lord Tennyson, Lewis Carroll, John Addington Symonds, and eight Fellows of the Royal Society including Alfred Russel Wallace.[2]

They all apparently believed that science could establish whether there was truth in the spiritualist claims. None seemed troubled by the fact that spiritualism itself came to birth in the age of science and offered apparently scientific 'proofs' for its validity – such as spirit photography. W.H. Mumler, principal engraver at the Boston jewellery firm of Bigelow Bros. & Kennard, was the first amateur photographer to receive the impression of departed spirits on his collodion plate, and though he was subsequently prosecuted for witchcraft in New York, and for obtaining money under false pretences, he was acquitted at his trial.[3] In the great majority of spirit photographs – usually ghosts hovering in smudgy form behind or beside the sitter – we have been assured by those who took and developed the plates that no tampering or dishonesty has occurred, allowing sceptics to scorn and believers to believe exactly as if no such scientific evidence had been produced in the first place.

What seems so characteristic of the age is the attempt to confirm one type of belief by means of an essentially alien mental process: enlisting science to verify the resurrection of the body and the life everlasting seeming as inappropriate as appointing mystics to a chair of physics. But the 1880s are an era of kaleidoscopic muddle when the future of Ireland or the Liberal Party is determined not by political discussion but by sex scandals. Aesthetes turn from wallpaper design to redesigning society. One of the most famous atheists of the age became a convert to Theosophy. And journalism, that ultimate fantasy magic-lantern, laid its first serious

claims to be not simply a purveyor of news, but a moral mirror to society as a whole.

We cannot hope in the space available to provide more than a series of snapshots of this extraordinary ten-year period. What is so striking is how often, as in some huge novel, the same characters recur in different incarnations. During this decade human visions and revisions took bizarre and violent forms: it is the decade when Marx died, Nietzsche published *Also Sprach Zarathustra* and socialism began to lead to riots and conspiracies worthy of Dostoyevsky's *The Devils*; when the Irish scene was peppered with assassinations and explosions and the British dreams of Empire shed much African blood; when modern America begins the relationship with Europe that will shape the twentieth century. Life became, for millions, more comfortable yet more constrained, and for yet more millions no less wretched than it had been for their grandparents. Not so much 'a low dishonest decade' like Auden's 1930s, as a decade that is high as one might be high on narcotics, and so painfully honest that parties and parliaments would rather tear themselves apart than compromise their idea of truth. It was a crazy, uncontrolled decade, over which Dostoyevsky, dying at the beginning of it, seems to hover like a godfather. Who, at the beginning of Queen Victoria's reign, could have predicted that the decade culminating in her Golden Jubilee would begin with intense parliamentary rumpus and debate about *atheism* and end with the most disgusting series of unsolved murders in the East End of London?

'The only way to start a revolution is to start with atheism,' maintains one of the characters in *The Devils*.[4] Charles Bradlaugh the social reformer and Jack the Ripper are both in their different ways like Dostoyevskian *emanations* – difficult to separate from fiction. The perennial task set for themselves by patient minds, of distinguishing Appearance and Reality, grew no easier as the nineteenth century hurtled on, a mad ghost-train out of control.

1 *Mumler spirit photograph, c. 1870.*

Dinner time at Marylebone Workhouse, London,
in the late nineteenth century.

Chapter Twenty-Five

The Plight of the Poor

The gulf between rich and poor and the numbers of the poor, the grinding degradation of their state and the ever-greater prosperity of the rich: these things escaped the notice of no one with eyes to see in the 1880s. If you did not dare to climb on an omnibus and ride through the poorer parts of a late Victorian city, you could read the articles by George Sims, reprinted in book form as *How the Poor Live* and *Horrible London*; or you could read the Congregationalist Andrew Mearn's pamphlet *The Bitter Cry of Outcast London*, or the punctilious sociological surveys of Charles Booth, whose multi-volume *Life and Labour of the People in London* showed that London could present a human being with sights every bit as troubling as those which caused Tolstoy moral exasperation in Moscow. The dirty, cramped living conditions, the disgustingly high rents, the foetid water supplies, the near impossibility of scraping together enough to eat in such places, let alone to pay for your child to go to school – all these daily humiliations were widely publicized.

Asked what was the most signal fact in contemporary history, shortly before his death in 1884, Mark Pattison replied without hesitation, 'The fact that 5,000,000 of our population possess nothing but their weekly wages.'[1] Florence Nightingale scribbled a pencil note: 'It is always cheaper to pay labour its full value . . . Labour should be made to pay better than thieving. At present, it pays worse.'[2] In a private letter of 1865 Gladstone had remarked on how much the privileged classes needed to remember 'that we have got to govern millions of hard hands; that it must be done by force, fraud or goodwill; that the latter has been tried, and is answering.'[3]

As the 1880s unfolded, however, the goodwill broke down, prompting in many areas, not just in Ireland, the question, Were merely extending the franchise, or offering elementary education, solutions radical enough to cope with an unsteady labour market, and a growing population? Jerry-built suburbs sprawled out of London, put up in a hurry by speculative builders in such places as West Ham, whose population rose from 19,000 in 1851 to 267,000 in 1880. Office-building, new streets and railways within the confines of the City of London led to a decline in the population here, which fell from 113,387 in 1861 to 51,439 in 1881. The construction of Farringdon Street alone displaced 40,000 people. But a survey by the Metropolitan Board found that many of the new suburbs were empty – in Tottenham, Stamford Hill, Peckham, Battersea and Wandsworth the jerry-built streets were unpopulated. There was no underground railway as yet. The unemployed could not afford to live there. Those employed upon precarious terms, either in manual or clerical work, needed to be able to walk to work, which led to gross overcrowding of areas within hailing distance of the City, such as Bethnal Green. The rebuilding programmes and the haphazard migrations of workers (and this was not a problem unique to London) took place without any central planning

Children sitting under a washing line in a slum area of London, 1889.

at all. No government or political party in England saw it as any part of its business to house the workers. 'They must put up with dirt, and filth, and putrefaction; with dripping walls and broken windows; with all the nameless abomination of an unsanitary hovel, because if they complain the landlord can turn them out at once, and find dozens of people eager to take their places who will be less fastidious.' That was George Sims, who said, 'Is it too much to ask that in the intervals of civilizing the Zulu and improving the condition of the Egyptian fellah the Government should turn its attention to the poor of London, and see if in its wisdom it cannot devise a scheme to remedy this terrible state of things?'[4]

The governing classes did not consider socialism to be an option. The debates within the upper echelons of the Liberal Party boil down to the alternatives spelt out by Gladstone in 1865, whether the rich govern the poor by force, fraud or goodwill. Even those, such as the younger

radicals Joseph Chamberlain and Sir Charles Dilke, who advocated a more radical social programme than the old Whigs or Gladstonians are deemed by at least some historians to be deliberately counter-revolutionary – killing working-class agitation with kindness.[5] In this they were entirely at one with Lord Salisbury, who began at this time to concern himself with the problems of housing, recognizing that the conditions described by George Sims, Charles Booth and others could not long endure without great social disruption.

And disruptions there were. Trade union militancy was common throughout the middle and late years of the century – there were frequent strikes, even before the official inauguration of the Trades Union Congress (1868)[6] and the change in legislation, under Disraeli's second term, by which peaceful pickets were not automatically deemed in law to be criminal conspiracies.

By the early Eighties, the socialist ideas of Marx had

Membership card for the Democratic Federation designed by William Morris, 1880. The design is an oak tree laden with acorns.

begun to reach an influential audience. Bernard Shaw read Marx in French translation at this date. So too did an Old Etonian called Henry Hyndman, who read the French *Das Kapital* on the way home from Salt Lake City in the 1870s.[7] In 1881 he founded the Democratic Federation, and asked radicals such as Helen Taylor (Mill's stepdaughter) and Professor Beesly to the preliminary meetings. Hyndman was an unintentionally absurd figure. Marx found his unsolicited visits to his house in Kentish Town a great bore, and many must have raised an eyebrow at the sight of Hyndman, who never abandoned his silk hat, frock-coat and silver-topped cane, addressing the toilers as his comrades.

William Morris joined the Democratic Federation in January 1883 because it was 'the only active Socialist organisation in England', not because he was attracted to Hyndman. The simple unfairness of life under capitalism, the poor becoming no better off in many quarters as the rich became richer, inspired Morris. It was not a carefully thought out but a deeply felt decision, more akin to religious conversion than reasoned argument.

Morris was to demonstrate in his own personal pilgrimage one of the key reasons why the Left took so long to become an effective political force in England in the years up to the First World War: namely a fatal tendency to sectarianism. The psychology of the rebel against the system is unlikely to be that of the team-player. However much he or she believes themselves converted to a system of universal comradeship, they are always likely to rebel against the actual comrades' way of going about things. The Democratic Federation was destined to splinter in the mid-Eighties, with Morris and others forming the Socialist League on 30 December 1884 (it included an old Chartist veteran), only to leave it three years later when it had drifted into the hands of anarchists.

Here was a second reason why socialism was slow to appeal to the British public – and especially to the British working class. Those who have lived in England since 1945 and the Labour government of Clement Attlee think of socialism as the imposition of order. For many in the nineteenth century, as the novels about socialism demonstrate – *The Devils, Germinal, The Princess Casamassima, The Secret Agent* – socialism was indistinguishable from anarchism.

There were three other cogent reasons why socialist ideas such as those of Marx and Morris had no hope of wide adoption in the early 1880s. The first is that while the condition of the poor was as truly awful, throughout Europe, as Tolstoy, Zola or Morris observed, the evidence about overall growth in wealth and prosperity is very mixed. It is demonstrable fact that in some industrial English towns, the average height of human beings – a sure indicator of nutritional and general well-being – went down between 1830 and 1880. But against this melancholy statistic must be placed the unquestioned fact that many felt more prosperous – not the unemployed, not the agricultural workers, not the day-labourers in the building or docking industry when trade slumped: but for many, even in the working class, and particularly in the upper working and lower middle classes, the opportunity of self-betterment, self-promotion, even against a cruel atmosphere of risk, was preferable to nihilism and ideas culled from foreigners with funny names. E.P. Thompson has suggested that when Morris became a socialist in 1883 probably no more

'Plundering and Blundering', cartoon depicting Gladstone as a pilgrim weighed down with burdens, which included Bradlaugh, c. 1880.

than 200 people made the same journey.[8] It is only because we know, with hindsight, how important socialism was to become that we note its burgeoning in such detail. In British political life *at the time* it was a minor issue. There were far more pressing things on the agenda – a crisis in Egypt, a very unsettled Ireland, and the preparedness of Gladstone's second government to work towards extending the franchise to all males. The 1884 Franchise Act increased the electorate from about 3 to 5 millions. (It was not until 1918 that everyone – all males, that is – got the vote.)[9]

This leads to the second reason why socialism was not a political option for the late Victorians. If the first was that the majority of voters were too prosperous to need or want it, the second is a double and contradictory fact: the strength of Liberal Radicalism during Gladstone's

second term of office. Over such questions as education, or extending the franchise, the Radical wing of the Liberal Party was strong, and represented by figures as diverse as Charles Bradlaugh and Joseph Chamberlain. But, as mention of the last name indicates, radicalism meant different things to different people. Gladstone's parliamentary majority depended on the old Whigs, on urban radicals like Bradlaugh, on Northern Methodists, on Chamberlain and the brass tacks contingent: none were sympathetic to the Irish Home Rulers towards whom Gladstone was inexorably moving.

But first, let us consider the figure of Bradlaugh. He had neither the gloss of the patrician Liberal Charles Dilke nor the flashiness of Chamberlain, the businessman who had transformed Birmingham. He stood for the little man being allowed to speak his mind, and for the poor man having as much say in the scheme of things as the rich. He was a quintessential English protestant, small p, allowing his questioning of any established authority to lead him to virulent atheism. He was also a republican. From the 1850s onwards, he had identified with the Polish nationalists against the Russians, the Italian nationalists against the Austrians and the pope, and the Irish nationalists.

He was also a keen Malthusian, but unlike the Reverend Thomas Malthus, Bradlaugh saw that the logic of attributing all social ills to overpopulation was to advocate birth control. In 1877 the British government decided to prosecute the English publisher of an American book – *The Fruits of Philosophy* – written by a physician named Knowlton and advocating birth control. Together with his friend Annie Besant, the runaway wife of an Anglican vicar and at that stage an unbeliever, Bradlaugh produced a new version of the book and after an absurd trial the jury decided, 'We are unanimously of opinion that the book in question is calculated to deprave public morals, but at the same time we entirely exonerate the defendants' – Bradlaugh and Besant – 'from any corrupt motives in publishing it.' They were sentenced to six months' imprisonment and fined £200 each, but the Court of Appeal quashed these sentences on a legal technicality.[10]

So this was the man who in the election of 1880 stood as a Radical candidate for Parliament for the seat of Northampton. He was elected – and Henry Labouchere, moderate Liberal, was elected for the other Northampton seat. Labouchere is perhaps a notorious figure nowadays, since in 1885 when Parliament was debating homosexuality he proposed a clause in the Criminal Law Amendment Act which made all forms of male homosexual activity, and not just buggery, illegal. It seems likely that Labouchere did this to demonstrate the absurdity of the law, but the effect of his amendment was, among other things, to send Oscar Wilde to prison

ten years later.[11] His other claim to fame, perhaps more cheerful, is the quip, 'I do not mind Mr Gladstone having an ace up his sleeve, but I do object to his always saying that Providence put it there.' To Bradlaugh, a man utterly different in background and outlook, he was a loyal parliamentary friend.

Bradlaugh arrived at Westminster in 1880 and refused to take the oath required of all sitting MPs. The idiotic Speaker of the House, Sir Henry Brand, could have easily allowed Bradlaugh to affirm, rather than take an oath, with a warning that he might be liable to prosecution. As it was, he referred the matter to the House – then to a private committee. At one crazy moment Bradlaugh was imprisoned in the Clock Tower by some arcane piece of medieval law. Meanwhile the Tories could make capital from the episode and waste hours and hours of parliamentary time, worrying the Irish members and many of Gladstone's Northern Methodist grocers with the imputation that the Liberal government was a Radical atheist sham.

It was an occasion which brought out the best in Gladstone, from the point of view of parliamentary theatre. He made one of the greatest speeches of his career rebutting the young Tory firebrands such as Lord Randolph Churchill and A.J. Balfour. Gladstone saw Bradlaugh as a 'parliamentary impediment'. Each time the House rejected him, the good people of Northampton re-elected him. Eventually, in spite of the vociferous extra-parliamentary intrigues of Cardinal Manning, the opposition of most of the Anglican bishops and the blustering fury of the Tories (Churchill said Bradlaugh – 'a seditious blasphemer' – was supported by 'mob scum and dregs'),[12] Bradlaugh was allowed to affirm rather than take an oath involving the mention of a God in whom he did not believe. He had won his case, and made a point, but it is questionable how far Bradlaugh had helped those who were, in political terms, his primary concern – the poor.

A crowd attends an open air Mass at a makeshift altar at Bunlin Bridge in County Donegal, 1867.

Chapter Twenty-Six

The Rise of Parnell

In January 1880 a correspondent from the *Daily Telegraph* – in those days a Liberal newspaper – visited Connemara and was shown round by the parish priest of a place called Ernlaghmore. Father Flannery pointed to a mound of rubbish by the roadside – heaps of soil, trash, a few domestic items. From this mound a little column of smoke emanated. The rubbish was inhabited by a man who had been evicted by his landlord. The journalist was amazed when, from this hole in the ground, a fine-looking woman emerged, holding a baby. A little way down the shore, Father Flannery found for the Englishman a small cave whose mouth had been stopped by a lobster pot from whose aperture, once more, a trail of smoke proceeded.[1]

Stories such as this could be replicated all over rural Ireland at the time – in Galway, in Connemara, in the Ballina district of Co. Mayo, where small tenant-farmers had been driven off their land by high rents. An average of 200 per week were leaving the port of Larne alone for the United States, and hundreds were crossing the Irish Channel for Liverpool or Glasgow.

Wales had escaped famine – unlike Ireland and Scotland. On the other hand, unlike these lands, it had a living language spoken by a significant proportion of the population, it had suffered from bullying landlords and agricultural depression and – in the winter of 1887–8 – the Hussars were used to quell Welsh riots.[2] But though resentment against the English would continue to be felt to this day by the Welsh, for a number of legitimate grievances, the separatist movement would never be so strong as to lead to the creation of a Welsh Free State or a Welsh Republic. Rather, within the United Kingdom, the Welsh would establish their distinct identity by cultural and linguistic means, and by identifying, when the Labour Movement took shape, with the left wing of socialist political programmes.

In Ireland things were otherwise. There was poverty, and hunger, and rage: there were the memories, folk memories and actual, of the Famine: there were the Fenians – a Gaelic brotherhood naming themselves after the Fianna army in the medieval saga of Fionn MacCumhail: there were also the murderers, the professional malcontents, the anarchists.

The Land League of Michael Davitt (1846–1906), heavily subsidized from America, was a pivotal agent in the story. Born during the Great Famine, Davitt had been evicted, with his father and mother, from a smallholding in Co. Mayo when still a boy. They emigrated to Lancashire, where he was put to work in a factory and lost an arm aged eleven. Unsurprisingly, when he grew up, he had taken part in the unsuccessful raid on Chester Castle and became involved in gun-running, for which he was sentenced to grim treatment in Dartmoor jail. Because he could not as a one-armed man break stones on the moor he had been harnessed to a cart like an animal.[3]

A husband teaches his wife how to use a revolver during the unrest caused by the formation of the Land League, c. 1880.

Captain Moonlight was a truly Dostoyevskian 'horror'. It was the codename of the Land League, and it meant what happened to tenants who did not conform to the Land League's patriotically rebellious attitude to landlords. Ricks were burned, cattle maimed, houses and barns torched – all at night by Captain Moonlight. Anyone taking a farm from which a tenant had been evicted was to be 'isolated from his kind as if he were a leper of old'.

The first man to do so was, in his rashness, to add a word to the English vocabulary. When Captain Boycott took over a farm in Co. Mayo not far from Knock, he was besieged by angry expelled tenants who henceforth refused to work or trade with him. An expedition of Ulster Protestants marched to rescue him. The first Boycott in history had taken place. Captain Moonlight dug graves beside traitors' back doors but at first there were no actual murders – at first.[4]

In 1882 the viceroy, Lord Cowper, and William Forster, the chief secretary, resigned and were replaced by Lord Spencer and the Duke of Devonshire's brother, Lord Frederick Cavendish. On 6 May Cavendish and an under-secretary, T.H. Burke, were walking in Phoenix Park in Dublin when a murder gang – the 'Invincibles'[5] – sprang out and hacked them to death with twelve-inch surgical knives. Even the Fenians were shocked by the brutality and brazenness of the outrages. The leader of the Invincibles was an Irish American, Edward McCaffrey. To murder anyone is undesirable: the murder of an amiable young man like Lord Frederick who had only just arrived in Ireland sent a good indication to the politicians that they had to deal here with something rather more formidable than the Welsh nationalists. In January 1881 a Fenian bomb had injured three people in Salford (Manchester); an unexploded bomb was found in the Mansion House in March; and again in the May of the following year. In 1883 bombs exploded in Glasgow and London, and the next year four London railway stations were closed because of terrorists, Irish conspira-tors attempted to blow up London Bridge, and the newly opened Underground Railway was closed by bombers.

It was against this background of anarchic violence

A battering ram is used to break into a house on the estate of Captain Hector Vandleur in County Clare during an eviction of tenants for the non-payment of rent. The tenants have stuffed foliage in the doors and windows to hinder entry, 1888.

that we are to understand Mr Gladstone's conversion to Home Rule for Ireland – just after the election of 1885 – as well as the extraordinary political career of Charles Stewart Parnell (1846–91), whose name, incidentally, was pronounced not Parn-*elle* but *Parn*-ull, with emphasis on the first syllable.

Parnell, a young Protestant landlord from Avondale, Co. Wicklow, was destined to die in his wife's arms in Brighton, in 1891, aged forty-five. It is hard for any British or Irish person to contemplate his early end, and his failure, without intense emotion; for we have lived through thirty and more disgraceful years at the end of the twentieth century in which the government of Ireland, in accordance with the wishes of its inhabitants, has been perceived, or made into, an intractable problem by generations of politicians and pundits. The nature of 'the Irish problem' in our time has been what to do about Ulster, prompting the question, had Parnell any idea of the strength of resistance to his Home Rule scheme which would have come from the hard-core Scottish Protestants of four Ulster counties?

We shall never know the answer to that. It was never put to the test. The story of Ireland, and of Parnell, dominates the 1880s, and this political genius, this inspired visionary, seems all the more impressive with the perspective of the years. His very great achievement was double-handed. First he persuaded the Irish nationalists, old and new-style, to rally behind his very conservative and in some respects ambiguous programme of Home Rule. That is, Ireland would have its own parliament, but remain part of the British Empire.

The finer details were never fully worked out. The point was that even 'Land Leaguers' such as Davitt joined up behind Parnell, and in the course of the 1880s not only the 'Irish party' at Westminster but in effect the whole Irish nation united behind him. This was never to happen again, with any other figure on the Irish scene, however skilled or attractive to his followers.

It would be out of place to tell the whole story at once, but it is necessary to realize that within a remarkably short space of time Parnell and his parliamentary party had moved from being imprisoned outlaws to coming within a whisker of 'pacifying Ireland' – Gladstone's long-cherished dream.

Parnell held on to his own revolutionary wing, his Captain Moonlight practitioners, his American desperado friends and potential bomb-makers, not by theatricality but by a genuinely radical attitude to the Land Act, brought in by Gladstone in 1881. He did not believe it went nearly far enough, and he was arrested and imprisoned at Kilmainham for urging Irish tenants to disregard it and withhold rents. It is perhaps necessary to labour the obvious and remind readers, who presumably would not be holding this book in their hands if they were not comfortable and well-fed, of the troglodyte existence forced upon Irish people by obdurate landlordism. The harvests of the late Seventies, so ruinous to many English agrarian workers, threatened in Ireland a repetition of the Great Famine. Parnell was not putting on an act to win over the Fenians when he resisted the Land Bill and landlordism. He defied it with every ounce of his political blood – which is largely why landlordism was defeated, even though he himself died a failure. After the Liberal government did him the favour of locking him up in prison, the Irish felt they could trust Parnell, Protestant and landlord though he be.

Partly through his own skill, partly as a matter of electoral good fortune, Parnell held a balance of power, both during Gladstone's second administration of 1880–5 and, after the 1885 election, during Salisbury's brief minority government (June 1885 to the beginning of 1886).

But it was at the end of 1885 and during that election that Parnell's most outstanding political achievement was, as we should say, 'leaked' to the public. That is, he had converted Gladstone himself to an out-and-out commitment to Home Rule. The 'leak' occurred in a characteristically eccentric fashion. Just before Christmas Gladstone's son Herbert (also his secretary) told several newspaper editors, and the National Press Agency, of his father's conversion.[6]

The timing of the 'Hawarden Kite', as this leak was dubbed – some say the coinage was Salisbury's – was perhaps designed to cheer up the Irish voters, and to flush out the Tories as proponents of coercion: that is forcing tenant farmers to either pay their rents or take to the hedgerows. But it was a bold move, the beginning of the boldest and noblest phase and aspect of Gladstone's career. Though we may think harshly of Gladstone, and might share the personal aversion from him felt by many of his contemporaries, in his Irish policy he was more enlightened than any British leader before or since.

Gladstone's conversion was to throw his own party, the English Liberals, into considerable disarray. His worst enemy within his own ranks, and whom he woefully underestimated, was the Flash Harry from Birmingham, Joseph Chamberlain, soon to begin the distinctive Odyssey which would take him from the Radical wing of the Liberal Party into Lord Salisbury's third Cabinet as a rabidly jingoistic colonial secretary. Other senior Liberals, most notably Hartington, by now 8th Duke of Devonshire, would leave the Liberals and as Liberal Unionists ally themselves with the Tories over the Irish issue.

Parnell in 1885–6 was in the ascendant. He was only forty, he had Ireland, and the most eminent of all British statesmen, on his side. He also, known to a handful of insiders, was having an affair with the estranged wife of Captain O'Shea, one of his own MPs. Triumphant as he was at this time, it is impossible to imagine that he did not view with foreboding the tragic case of Sir Charles Dilke, another extraordinarily talented parliamentarian – a Radical who was seriously spoken of in many quarters as a potential successor to Gladstone himself.

Dilke (1843–1911) was the youngest member of Gladstone's outgoing Cabinet. As a rich young man in Chelsea, Dilke was well-read, well-travelled and knew 'everyone'.

When Gladstone took office for the second time, Dilke and his great political ally Chamberlain had issued the old man with the joint ultimatum that neither would serve under him unless he appointed both to Cabinet office. After some humming and hawing they had accepted a compromise – Chamberlain was made president of the Board of Trade, and after a reshuffle in 1882 Dilke got the presidency of the Local Government Board. Moreover his friend of some years, Emilia Pattison, the much younger wife of the crabby old rector of Lincoln, was now a widow and had agreed to marry Dilke on her return from India.

But on Sunday 19 July 1885, Dilke heard the fateful news that Mrs Donald Crawford – sister of his brother's widow – had told her husband that after her marriage, Dilke had been her lover. Crawford was to sue for divorce, citing Dilke as co-respondent.

The case of *Crawford* v. *Crawford and Dilke* was heard before Mr Justice Butt on Friday 12 February 1886. The decree nisi was given by the learned judge, though he did not accept Mrs Crawford's fairly hair-raising testimony against Dilke. Indeed he appeared to accept the truth of Dilke's denial that he had slept with Mrs Crawford and as Roy Jenkins says in his biography of Dilke, 'the verdict appeared to be that Mrs Crawford had committed adultery with Dilke, but that he had not done so with her'.[7]

Mrs Crawford lied in court – of that there's no doubt. She lied in the divorce hearing, and she lied when, in the following July, Dilke tried to clear his name through a process whereby the evidence was presented to the Queen's Proctor. (In this he failed – and Mrs Crawford's decree was made absolute in the summer of 1886.)

Cardinal Manning is a figure in the story. As a political ally and social friend of Dilke's, he was taken into the confidence of the beleaguered politician. He maintained Dilke's innocence, and continued to associate with him, which one suspects he would not have done had he believed Dilke had lied about the matter in court.

Roy Jenkins's biography, sunnily at home with the complexities of political intrigue in the higher echelons of the Liberal Party and the social upper reaches of late Victorian London, whirls into eddies of incoherence when trying to come to grips with the psychology of this young woman. As his story stands – and it remains easily the best account of the case, and one of the best vignettes ever written of political life in Victorian England – the baffling figure of Virginia remains incomprehensible.

Some things are clear. She wanted to carry on a love affair with a Captain Forster, so she didn't confess it to her husband. Instead she named Dilke. In spite of all his protestations it looks as if he did have *something* going on with her, even if some of the incidents (such as three-in-a-bed with a maid) were either inventions or as Jenkins says *transferred*: i.e. happened in actuality with Forster. Presumably she blurted out her story to her husband because their marriage had become intolerable, but could not have dreamed of the terrifying cross-questioning from lawyers that lay ahead.

It would be a fair assumption that in the summer of 1885 very many distinguished figures in London were involved with affairs which would cause scandal if made public. Why was Dilke singled out?

The answer is, we don't know that he was, and the notion of any sort of conspiracy against him got up for political purposes has never been proved. But nor has the evidence of ex-Inspector Butcher ever been explained either. Two days before she made her confession to her husband, Virginia Crawford was spied upon by a detective, Inspector Butcher, calling at Joseph Chamberlain's house in London. Chamberlain had no previous acquaintance with Virginia Crawford. He did not tell Dilke, supposedly his dear Radical ally, about the visit, and when challenged about it, he never supplied an adequate answer.[8]

What we know in the political sphere at this time is that Dilke was Chamberlain's only serious rival as a leader of the Radicals and as a potential successor to Gladstone. Whether or not Chamberlain, or another, deliberately set up the Dilke scandal for political ends (and there are those who favour the theory that Rosebery was the instigator),[9] we shall probably never know. What is certain is that the Dilke case demonstrated how utterly the scandal of a divorce case could ruin a political career. To have affairs is one thing; to have them published in the newspapers is quite another. The incident would give powerful ammunition to those who knew of Parnell's love-affair with Katharine O'Shea and gave an ugly boost to what could be called the power of the Press. The Press, and the anti-Parnellite politicians, would use any weapon which came to hand to destroy the workability of Home Rule.

Chapter Twenty-Seven

The Fourth Estate –
Gordon of Khartoum –
The Maiden Tribute of Babylon

One of the strangest legacies left to the world by the Victorians is the popular Press – and by extension, the radio and television journalism which has largely modelled itself on 'the New Journalism'.

The need for 'news', an instantaneous impression of the world on a weekly or daily basis, evolved within a century or so of the invention of printing, but the great age of journalism in Britain was undoubtedly the nineteenth century. By then there was a plethora of locally produced daily newspapers, and in addition to the provincial press there were many London newspapers printed with a national audience in mind. Of these, *The Times* at 3*d*. was pre-eminent under the editorship of J.T. Delane. There were many other dailies selling for a penny, including *The Daily Telegraph*, *The Daily News*, *The Daily Chronicle*, *The Morning Post* and *The Standard*. One of the stories of the 1880s, and the direct result of Gladstone's Irish policy, was how many of these originally Liberal papers, such as *The Telegraph* and *The Morning Post*, became Conservative.[1]

In periodicals such as the *Fortnightly Review* or the Liberal *Spectator* under Hutton's editorship, or the *Westminster Review*, the Victorian upper and middle classes could mull over what they thought of the news, of science, of religion, literature and their place in the world. This higher journalism is one of the great evidences of their sophistication and moral literacy. But something which Matthew Arnold called 'the New Journalism' was on its way, and its most energetic exponent was William Thomas Stead (1849–1912).

Stead was twenty-two when he became editor of the *Northern Echo*, a daily paper published in Darlington, and he remained there until 1880. It was the articles he wrote on the Bulgarian Atrocities in 1876 which first brought him to notice, and which were crucial in demonstrating to Gladstone that there existed a 'constituency' who could be swayed on supra-political moral grounds. Stead had cheered when Gladstone promised to boot the Turks out of Bulgaria. But Gladstone when swept to power in 1880 did nothing about renegotiating the terms of the Congress of Berlin which trisected Bulgaria and left two of the three sections under Turkish rule.[2] Few of the subscribers to the *Northern Echo* would much care, because by then they had moved on to some other excitement.

In 1880 Stead became deputy editor in London on the *Pall Mall Gazette*, then editor in August 1883.[3] The type of journalism which he espoused and developed was to become an essential prism by which the modern world observed itself. It

Photograph of a newspaper boy holding a placard for the Pall Mall Gazette *of 21 October 1871. The placard contains the headlines of the day, including the Chicago Fire and the death of Charles Babbage (1792-1871), inventor, reformer, mathematician, scientist, philosopher, political economist and the father of modern computing.*

was based on a threefold alliance, between an eagerly opinionated public, a political class anxious to test and ride these opinions like surfers waiting for the next roller to bear them crashing to shore, and the conduit that brought these two together, the solicitors or procurers known as journalists. Of Stead it was observed, 'Nothing has happened to Britain since 1880 which has not been influenced by the personality of this extraordinary fanatic, visionary and philanthropist.'[4] The opinion was that of Reggie Brett (later Lord Esher), the private secretary of Lord Hartington. Brett had introduced Admiral Jackie Fisher to Stead – a meeting which led to the 'Truth about the Navy' articles.

In 1882–3 Brett's mind had turned to Egypt and the Sudan. The Cabinet was, as on most issues, divided about Imperial affairs generally, Egypt in particular, with the secretary for India (Hartington), the president of the Board of Trade (Chamberlain) and the first lord of the Admiralty (Northbrook) taking a hawkish and interventionist view; John Bright (chancellor of the Duchy of Lancaster) was the most extreme in the opposite direction, being a Quaker and a pacifist. Gladstone was chiefly worried by the possibility of spending public money, and still believed that the purchase of Suez Canal shares had been a risk not worth taking. But, as Frederic Harrison declared, 'a hollow and ghostlike laugh of derision' was to be heard from Disraeli's burial-vault as the Gladstone government of 1880–5 responded to events in Egypt.

Having spent the Midlothian campaign denouncing 'Beaconsfieldism' and opposing British involvement in Egypt, Gladstone had to recognize that the United Kingdom's commercial interests were intimately bound up with Egypt and the Suez Canal. Forty-four per cent of Egyptian imports came from the UK, and 80 per cent of Egyptian exports came to Britain. The canal was a vital route to India, for both commercial and military reasons. The political situation was, to put it mildly, unstable and the system of Dual Control – by which the khedive governed with the cooperation of Franco-British advisers – did not work well. For reasons which had more to do with French domestic politics than with Egypt itself, the French did not have the concerted will to persist with a policy of European intervention when the situation became complicated. The mutiny of the Egyptian army in 1879 had been followed by the uprising of Colonel Arabi Pasha in 1881 – which many French liberals saw as a legitimate nationalist aspiration. The French fleet which together with the British had been patrolling the waters of Alexandria harbour was withdrawn, leaving the British fleet alone. Alexandria saw

riots during the summer of 1882, with 50 Europeans killed and 60 wounded on 11 June. Gladstone with great reluctance sent in the army, under Sir Garnet Wolseley. It was a highly popular campaign with the public, the more so since Wolseley gave Arthur, Duke of Connaught (1850–1942), command of the 1st Guards Brigade. 'When I read that my darling precious Arthur was really to go, I quite broke down,' the Queen told her journal. 'It seemed like a dreadful dream.'[5]

But it turned out to be a triumph, one of the most successful small campaigns of the Queen's reign. The general took with him a group of brilliant soldiers known as 'the Wolseley gang' who had proved themselves in the Ashanti War of 1873–4 – Redvers Buller, who interrupted his honeymoon to take part, William Butler, Hugh McCalmont and others. 17,401 British troops with 61 guns and supplies were successfully shipped to Alexandria – which the navy bombarded. Bright resigned from the Cabinet – no one much minded. Wolseley marched westward across the desert and engaged Arabi's forces about 16 miles east of Zagazig at a village on the Sweetwater Canal, and beside the railway line, called Tel-el-Kebir. The Egyptian fortifications would, Wolseley saw, be a 'tough nut to crack', but it was a perfectly managed operation. The 'butcher's bill' for the battle was 57 British killed, 382 wounded and 30 missing, half the casualties being Highland Scots.[6] On 18 September Wolseley reached Cairo and found a letter from the Queen – 'as cold-blooded effusion as you have ever read'.

Gladstone's Cabinet intended to withdraw the troops as soon as possible. This, however, was one of the classic examples in history of how easy it is for a Western power to intervene in apparently anarchic situations abroad, and how difficult it is to withdraw. Over the next forty years sixty-six promises were made by British governments or their consuls announcing their firm intention of leaving Egypt. Somehow the moment was never quite right, and there was in fact a permanent presence of British troops on Egyptian soil until President Nasser drove them out in 1956.[7]

In September 1883 Major Evelyn Baring, who had been in India as a finance member of the viceroy's council for three years, was recalled to London, knighted, and sent to Egypt as British agent and consul-general. He would hold the post for the next twenty-three years.[8] Gladstone, of all unlikely people, had annexed Egypt, but he was not happy as a colonialist, still less as an imperialist.

Baring had set out for Egypt with the doubtless admirable intention of 'leading the Egyptian people from

The Black Watch at the Battle of Tel-el-Kebir, 13 September 1882.

bankruptcy to solvency, and then onward to affluence, from Khedival monstrosities to British justice, and from Oriental methods veneered with a spurious European civilization towards the true civilization of the West based on the principles of the Christian moral code'.[9] Alas, this good Liberal banker was immediately faced with a danger which was not obviously soluble by reasonable means. An Egyptian government official, a former slave-trader called Mohammed Ahmed, declared himself to be the Mahdi ('one who offers divine guidance in the right way'). He raised a rebellion in the Sudanese province of Kordofan. The khedive dispatched 10,000 troops under the command of General William Hicks: a good soldier, but one who was in an impossible position. The 10,000 Egyptians under him had not been paid, their morale was poor, their willingness to fight low. The Mahdi was established in the capital of Kordofan, El Obeid, a fortified city of 100,000 inhabitants, and though many of them were armed with nothing but sticks[10] they fought as those who had God on their side. By a series of clever ambushes, and the use of treacherous guides who

lured Hicks Pasha's men into wooded ravines, the Dervishes were able to massacre all 10,000 of the Hicks army.

This was the situation facing Baring when he arrived as consul in Cairo.

General Charles George Gordon (1833–85) – from the British point of view, destined to be the tragic hero of the unfolding drama in the Sudan – was in Jerusalem when El Obeid surrendered to the Mahdi. When the news came of the Hicks disaster, he had been in Palestine ten months, basing himself in a house at Ain Karim, a village three miles west of the city. By the simple method of walking about Jerusalem with a bible in his hand, this devout Christian soldier managed to persuade himself that he had identified the actual Place of the Skull at which the crucifixion of Christ occurred, and the very 'Garden Tomb' which was the scene of the Resurrection.

Mysterious are the ways of Providence – in which Gordon, Gladstone and the Mahdi all fervently believed. While in Jerusalem, Gordon read of the unfolding events in the Sudan and favoured granting it independence under native rulers. What neither Gordon nor Gladstone knew was that the Mahdi was to die of natural causes by the middle of 1885 and that the entire crisis occasioned by his uprising would thereby have been averted.

Gordon appeared to be destined for quite another sphere of glory, since while he was in Jerusalem the king of the Belgians offered him the governorship of the Congo. He was admirably qualified, having been in his time governor of the Sudan – he administered the place in happier pre-Mahdian times with almost no European troops – and the successful victor over the 'Celestial King' who had tried to raise the Taiping rebellion in China (hence his nickname – 'Chinese Gordon'). The very man to exercise a kindly Christian influence over the Congolese.

But pressure was mounting on the Gladstone government to do something about the situation in the Sudan. The British generals in Cairo advising Baring – General Stephenson, Sir Evelyn Wood and General Baker – were all of the view that the Egyptian government could not hold on to the Sudan, and it was essential to withdraw the garrisons.[11] It was a formidable, if not impossible operation. The combined number of Egyptians and British, civilian and military, at risk from the Mahdi in Khartoum was 6,000. How were they to be transported to safety?

When the news of the Hicks disaster reached England, a colonel in the Royal Engineers living at Folkestone remembered twenty years before seeing another fanatical horde in China collapse before the genius and skill of a young British officer. Colonel Edwards wrote to the inspector general of fortifications, General Sir Andrew Clarke RE, 'There is one man who is competent to deal with the question – Charlie Gordon.'[12] Clarke told his friend the chancellor of the Exchequer, who in turn told the foreign secretary, Lord Granville. On Sunday 1 December, Gladstone wired to Baring in Cairo, 'If General Charles Gordon were willing to go to Egypt, would he be of any use to you or to the Egyptian Government, and if so, in what capacity?'

The idea that 'Chinese Gordon' would save the day gathered force. It was once believed[13] that the Hartington 'party' within the Cabinet deliberately set up a meeting between Gordon and W.T. Stead, engineered by Reggie Brett, who had such belief in Stead's powers. The truth is, there was more chance, or Providence, at work than conspiracy. Gordon had accepted governorship of the Congo. Hartington and Granville were in correspondence about whether a commissioned British officer could legally accept such a post without resigning his commission and his pension.[14] Hartington would scarcely have been writing in confidence to a Cabinet colleague about Gordon's departure for the Congo if he seriously entertained hopes of nobbling him for the Sudan. Later, when Gordon was sent to the Sudan, Hartington was a supporter – but that was after two changes of mind.

Gordon went to Brussels, accepted governorship of the Congo from King Leopold and wrote resigning his commission in the British army. The next day, 8 January 1884, Gordon was staying with his sister in Southampton. An old friend, Captain Brocklehurst of the Horse Guards, was with him when a short bearded man presented himself at the door.

'Can I see General Gordon?' – 'I am General Gordon' – was the exchange which took place on the doorstep – itself a token of Gordon's eccentricity. How many other generals of this date would open the front door rather than wait for a servant to do it for them? For both men, it was a religious moment. Stead 'knew he was in the presence of one of God's doughtiest champions'. Gordon at first declined to speak of the Sudan, but once he started on the subject, it was difficult to stop him. The government policy of evacuation could not work, and he explained to Stead why. 'You must either surrender absolutely to the Mahdi or defend Khartoum at all hazards.'[15]

Before Stead left, Gordon presented him with a copy of *The Imitation of Christ*. The next day the *Pall Mall Gazette* had the headline *Chinese Gordon for the Sudan*:

> We cannot send a regiment to Khartoum, but we can send a man who on more than one occasion has proved himself more valuable in similar circumstances than an entire army. Why not send Chinese Gordon with full powers to Khartoum, to assume absolute control of the territory, to treat with the Mahdi, to relieve the garrisons, and to do what he can to save what can be saved from the wreck in the Sudan?

Gladstone's government worked on this advice. It was the most disastrous political mistake of Gladstone's career, and it was based on two fundamental errors. First, he could not decide – as Gordon earnestly desired him to do – whether Gordon in Khartoum was being sent as an adviser, or as an alternative executive. And secondly, he would not commit the government, until it was too late, to sending troops as a reinforcement for Gordon's mission. These two mistakes were compounded by dithering. After Gordon had set out for Khartoum, the government changed its policy. In January, Gladstone's

Gordon's Last Stand by G.W. Joy. It is an icon of Christian civilization, stoical in the face of anarchic savagery. It is also, paradoxically, an image of white supremacy and power, even though it is a picture of one quite small white man about to be speared by a gang of black men. Partly, the message of supremacy is reinforced by the fact that Gordon stands at the top of the steps while his assailants come up from below. But more than that, he stands as the emblem of what is necessary in the face of such murderous anarchy: calm discipline, goodness such as only the English can bring to the world. This is the message of this powerful picture: it justifies a British presence, not only in the Sudan, but anywhere else in the world where the indigenous population lack the self-discipline or restraint to conduct themselves according to the mores of North-West Europe.

son Herbert had made a categorical assurance that the British would *not* hand over responsibility for the crisis to anyone else. On 19 February Hartington shamelessly changed gear with: 'I contend that we are not responsible for the rescue or relief of the garrisons either in the Western or the Southern or the Eastern Sudan.'[16]

The Cabinet dithered about whether to send a relieving force to Gordon in Khartoum. When General Sir Garnet Wolseley was at length dispatched with the Wolseley gang, they had on their hands a much more difficult campaign than their victory over Arabi at Tel-el-Kebir. In January 1885 10,000 Dervishes struck a column led by Sir Herbert Stewart at Abu Klea, 45 miles from Korti – 'the most savage and bloody action,' accord-

ing to Winston Churchill, 'ever fought in the Soudan by British troops'. Colonel Burnaby was killed, with 8 other officers and 65 other ranks. Stewart was mortally wounded. Khartoum was by now besieged, when Sir Charles Wilson, an experienced staff officer but no commander, received the fateful message by Nile steamer from Gordon that men and women were dying in the streets and relief was desperately needed. Wilson delayed for three days – the most fateful three days of Gordon's life.

Two days before his fifty-second birthday, at 3.30 a.m., General Gordon lit a cigarette and sent that message to Wilson. By 5 a.m. he was dressed in his white uniform and his sword and holding his revolver. The noise of the

Dervishes in the streets had been echoing all night. He walked to the top of the stairs which led to the palace council chamber. A throng of Dervishes stood at the foot of the stairs brandishing spears. Their leader, a warrior called Shahin, advanced with his spear. Gordon shrugged before Shahin's spear hit him. As he spun round, another spear hit his back. He fell on his face and the other Dervishes attacked him. It was 5.30 on the morning of 26 January 1885.*

Gordon's death at the time and afterwards was seen as a martyrdom. If it could be used to justify later atrocities that is not Gordon's fault. Lytton Strachey looked ahead to the 'glorious slaughter of twenty thousand Arabs, a vast addition to the British Empire, and a step in the Peerage for Sir Evelyn Baring'[17] when General Kitchener conquered the Dervishes at Omdurman. These horrors are not to be denied, and we can see they were a combined consequence of the new generation's imperial ruthlessness, and the old generation's vagueness about intervening.

There is no doubt that Gladstone's perceived callousness to Gordon, and his inability to see why the death in Khartoum caught the imagination of so many people, was a symptom of his having lost political grip. Five days after the news of Gordon's death reached London, Gladstone went to the theatre, a gesture of indifference which caused public fury. 'No single event in Gladstone's career made him more unpopular.'[18] Quite apart from anything happening in Ireland, it was the beginning of his coming adrift and a major cause of his electoral failure in 1885. Of course, within six months of Gordon's death, the *Pall Mall Gazette* had forgotten the hero of Khartoum and moved on to something even more exciting.

There can be no doubt that in the eyes of Stead himself, his greatest journalistic coup was his exposé of child prostitution, 'The Maiden Tribute of Modern Babylon'.

Josephine Butler, the wife of a Cheltenham schoolmaster, George Butler, had been stung into public good works by bereavement, her agony following the death of her little daughter Eva in 1864. (She fell downstairs.) Mrs Butler never recovered her own health fully, but decided to reach out of her own suffering to help others.

She began by visiting the workhouse in Liverpool. (To escape the associations of their home in Cheltenham the Butlers had moved to Liverpool, where George had become principal of Liverpool College.) Sitting among

*The man who actually killed Gordon did not so much as know who he was. The Mahdi had decreed that he wanted Gordon taken alive. This did not stop the death of Gordon achieving instantaneous iconic status at home.

the women of the workhouse, and picking oakum with them, Josephine Butler began to understand the conditions of working-class women – and above all to feel anger at the Contagious Diseases Acts. The Report of the Royal Commission of 1870 to inquire into the workings of the Acts (of 1864, 1868 and 1869) saw the behaviour of those who visited prostitutes as 'the irregular indulgence of a natural impulse'. The law institutionalized the notion that to use a prostitute's services was 'natural' even though the woman who provided the service was wicked. In order for this institutionalized rationale of prostitution to be effective, it required, in the Contagious Diseases Acts, giving to the law the right to apprehend, and to examine, women at will.

It is hard to overstate the courage of Josephine Butler in bringing this abuse to the attention of the public. Decent women did not talk about sex in public – still less about sexual diseases, or the double standards employed by men when legislating about them. At the Colchester by-election of 1870, when Mrs Butler spoke in support of the Abolitionist who challenged Sir Henry Storks, Tory, a keen supporter of the Acts, her hotel was mobbed and its windows smashed. But Storks lost by 500 votes – 'bird shot dead' as Josephine Butler was told by a telegram. A Royal Commission was set up to review the Contagious Diseases Acts, to which Mill gave vital evidence, emphasizing that this was a matter of basic civil liberty. After years of campaigning by Mrs Butler and friends, the Acts were eventually repealed in 1886.

In the course of her campaigns to repeal the Acts, Josephine Butler came across many abuses in England and abroad. She went to Brussels, and exposed the kidnap of British children and young women for use in Belgian brothels. And what she found out so scandalized her that she decided to approach Stead and expose the fact that you could purchase a child on the streets of London for the purposes of sexual abuse. In Liège, she had been told, 'waggon-loads of girls had been brought into Belgium'.[19]

It was, from the point of view of those English puritans with a taste for such things, sublime 'copy'. But in order, as they say in the trade, to make the story stand up, it was necessary for an actual man to purchase an actual child-prostitute and be prepared to admit that he had done so. Who better than our Northern crusader himself, W.T. Stead?

Readers of the *Pall Mall Gazette* during the first week of July 1885 were warned not to buy the issue of 6 July, since it would contain matters to upset the squeamish.

Josephine Butler writing in her study.

Even without these inducements, 'The Maiden Tribute of Modern Babylon' would have been a sell-out – a full account of the sale or violation of children, the procuration of virgins, the international trade in little girls and the unnatural vices to which they were subjected. Headlines such as 'THE FORCING OF UNWILLING MAIDS' and 'DELIVERED FOR SEDUCTION' had all the hallmarks which this type of journalism has had ever since. That is, while professing to deplore what it describes, it offers the readers the pornographic thrill of reading all about it. Stead described a clergyman calling regularly at a brothel to distribute Christian literature, but with equal regularity succumbing to the erotic allure of the little girls. Whether or not this reverend gentleman existed in fact, he was an emblem of Stead and his readership, hovering self-righteously about unsavoury places to which they were irresistibly drawn.[20]

On Derby Day, 1885, Stead claimed he had witnessed a girl being purchased from her mother for £5. In fact, this sale was a masquerade. The girl was called Eliza Armstrong. She was taken to a brothel in Lisson Grove, Marylebone, and rested on the four-poster bed while Rebecca Jarrett, a retired prostitute now under the protection of the Salvation Army, administered chloroform. Around the curtains of the bed there now appeared our puritanical editor, Stead, holding a glass of champagne and a cigar as tokens of his status as a roué. He paid his money, and Liza was bundled off to a Salvation Army hostel in Paris, then on to Drôme in the South of France,

before being returned to Stead's house in Wimbledon. But Stead in his zeal had overstepped the law, and Liza's father, who did not have a part in the proceedings, brought a prosecution for abduction. During the trial it emerged that Rebecca Jarrett worked as a housemaid for Josephine Butler and that the whole story was a fabrication.

Rebecca Jarrett was sent to prison, the others involved in the fraud being let off – except Stead, who went to jail for three months. For every year afterwards he wore his prison clothes on the anniversary of his imprisonment, attracting some notice as he paced over Waterloo Bridge to his office in a jacket and trousers covered with arrows, and a badge with his number. The gesture, like the offence for which he was originally sentenced, was an expedition in the cause of some higher truth into the realms of fantasy. Although Stead had worn prison uniform on his first day in prison, as a 'first class misdemeanant' he was in fact allowed to wear his own clothes for the remainder of his sentence.[21]

There were a few attempts to revive the old sensationalist magic, some of which sold very well – especially *If Christ Came to Chicago* of 1892, in which Stead 'named and shamed' the brothel-owners. In latter years he became more and more obsessed by spiritualism and – as befitted a man with an eye for the headline – he did not die in his bed at home: he went down with the *Titanic* in 1912. He was last seen helping women and children on to the lifeboats.

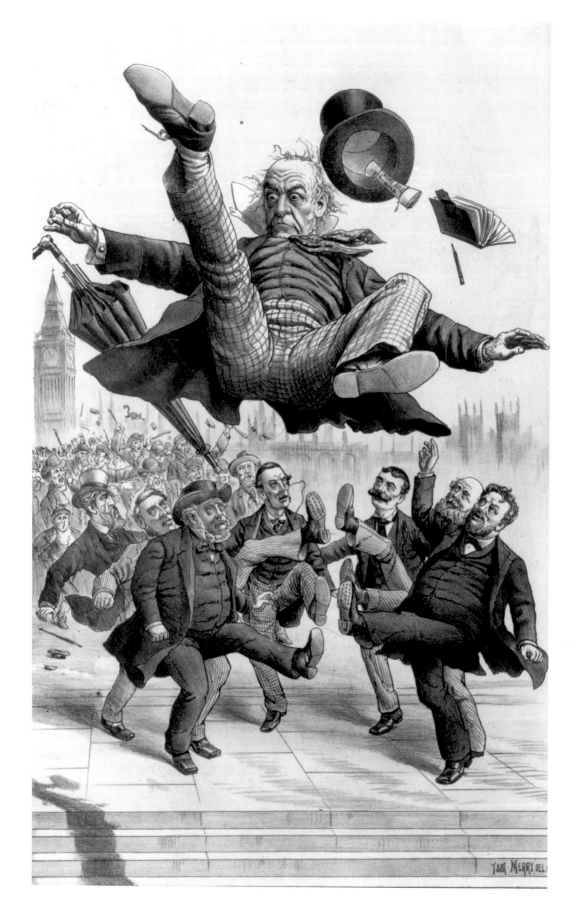

Chapter Twenty-Eight

Politics of the Late 1880s

The densely knotted drama of British political life from June 1885 to August 1886 will perhaps interest only the addict of the parliamentary roulette wheel. The general effect of what emerged from those crisis-ridden months, however, reverberates through British political life until the Second World War – arguably beyond it.

In outline what happened was this. Gladstone's second administration, which had been dogged by so many problems from the start – the Bradlaugh affair taking hours of parliamentary time, the unignorable Irish crisis, the problems of Egypt and the Sudan, the question of extending the franchise at home – ran into terminal trouble in the summer of 1885. The Cabinet was split over Ireland. But the ostensible reason for the collapse of the government was the budget which proposed a tax on beer and liquor. Behind the shield of this comparatively minor issue the shattered Liberal Party tried to disguise from itself the irreconcilable nature of its differences over the larger matter of Ireland. When Sir Michael Hicks Beach – what we would call the shadow chancellor of the Exchequer – moved an amendment on the budget, 76 Liberals abstained. The Irish members voted with Gladstone, giving him the tiny majority of 264 to 252 in the Commons. But the warnings were clear and Gladstone – who, remember, had not yet had his conversion to Home Rule and was still trying to hold the party together – resigned.

He went to Osborne to do so, and the Queen did not even offer him luncheon. Still less, during what both must have assumed to be his last audience in fifty-five years of political life, did she express one word of regret at his departure. On his way home across the Solent by the early-evening ferry, Gladstone was too absorbed in Robert Louis Stevenson's *Kidnapped*, just published, to feel much grievance.[1]

The Conservatives formed a minority government on 24 June 1885, but they knew that it could not last long. Parliament had voted the previous year to increase the franchise by 2 million individuals, and this could not fail to favour the Liberals. The procedures – establishing the names and addresses of the new voters, and the boundaries of the new constituencies – would take until November. In December 1885 the election led to a Liberal victory, as anyone could have predicted. A deep paradox was now going to unfold. Chamberlain, leader of the Liberal Radical wing, could boast that 'government of the people by the people . . . has at last been effectively secured'.[2] He could believe that a great programme of democratic reform would unfold – including abolition of the House of Lords and the monarchy. But as the election came to its slow conclusion, his leader, Gladstone, flew the Hawarden Kite and announced his conversion to Home Rule – anathema to Chamberlain, and to a significant proportion of Liberals, both old Whig and new Radical. When the results were counted in December 1885, the

A mob kicks Gladstone in the air over the Home Rule Bill in a cartoon called 'Away With Him', 1886, accompanied by the line from Tennyson 'The wild mob's million feet will kick you from your place.'

Liberals had 334 members, the Conservatives 250 and the Irish 86. It was clear that with the profound fissure in Liberal ranks caused by the Irish issue, Gladstone was never going to collect enough votes to secure Home Rule in the session of 1886. His Home Rule Bill came before the Cabinet in March 1886 – Chamberlain and Trevelyan resigned. In the Commons the Home Rule Bill was defeated by 30 votes – 341 noes against 311 ayes. Chamberlain had voted against his chief and changed sides – with extraordinary results both in his own career and in the history of politics. The short-lived third Gladstone government resigned, and Salisbury took office as prime minister in August 1886, and would serve a full term until the summer of 1892.

The question which forces itself upon our minds at the distance of one and a quarter centuries is how much of a true political shift took place as a result of the electoral reforms of 1884. Did the granting of a vote to 4,376,916 male adults (as opposed to 2,618,453) before the passage of the Representation of the People Act[3] appreciably change the way in which Great Britain was governed over the next few decades? Believers in Parliament might see British history as an unfolding progression of freedoms by which, as general election followed general election, more and more people – first the urban males, then the entire working class (males), then all adults, male and female – were empowered. But empowered to do what? To elect representatives who for the most part perpetuated the system which had placed them there.

If the majority of the population was working class, how did it come about that until the twentieth century there were next to no working-class parliamentarians thrown up by this supposedly democratic system? Was the Reform Act of 1884 a step in the direction of democracy, or was it a piece of legislation which allowed 4,376,916 male individuals to go into a ballot box and choose between two party candidates who in many fundamental areas had identical political aims? Is the reason that Irish Home Rule split the Liberal Party quite simply that it was the only issue about which the political classes were seriously divided, and the only issue, thanks to the solidarity of the Irish MPs, in which a vote cast in a ballot box might make an appreciable difference to the way politicians conducted public life?

Those who believe that Parliament is an institution with a serious political function might be surprised that the first woman member to take her seat did not do so until 1919 and that the proportion of men to women in Parliament is still in the twenty-first century overwhelming. But this is one of the many issues where the real agents of change were extra-parliamentary. Women's colleges, trade unions, the churches, the cells of non-parliamentary political groups and – in time of war – the meeting-together of people in ships, squadrons and regiments were all far more effective agents of change in Britain than any political party pre-1945 – arguably beyond. The function of Parliament was to preserve the power of the political classes; and this in effect meant the Rich.

Chapter Twenty-Nine

Into Africa

During the month of October 1885 – which saw the funeral of Lord Shaftesbury in Westminster Abbey, a general election in France, and the removal of 14 tons of rock by dynamite to form the tunnel in New York harbour known as the Hell gate, while a cyclone swept southern Italy, and a horse called Plaisanterie won both the Cesarewitch Stakes and the Cambridgeshire Stakes[1] – a thirty-eight-year-old Englishman was lying in a small hut in the East African region north of Lake Victoria Nyanza – Masai country. In his Lett's monthly pocket diary, measuring $4\frac{1}{2}$ inches by $2\frac{3}{4}$, he wrote, in a tiny handwriting, 'Eighth day's prison. I can hear no news, but was held up by Psalm XXX, which came with great power. A hyena howled near me last night smelling a sick man, but I hope it is not to have me yet.'[2]

Though he was not to be eaten by hyenas, the confidence of James Hannington (1847–85) was misplaced. His arrival as the newly consecrated bishop of the newly created diocese of Eastern Equatorial Africa had been full of hope and prayer. Docking at Mombasa, he had established his diocesan headquarters at Frere Town and then began a progress westwards through land which he had persuaded himself was 'his' diocese. The Masai were disturbed by the party – 226 strong – which the bishop took in his entourage, and the Christians suffered frequent attacks as well as bad weather and illness. At Kwa Sundu, in October, Hannington reduced the party to 50 – and pressed on towards Lake Victoria Nyanza, covering 170 miles in five days. All in all it had been an heroic trek – starting with a walk of well over 400 miles to plant the Cross of Christ on Kilimanjaro, and marching onwards down routes which had been trodden by traders – from Mombasa, through Taita by the lakes of Naivasha and Baringo to Uganda.[3] But the new young king of Ganda, Mwanga, found the advance of a white man along such a route undoubtedly threatening. The bishop and his party were surrounded, overpowered and arrested. The pocket diary reveals that Hannington applied to himself the words of the Psalmist – 'I had fainted, unless I had believed to see the goodness of the Lord in the land of the living. Wait on the Lord. Be of good courage. Wait, I say, on the Lord.' On 28 October, inquiring the reason why his custodians were drumming and shouting louder than usual, the bishop was told that he and his companions were to be taken to Uganda. As they set off, Hannington's party was surrounded by Masai. The bearded young man looked his murderers in the eye and bade them tell King Mwanga that he had purchased the road to Buganda with his life. Then he pointed to his own gun which was being brandished by a Masai warrior. The gun went off and, as his friend the Rev. E.C. Dawson put it, 'the great and noble spirit leapt forth from its broken house of clay, and entered with exceeding joy into the presence of the King'. The Masai then massacred, with spears, all but four of the fifty men accompanying the bishop.

Ugandan Christians revere Hannington as a martyr. He was not the last

The Massacre of an English Mission in Benin from Le Petit Journal *1897.*

Anglican martyr to meet a violent end there – in our own lifetimes President Idi Amin saw to that. Archbishop Janani Luwum was among the untold numbers massacred in the years 1971–9 in Uganda.[4]

It has been said by one of its liveliest historians that 'the scramble for Africa bewildered everyone, from the humblest African peasant to the master statesmen of the age, Lord Salisbury and Prince Bismarck'.[5] In a speech in May 1886, Salisbury stated that when he left the Foreign Office in 1880 'nobody thought about Africa', but when he returned to it five years later 'the nations of Europe were almost quarrelling with each other as to the various portions of Africa which they could obtain. I do not exactly know the cause of this sudden revolution.'[6]

The 'Scramble for Africa'[7] (a journalese phrase coined by *The Times* in September 1884) was the Victorian equivalent of the penetration of outer space for the superpowers of the twentieth century. It was of a piece with the Benthamite desire to control human groups and societies, and with the scientific desire to systematize, to classify, to museumize. To stick a label on something and to give it a Latin name is to comprehend it, to understand, to master.

Africa sat defiantly in the middle of the world throughout the Industrial Revolution, refusing to be classified,

Welsh explorer and journalist Sir Henry Morton Stanley, with his boy Kalula, posing in the clothes he wore when he met fellow explorer Dr David Livingstone in central Africa, 1871.

penetrated or understood. The extraordinary significance, for the Victorians, of David Livingstone, patron saint of missionary explorers, and of his St Paul, the American journalist Henry Morton Stanley, is that they had been where no white man had trod, and done it in a *scientific* spirit. Livingstone had died in May 1873 at a village in the county of Ilala, the very heart of the continent. They had sun-dried his body and brought it back for burial in the national Valhalla, Westminster Abbey. Stanley – the illegitimate son of Welsh-speakers who had been brought up in the local workhouse, St Asaph's near Denbigh, before going to America aged seventeen – saw Africa, as many explorers and missionaries did, as the metaphor for the uncharted territory of their own personal 'struggle'.[8]

The Scramble for Africa was not a plot. It was something which happened because of the nature of the times in which it happened. The restlessness and scientific curiosity and by their lights the wish to be helpful of some travellers and explorers went hand in hand with the commercial greed and appetite for power in others. Then again, these explorations took place at the time of growth in European nationalisms. Livingstone penetrated the Congo, but in so doing he found a world in which cannibalism, slavery and rampant sexual promiscuity were waiting to be abolished, tidied away and disapproved of. The King of the Belgians, Leopold II, was the first to give voice to the idea that '*Il faut à la Belgique une colonie*', Belgium must have a colony,[9] but it was not long before the other European countries were wanting

what he called 'a slice of this magnificent cake'.[10] *The Times* saw Central Africa as a land of 'unspeakable richness' only waiting for an 'enterprising capitalist'. Once on African soil, however, even some of the greediest Europeans felt the itch not merely to plunder but to improve the African.

No one can say that the post-colonial problems faced by Africans in the twenty-first century do not grow out of the preoccupations of the nineteenth-century conquerors. The artificial boundaries imposed on mapless tribal lands by analogy with European borders, the deliberate shattering of traditional sociopolitical structures among African peoples, and their exploitation by Western commerce continue to cause and to highlight the difficulty. But which Western observer confronted by child slavery in an East African cocoa plantation, or female circumcision, or rampant AIDS, does not feel the

impulses of benevolent Victorian missionaries to 'improve' and to 'civilize' the continent? The United Nations and the Commonwealth of Nations continue to assert the moral imperative of democracy for the new African states. Their fervour on the subject recalls the energy with which early missionaries attempted, with only limited success, to recommend monogamy.

None of us can entirely detach ourselves from the Imperial experiment and its consequences. At the same time, we cannot fail to wonder at the speed with which the European nations discovered Africa, mapped it, carved it up among themselves. France took the largest share geographically: the French Congo was a larger area than all Germany's African colonies put together.[11] By 1890 Salisbury and Bismarck had brokered deals with the other European powers and the 'map of Africa' was drawn.

Chapter Thirty

Kipling's India

The confidence with which white Europeans assumed racial superiority over the African or the Indian is one of the most shocking aspects of the Victorian sensibility. Bogus notions of racial stereotype, and fervour for the salvation of souls, sometimes combined in the same individual to produce an alarming cocktail of imperialistic motivation. The story of Gordon all but alone in Khartoum with his bible and his self-belief, or Livingstone penetrating the unknown territories of the Congo, or Bishop Hannington, with fifty bearers, confronting the angry warriors of King Mwanga, are all stories which suggest a primeval and physically equal struggle in which the white man's superiority to the black is demonstrated in moral terms. The truth is that the expansion of the Empire took place at a time of rapid technological advance. The new inventions changed everything, both in Europe and in the Imperial world: changed the pattern of trade, disrupted the normal pattern of political relationships both within and between nations, created a global economy, a global technological world with which politicians could only partially come to terms.

Technology is the vital factor in the Imperial story. We have already alluded to the fact that the British possession of the telegraph played a vital role in defeating the sepoy uprisings of 1857–8 in India. At the same time, Speke and Burton were setting out to discover the sources of the Nile, Livingstone to explore the Zambezi. Shallow-draft steamers were an essential part of the enterprise. Having begun his unlocking of the African mystery, Livingstone could also produce the bestselling book which would publicize it. Steam printing enabled him to roll off 70,000 copies of *Missionary Travels and Researches in South Africa*. Before its invention, 10,000 books sold would have been a prodigy.

Travel speeds, thanks to railroads and steamships, had now been reduced. This was the era when the world was divided into twenty-four time zones one hour apart, because it was now technologically possible 'to put a girdle around the earth', like Shakespeare's Ariel. Steel had replaced iron as the preferred material for boiler and hull construction.[1]

Petroleum fuelled the newly developed twin-cylindered engine developed by Gottlieb Daimler (1834–1900) of Württemberg.[2] In 1885 he devised his surface carburettor; and while he was designing his high-speed vertical engine, Karl Benz (1844–1929) of Mannheim was developing his first motor-vehicle[3] (his first four-wheeled car was constructed in 1893), though Daimler can take the credit or blame for inventing the internal combustion engine itself.

At the same time, wireless telegraphy was being developed by Heinrich Hertz (1857–94). Sir Oliver Lodge (1851–1940) pioneered the use of an induction coil as a means of tuning an electric resonator – a system he perfected in 1897, and whose commercial possibilities were almost instantly exploited by Guglielmo Marconi

The Ghats at Benares in India, late nineteenth century.

(1874–1937). Before that, Alexander Graham Bell (1847–1922), basing his experiments on the work of the German physicist Hermann Helmholtz (1821–94), had pioneered the telephone. The first telephone exchange was established in London in 1879.

The world of King Mwanga, of the Turkish sultans, or of the Reverend William Barnes in Dorset, was now to be replaced by another world altogether – petroleum-fuelled, steel-girdered, telephonically-connected, electric-lit.

'It is useless to rail against capitalism. Capitalism did not create our world; the machine did.'[4] Just as it could be said that the arms race got out of control merely because technology was unbridled, not because politicians willed it to do so, it could also be said that the Imperial expansion was part of the technological revolution. Those cultures with no such technology could not resist the incursions of those with Maxim guns, telegrams, railways and steel-framed steamships. One way of looking at this would be to say that the technologically advanced culture was dominant or even (as nearly all Victorians would have believed) superior. Another way of viewing matters, however, would be to suggest that the notion of 'control' was itself a patriarchal illusion. Much of the technological advance of the 1880s could be seen as a blind march to murder, arson, mayhem. In 1879 Alfred Nobel (1833–96) invented blasting gelatine – 92 per cent nitroglycerine gelatinized with 8 per cent of collodion cotton.[5] The initial difficulties of manufacture were great, but by 1884, with the use of soluble nitro-cotton (rather than collodion), large-scale production could begin. The human race now possessed the capacity to blast quarries, mines and dams on an unprecedented scale, but it had also taken an irrevocable stride towards the capacity to obliterate itself altogether.

The bard of the technological revolution, the artist who felt most instinctively, and understood with the most immediate intelligence, the connection between technology and imperial strength, was Rudyard Kipling (1865–1936). His Browningesque dramatic monologue 'McAndrew's Hymn' – a glorious poem almost better than anything, even, that Browning wrote – puts into the mouth of an old Scottish ship's engineer the bizarre thought:

> From coupler-flange to spindle-guide I see Thy hand,
>   O God –
> Predestination in the stride o' yon connectin'-rod.[6]

George Curzon pictured with his wife and His Highness the Nizam of Aina-Khana, 1900. Modern Indian historians can see the Raj, probably correctly, as based on notions of white racial superiority, but any Indian antiquary has reason to be grateful to Curzon for preserving and conserving so much.

And in 'The King' the poet sees Romance itself, the Boy-god who most poets teach us to suppose is vanished from the Earth, bringing up the nine-fifteen train.

His hand was on the lever laid,
His oil-can soothed the worrying cranks,
His whistle waked the snowbound grade,
His fog-horn cut the reeking Banks;
By dock and deep and mine and mill
The Boy-god reckless laboured still![7]

Kipling was also the first writer to admit the sexual appeal of imperial expansion. Whatever the political or economic motives of empire, its existence and its growth expanded the world for a great many people who could not conceivably have come into contact otherwise with races and cultures utterly different from their own. The 'Burma girl' who sits by the 'old Moulmein Pagoda' in 'Mandalay' offers delights which are not in the repertoire of the 'fifty 'ousemaids' dated by the common soldier-narrator since his return to London:

When the mist was on the rice-fields an' the sun was
    droppin' slow
She'd git 'er little banjo an' she'd sing 'Kulla-lolo!'
With 'er arm upon my shoulder an' 'er cheek agin
    my cheek
We useter watch the steamers an' the *hathis* pilin'
    teak.[8]

Kipling's reputation is one of the most complicated in the history of literature. It would be an obtuse reader who did not recognize his brilliance as a short-story writer – 'our greatest' according to the poet Craig Raine . . . 'our greatest practitioner of dialect and idiolect'.[9] It would also be hard to think of anything but priggishness or intellectual snobbery which refused to see merit in Kipling's enormous output of verse. Yet it is impossible to imagine the revisionist reader, however much under Kipling's spell, who could endorse the views in 'The White Man's Burden', with its picture of

> Your new-caught, sullen peoples,
> Half-devil and half-child.[10]

(A reference to the American conquest of the Philippines.) When Kipling's talent first shone upon the world, he was seen less as an imperialist than as an exotic. Those marvellous early stories in *Plain Tales from the Hills* opened up a world which many stuffier defenders of the Raj would probably have wanted concealed. He depicts in dozens of incomparable vignettes the silliness and triviality of English society in the hill stations, the casual adulteries and flirtations, and the continual allure, imaginative and sexual, of India itself.

In what is Kipling's most successful sustained evocation of Indian life, *Kim*, written when he had long since left India (1901), Kimball O'Hara, the son of an Irish colour-sergeant and (one infers) a Eurasian nursemaid, befriends a Tibetan lama and follows him on the religious pilgrimage to Benares and the river which will wash away sin. Contrasted with the lama and his essentially serious perception of things are the British intelligence agents who want to train Kim as a spy in 'The Great Game'. The most memorable and moving characters whom Kim and his Tibetan friend encounter, and the most realistic, are all Indians – Hindu and Muslim and Sikh.

The spies seem to have wandered into the 'felt life' of a masterpiece from adventure stories on a railway bookstall. One feels that Kipling's imagination has seen something to which his developed political brain is blind: namely the absolute inevitability that the Raj will one day end. In this story, everyone of course takes the Raj for granted. There are no Indian nationalists. Yet India itself in all its cultural abundance, in all its geographical varieties, its colours, lights and smells, comes alive in this book quite incomparably: larger and stronger than any temporary political system.

The inevitability that self-government would come is obvious to the eyes of hindsight. Lord Curzon, in some ways the greatest of all the viceroys, who took up his post in 1899, was the most out-and-out Imperialist, believing that 'through the Empire of Hindustan . . . the mastery of the world was in the possession of the British people'. Yet he sensed almost as soon as he got to India, in his fortieth year, that 'The English are getting lethargic and they think only of home. Their hearts are not in this country.'[11]

Curzon was one of the only viceroys with a deeply learned love of Indian language, lore, architecture and archaeology. In his antiquarianism and taste for old Indian artefacts, buildings, philosophy and literature, Curzon seems, like the muse of Kipling, both imperialistically arrogant and culturally humble. A large part of him bowed before a great Asiatic past, and seemed to know by instinct that British imperial ambitions would never have the power, or importantly the will, to dominate it.

'Right-wing' critics of liberalism in the Raj looked with satisfaction to the journalism of Sir James Fitzjames Stephen, who in 1883 famously said that the Raj was 'founded not on consent but on conquest'. Obviously, after the quite horrifying trauma of 1857–8, this was in part true. The reform of the Indian army after the Mutiny raised the ratio of Europeans to Indians in the armed services to about half by the mid-1860s.[12] But it must have been obvious to all that on another level, both the army and the ICS only functioned on a principle of consent. In the 1860s the army numbered 120,000 Indians and 60,000 Europeans, and it was the constant aim of penny-pinching laissez-faire British governments to cut these numbers. Once Indian nationalism became an even half-serious proposition, the Raj could not long endure. Racist, by any standards, it undoubtedly was; economically exploitative too, as nearly all modern historians wish to point out; but the British will to govern by force had its limits when consent was absent. The massacre of protesters at Amritsar by General Dyer – 379 killed and 1,200 wounded – on 13 April 1919, followed by a proclamation of martial law, was a disgrace from which the British Raj never recovered its semi-legitimate self-estimation for decency and justice. Thirty years before independence it sealed the Raj's fate, but one can now sniff the obsolescence of the imperial ambition in the wind much earlier – in the closing decades of Queen Victoria's reign.

Chapter Thirty-One

Jubilee – and the Munshi

To the crowds who assembled in London for the Queen's Golden Jubilee in June 1887, however, the British Empire was manifested as a visible pageant. As the Queen's carriage was drawn to Westminster Abbey for the Service of Thanksgiving on 21 June, it was preceded by an Indian cavalry escort, each member of which was presented with a special medal at Windsor Castle before going home.[1] The crowds gave rousing cheers to the brilliantly dressed Indian princes who attended the ceremonies in honour of their Queen-Empress. The Maharao of Cutch, his diamond-and-ruby-encrusted turban sparkling in the sunshine, received especially warm applause. The Maharaja Holkar of Indore was clad with equal magnificence. And there must have been gasps of wonder at the superb gold and silver trappings and saddle on the proud Arab stallion of His Highness the Thakor of Morvi.

One figure stood out from the grandees in their gilded epaulettes, sashes, uniforms, helmets, turbans. The Queen herself wore a black satin dress, and a bonnet trimmed with white lace. Many will have noted her corpulence, to which the previous day's luncheon (the actual anniversary of her accession) amply contributed. With its Potage à la Royale, its Filet de Boeuf au Macaroni, its Poulets, its Venison steaks, its lobsters, ducklings, jellies and *Reis Kuchen mit Aprikosen*, it was of a positively Hanoverian heaviness.[2]

One witness to the Abbey service remarked how apt it was that the Queen dressed so simply – 'she was mother and mother-in-law and grandmother of all that regal company, and there she was, a little old lady coming to church to thank God for the long years in which she had ruled over her people'.[3] A comparable observation was made once when she was being driven through Dublin, and a woman in the crowd remarked, 'Sure, and she's only an old body like ourselves.'

She was no such thing. Those admitted to her presence attested to her personal charm and strength of character, which was 'both shy and humble . . . But as Queen she was neither shy nor humble, and asserted her position unhesitatingly.' This could form no part of public perception of her character, however, since for most of the previous quarter-century she had been a recluse, squirrelling away the £400,000 per annum awarded to her as Head of State, and seldom seen. Journalists and those whose hobby was to 'follow' the royal family singled out particular members as 'popular', 'scandalous' and so on, but very little was publicly known about any of them, least of all about the Queen.[4] Even those who might be expected to have come across Her Majesty – such as the 3rd Marquess of Salisbury – found her character a total surprise when actually encountered.

The parade of the Queen's children, grandchildren and in-laws was distinguished neither by its beauty or health, nor by its morals. It was widely agreed in the Abbey that the most impressive figure was the German Crown Prince (Fritz) –

married to the Princess Royal. He had arrived at the ceremonies, with Vicky, arrayed in cuirass and silver helmet, from a hotel in Norwood where they were staying to conserve their strength for a summer at Balmoral.[5] They had also consulted Dr Morell MacKenzie of Harley Street, who had confirmed that Fritz had cancer of the larynx. (He died in 1888.) Their son Willy (the future Kaiser Wilhelm II) had been damaged at birth – one arm was crushed and he was deaf. He had also inherited the strain of madness in the family. His relations with his parents were of the most painful. In some moods he was so Anglophobic that once when he cut himself he hoped he would lose every drop of his English blood. Those who cheered the arrival at the Abbey of the governor general of Canada, the Marquess of Lorne, might have wondered why his wife, Princess Louise, had produced no heir. Did it have anything to do with the fact that she had been in love with the sculptor Edgar Boehm and that Lord Lorne was a promiscuous homosexual, much given to meeting guardsmen in Hyde Park until his exile to the land of the lumberjack? The Prince of Wales was a by-word for scandalous adulteries, and poor Prince Leopold was haemophiliac, a condition for which Princesses Alice (already ten years dead at the time of the Jubilee) and Beatrice were carriers – as was the Princess Royal. (They spread the disease through most of the royal houses of Europe.) This was no 'old lady like ourselves': it was an extraordinary matriarchy of medical and psychological oddities.

One of the more markedly eccentric – and to me attractive – features of the Queen's character was shown in her passionate partiality for individual servants. John Brown, the Highland ghillie, certainly enjoyed an intimacy with his royal employer which gave rise to gossip.[6] There was even a scurrilous pamphlet published – *Mrs John Brown*. Courtiers who saw them together were irritated by Brown's throwing his weight about. He 'could do practically what he liked with the other servants' and was impertinent to equerries, royal doctors and the like. But Frederick Ponsonby – son of the Queen's private secretary and himself a royal servant of long standing – was surely right to conclude that 'whether there was any quite unconscious sexual feeling in the Queen's regard for her faithful servant I am unable to say, but judging by what I heard afterwards . . . I am quite convinced that if such a feeling did exist, it was quite unconscious on both sides, and that their

A satirical view of Queen Victoria's Golden Jubilee, 25 June 1887.

ROYAL ARMS JUBILANT.

Queen Victorian writes a letter at a table piled with despatch boxes, while her Indian servant awaits orders, 1893. Victoria's idea to have not merely decorative servants in turbans but Indian members of the Household contrasts impressively with that of Elizabeth II, who during a period when her country became supposedly multiracial and multicultural employed not one secretary, equerry or household servant of an Asian or Afro-Caribbean background.

relations up to the last were simply those of employer and devoted retainer.'[7] The court grew used to the Queen's adopting Brown's locutions. When the Duchess of Roxburgh and Lady Stopford (a woman of the Bedchamber) were not on speaking terms, Sir James Reid, the Queen's doctor, suggested that the Duchess might visit her. 'Oh no,' exclaimed the Queen. 'There would only be what Brown calls Hell and hot water.'

Perhaps only those, in our own day, who have befriended old ladies who still employ servants can recognize how deep and close the bond between them can grow. The Queen had been in effect an only child – though she had a half-sister she was brought up as a solitary, uncertain of her mother's love and yet monarch of all she surveyed. She also inherited the classic Hanoverian distaste for her

heir, and she had the terrible misfortune to be widowed young. Neither from parent nor from first-born son could the consolations of affection be found, nor the even more deeply consoling qualities of dependability, obedience, affection for her whims. It is no surprise that she numbered her servants among her best friends.

When Brown died in 1883 she was devastated, and was still thinking loving thoughts of him on her deathbed nearly eighteen years later. No servant ever replaced him in her affections, but there was one 'about whom' – to quote from her doctor – 'the Queen seems off her head'.[8]

At the end of June 1887 she engaged her first two Indian servants – Mahomet Buksh, a plump smiling young man, and Abdul Karim, aged twenty-four, both of them *khidmutgars* (waiters). They were engaged to serve at table, but it was not long before the Queen had given her secretary a Hindi vocabulary to study. 'I am learning a few words of Hindustani to speak to my servants. It is a great interest to me for both the language and the people,' she said.[9]

Abdul Karim soon became the favourite. Evidently he was very charming, and he was the master of 'laying it on with a trowel', the prerequisite, as Disraeli had noted, when flattering royalty. Abdul was – to the amazement of the other courtiers – given John Brown's room to occupy, almost a sacred shrine in the Queen's eyes. He was – he assured Her Majesty – the son of a Surgeon General in the Indian army and it was most inappropriate for him to be waiting at table. Before long he was given the title of Munshi Hafiz Abdul Kasim – the Queen's official Indian secretary. Young Frederick Ponsonby, son of Sir Henry and now a member of the royal household, was dispatched to India to establish the credentials of the 'Surgeon General'. He found the Munshi's father was the apothecary in the jail at Agra. The Queen was furious with Ponsonby and told him he had met the wrong man. She did not invite Ponsonby to dine with her for a year.[10]

Historians and biographers have, alas, tended to share the snobbish and racialistic attitudes of the court to the Munshi; even, it has to be said, Lady Longford adopts a tone which implies that there is something inherently ridiculous about an Indian being a royal servitor. The Queen, who could be so maddening and so foolish on many levels, was also able to see that a capable and pleasant fellow such as the Munshi would have got nowhere if he had told the truth about his supposedly low origins. The Queen begged to inform Sir Henry Ponsonby that 'to make out that the poor good Munshi is so *low* is really *outrageous* & in a country like England quite out of place . . . she has known 2 Archbishops who were sons respectively of a Butcher & a Grocer'.

True, she was insensitive to the dangers of accepting advice on Indian affairs from a Muslim at a time when there were tensions – when were there not? – between Hindus and Muslims. Perhaps she saw some kinship between the moral and scriptural simplicities of the Mosque and the austere Presbyterian worship at Crathie, which she in every way preferred to the Anglican service. Not all her notions were crazy. Salisbury pooh-poohed the notion that he should send Mr Rafuddin Ahmed, a young friend of the Munshi's, to Constantinople as an attaché at the embassy.[11] Surely a Muslim voice representing Britain in the Ottoman capital was perfectly sensible.

So, the Golden Jubilee passed away – with a children's party for 30,000 in Hyde Park, a review of the fleet at Spithead, and well-wishers from all over the three kingdoms, and all over the Empire, saluting their sovereign with bunting and telegraph messages and songs. To read the Queen's own, and understandably self-satisfied, account of the matter in her Journals you could be forgiven for believing that 1887 had closed in a glow of happiness, with the Empire calmly and prosperously in love with its sovereign and – to borrow a phrase from a modern politician – 'at ease with itself'. Nothing could have been further from the truth.

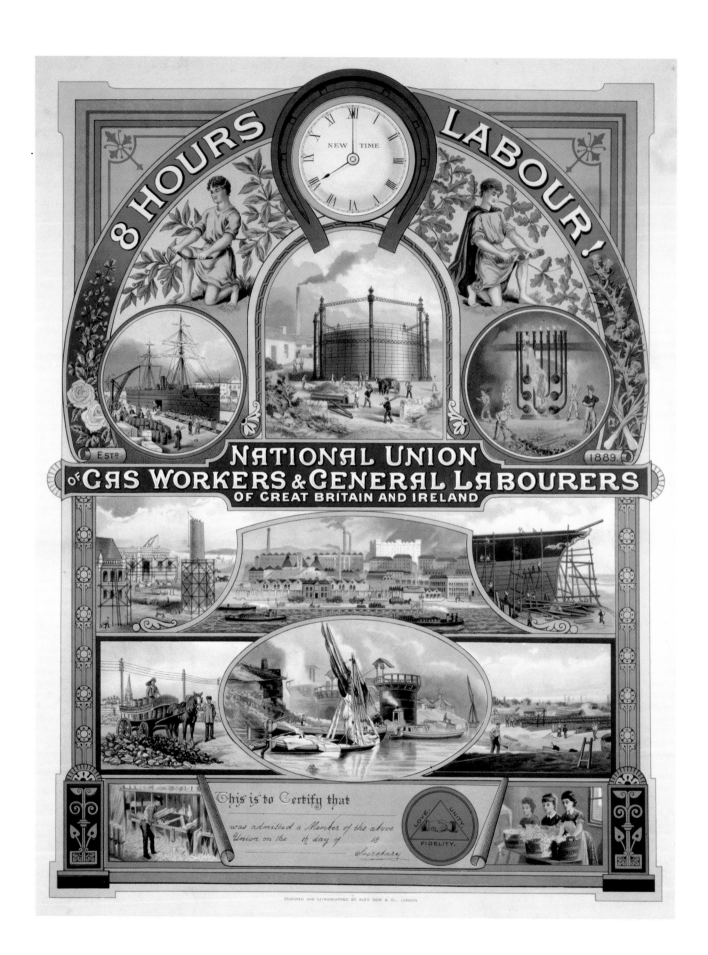

Chapter Thirty-Two

The Dock Strike

In May 1887, the Queen had been to the East End of London and heard what she described to her prime minister as a 'horrid noise (*quite* new to the Queen's ears) "booing", she believes it is called'. Salisbury was 'much grieved to hear it', but explained to his Sovereign that 'London contains a much larger number of the worst kind of rough than any other great town in the island; for all that is worthless, worn out, or penniless naturally drifts to London.' He opined that the 'booing' almost certainly emanated from socialists or the Irish – 'very resentful men who would stick at nothing to show their fury'.[1]

Poster for the National Union of Gas Workers and General labourers, 1889.

The only plausible political group within the parliamentary system who might have represented the interests of the poor against the views of Lord Salisbury were the Liberal Radicals. Yet their leader Joseph Chamberlain had brought down Gladstone over the question of Ireland and would himself one day serve in a Salisbury Cabinet. The split in the Liberal Party put the Conservatives in power for most of the rest of the reign.

As will always happen eventually when strong interests are not represented within the political system, people took to the streets. Under Gladstone's government, a new word had been coined to describe the dreadful effects of the slump – 'unemployment';[2] it was matched by the conditions already described in rural areas – devastation in Ireland, and to a small extent in England, too. The people described as 'worthless, worn out and penniless' did indeed come to the cities in a desperate attempt to find work, and in the Jubilee Year they were not always very successful. In the winter of 1886–7 there had been almost daily demonstrations organized by the Marxists, in which lines of ragged men marched out of the East End.[3]

During the autumn they had tended to congregate in Trafalgar Square – 'the most convenient place in all London for an open air meeting' according to William Morris, but dangerously near the Westminster Parliament at the end of Whitehall, or Buckingham Palace at the end of the Mall. The newly appointed chief of the Metropolitan Police was instructed by Salisbury to crack down on demonstrations. It was Salisbury himself who conceived the idea of railing in the Square – 'with gates of course',[4] so that in the event of trouble the agitators could be penned in.

On Sunday 13 November – it was to earn the sombre nickname of 'Bloody Sunday' – the Radical Federation announced that it would hold a demonstration to protest against coercion in Ireland, and to demand the release of William O'Brien MP. Both sides, the socialists and the police, had a strategy in place. The demonstrators tried to baffle the police by approaching in many different groups from all sides of the Square. Morris and Annie Besant marched from Clerkenwell Green. Another group marched from Holborn and were met at Charing Cross station by the Radical MP and author R. Cunninghame Graham and John Burns the trade

Policeman fighting a contingent from Clerkenwell Green during a riot in Trafalgar Square, 13 November 1887.

unionist. Others, trying to march from Bermondsey and Deptford, met with mounted police on Westminster Bridge – where twenty-six people were so badly injured that they were carried back across the river to St Thomas's hospital. What the demonstrators did not realize was that the police, tipped off by spies, had surrounded Trafalgar Square at points in a radius of about quarter of a mile and that behind them were two squadrons of Life Guards with fixed bayonets. Once the marchers had passed through the strategic points marked out by the police they were surrounded and at their mercy. *The Times* reported that 'the police, mounted and on foot, charged in among the people, striking indiscriminately in all directions and causing complete disorder in the ranks of the processionists. I witnessed several cases of injury to men who had been struck on the head or the face by the police. The blood, in most instances, was flowing freely from the wound and the spectacle was indeed a sickening one.'[5]

Part of the trouble was that the demonstrators, in so far as they were organized at all, imagined that they could fight well-coordinated troops and police against whom they stood no chance. They would have been much better advised to conduct the sort of non-violent resistance to the police pioneered by Gandhi in South Africa – inspired in part by the pacifist writings of Tolstoy.[6]

The police numbers were so great – probably 2,000, backed up by 400 armed soldiers – that the 10,000 marchers, many of them beaten up, dispersed without a shot being fired. Cunninghame Graham and Burns, having been badly clubbed, were arrested – and subsequently imprisoned for six weeks. The following Sunday, a smaller number tried to hold another demonstration in Hyde Park. At the same time police in Northumberland

Avenue, just south of Trafalgar Square, knocked down a young law-writer named Alfred Linnell, who subsequently died. After some weeks of legal wrangling about whether he had died as a result of injuries caused by a horse kicking him, Linnell's body was released for burial. It was decided to make the funeral held on 18 December a demonstration.

It was choreographed by Annie Besant.[7] To the solemn music of the Dead March from *Saul*, fifty wand-bearers, veterans of the Chartist agitation, preceded the coffin, which was emblazoned with the legend, 'Killed in Trafalgar Square'. They set off from Soho with an open hearse, four horses and six pall-bearers – William Morris, Cunninghame Graham, W.T. Stead, Herbert Burrows, Frank Smith and Annie Besant herself.[8] Huge crowds (Mrs Besant reckoned 100,000 people) lined the wayside to the Mile End Road, and the cortège did not reach the cemetery until half-past four. It was nearly dark and rain fell as the burial service was read by Christian Socialist leader the Rev. Stewart Headlam. Orations and laments were spoken, by the light of lanterns, to a vast crowd. Eleanor Marx might have reflected on the strange fact that when her father had been buried in Highgate cemetery in March 1883 only a huddle had collected in Highgate to hear Engels' panegyric. The obsequies of an unheard-of clerk, however, symbolized for hundreds of people present why the struggle was so important.

Morris's hymn 'A Death Song', set by Malcolm Lawson to music, was not his most accomplished effort but its refrain sent out a message to 'the rich':

*Not one, not one, nor thousands must they slay
But one and all if they would dusk the day.*[9]

Demonstration during the London Dock Strike, 1889.

Quite how the revolution might be accomplished or prevented would occupy the politically minded for the next half-century. In England, on the Left, the debate at first was between those who sought purely political remedies, and by revolutionary means – Morris, Eleanor Marx, Hyndman in their differing ways – and those such as Bernard Shaw and ultimately Beatrice (née Potter) and Sidney Webb who advocated gradualism – Fabianism. But it is hard, when reading the writings of the Fabians, to avoid the conclusion that they shared with the bossy Benthamites at the beginning of the century an essential distrust of the working classes; their ambition was not merely to improve the conditions of society but to improve the members of the lower orders themselves. Shaw mocked the Social Democratic Federation as Chartism 'risen from the dead'; they could have replied that he was Jeremy Bentham with a long red beard. Beatrice Potter, not yet either Mrs Webb or a fully-fledged socialist, but a close chronicler and

observer of the lives of the poor in dockland and among the sweatshops of the new Jewish immigrants in the East End, did not believe that the working classes were capable of organizing themselves.

The events of the next few years would prove her wrong. 'The strike,' she told her diary, of the Dock Strike in 1889, 'is intensely interesting to me personally, as proving or disproving, in any case modifying my generalizations on "Dock Life". Certainly the "solidarity of labour" at the East End is a new thought to me.'[10]

One of the first triumphs for organized labour happened at the Bryant & May match factory in the East End. The development of the lucifer match in the 1860s had been so successful that Bryant & May had added an extra storey to their factory, thereby destroying the ventilation. Phosphorus fumes filled the premises, and many employees – they were nearly all female – developed 'phossy jaw', a form of bone cancer, or skin cancer. The hours were long – in summer, 6.30 a.m. until 6 p.m., in winter starting at 8 a.m. Latecomers were fined half a day's pay. There were also fines for dropping matches, talking, or going to the lavatory outside of two short mealtimes. Eating happened on the premises, so that phosphorus was ingested, and those with rotten teeth had them pulled, often against their wishes, by the foremen. Piecework could make a girl 5*s*. or 9*s*. per week – many started as young as six. A really hard-working adult could make between 11*s*. and 13*s*. It was Annie Besant who drew attention to conditions in this factory (where Karl Marx's illegitimate son Freddy Demuth worked as a foreman) and her three informants were promptly identified and sacked. In late July 1888, Annie Besant announced that a Matchmakers Union had been formed. They went on strike, and within three weeks the employers had conceded most of their demands – shorter hours, better pay and some improvement in working conditions.[11]

In March 1889 there was formed the National Union of Gasworkers and General Labourers of Great Britain and Ireland. After their strike of 1889, initially over the disgusting working conditions at the Beckton Gas Works, they made history, being the first to win the concession of working only an eight-hour day.

Gasworkers were busy in the dark cold months of winter, but in the summer months, when people needed less heat and light, the workers were laid off. Similar problems faced the London dockers, and after their strike in the late summer of 1889, relations between labour and capital were never again the same. The power of peaceful organized labour had been demonstrated, and it was not a forgettable lesson. Much of its drama stemmed from the fact that, as has already been observed, London's docklands exhibited with hyperbolic forcefulness the contrasts and injustices of the capitalist system. Thanks in part to the surveys of Charles Booth – *The Life and Labour of the People in London*, for which some of the research was done by Beatrice Potter – and thanks also to photographic evidence, and to the anecdotal recollections of those who worked with the priests mentioned earlier, in chapter 20, we know in profound detail about the lives of the poorest of the poor in the capital of the richest city in the world. The great ships which came into London Docks from all over the world, bringing to their owners, and to the investors and merchants who profited from them, colossal wealth, were unloaded by men who worked piece-rates. When trade was slack, the men were paid nothing. The pay was variable. In August, the strike began for 6*d*. an hour.

You can't separate the three big things going on at once in the political life of Britain at the end of the 1880s – Ireland, the growth of organized labour in trade unions, and Imperialism. They are all intertwined. The Imperialists saw the Empire as the ultimate dumping-ground for troublemakers, and the best solution for hunger and discontent caused by overpopulation at home. (Without it, Cecil Rhodes believed there would be a civil war in England.) Yet the desire of the Irish for independence cut at the vitals of English power and unity. If a Westminster government could not even hold together a tiny United Kingdom, how could it sustain an empire stretching across the world? Of course it could not, and the ill-starred 'scramble for Africa' which took place within a few decades produced an Imperial experiment which could be neither administered nor paid for. The wonder is that it lasted the sixty or seventy years it did before coming apart. (Just about as long as that equally ill-starred venture, the Union of Soviet Socialist Republics.) It could only work economically by a system of exploiting markets and labour at home and abroad. In India, for example, the shoddily produced cotton fabrics of Lancashire factories or the gimcrack metalwork of Birmingham were bought by an artificially created 'market' while indigenous textile or metalworkers were sweated for cheap export.

The place where all this came home, in every sense of the phrase, was the dock; nor was it entirely accidental that those poor enough to be driven to accept the lousy wages for loading and unloading – the stevedores – were overwhelmingly of Irish extraction.[12] The strike was led by Ben Tillett (1860–1943), himself an itinerant labourer, an English-born Irishman, a slight man with the gift of impassioned oratory. Beatrice Webb said he had the face of a 'religious enthusiast'.

It was easy enough for Tillett to call the strike; altogether more difficult to persuade perhaps 30,000 strikers, with no previous tradition of solidarity or union discipline, to stay on strike for no pay for as long as the dispute with the directors lasted. (And it lasted five long weeks during which some men were close to starvation, in spite of the soup kitchens set up by well-wishers and the funds collected from as far afield as Australia.)

Tillett could not have led such a mighty movement on his own. He owed much to the help of Will Thorne (1857–1946), Tom Mann (1856–1941) and John Burns (1858–1943), all members at one time of the SDF. Thorne was the leader of the Gasworkers Union, and could offer the benefit of his experience of a successful strike. Mann had helped – and he alone of the group remained to the end of his days a Marxist, being a founder member of the Communist Party of Great Britain in 1920.

In some ways, though, the most powerful figure among the strike-leaders was John Burns – he who had been arrested on Bloody Sunday. His Scottish father died when he was young. One of eight children, he grew up in poverty in South Lambeth. On his re-election as a Member of Parliament he said, in a speech in 1901 in the Commons, 'I am not ashamed to say that I am the son of a washerwoman. Two of my sisters used to be the ironers in the laundry which now does the laundry work for the House of Commons.' He trained as an engineer, but all his life he was not merely bookish but a voracious collector and reader of books.

As a foreman engineer, the teenaged Burns, like some character in Conrad, sailed the West African coast. He once dived into the sea to rescue the cook, who had fallen overboard, and it was while recuperating that he read John Stuart Mill's *Political Economy*. The chapter on communism converted him to socialism.[13]

By the mid-Eighties, he returned to London. Burns was an active trade unionist and a keen orator, advocating universal adult suffrage, an eight-hour working day, legislative independence for Ireland, and the power of making war or peace vested solely in the democratic vote of the people. There were two significant contributions he made to the success of the Dock Strike.[14] One – a conspicuous figure now in his white straw hat and black beard – was his organization of processions through the City of London. Probably not since the reign of Mary Tudor had the Square Mile seen such an array of banners, with floats and carts like some Corpus Christi Miracle Play. Only instead of religious tableaux, here were coal-heavers with their baskets on poles, and the Social Democratic Federation – 'Justice not charity' the motto on their bright banners – and tens of thousands of followers. The second thing on which Burns insisted in his speeches was that workplaces be picketed and those who continued to work, the scabs, be verbally and physically abused. The intimidation was effective. Burns was later regarded as a renegade to the Labour movement, when in 1905 he accepted a seat in Sir Henry Campbell-Bannerman's Liberal Cabinet, but he has his place in the history books as the first working man to become a government minister. The docks directors and the City bosses, when they heard his speeches, did not see a future Cabinet minister and bookman – they saw a revolutionary.

If the directors had been callous enough to hold out until the winter they might have broken the strike. It was essential that the strikers should find a friend in the 'establishment' who would negotiate a settlement. Disraeli, if he witnessed the strike from the Empyrean, would have smiled to see who these workmen, many of them Irish, chose. It was the same man who had been the confidant of Charles Dilke, a go-between for Gladstone and the Irish bishops, a furious opponent of Bradlaugh, an unpopular advocate of Papal Infallibility – in short the cardinal with a finger in every pie – just like Disraeli's Cardinal Grandison – Henry Edward Manning. He it was, together with the MP Sydney Buxton, whom both sides – strikers and directors – felt they could trust. After five weeks out on strike, the men got their sixpence an hour (eightpence overtime) and the greatest port in the busiest and richest capital in the Empire was once more open, and operative. In unfurled silk which would not look out of place in a Catholic cathedral, the Amalgamated Society of Watermen and Lightermen (Greenwich branch) wove an image of Manning into their banner.[15]

Chapter Thirty-Three

The Scarlet Thread of Murder

Eighteenth-century London carried its poor in its midst. To walk with Garrick or Johnson through Covent Garden or down to Fleet Street would be to pass courts and alleys crammed with crime, poverty and disease, cheek by jowl with the houses of the rich. As Manning knew, surrounded by the poor of Westminster, there was still great poverty in central London. The Victorian Age, however, witnessed London being laid out along the social classifications which the capitalist revolution had created and enforced. The genteel squares of Belgravia and Mayfair were gated against the intrusion of undesirables. The world of shops and theatres, lights and delights, became for the rest of London the mythical 'West End'. To visit them was to go 'up West'. In turn, the villages and suburbs of an earlier age – Hoxton, Hackney, Shoreditch, Stepney, Bethnal Green – swarmed with overpopulation: the 'East End', no less mystic to the half-London who did not live there. This was the world which the Salvationists tried to win for God, and which the disciples of T.H. Green and Toynbee wanted for democracy: a hard, brick-built, low-lying, gin-soaked world out of whose gaslit music halls and fogbound alleys mythologies developed. Here Dan Leno and Marie Lloyd began their careers, here Jack the Ripper lurked, and from time to time Mr Sherlock Holmes emerged from a four-wheeler, sometimes heavily disguised.

The music halls developed out of pubs. By the 1850s, many taverns had their song-saloons – so popular that busybodydom required them to have a theatrical licence, which permitted the performance of popular music but forbade the playing of Shakespeare.[1] This was scarcely a hardship to the thirsty patrons of 'the halls', who did not go out in the evening with a burning desire to see *Measure for Measure*.

Mayhew believed that the theatres of the East End 'absorb numbers of the inhabitants, and by innocently amusing them, soften their manners and keep them out of mischief and harm's way'. He approved of the pyrotechnic displays at the Effingham Theatre in the Whitechapel Road – 'Great is the applause when gauzy nymphs rise like so many Aphrodites from the sea and sit down on apparent sunbeams midway between the stage and theatrical heaven.' (The theatre burnt down in 1879 and was rebuilt as a theatre for Yiddish plays that appealed to the huge new influx of refugees from Russia and Poland.)[2]

It was another matter at the 'Penny Gaffs', theatres which had a series of 'variety' turns, and where the audience was crammed with teenaged criminals picking pockets and undercover policemen trying to catch them doing so. The act which most revolted the normally unshockable Mayhew was performed by a fourteen-year-old boy, dancing 'with more energy than grace' and singing a song 'the whole point of which consisted in the mere utterance of some filthy word at the end of each stanza'. The audience loved it and cried for more, being rewarded with

The cover of a programme for the Empire Theatre in London, August 1889. The bill featured comedians including Dan Leno and 'Cleopatra, A Grand Ballet Divertissement'.

a song called 'Pine-apple Rock', with a rhyme which can easily be reconstructed.

It was to appeal to audiences with comparable tastes that the music halls evolved, though the best performers – from Marie Lloyd to Max Miller in the middle years of the twentieth century (the last great music-hall artist) – depended on double-entendre rather than the blatant crudity which so upset Mayhew.

Marie Lloyd was born as Matilda Alice Victoria Wood on 12 February 1870 at 36 Plumber Street in the slums of Hoxton. It was a large, poverty-stricken family. Her father, John Wood, made artificial flowers for an Italian who paid him 30 shillings a week, and he worked part-time as a waiter at the Royal Eagle – the tavern in Bethnal Green immortalized in 'Pop Goes the Weasel' ('Up and down the City Road, In and out the Eagle'). It was here when she was fourteen that Matilda Wood did a turn under the name Bella Delmare and won instant success. She went on to perform at the Falstaff Music Hall in Old Street, and when her talent was spotted by George Belmont, a music-hall impresario, she was taken on by a big music hall in Bermondsey. By the time she was sixteen she was on tour and earning £10 a week. Soon she was earning £600 a week.

She died in the year that T.S. Eliot published *The Waste Land*, 1922. 'Although I have always admired the genius of Marie Lloyd,' Eliot wrote, 'I do not think that I always appreciated its uniqueness; I certainly did not realize that her death would strike me as the important event it was. Marie Lloyd was the greatest Music Hall artist of her time in England; she was also the most popular.'[3]

She had a rough life. She was alcoholic. Her third husband, a jockey, beat her, and they were arrested when they tried to disembark at New York harbour posing as man and wife before they were actually married. Her life from the grinding poverty of its origins to the alcoholic pathos of its end had the carelessness for safety which is often the ingredient of an artist's career that distinguishes talent from genius. The capacity to let rip, to let go, must have been part of what enabled this weird-looking girl with buck teeth and thin hair to electrify an audience of cynical drunks from the moment she got up and sang 'The boy I love is up in the gallery'.

Apart from the release of risqué humour, she provided the audience with a reflection, an embodiment of their own hideous lives. It was humour based on staring into the abyss. Some of her most famous songs are about bankruptcy, drunkenness, dereliction.

Her wit was shown at its best in

Outside the Cromwell Arms last Saturday night,
I was one of the ruins that Cromwell knocked about a bit.

It was very much a humour for hard, cynical Londoners. She could 'bomb' in the provinces. In Ardwick, Manchester, she shouted, 'So this is Ardwick, eh? Well, to hell with the lot of you.' And to the good people of Sheffield, after a cool reception, she yelled, 'You don't like me, well I don't like you. And you know what you can do with your stainless knives and your scissors and your circular saws – you can shove 'm up your arse.'[4]

Dan Leno (1860–1904) – his real name was George Galvin – made his first stage appearance as an adult on 5 October 1885 at Forester's Music Hall in Mile End – but he had been on the stage since he was three ('Little George, the Infant Wonder, Contortionist and Posturer'). His humour was much more fantastical than Marie Lloyd's. There is something almost Blakean about his mad song about a wasp who loved a hard-boiled egg –

But not one word said the hard-boiled egg,
The hard-boiled egg,
The hard-boiled egg,
And what a silly insect the wasp to beg
For you can't get any sense out of a hard-boiled egg![5]

He was a legendary pantomime dame – hurling himself into the parts with quite literally manic energy. He went mad while playing Mother Goose. He was a broken and exhausted man at forty-three: 'the funniest man on earth' as it said on the posters. 'Ever seen his eyes?' asked Marie Lloyd. 'The saddest eyes in the whole world. That's why we all laughed at Danny. Because if we hadn't laughed, we should have cried ourselves sick. I believe that's what real comedy is, you know. It's almost like crying.'[6]

We can still hear Dan Leno on record – but the magic was to see him on stage. Max Beerbohm, when asked by foreign visitors to show them something inherently British, would take them first to see the Tower of London or Westminster Abbey – and then to a music hall to see 'the big booming Herbert Campbell, and his immortal, nimble little side-kick, Dan Leno'.[7]

Part of the attraction of music hall for the middle class was its sheer entertainment value. When one considers that there were no plays of any interest or quality written in English between the death of Sheridan and the emergence of Oscar Wilde (both Irish, note well) it is not surprising that many middle-class theatregoers flocked with rapture to Little Tich, Marie Lloyd or Dan Leno. They were superb performers, artists of first-rate

quality. But for someone of the class of Max Beerbohm or T.S. Eliot to frequent the halls there was also an element of excitement – tasting a bit of rough.

The enchantment of the alien, the half-thrilling terror of violence lurking in such 'hell-holes', the cheap excitement of knowing that such 'scores of women' are readily available, masculine self-hatred at the thought of prostitutes, transferring into hatred of the women themselves – all these factors are present in the pornographic fascination of the Jack the Ripper murders. There would seem to be no end to the appetite of so-called Ripperologists for more films, more books and more crazy theories about 'the autumn of terror' in 1888 when over ten weeks – from 31 August to 9 November – five women had their throats slit. In two cases, organs were removed from the victims' bodies with sufficient skill to suggest on the murderer's part an at least rudimentary knowledge of anatomy. The murders became increasingly savage, culminating with a blood-saturnalia of dismemberment on 9 November – the murder of Mary Jane Kelly. This was the only killing to occur indoors – the others took place in darkened alleys. All the victims

THE WHITECHAPEL MYSTERY.

– Mary Ann Nichols (42), Annie Chapman (47), Elizabeth Stride (45), Catherine Eddowes (43) and Mary Kelly (25) – had been married. Between them they had twenty-one children. They were all prostitutes.

This undoubtedly quickens the interest of those who are obsessed by these murders. Their imaginations running riot, the 'Ripperologists' have supposed that the women were killed by a Harley Street physician taking revenge for the death of a beloved son from syphilis, or for reasons of religious zeal. (Anti-semites can imagine

that the women were killed by methods of kosher slaughter.) Conspiracy theorists imagine a royal murderer (the Duke of Clarence is the favourite) or a cabal organized by Lord Salisbury himself. But the key excitement of the unsolved crimes is the professional activity of the women themselves.

Part of the excitement stems from the cliché of the Victorian Age as being excessively puritanical or buttoned-up in relation to sex. For those who believe this, or who imagine that the Victorians were so prudish that they draped their chair-legs (whence stemmed *that* bizarre fiction?), a key text is the pseudonymous pornographic work *My Secret Life*, privately printed by Auguste Brancart of Brussels *circa* 1890. Far from lifting the lid on the actual behaviour of Victorian middle-class life, this crazy account of some 1,500 relations by a married man called Walter has all the hallmarks of porno-fantasy. It has lately been suggested that 'Walter' was Henry Spencer Ashbee,[8] bibliophile father of the Arts and Crafts designer and teacher Charles Ashbee.

The Whitechapel murders unfolded before the newspaper-reading public like a detective story of the grisliest kind, with the arrest and release of suspects, the letters to the police purporting to come from 'Jack' himself – ('I send you half the Kidne [sic] I took from one woman prarsarved [sic] it for you tother piece I fried and ate it was very nise [sic].' Everyone had a theory, everyone wanted to chip in with advice.

The trouble was, that although the Whitechapel murders acquired instantaneous mythic status, the authorities relied on the services of real-life policemen, the equivalents of Lestrade and Gregson in the Sherlock Holmes stories. Holmes himself was required.* It was in fact one month before the first of the Whitechapel murders – in July 1888 – that *A Study in Scarlet*, the story in which the greatest detective of them all makes his début, was first published in book form, though its author, a young doctor called Arthur Conan Doyle (1859–1930), first published the tale the previous year in *Beeton's Christmas Annual*.[9]

Sherlock Holmes was very much a thinker of his time, his view of the nature of things absolutely in tune with the English Idealists F.H. Bradley and T.H. Green.

A logician could infer the possibility of an Atlantic or a Niagara without having seen or heard of one or the other. So all life is a great chain, the nature of which is known, whenever we are shown a single link of it. Like all other arts, the Science of Deduction and Analysis is one which can only be acquired by long and patient study, nor is life long enough to allow any mortal to attain the highest possible perfection in it.[10]

*In December 1965 the BBC broadcast 'The Case of the Unmentioned Case' by L.W. Bailey, which points out that when the entire police force was at its wits' end trying to solve the Whitechapel case, Holmes was not consulted. Inevitably, Bailey suggested that Holmes, with his rudimentary knowledge of anatomy and supposed misogyny, was the Ripper – a thesis which more than one listener was right to find 'shameful': the essence of Holmes's appeal consisting in his virtue. See Wilson & Odell, p. 191.

When common-sense Dr Watson reads this article in a magazine he exclaims, 'What ineffable twaddle!' He cannot believe, as the article suggests, that 'By a man's finger-nails, by his coat-sleeve, by his boot, by his trouser-knees, by the callosities of his forefinger and thumb, by his expression, by his shirt-cuffs – by each of these things a man's calling is plainly revealed.'[11]

Needless to say, it transpires that the author of the article is the man with whom Watson is sharing lodgings at 221B Baker Street. He immediately demonstrates his skills by 'deducing' – from merely looking at him across the street – that a man on the pavement is a retired sergeant of the Marines. He has no sooner met Watson than he can *know*, by his supposedly scientific method, that he had been wounded in Afghanistan. In a later story, *The Sign of Four*, he enrages Watson by telling him that his brother was 'left with good prospects; but he threw away his chances, lived for some time in poverty with occasional short intervals of prosperity, and finally, taking to drink, he died'. All this is inferred by looking at the dead brother's gold watch and noticing its scuffed appearance and the pawnbroker's number scratched minutely on the case.

Holmes evolves through several stories. In *A Study in Scarlet* we find him in a laboratory – he never seems to return to it in the *Strand Magazine* short stories which – reprinted as *The Adventures of Sherlock Holmes* in book form – are the best in the collection. Also in *A Study in Scarlet* Holmes does not wish to clutter his brain with general learning which does not relate to his profession. He says he is ignorant of the work of Carlyle (while going on to quote him) and, less probably, ignorant of the Copernican theory of astronomy. In later tales, Holmes has become a polymath. ('Breadth of view . . . is one of the essentials of our profession' – *The Valley of Fear*.) In *A Study in Scarlet* Watson dismisses the notion that Holmes was 'addicted to the use of some narcotic' because 'the temperance and cleanliness of his whole life'[12] forbade such a notion. In the later stories we discover that Holmes is a cocaine addict and frequents opium dens.

Yet in spite of all the inconsistencies, Holmes comes before us as totally real. T.S. Eliot said that 'when we talk of him we invariably fall into the fancy of his existence'.[13]

Much has been written about the evolution of Holmes in the mind of his creator. His deductive method owes a lot to similar tricks performed by the Edinburgh surgeon Joseph Bell when Doyle was a medical student; his relationship with Watson is partly derivative from Boswell and Johnson. But he is also archetypically of his time.

Chapter Thirty-Four

The Fall of Parnell

Arthur Balfour, Lord Salisbury's clever nephew, succeeded Hicks Beach as Irish secretary in March 1887 and was immediately faced with the prospect of dealing with the so-called 'Plan of Campaign', which called on tenants all over Ireland to organize, and to treat with landlords as if they were a united body. Parnell privately disapproved of the Plan of Campaign. Important as the Land Issue was to him – the basic issue of how the Irish rural population could till the land, and eat, without being squeezed into unbearable poverty – he never lost sight of the larger political dream, from which agitation over Land Acts detracted. Balfour was his uncle's stooge, but he was also highly ambitious, and he was anxious to use the Irish situation to prove himself.

On the one hand he allowed some concessions to the tenants, but on the other he brought in a new Crimes Act – the Criminal Law and Procedure Act, 1887 – which was much more drastic than any previous legislation. Boycotting, resistance to eviction, intimidation and conspiracy now carried much heavier penalties. Suspects – before they had committed any of these offences – could now be held and examined. Those accused could be moved away from their own districts for trial. Six months' hard labour was the maximum sentence.[1]

Salisbury wanted even tougher measures. Ireland was the test case, before the eyes of the world, of British competence to govern. If Britain could not rule Ireland, 'what right have we to go lecturing the Sultan as to the state of things in Armenia or in Macedonia?'[2]

'Loot, loot, pure loot, is the sacred course for which the Land League has summoned the malcontents to its standard,' Salisbury had written in the *Quarterly Review* in 1881. If the government surrendered to 'land hunger', why should not governments give way in the future to 'house hunger', 'consols hunger' or even 'silver plate hunger'? Salisbury was not himself a harsh landlord. When times were bad, he entirely remitted rents on his 20,000 acres, all of which were held in England. His opposition to the Irish and 'the amiable practice to which they were addicted of shooting people to whom they owe money' was deep, and his Irish policy drew on his wells of cynical pessimism.

One remedy to mutual hatred is divorce, but for the Imperialist reasons already stated, Salisbury was unwilling to contemplate Home Rule. He was astute politically and could see that the Irish Party and the Irish 'question' possessed a vulnerable, not to say spurious, unity. Land agitation and individual cases of hardship were not the same as an ideal for political independence; Fenian nationalism had been different in texture from Parnell's Home Rule idea – and the differences between Parnell and some of his followers could be exploited. Destroy Parnell, and the Tories would have managed in large measure to divide the enemy. It would not make the problem of Ireland go away but it

Portrait of Charles Parnell, 1892. The era of 'Parnellism' in Irish politics was one in which issues were subsumed in one superbly attractive personality, Parnell himself, who by masterful political manoeuvre and charm, deployed in equal measures of skill, had managed to unite the various aspirant Irish nationalists and Irish liberals with the English Liberal Party, itself a coalition.

would make it – which was Salisbury's ideal – utterly insoluble.

So, while Balfour with great parliamentary aplomb was seeing his contentious Crimes Bill through the Commons, *The Times* printed what purported to be the facsimiles of letters from Parnell condoning the Phoenix Park murders of Lord Frederick Cavendish and his secretary. The old slur – that by associating with Irish nationalism you were rubbing shoulders with murderers – was very much helped by *The Times* 'revelations'. Parnell immediately denounced them as a 'felonious and bare faced forgery'.[3] Salisbury and Balfour must have had their suspicions that this was the case, even if they did not know it for certain. Would so highly literate a man as Parnell spell the word as 'hesitency'? At the time, it suited them very well to believe so. The Crimes Bill became law – nicknamed the 'Jubilee Coercion Act' by its enemies.

In September 1887, at the opening of the trial of William O'Brien, MP – this nationalist with strong links to the Irish in Chicago was being prosecuted under the new act for inciting tenants to resist landlords and to boycott those who moved into farms where these had been evicted – O'Brien's parliamentary colleague John Dillon, another nationalist, was addressing the crowd of 8,000 who had congregated at Mitchelstown, County Cork. A scuffle broke out, the police moved in, and as they were driven back by the crowds, a number of officers opened fire. One man was killed, several others injured.

Edward Carson (1854–1935), the thirty-three-year-old counsel for the Irish attorney general, told 'Pretty Fanny' Balfour, 'It was Mitchelstown that made us certain we had a man at last.'[4] Others were less impressed. A coroner's jury found wilful murder against the county inspector and five constables. The Queen's Bench in Dublin, five months later, quashed the verdict on technical grounds.[5] The lengths to which the Tory Unionists in government were prepared to go had been revealed. Gladstone, addressing a rally in England that Jubilee autumn, declared, 'I have said and say again, "Remember Mitchelstown!"' Salisbury did not mind. When he arrived in Oxford and found three-foot-high posters reading 'Lord Salisbury is coming. Remember Mitchelstown', he was perfectly happy that the people should do so.

Unfortunately for Salisbury and Balfour, Parnell insisted on a Special Parliamentary Commission to look into *The Times* forgeries. He also took legal action against the newspaper for its articles 'Parnellism and Crime'. He was vindicated. The letters were shown to be the work of a clever forger called Richard Pigott (not so clever as to be able to spell hesitancy), who admitted his crime in the witness box. Pigott's humiliation caused him to flee abroad, to Madrid. There he committed suicide.[6]

Parnell now, in the period of 1889–90, enjoyed unprecedented popularity and public support. His truthfulness had been proven by a Special Commission to Parliament. When he first appeared in the House after the collapse of Pigott, the entire Opposition, including Gladstone, rose to their feet and cheered for some minutes. He found himself a hero not only in Ireland but among the English public.

Yet Parnell's triumph was short-lived. On Christmas Eve 1889, Captain William O'Shea, the MP for Galway, filed for divorce, citing Parnell as co-respondent. The trial of the case came up nearly a year later, in November 1890, and though O'Shea clearly lied in pretending that his wife's relations with Parnell were very shocking to him, and that he had heard about them only shortly before filing for divorce, the central fact was not contested. Parnell and Mrs O'Shea were lovers.

Gladstone had known about it for years, and often used Mrs O'Shea as a go-between when negotiating with the Irish Party. Given the willingness of Salisbury's government to make political capital out of the Dilke divorce, and the Pigott forgeries, one does wonder whether they made it worth Captain O'Shea's while to destroy Parnell. After all, O'Shea had been totally complicit for ten years. Three of his wife's children were Parnell's.

There are many remarkable things about the whole story, which, because it has passed into legend, is difficult to deconstruct. For something approaching a year – from January to November 1890 – the Irish Party was in suspense, awaiting the outcome of the trial. Parnell assured his close supporter Michael Davitt that 'he would emerge without a stain on his reputation'.[7] Either this was a simple untruth, or we are to assume that Parnell meant he had not broken the code of a gentleman; he had not *deceived* O'Shea. The Press, in Ireland and England, was not silent, and for this whole period there was plenty of time for the implications of the story to sink in. Yet almost all Irish public bodies, all the MPs and the Catholic bishops remained loyal and expressed confidence in Parnell's leadership. When one considers how extremely puritanical the Irish were (until our own generation) about such matters, the loyalty, and the political maturity, thus demonstrated is all the more extraordinary.

The crisis came in the middle of November 1890, when Mrs O'Shea accepted in court that she had been unfaithful to her husband. The leader of a parliamentary party was now legally defined as an adulterer.

Cardinal Manning, less than a week after the O'Shea

Charles Parnell mobbed when leaving Castlecomer during the Kilkenny by-election at the time of his disputed leadership of the Irish Party, 1890.

divorce proceedings, urged Gladstone to repudiate Parnell, and much more importantly he had advised the Irish bishops that Parnell could not survive politically, and that on their part, 'plain and prompt speech was safest'. 'We have been slow to act,' the archbishop of Dublin telegraphed to one of the Irish members, 'trusting that the party will act manfully.'

Yet although W.B. Yeats, in common with many Irishmen, believed that

The Bishops and the Party
That tragic story made . . .

this was not strictly true. At least in chronological terms, it was the English Liberals who at first made it clear that they would no longer continue supporting Parnell. It so happened that there was a Liberal convention meeting in Sheffield on 22 November, from which Harcourt reported back that the assembled Northern grocers and Methodistical aldermen with their silver watch-chains could not tolerate co-operation with Irish Home Rulers so long as they were led by an adulterer. Gladstone thereafter wrote a letter – which he subsequently had published – to John Morley conveying the views of the Liberal Party and saying that Parnell's continuation as leader would render Home Rule 'almost a nullity'. Davitt meanwhile was writing articles complaining about the silence of the Catholic bishops on the subject.

The real drama of the story began when Parliament reassembled and the Irish MPs met in Committee Room 15 to ratify Parnell's leadership for the next session. On all previous occasions this had been a mere formality. After an agonizing week, forty-five members withdrew from the Committee Room, leaving Parnell with twenty-eight followers. The Press Association summarized the situation with the words, 'the old Irish party no longer exists'.[8]

Almost as soon as the vote had gone against him, Parnell went over to Ireland to help one of his candidates fight the Kilkenny by-election. Parnell had a good candidate, and in one district of the constituency he was even supported by the parish priest, but he was beaten by two to one.

Parnell was a brave man, but vanity played its part. He was thunderstruck by the defection of Irish MPs and fought two more gruelling by-elections, hoping to prove a point. He was humiliated on both occasions, at North Sligo in April and at Carlow in July. In June 1890 he married Katharine O'Shea, a step which placed him finally beyond the pale in the eyes of the Catholic bishops who had always been prepared to overlook his Protestantism and his unbelief. 'You cannot remain a Parnellite and remain a Catholic,'[9] a priest told his flock the following year in Meath, and the truth or otherwise of this contention exercised many an angry Irish household or bar in the years to come, as readers of Joyce's *Portrait of the Artist as a Young Man* will recollect.

Parnell himself was exhausted. On 27 September 1890 he addressed a meeting in the rain, while suffering from rheumatism. He came over to England gravely ill, joined his wife at Brighton and died in her arms on 6 October.

To this day one has an overpowering sense, reading his story, that Parnell was a greater man than any of those who took part in the tragic drama of his downfall, a man of epic status, whose fall was not merely a private tragedy but also a great national calamity.

Part Six

THE EIGHTEEN-NINETIES

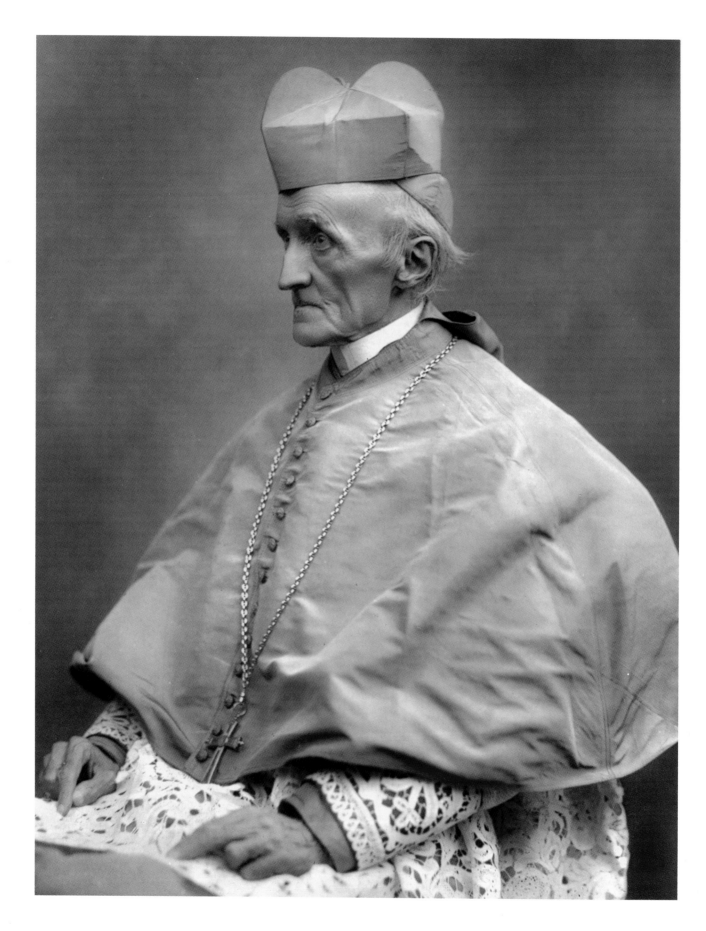

The Victorian Way of Death

The English, who in our day are so diffident about funerals, positively revelled in the trappings of death during the nineteenth century; and the 1890s 'witnessed the golden age of the Victorian funeral'.[1] The most elaborate ceremonials, of a kind which today would appear extravagant for the obsequies of a head of state, were matters of routine when burying a grocer or a doctor.[2] The hearse would be a glass coach groaning with flowers, but smothered in sable and crêpe. Four or six horses nodding with black plumes would lead the cortège, preceded by paid mutes who, swathed in black shawls and with drapes over their tall silk hats, make an alarming spectacle to the modern eye: medieval Spain could hardly produce images more macabre. Behind the coffin in their carriages would follow the mourners, in new-bought black clothes, bombazine and crêpe and tall silk hats and black gloves and bonnets – all a tribute to how much money the mourners had, and how highly they considered themselves to have climbed in the ladder-game class-system created by democratic capitalism. The more the funeral became a social status symbol, the more in turn it grew to be big business, with many undertakers in the larger cities becoming people of substance on the strength of it.

If private families went to such impressive lengths to ensure costly funerals for their loved ones, public figures could be sure of huge shows. The one which stayed in everyone's mind from the middle of the century was that of the Duke of Wellington. The funeral of Cardinal Manning, on Thursday 21 January 1892, attracted even larger crowds – possibly the largest ever to assemble for any such event in London. The greatest promoter of Roman Catholicism in Britain who has ever lived – the man who ensured that his religion would be followed and believed by millions, and respected by ten times that number – died before there was a cathedral for his branch of Christianity in London.

Manning's genius was human, organizational. He wasn't an intellectual – but this should not imply that Manning's mind was not sharp and serviceable. He had the true statesman's faculty of quick adaptability – witness his immediate recognition, once the kingdom of Italy was created, that claims for the Temporal Power of the Papacy should be dropped. Always the clever Balliol man, he had in common with one of a later generation, Thomas Hill Green, the rare quality of applied intelligence – whether he was thinking about the personal and political implications of the Dilke case, or the solution to the Dock Strike.

It was probably true that Manning was driven out of the Church of England by quasi-political factors. 'If Manning leaves us it will be because his trust in our being a true branch of the Church Catholic is killed – & this will mainly be the work of Lord J Russell,' Soapy Sam Wilberforce had written bitterly in October 1850.[3] What a world away that was from the urban, industrialized, politicized London of the 1890s which – on one level so surprisingly – had taken to its heart this

Cardinal Manning, 1890. Hilaire Belloc saw Manning as the greatest figure of his age. 'The poor of Jesus Christ whom no man hears/Have waited on your vengeance much too long', Belloc wrote, in a poem about the London poor. It was these people that, without any desire to cut a figure for himself, Manning represented. He was sufficiently a gentleman to know that Roman Catholicism in England was utterly not the religion of gentlemen. If a member of his own class visited him in the early days of his Catholicism he would apologize for his clothes – the 'Roman Collar' now worn even by Protestant clergymen. But once he had lost his self-consciousness, he could make the joyful claim, 'If I had not become Catholic I could never have worked for the people of England, as in the last year they think I have worked for them. Anglicanism would have fettered me.'

The Prince George at Spithead during the Naval Requiem of Queen Victoria, 1901.

etiolated, severe, early Victorian parson turned Roman prince and prelate. It was surely because people recognized that he was one of the few establishment figures who had dared to leave the establishment, and who was genuinely moved by principles to which they would have liked to aspire.

So it was, after the solemn requiem at the Brompton Oratory, that pastiche of a Roman city church set down in the middle of Knightsbridge, attended by sixteen bishops, that they took their cardinal to be buried. Many Londoners had never seen such a sight – hundreds of priests, monks and friars in their medieval habits, singing their solemn Gregorian chant, set out in procession to Kensal Green cemetery. But these enchantments of the Middle Ages were accompanied by figures quite new in history: behind the Funeral Car were the National League, United Kingdom Alliance, Trades Unions of London, Dockers' Societies, Amalgamated Society of Stevedores, Federation of Trades and Labour Unions, Independent Order of Good Templars and Universal Mercy Band Movement. How strange they would have seemed to Manning's parishioners if they had appeared half a century earlier to greet him in his Protestant incarnation, and had appeared on the lawn of the archdeacon of Chichester at Lavington. Now they marched on, they the future, taking the old Victorian to his grave. And for every step of that four-mile journey, the pavements were thickly lined with crowds. At some points, they were so dense that the procession was halted.

It was twilight, on that dim January day, when they finally reached Kensal Green. The bishop of Birmingham said the final prayers, the acolytes held up their twinkling tapers, and the choir sang a Miserere, as they buried him in the Catholic plot, near Wiseman, and near that heroine of the Crimean War, Mary Seacole.

Kensal Green, the first public cemetery (as opposed to churchyard or church-owned burial-ground), was the inspiration of a barrister called G.F. Carden, who had been impressed by the new general cemeteries in Europe, especially Père Lachaise in Paris. Carden first attempted to take over Primrose Hill. He engaged Thomas Wilson to design a vast pyramid on the site, capable of housing 5 million bodies, but in the end the General Cemetery Company established itself at Kensal

Green in 1831. There were soon public cemeteries in Norwood (1837), Highgate (1839), Nunhead, Abney Park and Brompton in 1840, Tower Hamlets in 1841. It was initially the custom to pay sums ranging from 1s. 6d. to 5s. to one's parish clergy in compensation for the funeral fee which would have been paid had the burial occurred on consecrated ground. The truth was, though, that the Malthusian principle operated in death as in life. There was simply no room for any more dead in the old burial grounds, and the new public cemeteries – which of course could provide interment for those who owed no loyalty to the established Church – soon filled up.

A very obvious solution lay to hand but there were objections – emotional, theological, and even legal – to the sensible idea that in an overcrowded world, riddled with disease, dead bodies should be consumed by fire, rather than buried in the earth.

Sir Henry Thompson (1820–1904) was one of the first to pioneer the idea of cremation as an alternative to burial, in an article in *The Contemporary Review* in January 1874, and went on to form the Cremation Society with a number of friends, including Sir John Tenniel of *Punch*, the illustrator of *Alice*.

Though the habit of cremation was slow to be adopted, the notion of it, as the most efficient means of disposing of the dead, had certainly entered public consciousness. When the English cricket team lost heavily in the Test match against Australia in 1882, the result was not the Coffin of British Luck – but the Ashes. (The joke appeared first in *The Sporting Times* – 'In affectionate remembrance of English cricket, which died at the Oval, 29th August, 1882, deeply lamented by a large circle of sorrowing friends and acquaintances. RIP. NB The body will be cremated and the Ashes taken to Australia.')[4]

It remained an open question whether cremation was yet legal. When a Captain Hanham of Blandford, Dorset, cremated both his wife and mother (at their own request) in a privately constructed furnace, it was felt that the law had been infringed, but nothing was done about it by the then home secretary.[5]

It was a Welshman who, in 1884, was bold enough to take an action which, eventually, made clear what the law actually was. William Price, eighty-three years old, was an outspoken radical, a medical doctor, a fervent Welsh Nationalist and a Druid. When his five-month-old son – whom he had christened Jesu Grist (Jesus Christ) – died, Dr Price placed the infant in a barrel of petrol on a hillside at Llantrisant and ignited it.[6] He was prosecuted for the common law offence of burning, not burying, a body, and the case came before Mr Justice Stephen at the

Funeral of Cardinal Manning – the Requiem Mass at Brompton Oratory. Illustration from The Graphic *30 January 1892.*

Glamorganshire Assizes, Cardiff, on Tuesday 12 February 1884.[7] The judge ruled that 'a person who burns instead of buries a dead body does not commit a criminal act unless he does it in such a manner as to amount to a public nuisance at common law'.[8]

Thereafter the way was open, and the Society carried out its first cremation at Woking in March 1885. There were only 3 that year, 10 in 1886, 104 in 1892. Even by 1914 there were just 1,222 cremations, 0.2 per cent of the 516,000 deaths that fateful year. The baleful Edwardian and Victorian legacy of the huge public cemetery is with us yet, and every large city in Britain has its miserable hinterland, now ruinous, bramble-grown and strewn with our own contemporary detritus, of mile on mile of damp vaults, sunken tombstones, chipped stone angels and illegible headstones, monuments to the forgotten Victorian millions.

☞ *The Necropolis graveyard in Glasgow, c. 1890.*

HOW TO BECOME A MAHATMA!

Chapter Thirty-Six

Appearance and Reality

One of the strangest spiritual Odysseys of the age was that of Annie Besant (1847–1933), the vicar's wife who was brave enough, aged twenty-seven, to run away from a cruel husband and a religion in which she no longer believed. She risked losing her children (though in the event, the deed of separation, dated 25 October 1873, gave her custody of her daughter Mabel). With atheism and political radicalism she espoused, as an ineluctable consequence, poverty and social ostracism.[1]

She became the friend and collaborator of Charles Bradlaugh, leader of the National Secular Society. As an advocate of birth control and a distributor of *The Fruits of Philosophy* (an inappropriately titled tract about how to limit procreation) she was arrested, tried and condemned, though on appeal she escaped imprisonment. But then she began to drift away from Bradlaugh's secular radicalism in favour of socialism. The arch-cad and con-artist Edward Aveling, medic, actor, Marxist, helped to effect this transition. She was rescued when he subsequently fell in love with Eleanor Marx, whose life he quite literally destroyed – luring her into a 'suicide pact' without keeping his side of the bargain. In the socialist circles of Aveling, Bernard Shaw and the rest, Annie flourished. She was immensely brave as an agitator, as we have seen in our account of 'Bloody Sunday' – November 1887 – and she was also a superb public speaker.[2] Something, however, was lacking. In W.T. Stead, of all people, she briefly found a father-figure. Atheism, she admitted, had brought peace from the torment of believing in an unjust God, but it left her 'without a Father'.[3]

Where would such a figure go? Beatrice Potter, after her marriage to Sidney Webb in 1892, was another woman of essentially religious disposition, who poured her longing for a 'cause' into socialism. She and her husband would be seen as key figures in the story of the British Labour Movement. Certainly, Shaw and the Webbs remained forever scornful of the direction in which Annie Besant chose, by contrast, to move, but in its way it was no less revealing, no less characteristic of its time.

In January 1889 Stead took her to meet the founder of the Theosophical Society, Madame Blavatsky (1831–91), on one of the sage's visits to London. The obese, pop-eyed Russian aristocrat (naturalized American since 1878) talked 'easily and brilliantly' of her travels.[4] 'Nothing special to record, no word of occultism, nothing mysterious; a woman of the world chatting to her evening visitors.' But when they rose to go, Madame Blavatsky, with a 'yearning throb' in her voice, said, 'Oh my dear Mrs Besant if you would only come among us.' Annie felt an overwhelming urge to bend down and kiss Blavatsky, but she resisted, and made her *adieux*.[5] Within a few months, Annie Besant had found her vocation and her life's work. Although in April 1889 she accepted re-election as a member of the Fabian

'HOW TO BECOME A MAHATMA!' A satire on Annie Besant's career from social reformer to birth control advocate to spiritual guru, 1891.

Elena Blavatsky and Colonel Henry Olcott from Histoire Authentique de la Société Théosophique *by Olcott, 1908.*

executive and was still aligning herself with such secular figures as Shaw and the Webbs, her eyes were now upon the distant horizons of the Orient. Like the soldier in Kipling's 'Mandalay', she could hear the temple bells a-calling. By the time she had attended the funeral of her old comrade Charles Bradlaugh she had put on Madame Blavatsky's ring – the symbol of esoteric power – and became one of the great prophets of Theosophy. (One of the young Indians she befriended and who attended Bradlaugh's funeral was Mohandas Karamchand Gandhi, who had visited Madame Blavatsky at Annie's house in St John's Wood.)[6]

Blavatsky has been much ridiculed, and her credentials are often questioned. She claimed that she had achieved enlightenment and initiation into the esoteric mysteries after seven years wandering alone in the Tibetan mountains. Even after the Younghusband expedition of 1903–4, Tibet remained closed to all but a very few travellers, so a white female traveller would, one would have supposed, have encountered some difficulties. As it happens, Blavatsky was so obese as to

have difficulty climbing the stairs: another reason sceptics have cast doubt on her claims to have ascended Himalayan heights in quest of wisdom.

By pioneering, or inventing, Theosophy, however, Helena Blavatsky was giving shape and voice to a yearning which lies buried in many human souls, the notion or wish that all faith is really one. True, the nineteenth century was an era of faith quite as much as it was one of doubt. While sophisticates abandoned the old Bible, new bibles were in the making. An angel called Moroni directed Joseph Smith, a teen-aged labourer from New England, to find, in 1827, those Golden Plates which would contain the new gospel, the *Book of Mormon*. In 1875, Mary Baker Eddy (1821–1910) was to publish *Science and Health*, later named *Science and Health with Key to the Scriptures*, which, as the central document of the new religion of Christian Science, was in effect to be a further testament, assuring believers that disease and indeed evil itself were illusory. Blavatsky's new Scripture, *Isis Unveiled* (1877), was written by invisible Spirit hands. Half a million words long, it began

Satire on Theosophy, c. 1890.

by denouncing the scientific materialism of Darwin and Huxley, and went on to expound its key doctrine, namely that all wisdom is One, that science is not opposed to religion, and that religious differences are man-made. Anyone who has nursed the thought that 'deep down all religions are saying the same thing' is more than halfway towards Theosophy.

Henry Olcott (*c.*1830–1907), Blavatsky's heavily bearded sidekick, was to be one of Annie's close theosophical allies. A farmer from Ohio, who had been a signals officer in the Union army, Olcott was of good New Jersey stock, claiming descent from the pilgrims. Whereas Blavatsky was visited by Hidden Masters from the ancient Egyptian dynasties of Luxor, Olcott's spiritual visitants came from India. A dark stranger from the Himalayas in an amber turban and white robes laid his hands on the colonel and told him he would do great work for humanity.[7] It was largely through Olcott that Annie Besant visited India – a revelation which changed

her life – in 1893. And it is in the Indian context that one sees *some* of the appeal of Annie's new mystical creed for her old radical self. In Ceylon, the British officials regarded Theosophy as seditious. It questioned one of the very bases for a European presence there: namely the superiority of Christianity over Buddhism. Olcott and Blavatsky actually 'took pansil' – a form of Buddhist confirmation – in Colombo. Olcott wore sandals and dhoti. He identified with the Buddhist protests against Christian missions – 805 Christian schools against four Buddhist ones; Christian marriage the only legal form of marriage. In promotion of Buddhist parity with Christianity there was a cause which would certainly appeal to Annie Besant's rebellious heart. There is an Olcott Street in Colombo. In 1967 the Singhalese prime minister said that 'Colonel Olcott's visit to this country is a landmark in the history of Buddhism in Ceylon'.[8] At the very time in history when the white races were imposing Imperialism on Egypt and Asia, there is something

William Butler Yeats with Charles and Thea Rolleston, 1894.

gloriously subversive about those Westerners who succumbed to the Wisdom of the East, in however garbled or preposterous a form. The political implications of this were not lost on Gandhi, who welcomed Annie Besant's support for Indian nationalism even when he rejected her spiritual teachings. (She in turn deplored his *satyagraha* – soul-force – policies of resistance to the Raj, believing, by the closing decades of her life, that change would come to India by means of spiritual revival, not political agitation. Such was the revolution which had come about in thirty years in the heart of the heroine of Bloody Sunday.)

Annie Besant was an exotic, and if all her life showed was one woman's journey from socialism to theosophy, then she would hardly seem typical. But though her individual journey was distinctive, in many respects she was a mirror of her age – the wronged feminist of the Seventies, the political activist of the Eighties and, in the

Nineties, the seeker after mystery, the grasper of some Greater Whole.

W.B. Yeats, who moved in some of the same circles as Annie Besant, has described in his unforgettable *Autobiographies* the liberating effects of what might seem – to a reader of our times – to be mumbo-jumbo. He too met Madame Blavatsky. And though he did not take her particularly seriously, he by no means scorned the pursuit of 'psychical research and mystical philosophy'. He saw it directly as a reaction against his own father (a genial artist) and the generation who had believed in both John Stuart Mill and 'popular science'.[9] For Yeats it was an epiphany when he met, in the British Museum Reading Room, 'a man of thirty-six, or thirty-seven, in a brown velveteen coat, with a gaunt resolute face, and an athletic body, who seemed before I heard his name, or knew the nature of his studies, a figure of romance'. This was Liddell Mathers, author of *The Kabbala Unveiled*, who introduced Yeats in 1887 to a society called 'The Hermetic Students' – where, after his initiation in a Charlotte Street studio, the Irish poet met alchemists, necromancers, readers of Henri Bergson, symbolists, fantasists. The magic, and the wisdom of the East, and the Kabbalistic-mystery side of Yeats were all usable, as were the Irish politics and the friendships, in the fashioning of his mighty poetic achievement: he remakes them in his later verse, just as the Grecian goldsmiths in his Byzantium hammer 'gold and gold enamelling'.

The 1890s were apprentice years for Yeats. Though he played with Indian and Irish mythology, his symbolism really developed later. The decade was for him, as a poet, the years of lyric, of the Rhymers' Club, of those contemporaries whom he dubbed the 'tragic generation'. 'I have known twelve men who killed themselves,' Arthur Symons looked back from his middle-aged madness, reflecting on the decade of which he was the doyen. The writers and artists of the period lived hectically and recklessly. Ernest Dowson (1867–1900) (one of the best lyricists of them all – 'I cried for madder music and for stronger wine') died from consumption at thirty-two; Lionel Johnson (1867–1902), a dipsomaniac, died aged thirty-five from a stroke. John Davidson committed suicide at fifty-two; Oscar Wilde, disgraced and broken by prison and exile, died at forty-six; Aubrey Beardsley died at twenty-six. This is not to mention the minor figures of the Nineties literary scene: William Theodore Peters, actor and poet, who starved to death in Paris; Hubert Crankanthorpe, who threw himself in the Thames; Henry Harland, editor of *The Yellow Book*, who died of consumption aged forty-three, or Francis Thompson, who fled the Hound of Heaven 'down the nights and down the days' and who died of the same disease aged forty-eight. Charles Conder (1868–1909), water-colourist and rococo fan-painter, died in an asylum aged forty-one.

Arthur Symons might be said to have defined the Ethos of the Decadence when he came back from Paris and announced to his friends in the Rhymers' Club, 'We are concerned with nothing but impressions.'[10] Yeats provides many archetypical vignettes of the set. One of the most memorable is of Lionel Johnson in his rooms in Clifford's Inn: the walls covered with brown paper, the curtains (over door, window and book-case) grey corduroy; a portrait of Cardinal Newman hung on the walls and a religious painting by Simeon Solomon, a friend of the Swinburne–Rossetti circle until they rather priggishly dropped him after an incident in which he was arrested by the police for homosexual indecency. Yeats

went to see Johnson at 5, but he never rose before 7 p.m., having his breakfast when others dined and spending the night reading theology, writing lyrics and – chiefly – drinking. 'As for living,' he said languidly, quoting from Villiers de l'Isle-Adam, 'our servants will do that for us.'

Johnson was as it happens a gentleman, but this absurd remark should not lead a later generation into supposing that the appeal of the Decadence was limited to those who could afford servants. What it offered was the capacity for self-reinvention, for making the world into anything you wanted it to be. For that reason it was actually of particular appeal to those whose incomes did not run to employing many servants, and whose outer lives were limited by the crushing restraints of petty bourgeois semi-poverty. It is no accident that Arthur Machen (1863–1947) or Frederick Rolfe (1860–1913) should have flourished at the same time as Mr Pooter. Their exotic sorties into the world of the Occult in Machen's case, and in Rolfe's into full-blown fantasies first about himself becoming pope (his novel *Hadrian the Seventh*, 1904, is very nearly a work of genius), then about pursuing boys in Venice (the posthumous *The Desire and Pursuit of the Whole*), are surely admirable protests against the dingy worlds which both men in fact inhabited. They were the camp equivalent of Kipling's 'British soldier' pining for the 'Burma girl' in Mandalay, sun-drenched or incense-drowned dreams to blot out the hell of suburban boredom. Rolfe's background – the son of a piano-maker, he became a teacher before beginning his extraordinary career as would-be priest, failed seminarian, con-man and sponger – more than justified his decision to transform himself into Baron Corvo, a distressed nobleman of the Holy Roman Empire.

Lionel Johnson drank, and kept himself locked in his nocturnal rooms, to escape those very demons who led Baron Corvo to the darkened *calle* of Venice in pursuit, not merely of the Whole, but of young gondoliers. The grandson of a baronet (General Sir Henry Johnson) and the son of an infantry officer, Captain William Johnson, the boy went to Winchester, and on to New College, Oxford. It was there that the insomnia began, and a doctor recommended alcohol as a palliative. And it was at Oxford that he fell under the influence of Walter Pater (1839–94), who had been a fellow of Brasenose since 1864.

Yeats tells us that 'if Rossetti was a subconscious influence, and perhaps the most powerful of all, we looked consciously to Pater for our philosophy'[11] – and this philosophy, in a few words, was *l'art pour l'art*. When he came to compile *The Oxford Book of Modern Verse* in

1936, Yeats began it with a passage of Pater's prose, which he divided into broken lines as if it were verse.

> She is older than the rocks among which she sits:
> Like the Vampire,
> She has been dead many times,
> And learned the secrets of the grave . . .[12]

Many who heard these words read aloud would not instantly, from the word-picture they create, form a picture of Leonardo da Vinci's *La Gioconda* in their minds. But for the generation who were young in the last quarter of the nineteenth century, Pater's *Studies in the History of the Renaissance* (1873), from which the Mona Lisa passage is taken, and his historical novel *Marius the Epicurean* (1885, set in the period of Marcus Aurelius) were revolutionary. They were the beginnings of the modern. They helped a whole generation to lose their faith in Bentham and Mill and Utilitarianism and to embrace the notion that Imagination fashions the world. As the more scornful and disapproving critics of Pater would insist, this would also suggest that morality, if adopted at all, was something we can make up as we go along. No wonder it appealed so strongly to the young. He saw religion as purely aesthetic, and aestheticism was his religion. No wonder those disciples who feared the consequences of this in their own lives, such as Lionel Johnson or the slightly older Gerard Manley Hopkins (1844–89), embraced the disciplines of a religious life. For those who drank Pater undiluted it could be heady stuff. Oscar Wilde (1854–1900) when he first met Yeats described Pater's *Renaissance* as 'My golden book; I never travel anywhere without it; but it is the very flower of decadence: the last trumpet should have sounded the moment it was written.'[13]

If Pater was the godfather of the Nineties, then undoubtedly its most precocious child and greatest visual genius was Aubrey Beardsley (1872–98), and *The Yellow Book*, the artistic quarterly which he helped to found with his friend Henry Harland, its Scripture. When he took a bundle of drawings to Burne-Jones's studio in Fulham, the older artist told Beardsley, then aged eighteen, 'Nature has given you every gift which is necessary to become a great artist. I *seldom* or never advise anyone to take up art as a profession, but in your case *I can do nothing else*.'[14] Whistler, whose relations with Beardsley were much edgier, made a generous admission in 1896 when he saw Beardsley's brilliantly clever illustrations to Pope's *Rape of the Lock* – 'Aubrey, I have made a very great mistake – you are a very great artist' – a tribute which reduced the consumptive (and not always sober) genius to tears.

Art historians can spot the influences on Beardsley's work – some William Morris here, some Japanese prints there. Beardsley's drawings, however, do not merely illustrate, they define their age, as with his design for a prospectus of *The Yellow Book*, showing an expensively dressed, semi-oriental courtesan perusing a brightly lit bookstall late at night while from within the shop the elderly pierrot gazes at her furiously, quizzically. Half the square is black; the whitened spaces, of books, shop window, lantern, seem shockingly bright. She is an emblem of new womanhood, and of erotic power. The candour with which Beardsley evokes erotic feeling in both sexes made his designs 'shocking' to his contemporaries: and it was partly on this shock value that his reputation rested. After he lost interest in *The Yellow Book* he started a new periodical called *The Savoy*, the prospectus for which depicted John Bull, emblem of bluff Englishry, with a notable erection. His illustrations for *Lysistrata*, with their fleshy-calved, full-breasted women whose pubic hair peeps from behind silks and feathers, capture the erotic power of the work they illustrate, and deliberately cock a snook at the suburbs.

But Beardsley is a much greater artist than these naughtinesses might imply. It is hard to think of any British artist who had a more certain sense of composition. Every small square and oblong is an innovation, an experiment in how to arrange black and white shapes. The draughtsmanship is impeccable. And, as is the case with all great art, no one who has imbibed these drawings is quite the same person as before. After Beardsley, no 'modern art' – not Picasso, not the Dadaists nor the Surrealists of the twentieth century – is a surprise. He has been there before. But he has also seen into the tired old soul of his age. The illustration of Juvenal's *Sixth Satire – Messalina Returning from the Bath* is an astonishing piece of work. A woman (or can we dispense with the indefinite article?) angry and sexually dissatisfied stomps upstairs after an unsatisfying quest for pleasure, her taut nipples bare, her hair loose over her shoulders. Her placing to the left of the picture, while the carefully drawn balustrades are all that occupy the right, is a good example of Beardsley's impeccable sense of space. But it is much, much more than a piece of book-illustration. When he was dying of consumption, the poor young man, who had converted from Anglo-Catholic to Roman Catholic piety, wrote to his publisher Smithers, 'Dear Friend, I implore you to destroy *all*

Artist and illustrator Aubrey Beardsley, 1895.

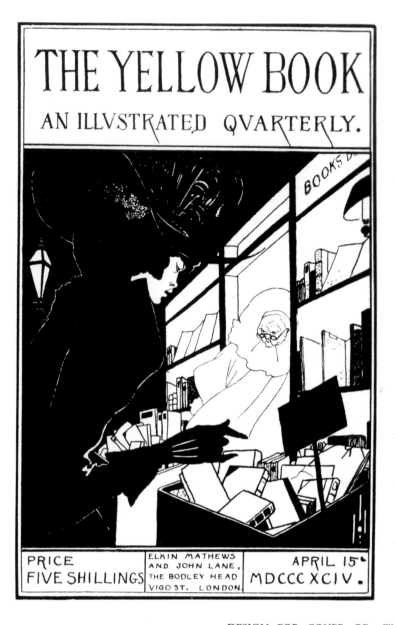

Front cover by Aubrey Beardsley of the prospectus for The Yellow Book, *1894.*

Plate 5

DESIGN FOR COVER OF " THE YELLOW BOOK " PROSPECTUS

copies of *Lysistrata* and bad drawings . . . By all that is holy *all* obscene drawings. In my death agony.'[15] One is grateful to Smithers, publisher to the Decadents, for ignoring this prayer. Perhaps in any case he realized, as we must do, for example, if we walk into an Arts and Crafts Nineties church such as Holy Trinity, Sloane Street, in Chelsea, that the religion of those times was more than a touch decadent, and the decadence of Beardsley's drawings more than a little religious.

One feels the same sentiments when leaving Beardsley's Bohemian world of Soho restaurants or the

flats he shared with his sister Mabel, and turning to the country houses of the group known as the Souls.

Arthur Balfour, the languid nephew of Lord Salisbury, who would succeed as Conservative prime minister on 12 July 1902, felt within himself a superficiality, a frivolity against which he forced himself to guard. He told his niece Blanche Dugdale in the late 1920s that in his youth he had taken his philosophic writings and musings very seriously indeed. This activity 'was my great safeguard against the *feeling* of frivolity'.[16] Balfour's philosophy is not much read now, though the still popular C.S. Lewis provides what is in effect a *rechauffé* version of Balfour's *The Foundations of Belief* in his writings, especially in *Mere Christianity* and *Miracles*. Some of the more light-weight biographical coverage of Balfour and his circle has, by reading only one famous extract from that book, formed the impression that his philosophical position was one of despondency and unbelief, an impression confirmed by his confusingly titled book *A Defence of Philosophic Doubt*. But what Balfour took leave to doubt was not religion but the pretensions of scientific materialism.

For Pater, the natural response to the dark godless universe suggested by Victorian science was to live in myth, and in art. It is in the creation of art that humanity retains its dignity.[17] But for the nephew of Lord Salisbury, this was not quite enough: Balfour tried nobly to create an intellectual justification for *not* believing in the nihilism suggested by Darwin, *not* believing in a godless universe – and by implication, therefore, for accepting Church and State by Law, and by God, established. The atmosphere at Hatfield, during the lifetime of Balfour's uncle, the great prime minister, was distinctly pious. Gladstone liked the feeling in the chapel where Lord Salisbury prayed every day, saying it was 'hearty' – by which he meant full of felt piety, not in the modern sense alive with the noise of tambourines. One of Balfour's biographers describes the 3rd Marquess's children as 'fanatical Anglicans'.[18]

Balfour, though a believer, could never be so described. His 'set' – nicknamed the Souls – had a different ethos altogether. They were aristocrats who deplored the philistinism of their kind. Mention has already been made of George Nathaniel Curzon's knowledge of languages, architecture and art in East and West – demonstrated with panache when he became viceroy of India. Other 'Souls' included Violet, Duchess of Rutland, who described herself in one word in her *Who's Who* entry as 'artist' – her sculpture of her nine-year-old son lying dead on his tomb at Haddon is testimony of how worthy she was of the name. Another was her lover Harry Cust, minor poet, dashingly handsome man of letters. Wilfrid Scawen Blunt was the oldest member of the circle, a man of enormous accomplishments and a scurrilous pen whose diaries continue to confuse historians with their questionable gossip about upper-class life. A keen Arabist (his wife painted him in Arab costume), he also espoused Irish nationalism (and was imprisoned for a while in consequence). His great house Clouds, now famous as a fashionable clinic – he

commissioned Philip Webb to build it at a cost of £80,000 – was often so full of guests that Blunt camped in an Arab tent on the lawn. While the 'Crabbet Club' which Blunt had founded were staying, all twenty of them at once, his wife Lady Anne (Byron's granddaughter) asked guests to share, three to a room. It was a magnificent house – Webb's masterpiece, built of green sandstone, with interiors chiefly white, with here and there a splash of colour provided by Morris carpets or tapestry.

Other 'Souls' houses included the manor house at Mells where the beautiful Frances Graham, subject of many a Burne-Jones canvas, had married the lord of the manor, John Horner. Mells was said to be the 'plum' pulled out by Jack Horner in the rhyme – formerly it was the summer residence of the abbots of Glastonbury. (The Horners had lived at Mells since the Reformation.) Then there was Stanway in Gloucestershire, the superb Jacobean house where Mary Wyndham became the chatelaine, marrying Hugo Charteris, Viscount Elcho, and conducting a lifelong *amitié amoureuse* with Balfour. Far less beautiful architecturally, but no less alive with bright conversation and clever Souls, was Taplow Court near Maidenhead, where the ethereal, sad-faced Lady Desborough presided.

Though Burne-Jones was besotted with Frances Horner, Sargent was the painter who captured the essence of the Souls, as in his stupendous portrait of *The Wyndham Sisters* – Lady Elcho, Mrs Tennant and Mrs Adeane – of 1900. It depicts a world of immense privilege and lightheartedness, but one of dazzling talent too. Yeats, thinking of the rather comparable world of his aristocratic friends in Ireland, saw that country-house life did provide a very special opportunity for a very few clever, nice people to lead lives of the mind, and to be detached from *la vie quotidienne*. By so doing they did not produce works of philosophy to rival Plato or poetry to arouse envy in the shade of Alexander Pope, but it is hard to think of any way of life in any period of history which more deserves the epithet civilized.

Wilde, was often in, though not of, this set. Lady Desborough admired the way he would seek out the most prosaic person in the room and 'conjure him into being a wit'.[19] It is strange to think of him being the guest of Herbert Asquith – home secretary who for eight years was married to Margot Tennant, a great Soul.[20] At one moment, Asquith basks in Wilde's wit at his table. At the next, as home secretary, Asquith was ultimately responsible for prosecuting him on a criminal charge and sending him to prison.

Oscar Wilde, as Yeats reminds us, 'hated Bohemia'[21] and was happier in the houses of the rich. 'Olive Schreiner,' he once said to Yeats, 'is staying in the East End because that is the only place where people do not wear masks upon their faces, but I have told her that I live in the West End because nothing interests me but the mask.'[22]

What lay behind Wilde's mask is anybody's guess. The mask itself, the persona presented to the world, was clear for all to see, which is why one takes with a pinch of

The Adoration of the Magi *designed by Sir Edward Burne-Jones, tapestry made by William Morris and Co., late nineteenth century.*

During his lifetime, he could be seen as a man of incomparable wit who had written some jolly plays and one masterpiece – *The Importance of Being Earnest*. The fairy stories, the creakingly obvious *Picture of Dorian Gray*, the unsuccessful lyrics, can surely only be savoured by the most enthusiastic devotees. As for his private life – he chose not to make it private. A case could be made out for the Victorians being more prudish than we are. An equally strong case could be made for their retaining what is necessary to be retained in order to lead a sane or civilized life: namely, a sense that while there are some things which one would say or do in private, they change their nature if made public. By so incomprehensibly choosing to make an exhibition of himself in court, Wilde made life measurably more uncomfortable for all the homosexuals in Britain, many of whom fled abroad after the second trial. On the day that Wilde was bound over at Great Marlborough Street Police Court, London was placarded with his name on news-stands. 'Well,' a friend remarked to him, 'you have got your name before the public at last.' 'Yes,' Wilde laughed. 'Nobody can pretend now not to have heard of it.'[23] He showed extraordinary courage, but the trials did not do much except create an impression in the public mind of a murky homosexual underworld in which fairly sordid things took place, often with boys who were legally minors.

Yet while the Victorians made the crude moral mistake of treating Wilde like a criminal, our generation has made the almost more mysterious mistake of seeing him as part martyr for sexual liberation, part great thinker.

What cannot be doubted is that Wilde's trial and conviction made a profound impact on his times. It did not necessarily change the way Victorians thought about homosexuals, or the Irish, or prisons, or prostitutes, or relations between the propertied and unpropertied classes. All these ideas have been put forward to attach significance to the Wilde trials, but this is to impose rational shape on something which at the time was upsetting in different ways.

On 18 February 1895, the 8th Marquess of Queensberry, a choleric nobleman with only a slender hold on what others would consider sanity, called at the steps of Wilde's club, the Albemarle, and left a visiting card on which he had written, 'To Oscar Wilde posing as

salt the clever modern interpretations of the plays as metaphors for a hidden homosexual life – Bunburying being such a metaphor for example. What amazed Wilde's contemporaries was not furtiveness – which was alien to his nature – but his exhibitionistic candour.

a Somdomite' (*sic*). The hall porter at the club read the words as 'ponce and Somdomite'.[24]

The behaviour was entirely characteristic of the Scarlet Marquis (as Wilde called him). His elder son, Lord Drumlanrig, had become private secretary to Lord Rosebery, Gladstone's foreign secretary. In 1893 Rosebery suggested a promotion for the young man by making him a lord-in-waiting to the Queen, but this involved giving him an English peerage. Scottish peers elected from among their number those who could sit in the English House of Lords. When Drumlanrig got an English peerage, entitling him to sit there as of right, Queensberry was wild with rage. He had himself not been elected by his fellow peers, on the reasonable grounds that he refused as an atheist to take an oath to the Queen and had made a nuisance of himself, littering the red leather benches of the chamber with his atheistic pamphlets.

Furious at his son's promotion where he had failed, Queensberry also sniffed out a homosexual tinge to the relations between Drumlanrig and Rosebery. He pursued Rosebery to Homburg, where he had retreated on health grounds, offering to horsewhip the foreign secretary on the steps of his hotel. Perhaps to quieten the rumours, poor dim Drumlanrig proposed marriage to a general's daughter. This did nothing to appease Queensberry's wrath. 'It makes the institution of marriage ridiculous,' he spluttered. On 18 October 1894 Drumlanrig was found dead during a shooting party at Quantock Lodge in Somersetshire. He was lying with his head in a bramble bush and the double-barrelled gun lay on his chest. Though the doctor told the inquest that Drumlanrig had been shot through the mouth, the coroner decided that it was an 'accidental death', and that the gun had gone off while Drumlanrig was climbing the hedge to join his shooting chums.[25]

The death of this unfortunate young man removed a very considerable occasion of scandal from the public scene. Quite what Drumlanrig and Rosebery ever did when they were alone together we shall probably never know, but they were widely believed to have been lovers, and the belief is far from implausible, given the temperament of both men. Six months before the shooting, in March 1894, Gladstone had resigned as prime minister and Lord Rosebery had succeeded him. Even in today's relaxed and tolerant climate there would surely

be misgivings about a prime minister who had promoted his apparently talentless and very young secretary to a peerage.

It is against the background of the scandal which never quite happened – Rosebery and Drumlanrig – that Queensberry was able to highlight the scandal which did, the unsuitable friendship of Drumlanrig's younger brother, Lord Alfred Douglas (1870–1945), and the famous playwright and aesthete, Oscar Wilde. The fateful pair met in 1891 when Lord Alfred (known as Bosie) was twenty-two and Wilde thirty-eight. Lionel Johnson brought the young man to tea at Wilde's house in Tite Street and the rapport was instantaneous, quickly developing into a mutual obsession. Letters, notes, presents of all kinds were soon being showered upon the young man.

In the long letter to Douglas sent from prison and entitled *De Profundis* by Wilde's friend Robert Ross,[26] Wilde makes it clear that even in the midst of the most besotted feelings of love for Bosie there was also deep boredom. The young man needed constant amusements – bicycling holidays, golfing holidays, treats, nights out. To a working artist, such distractions must have been torture. Great loves of this kind involve sexual feeling, but sex is not a big part of what is going on. Douglas afterwards said, 'I did with him and allowed him to do what was done among boys at Winchester [Douglas's school] and Oxford . . . Sodomy never took place between us, nor was it attempted or dreamed of . . .' It would seem, though, that both men had a taste for going in search of the young male prostitutes who were so plentiful in Victorian London. Wilde's large income – over £3,000 p.a. by now – and lavishly generous nature involved many a hotel room or suite, or restaurant table, at which these young men would indulge in what seems to have been sordid, but fairly mild, sexual activity for Bosie's amusement.[27] It would seem as if Wilde's part in these proceedings was largely, if not entirely, voyeuristic. Rumours circulated. Blackmailers stole some of Wilde's more extravagantly phrased letters to Douglas. The furious marquess left his card at Wilde's club.

It was then that Wilde made his incomprehensible mistake of suing Lord Queensberry for libel. One of the most popular dramatists of the age suing one of the most colourful noblemen! It was bound to attract the enormous attention which both men so mysteriously needed. Equally, by the time of the trial Queensberry's defence counsel, Edward Henry Carson (1854–1935), was bound to accumulate evidence which would reveal the nature of Wilde's life to the world. His love letters to

Oscar Wilde and Lord Alfred Douglas, 'Bosie', in 1894, the year before the trial.

Bosie would be read out in court; the rent-boys would be subpoenaed; no jury of the time would have found for the plaintiff in such a case. Moreover, when one remembers that all Carson had to prove was that Wilde was 'posing as a Somdomite', one might think that the plaintiff did the counsel for the defence's own work. Asking Wilde about Walter Grainger, Douglas's servant at Oxford, Carson said:

'Did you ever kiss him?'
'Oh, dear no! He was a peculiarly plain boy. He was, unfortunately, extremely ugly.'[28]

When Wilde's libel case collapsed, as it inevitably did, it was only a matter of time before he himself was arrested for infringements of the Criminal Law Amendment Act (1885). The magistrates gave Wilde time to escape. The manager of the St James's Theatre, where *The Importance of Being Earnest* was still showing, urged him to go abroad. 'Everyone wants me to go abroad. I've just been abroad. One can't keep going abroad, unless one is a missionary, or, what comes to the same thing, a commercial traveller.'

Bosie even rounded on Shaw and Harris, both of whom urged flight – 'Your telling him to run away shows that you are no friend of Oscar's.'[29]

There are a number of explanations for his reckless decision to stay in England and stand trial. Likeliest, surely, is that Bosie wanted him to do so and – such is the madness of love – Wilde was in Bosie's thrall. He also surely knew that if he told the full truth in the witness box he would be acquitted, but he could only do so by admitting that he had witnessed various indecent acts, but performed few, if any. Indeed, the mad Marquess surely had a point when he said that 'I do not say you are it, but you look it, and you pose as it which is just as bad.' Wilde, who was sent to prison for two years' hard labour for being indecent, was actually much more accurately to be described as decent. The real reason this camp, sentimental man suffered was to protect his friend.

As the many public scandals of the nineteenth century show, the Victorians enjoyed such things as much as we do. But they were perhaps more conscious of their destructive effect.

The Irish people, many of them highly puritanical in private life, were prepared to overlook the scandal of Mrs O'Shea's divorce; it was the English puritans who initiated and confirmed the destruction of Parnell. There are some who to this day believe that the Wilde trials were likewise brought to pass to discredit yet another Irishman. All the evidence, though, is that Wilde destroyed himself. Many puritans then, and some now, must be shocked by the details of homosexual life which emerged in evidence during the trials – the stained sheets at the Savoy Hotel being the most distressing. But though for a modern reader of these transcripts Wilde might seem like a gay martyr, to the Victorians his real crime was appalling frankness. 'Things are in their essence what we choose to make them' – the lesson he tried in his long vituperative letter to Bosie to expound from the prison cell was not really a doctrine he preached. Without a measure of hypocrisy, a blurring of the edges between Appearance and Reality, societies cannot function.

Chapter Thirty-Seven

Utopia: The Decline of the Aristocracy

Utopia Limited opened at the Savoy Theatre on 7 October 1893 and ran for 245 performances. It marked the reconciliation of Gilbert and Sullivan after one of their celebrated tiffs. Perhaps the reason that it is not performed as often as some of their other operas is that Sullivan was not really on form: the music does not match the amusing plot, in which a South Sea island – Utopia – decides to improve itself by modelling its constitutional and political arrangements on 'a little group of isles beyond the wave'.

The audiences of this satire would have returned to their suburban homes reminded that the late Victorian political scene was an extraordinary phenomenon.

The 1884 Reform Act had extended the possibilities of parliamentary democracy. The electorate was now enlarged to 5 million (or thereabouts), and included agricultural labourers and the urban working classes. Such was the cleverness with which Lord Salisbury had negotiated the borders of constituencies with the Liberals that this did not materially threaten his party's dominion over Parliament, nor his class's dominion over his party. The radicals and socialists made a little headway in the late Eighties, but the suburbs had been conquered by the Conservative Party. The split in the Liberal Party over Home Rule went very much in favour of the Unionists – as witnessed by the fact that when Gladstone resigned as prime minister in 1894 he was replaced by a Liberal Unionist, Lord Rosebery. Lord Salisbury formed a government in June the following year and the Conservatives remained in office for the next ten years.

While the Independent Labour Party, formed in 1893, raised many hopes, it did not do very well electorally. One of its founding fathers, Philip Snowden, believed that its formation was 'the most important political event of the nineteenth century'.[1] The three ILP candidates – John Burns, Keir Hardie and James Havelock Wilson – who won as independent socialists seats in the 1892 election lost them again as ILP candidates in 1895. That election saw Hardie himself, the leader of the ILP who had so movingly taken his seat in the Commons wearing his working clothes and his tweed cap and his boots, defeated by the Conservative at West Ham. The ILP fielded 28 candidates in that election, the Social Democratic Federation 4. They were all defeated.

While the beginnings of the ILP were important, then, some might question whether it was 'the most important political event' of a century which contained three very major reforms of parliamentary franchise; three major (and innumerable minor) wars; the extension of the British Empire to a position of previously unimaginable extent, scope and strength; and the beginning of the parliamentary career of David Lloyd George.

It was the failure of socialism to take hold in Britain which was really of significance. As for the strength of the aristocracy, or its apparent strength during the

VOTE FOR

Home Rule.

Democratic Government.

Justice to Labour

No Monopoly.

No Landlordism

Temperance Reform.

Healthy Homes.

Fair Rents.

Eight-Hour Day.

Work for the Unemployed.

KEIR HARDIE.

An election campaign poster for Keir Hardie, c. 1895. Hardie was the architect of the Labour Party and its most outstanding political inspiration in its first twenty years.

years of Lord Salisbury's premiership – this too is not all that it seems. Any simplistic, or blanket, explanation for the political climate in the 1890s is going to distort reality. Had England ceased, since the passing of the 1884 Reform Act, to be a country governed by the aristocracy? Was it now a true democracy? Were the poor, the working class and the lower middle class represented by the political system? And what had happened to the Liberal Party since the split over Home Rule?

Utopia, Limited or otherwise, Lord Salisbury's Britain certainly wasn't. Viewed in many lights it seems like a country in crisis: at the very least a *deluge* which that consummate Conservative was postponing until he had left the stage.

In *My Apprenticeship*, published in 1926, Beatrice Webb drew on the diaries and punctilious records which she kept in the last quarter of the nineteenth century to explain the question 'Why I became a Socialist'. Since, with her husband Sidney Webb, she was one of the greatest architects and prophets of the British Labour Movement, the question is broader than the merely personal. This was not just the question of how one clever, guilty rich young woman chose to become left-wing to appease feelings of awkwardness about her father's wealth. It was the exposition, by a deeply informed political intelligence, of the nature of the nineteenth-century problem, and the most plausible solution – as she came to see it. It is all the more interesting because of her character – its innate conservatism, its essentially religious bent, and its intense seriousness.

Slowly, during the late 1880s, Beatrice (still Potter) had become involved with trade unions and with the Co-operative Movement (which had begun in 1844 in the small Lancashire town of Rochdale). The twenty-eight flannel weavers known as the Rochdale Pioneers pooled a proportion of their earnings to buy groceries at wholesale prices. The more people who joined the Co-operative the wider the range of goods offered and the lower the prices. This in turn developed into a nationwide English Co-operative Society, with department stores and simple banking arrangements for its members, and, since it was run on a non-profit-making basis, a dividend (or 'Divvy') handed back to members each year in proportion to their contribution.

What the Co-operative Movement had done was to treat all its members not as Nibelungs toiling to produce some supposed value, but as consumers. 'To organize industry from the consumption end, and to place it, from the start, upon the basis of "production for use" instead of "production for profit", under the control and direction not of the workers as producers, but of themselves as consumers, was the outstanding discovery and practical achievement of the Rochdale Pioneers.'[2]

If it had been possible to construct society as a whole on the model of the Co-operatives, using compulsory tax rather than voluntary contributions of 'Co-op' members, then there might be the means to alleviate poverty, and to provide public services.

'Man does not live by bread alone'; and without some 'socialism' – for instance, public education and public health, public parks and public provision for the aged and infirm, open to all and paid for out of rates and taxes, with the addition of some form of 'work or maintenance' for the involuntarily unemployed, even capitalist governments were reluctantly recognizing, though hardly fast enough to prevent race-deterioration, that the regime of private property could not withstand revolution.[3]

This, then, was her blueprint; and when she had abandoned her unfocused radicalism and joined herself quite definitely – and literally, by marriage – to Fabian socialism, she had not merely discovered her aim but agreed the best means of achieving it. By 1898 she and her husband had founded the London School of Economics as the seminary of the new creed. *The New Statesman and Nation* was its unfolding scripture, disseminated to 2,500 subscribers in the first issue, and soon to be much the most influential of all left-wing periodicals in the English language.

The Labour Movement's strength was not simply in its alliance between 'workers' and 'intellectuals'. Such supposed friendships were the commonplace of all continental revolutionary or democratic movements. What solidified the Labour Alliance in Britain was the perception that the underlying idea, the Co-operative Movement, derived from the working classes themselves. In its own 'personal myth', therefore, the Labour Party could not have been more different from Marxism. The communist faithful absorbed their wisdom from the sacred texts written by Marx and expounded by Engels. In the Fabian socialist movement Mrs Webb attributed her conversion to socialism to the Rochdale pioneers (though she did so with back-handed condescension, believing they did not realize the economic or political implications of what they had demonstrated).

The Independent Labour Party was founded in Bradford in 1893. Keir Hardie, who had won the parliamentary seat of West Ham, chaired the first conference and was elected its first leader. The illegitimate son of a Lanarkshire farm servant, he began work in a Glasgow printing works at the age of eight and became a coal miner at the age of ten. He was a working collier until he was twenty-three, and entered politics by becoming active in trade unionism. The Labour Party was always a marriage of contrarieties, and some of these oddities reflect the strangeness of Hardie's own character. He was always much more of a Bohemian than a stereotypical member of the working class, affecting a Sherlock Holmes-style deerstalker hat as often as the famed cloth cap which he wore for his first entry to the Commons. In summer months he defied convention yet further, and while other Honourable and Right Honourable members still wore their black frock-coats and stiff collars he wore a 'Japanese kaftan' (a kimono we must assume) and nothing on his feet.

Hardie's ideological credentials were as eclectic and perplexing as his clothes. Sometimes he claimed to be a disciple of Marx, discovering in the writings of the German revolutionary a quiet gradualism, a belief in socialism by degrees, which was surprising to doctrinaire Marxists. Having insisted with great bravery that the Labour Party must be Independent of even the most sympathetic Liberals at the beginning of the Nineties, by the end of the decade he was making common cause with Lib–Labs over the issue of the Boer War. Having begun as an ardent trade union activist, he lost all sympathy with the unions and by the late Nineties he was referring to the hero of the Dockers' strike as 'that dirty little hypocrite' Ben Tillett. At times he seemed to speak as if socialism was Class War or it was nothing; at others, as if it was a creed to unite all classes behind a common cause. Certainly in the initial decade of his leadership the ILP lost members at an alarming rate. (10,720 members in 1895 had shrunk to 6,084 in 1900, and its appeal was increasingly to the middle classes.)

Yet the fact remains that Keir Hardie was there in the Palace of Westminster. The man who had worked down the pits for thirteen years was sitting on the green leather benches beside the (still overwhelmingly) upper-class Tory and Liberal MPs. Not until the Liberal landslide of 1906, when the Tories lost not merely seats but a hold on the political scene, could the Labour Party make a significant *parliamentary* advance. (In that election they won 29 seats and could begin to look like an alternative radical party when the Liberals disintegrated.) In the 1890s, Hardie was right to see that his role in the Commons was primarily a prophetic, symbolic one. Socialism is, as he observed, 'much more an affair of the heart than of the intellect'; and although with his thick bushy beard he bore a passing resemblance to Marx, he liked to reflect that long before he had heard of *The Communist Manifesto* he had learnt what *he* called socialism from the ballads of Robbie Burns, with their message of the brotherhood of man and their acerbic distrust of the rich or the 'unco guid'.

One of the more momentous surprises in *A la recherche du temps perdu*, Proust's masterly description of French aristocratic life from 1870 to 1919, is the fact that the Princesse de Guermantes in the final volume turns out to be none other than our old friend Madame Verdurin from the beginning of the story. The absurdly posturing social climber, with her '*petite bande*' of largely unimpressive friends, has become a high aristocrat. Victorian England could boast many such elevations and transformations, as we have already seen. The very class who had supposedly ousted the aristocracy from their seats of power by the Industrial Revolution and by the Reform Acts of 1832, 1867 and 1884 discovered, when they had made their millions, that there were few more agreeable things to do with them than to acquire lands, and having acquired lands to acquire the manners, daughters and titles of the old landed class. Between 1886 and 1914 two hundred and forty-six new titles were granted. Discounting those who were members of the royal family, or who were being promoted within the peerage, two hundred of these were entering the nobility for the first time and some seventy of these were new money made from business or industry. Lord Salisbury, who had

fought so hard to defend the landed interest in 1866–7, quickly saw that this cause was lost, and that Conservatism henceforward was to be of a different complexion. In his first brief ministry he made a Burton brewer, Henry Allsopp, into the first Baron Hindlip. In his second administration he made a second Guinness peerage – that of Iveagh; the silk broker H.F. Eaton became Lord Cheylesmore and the wool-comber Samuel Cunliffe-Lister became Lord Masham.

In this Indian Summer of aristocratic life, then, in the thirty years before the outbreak of the First World War, the aristocracy could be said to have shown Darwinian skills at adapting and modifying itself to survive. In so doing they were able to bring money to prop up the system.

England had changed deeply and fundamentally since the Queen came to the throne, and the two doomed categories, sociologically and politically, were the old Whig aristocracy and the squires. The Whig idea – upheld by all the great aristocrats who supported the Reform Bill of 1832 – was that they governed *for* the People. The democratization of the representative system, albeit a very modified democratization, finished the notion of Whiggery. Because the voting systems introduced since 1884 are based on a 'first past the post' system, and because the electorate remained quite small, the new political castes could borrow from the Whigs the convenient cloak of being 'representative' when they least wished to consult the populace or its wishes. They do so even today. But the ethos of Whiggery, with its base in the educated aristocracy, was doomed by extending the franchise.

As so often since in England, it was a Conservative government which delivered the *coup de grâce* to some venerable old aspect of national life.[4] Lord Salisbury appointed Charles Thomson Ritchie (1838–1906) as president of the Local Government Board, and he was the architect of the Local Government Act 1888. Ritchie, the fourth son of a Dundee merchant and jute-spinner, was himself a banker. He would rise to be chancellor of the Exchequer and home secretary. His Act was 'distasteful' to Salisbury, who did nothing to prevent it going through. Salisbury's were crocodile tears. In the end selfishness and greed overcame the attractive Anglican pessimism in this mixture of a man. The most important fact about the Cecils and the other great aristocrats was, after all, that they were richer than anyone else. It was quite natural that Salisbury should ditch the old Tory squirearchy and chum up with New Money. Britain was a rich man's club, sharing the 'business sense' of

Minister=Rennen in England.

(Kampf des Derby-Siegers Rosebery mit dem alten Herren-Reiter Salisbury.)

Auch in England kann sich das liberale Prinzip auf den Kopf stellen, — der Konservative langt doch immer als Erster am Posten an!

'*Ministerial Championship in England – a battle between Derby-winner Rosebery and the old Gentleman-Jockey Lord Salisbury*'. A German view of British elections. 'In England', says the caption, '*Liberal principles get stood on their head . . . and the Conservatives are always first past the post*'.

Birmingham radicals. Naturally it must be forced to 'modernize'. Sixty-two county councils were created. County boroughs and counties were divorced. The London County Council took over the administration of London. In the country, the squires were for the most part elected to the new councils, committees and boards set up by Ritchie's bureaucracy; but something had been lost. As Gladstone said, the public had confidence in the existing county authorities: their duties had not only been 'well discharged, but unselfishly, wisely and economically'. Ritchie took away from the quarter sessions and gave to the county councils the task of administering almost all the things which affected the lives of those living in the counties: finance, county buildings and bridges, the provision and management of lunatic asylums, the establishment and maintenance of reformatories and industrial schools, the diseases of animals acts, main roads, liquor licences, the police.

Henceforward, there was no particular reason for any local authority to be local. The squire, displaced economically from his land, was now politically redundant in his ancestral locality. Ritchie's legislation was both deeply bureaucratic and profoundly destabilizing. Manning thought it the most radical legislation since 1833, and it certainly put the seal on Old England. The country which had, in the Queen's girlhood, been a primarily rural community governed at local level paternalistically, at a national level aristocratically, was now an industrial country governed nationally by plutocrats, locally by bureaucrats.

Having lost rents and status and political power, the minor landowners were to be hit finally by the Liberal chancellor of the Exchequer, Sir William Harcourt (1827–1904), introducing death duties in his budget of 1894. For those whose wealth was primarily bound up in land, this measure more or less guaranteed that inherited estates would diminish, or be broken up.

All these measures, calculated to destroy the power

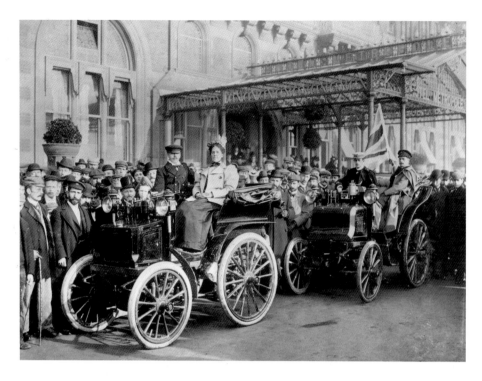

Two Panhard cars complete the first London to Brighton run, outside the Metrople Hotel in Brighton, 1896. This was known as the 'Liberation' or the 'Emancipation' run as it celebrated the repeal of the law requiring all motor vehicles to be preceded by a man walking with a red warning flag.

and stability of the old landed class, were put in place when that class, and the aristocracy which largely depended upon it, were supposedly in power.

Tennyson returned in 'Locksley Hall Sixty Years After' to the fictitious Lincolnshire manor house which had been his theme in 1842. The trochaics of the young man's poem had lamented the loss of his beautiful cousin Amy to the local squire.[5]

> As the husband is, the wife is; thou art mated
> with a clown.

Returning to Locksley as an old man, the poet sees this 'clown' as the embodiment of the good old ways, who

> Served the poor, and built the cottage,
> raised the school, and drained the fen.[6]

The poem is a hymn of hate to the modern world, seeing the country run down, the cities riddled with vice and injustice. He laments

> Poor old Heraldry, poor old History, poor old
> Poetry, passing hence
> In the common deluge drowning old political
> common-sense.[7]

It was indeed an age of commoners, and as if to prove it, on 4 May 1896 a young Irishman called Alfred Harmsworth (1865–1922) launched a new newspaper called *The Daily Mail*.[8] It was designed to encapsulate world news in bulletin form. The first issue sold 397,215 copies, so many more than predicted that it was necessary to hire the use of machinery from two evening newspapers to meet the demand. With his brilliant editor, Kennedy Jones, Harmsworth provided the public with an easily assimilable newspaper, with plenty of crime stories, football, racing and cricket. Lord Salisbury sent Harmsworth a congratulatory telegram, while famously sneering at the venture in private: Thackeray's *Pendennis*, said the prime minister, produced a newspaper 'by gentlemen for gentlemen'; the *Daily Mail* was 'a newspaper produced by office boys for office boys'.

Salisbury's acute political judgement would not have pursued 'villa Conservatism', against every aristocratic instinct, if he had not known that the new England had a very great number of office boys in it. They in turn had wives – leading Alfred Harmsworth to found the *Daily Mirror* in 1903, with an all-woman staff for an all-woman readership.

The balance of the electoral system, and the lack of cohesion or political sophistication, partly explained, perhaps, the reluctance of the urban working classes to rally in greater numbers to the Independent Labour Party. Many of them in any case were arch-Jingoes who preferred Lord Salisbury. The Whigs and the Tories of the old breed had both of them passed or

Lord Tennyson, c. 1886.

were passing into oblivion. Except in Ireland, where the collapse of Parnell had badly weakened the cause of Home Rule, and the merest threat of its success had solidified Unionist opposition in the Protestant North, the political parties were losing touch with what could be seen as their natural constituencies. The field was open for a new type of politics altogether, based less upon identifiable interest and more on a kind of adaptable energy, prepared to ride the wave and watch the wind.

Surely much the most interesting political career, after Parnell's fall, is that of David Lloyd George (1863–1945), who would succeed Asquith as prime minister in 1916, and whose radical budgets when chancellor of the Exchequer – introducing welfare benefits, old age pensions and so on – did more for the working classes than Keir Hardie's rhetoric before the Labour Party had a chance of power or Ramsay MacDonald's incompetence after he'd been given that chance and squandered it.

Maynard Keynes's description of Lloyd George is that of a clever young man lampooning a wartime prime minister whose party broke into smithereens after the peace of 1918. It is well-known because it is so funny and so well-expressed; and it is only half-true – 'How can I convey to the reader, who does not know him, any just impression of this extraordinary figure of our time, this syren, this goat-footed bard, this half-human visitor to our age from the hag-ridden magic and enchanted woods of Celtic antiquity? . . . Lloyd George is rooted in nothing, he is void and without content; he lives and feeds on his immediate surroundings.'[9]

Lloyd George was not, in fact, rooted in nothing. He was rooted in something which was harder perhaps even for the economic genius of the great Keynes to fathom: namely, Victorian North Wales.

A Welsh-speaker and, in his earliest manifestations as a political being, to all intents a Welsh nationalist or at least a Welsh Home Ruler, Lloyd George belonged to a very different Wales from that of the pits and the valleys of the South. Though born and reared in poverty, he belonged to the tradition of teachers, preachers, dreamers and ranters who owe spiritual kinship to the Bards. Yet, such is the strangeness of David Lloyd George that he always transcended his background.

He was actually born in England – in Manchester, on 17 January 1863. His father had been a schoolmaster, a career he abandoned in favour of farming, but he died when his son was seventeen months old. Thereafter, David and his infant brother were brought up by his mother and Uncle Lloyd – their mother's brother, a shoemaker and pillar of the Baptist Chapel at Llanystumdwy.

Social class in Wales was not as crudely stratified as in industrial England. A clever, literate shoemaker was poor, but not the lowest of the low. The Idealist philosopher Sir Henry Jones (1852–1922) – Fellow of the British Academy, Companion of Honour, professor at Glasgow – was born the son of the village shoemaker at Llangernyw, Denbighshire, left school aged twelve, but grew up in a world which respected learning. Lloyd George received a good education at the local school – which was a Church school. In the early part of his political career, his preoccupation was the superficially parochial one of Church tithes. Since the (Anglican) Church in Wales was not (as the Irish one had been in 1859) disestablished, all local farmers and householders were obliged to pay a tenth of their income in tax to the parson. As in Ireland, so in Wales (where the majority of the population were Christians of a different complexion), the Established Church was deeply resented. The apparently small question of whether a shoemaker or a dairyman who attended the Baptist chapel should be made to pay money to the (Anglican) parson actually encapsulated the much bigger question of the powers of the state over the small nation and the small man.

In essence, surely, this is why Lloyd George never became a socialist. He saw the state as an enabler of private destinies, not as the paternalistic substitute for Church, mill-owner or landlord. When he was a well-established politician, in 1906, he told an audience in Birmingham that Joseph Chamberlain's Tariff Reform 'has focused the opera-glasses of the rich on the miseries of the poor. Once you do that, there is plenty of kindness in the human heart.'

Dickens could have said that: and Lloyd George has strong elements of the Dickensian in his nature – the hyper-energy, the tendency to fantasize, the essential benignity. He saw the great Liberal victory of 1906 as a chance to do the decent thing by the poor without the collectivist solutions of the Independent Labour Party.

From the very beginnings, Lloyd George had a Napoleonic confidence in his own destiny. At eighteen, three years before he so much as qualified as a solicitor, he made his first visit to London to take his Intermediate Law exams and visited a House of Commons which was

David Lloyd George with his dog in the garden, 1904. He was first Chancellor of the Exchequer and then Prime Minister.

CHECKMATE.

'Checkmate', Joseph Chamberlain in dire straits during talks with Paul Kruger of South Africa, 1896.

empty – it being a Saturday. In his diary of 12 November 1881 he wrote, 'I will not say but that I eyed the assembly in a spirit similar to that in which William the Conqueror eyed England on his visit to Edward the Confessor, as the region of his future domain.'[10] His letter to the woman he would marry, Margaret Owen, written perhaps in 1886, is chilling in its candour. 'My supreme idea is to get on. To this idea I shall sacrifice everything – except I trust honesty. I am prepared to thrust even love itself under the wheels of my Juggernaut if it obstructs the way.' No one could say she had not been warned – though, poor woman, she could not have guessed how highly sexed he was, nor how unfaithful he was capable of being. Carlyle would have been shocked by Lloyd George's lapses from honesty and chastity, but he would surely, had he lived to witness it, been impressed by the way in which the small-town solicitor

from Criccieth would emerge, with the apparent naturalness of a Muhammad, a Cromwell or a Frederick, as a Leader of the Leaderless.

So long as his sphere was domestic politics, David Lloyd George could appear marginal. The Liberal Party was defeated in 1895 and would be out of office for a decade. Lord Salisbury and his government cared little for Welshmen and their local concerns. But it was as a spokesman on a much wider theme that Lloyd George was to rise to prominence.

In South Africa Britain had annexed the territory east of the Orange Free State known as Griqualand West, in order to secure the diamonds of Kimberley. Then gold was discovered in the Transvaal, on the Witwatersrand, and a group of foreigners (Uitlanders) were threatening the old-fashioned Bible-based way of life of the Boers. Paul Kruger, the president of the Transvaal Republic, resisted the demands of the Uitlanders for political rights.

In December 1895 the young prime minister of the Cape, Cecil Rhodes, tried to engineer an uprising of the Uitlanders at Johannesburg, which would be joined by a flying column of Cape Chartered Company police, under the direction of his friend Dr Jameson. The new colonial secretary in Salisbury's government, Joseph Chamberlain, knew about this illegal, reckless scheme. The 'Jameson Raid', however, was an ignominious failure. Dr Jameson moved in too fast and had to be disowned; the Uitlanders did not rebel. Rhodes fell from power and the confidence he had tried to build up between Boers and British was destroyed.

The British Imperialists had been made a laughing-stock, and the rest of the world did not restrain its ridicule. A Welshman who had witnessed decades of English interference in his province (Welsh-speaking children were forced to carry a large letter W on their back in the schools where English was enforced) could not but be pleased. The Boers, Bible Protestants, hill farmers, were a more stolid lot than the Welsh, but there were obviously areas in common. 'In South Africa, a small republic, with an army the size of that of an ordinary German principality, has been able to defy the power of Great Britain,' Lloyd George could tell an audience at Penarth, on 28 November 1896. In the closing years of Queen Victoria's reign, all British eyes now turned towards South Africa.

Chapter Thirty-Eight

The Boer War

Cecil Rhodes, the son of a Hertfordshire parson, first sailed for Africa – the east coast – when he was seventeen, in 1870. It was in the fates that he would give his name to two great African countries, Northern and Southern Rhodesia (now Zambia and Zimbabwe). Whether he actually placed his hand on the map of Africa and said, 'That is my dream – all British'[1] – or in another version, 'all red'[2] – he certainly believed that in an ideal universe, Britain would hold dominion not merely over the Dark Continent, but over the world itself. In his 'Confession', written when he was a very young man, Rhodes even dreamed of the readmission of the United States to the Empire. True, 'without the low-class Irish and German emigrants' that great nation would be a greater asset. 'If we had retained America there would . . . be millions more of English living . . . Since we are the finest race in the world and that the more of the world we inhabit the better it is for the human race.'[3]

It is probably safe to say that there is no one alive on the planet who now thinks as Rhodes thought. Of course, there are those who, in an attempt to shock or amuse, might *pretend* to be British Imperialist, though with only a few outposts of rock in St Helena, Gibraltar or the Falkland Islands remaining of the Empire, it must be difficult, even as an affectation, to sustain the Rhodesian vision. Equally, there would be those, in far larger numbers, and not merely British or white, who might wish for a balanced view of the Empire. They might say, 'True, attitudes were expressed by the Empire-builders which shock a modern sensibility; and some unpleasant things happened; but the Empire brought good as well as bad to almost all the countries under its sway. There were countries which positively benefited from the educational system or the railway or the administrative skills into which they were initiated by the well-meaning British.' But while these views in themselves would be shocking to many of our contemporaries, they come nowhere near Rhodes's almost mystic sense that the British would inherit the Earth. A.C. Benson's great anthem, 'Land of Hope and Glory', however, 'Wider still and wider, shall thy bounds be set! God who made thee mighty – make thee mightier yet!' – bellowed now with some irony at the Last Night of the Prom Concerts each year in the Albert Hall – was once sung seriously. It was a creed for two generations of Englishmen, and fashioned the foreign policy of British governments and the general attitude of the British public down until 1945.

Those who witnessed the demolition of the statue of Rhodes in the middle of Harare (formerly Salisbury, the capital of Southern Rhodesia) in August 1980 saw something which in the Western world was comparable to the removal of the representations first of Stalin, next of Lenin in the old Soviet Union. To many a young Russian, it must seem hard to understand how the older generation were 'brainwashed' into admiring Lenin; it would be harder for him or her to see that by

British soldiers defend their position during a battle at Honey Nest Kloof, c. 1900.

absorbing the new anti-communist ideology they had also submitted to a set of doctrines – for example that capitalism spells freedom – which might seem quaint to a later generation.

Likewise the post-colonial Britain is in a poor position to understand Rhodes and his generation, not least because though popular with the majority, he and his vision of Empire were deplored by some of his contemporaries. 'Rhodes had no principles whatever to give to the world. He had only a hasty but elaborate machinery for spreading the principles he had not got. What he called his ideals were the dregs of Darwinism which had already grown not only stagnant but poisonous' – G.K. Chesterton.[4] Beatrice Webb, though she believed war, when it came, inevitable, blamed it on 'the impossible combination in British policy of Gladstonian sentimental Christianity with the blackguardism of Rhodes and Jameson'.[5]

The diamonds which so fired Rider Haggard's imagination in *King Solomon's Mines* (1885) had begun to be discovered on Afrikaner farms in 1866. Between 1870 and 1880, gems of vast size and value had been found in the midst of country farmed for generations by Dutch settlers. Of course, ownership of the diamonds was contested, and of the land in which they were found. By 1870 5,000 diamond-seekers had arrived to look for jewels in the rivers. Cecil Rhodes arrived at the diggings in 1871, coming from his brother's cotton farm in Natal. Within months of establishing himself at the mine (named Kimberley after the British secretary of state for the colonies) Rhodes had gone into partnership with a man called Charles Rudd. In 1873 they had an ice-making machine in operation, in 1874 they imported heavy-duty pumping machinery from Britain, transporting it 600 miles by ox wagon from the Cape. They won the water-pumping contract for the whole mine. By 1887 Rhodes's De Beers Mining Company had full control of the large De Beers Mine, and he soon had control of the Kimberley mines too.

The pickings, or winnings, were prodigious. In 1886 there had been a rumour of gold, discovered along the ridge known by the Afrikaners as the Witwatersrand (white water ridge) near Pretoria. In fact the ore was low-grade, but the Kimberley diamond magnates could afford to invest in heavy machinery to mine at a depth of two and a half thousand feet where the best gold was found. Rhodes was there, forming the Consolidated Goldfields of South Africa in 1892.

Rhodes and Rudd wanted to exploit the gold potential in Matabeleland, and they approached King Lobengula with the so-called Rudd Concession. They agreed to pay the king and his heirs £100 per month, as well as 1,000 Martini-Henry breech-loading rifles and cartridges and a steamboat with guns, in effectual exchange for all the mineral wealth in his territory.

You can measure Rhodes's achievement by surveying the map of Southern Africa in 1870 and comparing it with the same in 1895, when he had annexed, with the blessing of the British government and Crown, Mashonaland, Matabeleland, all the territory which is now Zambia and Zimbabwe. He also notoriously had his eye on the Afrikaner territories in Bechuanaland, where the unsuccessful Jameson raid took place at the end of 1895. It was the beginning of the end for Rhodes – he was forced to resign as prime minister of the Cape. But in another sense, it did his career and reputation no harm at home. The public was openly pro-Jameson. The new colonial secretary, Joseph Chamberlain, encouraged Rhodes to create the new territories of Rhodesia and to move towards the dominance of South Africa as a whole. It is not surprising that the Boers, the descendants of those Dutch settlers who had first come to the Cape in 1652, should have viewed with dismay those they called outsiders or Uitlanders.

The Afrikaners, back in the 1830s, had made a mass exodus from the Cape Colony. About 10,000 of them had made their way to the Transvaal for an independent life. Those who had made the Great Trek were known as the Voortrekkers, the pioneers. One of these Voortrekkers, who had left the Cape Colony with his parents in 1835 when he was ten years old, was the formidable president of the Transvaal: Stephanus Johannes Paulus Kruger, a strange giant of a man who with his hooded eyes, his whiskers, his stoop and his air of religious melancholy bears in some photographs a striking resemblance to Lord Salisbury himself. Whereas Salisbury was a High Church Anglican, who irritated Archbishop Benson by his cynicism and flippancy, Kruger was a fervent adherent of the 'Doppers', the most uncompromising of the three South African Reformed Churches. He knew much of the Bible by heart and believed in the literal truth of its every word. The annexation of the Transvaal by the British in 1877 had been a bitter blow to him, and independence of them had been his long-cherished political ambition.

With the discovery of gold in the Witwatersrand,

☞ *Cecil Rhodes caricatured as a colossus bestriding Africa,* Punch, *1892.*

THE RHODES COLOSSUS

STRIDING FROM CAPE TOWN TO CAIRO.

biblical images of blessing must have flickered through his mind; and when the little mining camp of Johannesburg sprang up into being a multinational town ('a kind of Dodge City on the veld') other biblical metaphors might have been supplied – of tribes inimical to the Lord being put to the sword, or consumed by divine wrath for their iniquity. For by 1898 the gold mines of the Transvaal were producing £15 million worth of gold each year. In 1899 this would be £20 million, with reserves conservatively estimated at £700 million. A British minister said it was 'the richest spot on earth'. In fifteen years, what had been a row of tents had become a city with 50,000 European inhabitants. Then the mines became organized. The gold rush died and an industrial pattern asserted itself. In the rich part of the town where the richer whites lived, there were broad gaslit pavements, big houses, theatres, hotels, nightclubs, brothels. In the poorer industrial hinterland 88,000 Africans lived in appalling conditions where typhoid and pneumonia were rife and home-made liquor, often literally deadly, was the only narcotic to numb the pain of existence. For all its mixture, Boer and Jew, black and brown, Johannesburg mysteriously felt British – both in its cruelly depressed slums, and in the street names of its salubrious quarters: Anderson Street and Commissioner Street.

No wonder Kruger and his government wished to deprive these invaders, these intruders, of as much as possible of their plunder by taxation: no wonder he wanted to withhold from them any political rights, such as a vote. And no wonder the British yearned to be the sole masters of the gold, as of the diamonds: the lords of a united South Africa under the British flag.

That is what the Boer War was about. The Jameson Raid of 1895 was a hasty, illegal operation for which the perpetrator received a token prison sentence in Holloway. But Rhodes and Jameson had only done with vulgar haste what Chamberlain – and Salisbury – wanted to do by negotiation or conquest: acquire Johannesburg. This is, as Rhodes wrote in a secret letter to Alfred Beit in 1895, 'the big idea which makes England dominant in Africa, in fact gives England the African continent'.[6]

In the days when the British Empire was still growing, or when people could conceive of it coming into being in a fit of absence of mind,[7] then individual losses of face or territory in different parts of the globe could be shrugged off. Paradoxically, when the idea of Rhodes took hold – that Britain should rule not just some parts

of the Earth, but the entire planet – then even the smallest rebellion here, military disaster there, could be seen as a threat to the whole. This perhaps explains in part, if anything can explain it, the growing ruthlessness of the British Imperial machine as it reached its zenith. Compare Gordon's campaign in Khartoum in 1884 and Kitchener's in 1898. Gladstone's government had sent Gordon to Khartoum not as a soldier but as a governor, with instructions to evacuate in the face of the Mahdi's insurgent popularity. Salisbury's Unionist government, with Chamberlain as colonial secretary, had very different ideas. So did Sir Herbert Kitchener (as he then was) who, against the advice of Lord Cromer, the consul-general in Cairo, wanted to reconquer the Sudan in the face of Dervish fighting against European forces.

Presumably if Kitchener's campaign in the Sudan happened today there would be an international tribunal and he would be summoned to The Hague to answer charges of war crimes and genocide. As far as the British public was concerned he was the gallant conqueror of Khartoum. The Dervishes fought with rifles and bayonets and spears. Kitchener's army had machine guns, which could explain the casualties. At the battle of Atbara Kitchener's force lost 125 white men, and 443 blacks. The Dervish Khalifa's army lost 2,000 dead, and a further 2,000 were taken prisoner.

The second Sudan War was a *locus classicus* of the new Imperialism. No one doubted that the system of the Khalifa, based on slavery, was cruel. Few doubted that in the best of all possible worlds, the Dervishes would be converted to Western Liberal Agnosticism, with a devotion to Free Trade and Cricket. What was new was the preparedness not merely to fight, but to eliminate the enemies of the Empire. At the battle of Omdurman the Dervishes had two machine guns, Kitchener fifty-five. His forces were transported by steamer and railroad, which was just as well, since the boots issued were unwearable and had fallen to pieces on arrival. (Many British soldiers in Kitchener's army marched barefoot in this campaign.)[8] By the evening of 2 September 1898, Kitchener thanked 'the Lord of Hosts who had brought him victory at such small cost in British blood'. The casualties were 23 British dead, 434 wounded, and a staggering 11,000 dead Dervishes. A further 16,000 Dervishes, many of them wounded, were taken prisoner.[9]

Yet it would be a mistake to imagine that the Europeans had it all their own way, or even that in all their imperial wars they had all the technological superiority. Menelik's forces at Adowa in 1896 had overwhelmed 30,000 Italians,

Charge of the 21st Lancers at the Battle of Omdurman, 2 September 1898.

and were armed with more than 14,000 muzzle-loaders and similar rifles. The arms trade which made Armstrong and others into millionaires knew little of territorial restraint. By 1899 Paul Kruger's Boer Republic had an arsenal of 31 machine guns, 62,950 rifles, 6,000 revolvers and sufficient ammunition for a protracted campaign.

They would also be helped by another factor: the sheer incompetence of quartermasters, suppliers and others, the human capacity to make mistakes. Belloc was a master of the witty epigram – 'Whatever happens, we have got/The Maxim gun and they have not.' The truer picture of Imperial warfare is probably given by Sir Henry Newbolt with his 'The Gatling's jammed and the colonel dead'.

Much of this bad luck and incompetence was on display in the opening months of the Boer War. So too was the resourcefulness of the Boers and the skill and courage with which they used their vast arsenal. So, ultimately, was that sheer ruthlessness which Kitchener had displayed at Omdurman.

In 1897, Chamberlain had appointed Sir Alfred Milner (1854–1925) as high commissioner for South Africa. He was a journalist – he had been a deputy editor to Stead and Morley on the *Pall Mall Gazette* – a barrister, a Liberal and a Balliol man. It would have been hard to find anyone with a mindset more different from Kruger's, who in an election of 1898 was returned as president of the Boer Republic with an overwhelming majority.

In the negotiations about the position of the Uitlanders which took place between Kruger and Milner, the Boer position hardened and the commissioner became increasingly exasperated. Every time Milner (on

GENˡ JOUBERT ᴀᴺᴰ STAFF ᴀᴛ NEWCASTLE, NATAL. Oᴄᴛ 17ᵀᴴ 1899.
PHOTO ᵇʸ GELL.

Afrikaanes General Piet Joubert and his staff at Newcastle, Natal, 17 October 1899. An American newspaper correspondent, Howard Hillegas, commented: 'To call the Boer forces an army was to add unwarranted elasticity to the word, for it has but one quality in common with such armed forces as Americans or Europeans are accustomed to call by that name. The Boer army fought with guns and gunpowder, but it had no discipline, no drills, no forms, no standards, and not even a roll-call.'

the Cabinet's instructions) made a minor concession to Kruger, the old man in his top hat upped the ante – for example by wishing to ban the immigration of Indians to Johannesburg. The dispute played out between the smooth, intelligent Milner and the stubborn, serious old Voortrekker was nominally concerned with the voting rights or residency permits of 'foreigners' in Johannesburg. It was really seen by everyone as something much bigger.

When Kruger had repelled the Jameson Raid, no less a person than the Kaiser, Wilhelm II, had cabled the Transvaal president on 3 January 1896: 'I sincerely congratulate you that, without appealing for the help of friendly Powers, you, with your people, by your energy against the armed hordes which as disturbers of the peace broke into your country, have succeeded in re-establishing peace and maintaining the independence of your country against attacks from without.'[10] When war eventually came, about 1,600 volunteers formed the 'foreign brigade' to help Kruger: Irish, Americans, Germans, Scandinavians, French, Dutch and Russians. (Among the European aristocrats were Count Sternberg and Prince Bagration of Tiflis, who was accompanied by two Cossack servants.)[11] The British, equally symbolically, drew on their Empire to supply them with troops – a Canadian regiment raised by Lord Strathcona, Australians, New Zealanders and Indians.[12] For this was to be a war which enabled other nations to deliver a verdict on the power of the British Empire.

That was why Milner believed that 'Krugerism' had to

A British concentration camp for Boer Civilians, 1901.

be checked. It was why he could stigmatize the prime minister of Natal (an English South African) as 'disloyal' for so much as sending a message of congratulation to Kruger on his re-election. It was why in a celebrated memo to the Westminster government, Milner flamboyantly said:

> The case for intervention is overwhelming . . . The spectacle of thousands of British subjects kept permanently in the position of helots, constantly chafing under undoubted grievances, and calling vainly to Her Majesty's Government for redress, does steadily undermine the influence and reputation of Great Britain and the respect for the British Government within its own dominions.[13]

By September 1899 the garrison in South Africa was reinforced from 12,000 to 20,000 troops and war became inevitable. The Orange Free State publicly allied itself with the Transvaal and war was declared on 11 October.

The Boers wore no uniform. When one field cornet of the Kroonstad commando insisted on holding a morning roll-call and a rifle inspection, the men complained to a higher authority, and he was told to stop harassing them.[14]

In the initial stages of the war, though, the Boers had all the advantages. They were familiar with the country, which was certainly not true of the 20,000 British troops lately arrived in the Cape, or the 10,000 Indians drafted in.[15] They also, in the opening stages of the war, heavily outnumbered the British. They had 50,000 mounted infantry, and enough ammunition for 80,000. Their marksmen were extremely skilled and the Krupp guns they used were superior to British weapons.[16]

Initially, when they invaded Northern Natal, the Boers had great success. By the end of October, Joubert had outmanoeuvred Sir George White at the battle of Ladysmith, which was to be besieged until 28 February 1900. Kimberley, on the northernmost border of Cape Colony, the western border of the Free State, was also besieged, and so was Mafeking. Three important British forces were thereby immobilized and the Boers had the opportunity to press on through the Cape Colony and take Cape Town. Had they done so, they would have forced Britain to make terms. Instead, with their desire to capture Durban and give themselves a seaport, they made a tactical error which allowed the British time to land a formidable army at Cape Town at the end of October under Sir Redvers Buller as commander-in-chief.

Buller was a stupid man, and his initial actions led to heavy casualties. In December there was the 'Black Week' in which Lieutenant General Sir W.F. Gatacre was defeated at Stormberg; a day later on the 3rd Lord Methuen was disastrously repulsed by Cronje at Magersfontein; and four days later Buller, advancing to relieve Ladysmith, was defeated by Louis Botha at Colenso. The only son of Lord Roberts was killed in the action. Buller then lost his nerve. He signalled to White that Ladysmith should surrender and cabled the same to the Cabinet in London.

The Cabinet's response was to sack Buller and make Roberts commander-in-chief and Kitchener his chief of staff. Roberts was sixty-seven years old. Three years before he had retired from the Indian command. He and Kitchener landed at Cape Town on 10 January 1900.

Roberts gave categorical orders to Buller that he was to do nothing until they had arrived, but the ambitious Buller attempted one last chance of a victory which was his and his only. The disastrous battle of Spion Kop was fought on 24 January – witnessed by a twenty-four-year-old war correspondent called Winston S. Churchill. 1,200 men were killed or wounded, both sides fought with outstanding valour; it was one of the worst defeats inflicted on British troops since the Crimea. The next morning the Boers photographed the British dead on the battlefield and published the pictures all over the world. They caused uproar in England.

When Arthur Balfour referred to the disastrous setbacks, the Queen upbraided him with: 'Please understand that there is no one depressed in this house; we are not interested in the possibilities of defeat; they do not exist.'[17]

Under Roberts's command, the British army turned round the disastrous position into which Buller had led it. 1900 saw the relief of Ladysmith and Mafeking, the capture of Bloemfontein, Johannesburg and Pretoria and – by October 1900 – the formal annexation of the Transvaal. Roberts returned to England and Kitchener succeeded him as commander-in-chief on 29 November.

It might have been supposed that the war was all but over. Rather, it had eighteen terrible months to run, with the Boers fighting a resourceful guerrilla campaign and Kitchener responding with a dreadful ruthlessness. The first part of his strategy was to set up a line of prefabricated blockhouses – constructed out of stone, with corrugated iron roofs – from Kapmurden to Komatipoort, as lookout posts to defend the railway from commando attack. His second move was to clear the land. Women and children were to be separated from their menfolk and herded into concentration camps. Their farms were to be burned or blown up. Crops were to be burnt, livestock killed. Several million horses, cattle and sheep were shot. Barbed-wire fences totalling 3,000 miles were set up to corral the Boers into the camps, with a blockhouse to observe them every few hundred yards.

From then onwards in the war the function of the British army had become the collection of non-combatants and livestock. Lieutenant Colonel Allenby commanded 1,500 men at the beginning of 1901, one of eight columns 'driving' the Transvaal. At the end of three months, his 'bag' was 32 Boers killed, 36 captured, 154 surrendered; 5 guns; 118 wagons; 55 carts; 28,911 rounds of ammunition; 273 rifles; 904 horses; 87 mules; 485 trek oxen; 3,260 other cattle; and 12,380 sheep. He also imprisoned some 400 women and children.

The plight of those in the camps was brought to the public eye by Emily Hobhouse, who went to South Africa on behalf of the Women and Children's Distress Fund. While the military ran the camps (until November 1901) the death rate was 344 per 1,000, falling to 20 per 1,000 in May 1902. The families were deprived of clothes, bedding, cooking utensils, clean water and adequate medicine.[18] Children often had to lie on the bare earth exposed to unbearable heat. By October 1901, 80,000 Boers were living in these camps – a number which swelled to 117,871 in the eleventh month. 20,177 inmates died, most of them children.[19]

Kitchener appears to have been indifferent to the suffering he caused in South Africa. Like many who enjoy inflicting pain on their fellow men, or from whose natures compassion has been mysteriously excluded, he was a keen animal-lover. He had a pet bear in Cyprus. He instantaneously 'bonded' with horses and camels on campaign. His true mania, however, was for dogs. When he had finished tormenting the South Africans this cruel

A German view on the war in South Africa. The caption reads 'War and Capitalism or the transformation of human blood into gold.' (1899)

bugger – there is enough evidence, surely, to justify both the noun and the epithet – doted on four cocker spaniels named Shot, Bang, Miss and Damn. When he was in India he bought a house, something he had never done before: 'I need somewhere for my dogs to live.'[20]

No such shelter was offered by the field marshal to the Afrikaner women and children whom he had starved, or allowed to die of dysentery and typhoid, in the midday sun of the High Veld. The photographs of the children in those camps, skeletal as the inmates of Belsen,[21] are the silent footnote to the South African war. Six days after the peace was signed at Vereeniging on 31 May 1902 Kitchener was awarded £50,000 by Parliament. He was given the Order of Merit and created a viscount.

The Victorian age, haunted by the dire warnings of Malthus, had begun with the erection of workhouses on home territory. It ended with a war which was no more than a scramble for gold and diamonds. The war cost Great Britain £222 million. 5,774 British troops were killed, 22,829 wounded, and some 4,000 Boers died in battle. The war was hugely popular. The reliefs of Mafeking and Ladysmith were the occasions of wild public rejoicing. The songs of the war had an infectious music-hall brio. And Britain may be said to have won handsome returns on her expenditure. For her £222 million she had won control of the richest spot on Earth. Yet as in a morality tale, she had gained diamonds and gold and lost something in return. A people who built workhouses at the beginning of an era and concentration camps at the end might have gained the whole world, but they had lost honour, and soul.

Chapter Thirty-Nine

Vale

Life at the court of Queen Victoria can never have been exciting, but as she entered the deeper, mistier recesses of old age, the tedium for her attendants was scarcely tolerable. At Osborne in the winters, there was so little to do that the equerries tried playing golf in the snow with red billiard balls: 'but the greens are of course useless. We share a great deal . . . We have had some good hockey.'[1]

The numbers dining with the Queen were small: usually just Princess Beatrice, sometimes Princess Louise ('the petticoats' as the equerries dubbed them) and one or two courtiers. The old lady liked to eat off gold – even her eggcup at breakfast for the royal boiled egg was gold plate – and she maintained a Hanoverian level of greed.

In this last phase of decrepitude her eyesight grew dim, and she became querulous about the darkened rooms (as they appeared to her) at Osborne, and the faintness of modern ink. She continued to be punctilious about overseeing the affairs of state and reading the boxes of state papers sent down by ministers. When she entered the very final stage, and was too ill to read them for just one week, Arthur Balfour 'was astounded at the accumulation of official boxes that had taken place during the last week and said it showed what a mass of routine work the Queen had to do'.[2]

She took a keen interest in the progress of the Boer War, and kept an album of photographs of all the officers killed: an agonizing task for the equerries who had to write to all the widows asking for these pictures. Having compiled it for a year she tired of it, saying it was too sad to look at.

The last official engagement she performed was on Monday, 14 January 1901, when she received Lord Roberts on his return from South Africa. She was wheelchair-bound and very frail. She conferred on him an earldom, and since his only son had been killed in the war she allowed him the privilege of the title passing to his daughter. (The Queen herself had lost a beloved grandson in the fighting: Prince Christian Victor, Helena's boy, who died of enteric fever in Pretoria.) She also made 'Our Bobs' a Knight of the Garter.

Not long after this audience, she began to sink. On Wednesday 16th, for the first time in twenty years as her personal physician, Reid saw the Queen in bed: she remained there all day, only rising to dress at 6 p.m.[3] Over the next few days, Reid and the courtiers began to warn those most intimately connected with her that the Queen's life was coming to an end. The government needed to be told: no one could remember the procedures for summoning an Accession Council or for swearing in a new monarch. The bishop of Winchester, Randall Davidson, was summoned to the Queen's bedside. The Prince of Wales was telephoned at Marlborough House,[4] and set off for the Isle of Wight.

Much against the advice and wishes of 'the petticoats', the Kaiser in Berlin had been informed and had set off at once to see his grandmother. When he arrived at Osborne House, he said to the petticoats, 'My first wish is not to be in the light, and I will return to London if you wish. I should like to see Grandmama before she dies, but if it is impossible, I should quite understand.'[5] Everyone was impressed by how well he behaved. She spent the last two and a half hours of her life leaning on the Kaiser's immobile arm, with Reid supporting her other side. She finally died at half-past six in the evening on 22 January 1901.

She died clutching a crucifix, but like so much else about Queen Victoria, her religion was *sui generis*. The 'Instructions', written out on 9 December 1897 and carried out by Reid to the letter,[6] insisted that she should be placed in her coffin with an array of trinkets worthy of an Egyptian pharaoh. Rings, bracelets, lockets, shawls, handkerchiefs and plaster casts of her favourites' hands were all placed in the casket. When all the royalties had come to pay their last respects to the body ('no smell')[7] and to look at that face – 'like a lovely marble statue, no sign of illness or age, and she looked *"the Queen"'*[8] – it was time for the doctor to cram more souvenirs into the casket – Prince Albert's dressing-gown: and in her left hand a photo of John Brown and a lock of his hair in tissue paper which the doctor tactfully covered with Queen Alexandra's floral tribute.[9] The new king kindly allowed the Munshi to come and look his last on the Empress of India, and finally two men came in and screwed down the coffin lid.[10]

To the end, she could indulge her love of clutter. The little body would now begin its stately journey to Windsor where – in accordance with her wishes – it was given a military funeral. The war in South Africa, still in progress as the Queen's military funeral took place, and as the cortège went to Paddington Station for its journey to the Mausoleum at Frogmore (where at last she would be reunited with the Prince Consort), reinforced the point that the genial power of the Victorian aristocracy,

Queen Victoria's funeral. The gun carriage is led past the crowds at Green Park, 1901. 'Oh! Dearest George,' wrote the Queen's cousin, Princess Augusta of Strelitz, to the Duke of Cambridge, 'what a calamity! . . . anxiety terrible as to what poor England will have to go through now! God have mercy on us all.' There were indeed terrible decades ahead – a First World War, decades of poverty and unrest, another war killing millions of Europeans, in addition to all the postcolonial problems visited upon the former dominions of the British Empire.

transforming itself slowly into parliamentary democracy, was underpinned by force. Ask – given the sickness and poverty of hundreds of thousands of Londoners on that cold February day, as the gun carriage bore the coffin through the silent streets – ask why they did not rebel, why they did not riot, why they did not behave like the Paris Commune of 1870 or the Bolsheviks of 1917. They had as much provocation, but part of the answer to the mystery of their submissiveness is supplied in those troops and those guns, following the procession. No one could doubt for a single second that at the first sign of trouble from the populace, pious old Salisbury and dear 'Old Bobs' – now an earl and KG – would turn the guns on the crowd, with all the confidence shown by the Chinese authorities eighty-eight years later in Tiananmen Square.

The other fact about the Victorians, however, which explains why the reign of the Queen ended in reverence and (domestically at least) peacefulness is more benign. From the first, the Victorians possessed the capacity for constructive self-criticism. Those who opposed the Boer War, or who had their doubts about this phase of the Imperial adventure, were not, as they would have been in a truly autocratic system, moved underground, silenced or imprisoned. The mercurial figure of Lloyd George made his career out of opposition to the war. 'The man who tries to make the flag an object of a single party is a greater traitor to that flag than any man who fires at it,'[11] said the great Welshman, replying to Tory accusations of treachery. All allowance should be made for Lloyd George's opportunism – not to say, in his later years at least, his downright dishonesty and corruption – but a country which enabled a man who grew up in a small shoemaker's cottage to rise in less than fifty years to be chancellor of the Exchequer was not a country which was entirely repressive. Against all the cruelty and the blunders – the workhouses, the oppression of Ireland, the blatant racism and butchery of the colonial wars – must be set a vast social (as well as technological) resourcefulness, a willingness to regroup and reorganize on behalf of the governing classes, which was guided by enlightened self-interest.

It is easy for those who come in after time to say what is wrong with a society, or a country, not their own. Those who have lived through a twentieth century whose wars slew and displaced tens of millions can easily, for some reason, turn a blind eye to the faults of their own generation and excoriate the Victorians, whose wars killed thousands. By the same token, life for a working-class Irish family in the slums of Liverpool in, let us say,

1880 may have been terrible; but it is only fair to add, terrible compared with what, and with whom? The nineteenth century was by many modern standards a cruel age. Those refugees, from Karl Marx to the Emperor Napoleon III, who fled to London from Europe suggest to us that with all its faults, Victorian England was more genial and tolerant than many other places at the same date. The Victorian Age saw floggings of sailors and soldiers, it saw children working down the mines; it also saw these abuses, and hundreds like them, reformed and abolished.

The gun carriage making its way to Paddington Station across Hyde Park was followed by King Edward VII, Kaiser Wilhelm II, King George I of the Hellenes and King Carlos of Portugal. In the procession were Crown Princes of Romania, Greece, Denmark, Norway, Sweden and Siam. The Duke of Aosta represented the King of Italy, Grand Duke Michael Alexandrovitch the Tsar of Russia, and Archduke Franz Ferdinand the Emperor of Austria. Almost all these characters, in their uniforms and feathered hats, presided over countries where the poor were even more miserable than in Victorian England, where political dissent was vigorously denied, and where technological and social change had been slower than in England. Almost all of them (not the Scandinavians) oppressed minorities within their own borders and were cruel colonial masters to those in Africa and Asia whom they had subdued. The huge proportion of them would, during or after the First World War, be toppled by republican movements which were even less humanitarian, and even less efficient.

Though dreadful mistakes were made by the Victorians, the comparative stability, comparative strength (military and political) and comparative benignity of England in the half-century after her death owed much to the Victorians. They even owed something to the tiny, round-faced woman trundling towards her last resting place with her coffin-load of mementoes.

'Vale desideratissime,' she had had inscribed over the doors of the Frogmore Mausoleum: 'Farewell, most beloved. Here at length I shall rest with thee, with thee in Christ I shall rise again.' That journey was hers, hers alone. Fascinating as it is to visit the mausoleum on open days, one always feels there something of an intruder. Let us, rather, take leave of 'the little old woman' before she leaves her island home for the great public funeral.

The gun carriage was drawn from Osborne House down York Avenue, East Cowes; the occupants of these villas, whose grandparents would not have had the vote, possessed not merely a share in parliamentary democracy but, in all probability, a savings account and a bicycle. The coffin was carried aboard the *Alberta* at Trinity Pier opposite the post office as a dull roll of forty drums rumbled. The royal family with their attendants boarded the royal yacht *Victoria and Albert* and set out, through the clear blue wintry air of the Solent, on the short sea-voyage to Portsmouth harbour. They sailed through an eight-mile-long allée of steel, in which the British fleet was joined by foreign warships, spaced at two and a half cable lengths, about 1,500 feet apart. They glided past *Australia*, between the *Camperdown* and the *Majestic*, the *Trafalgar*, the *Nile*, and the *Benbow*, the names of the ships recalling a vanished naval era, much at variance with the massy walls of gun-metal grey which they adorned. And here, still at peace with one another for another ominous thirteen years, were the *Dupuy de Lorne*, representing France, the *Dom Carlo I* from Portugal, the Japanese battleship *Hatsuse*, and four huge grey-masted ironclads flying the red, white and black German ensign, vastly overshadowing the others in strength and size.[12]

Notes

Unprinted sources are given in full, including the number of the manuscript and the folio number – e.g. Gladstone Papers, BL Add. MS 44790 f.177.

Notes on printed sources refer to the Bibliography. E.g. Litten (1991), p. 170 refers to Julian Litten's *The English Way of Death. The Common Funeral since 1450*. In cases where more than work by one author appears in the Bibliography, the reader should be guided by the date. E.g. Gash (1976) would refer to Norman Gash's *Peel*, published in 1976. Gash (1977) refers to *Politics in the Age of Peel*, 2nd edition, 1977.

In any case which could conceivably be confusing, the full title is cited. References to periodicals are self-explanatory. E.g. *The Law Journal*, 1884, can be found in any good reference library. References to signed articles in periodicals will, in general, be made to the author by name.

Thomas Curson Hansard was the printer of the Parliamentary Debates. This voluminous monument began as Cobbett's *Parliamentary History of England from the Norman Conquest to the Year 1803*, and was first published in October 1806 in thirty-one volumes. It continued as a record of Parliamentary Debates from 1812 onwards, *The Parliamentary Debates from the Year 1803 to the Present Time*, published under the Superintendence of T.C. Hansard in 1812. Thereafter the volumes are always popularly known simply as 'Hansard'. This series of forty-one volumes continues until February 1820. The next series, from 21 April 1820 to 23 July 1830, covers a further thirty-five volumes. Most of our period is covered in the Third Series, which extends to 5 August 1891. Reference in the notes is simply to Hansard, the number of a volume in Roman numerals and a column number in Arabic numerals. So 'Hansard, XXVI.3' would refer to Hansard's Parliamentary Debates, Third Series, volume XXVI, column 3. The date will only be added if it is considered of especial significance.

The Annual Register, now published by Keesing's Worldwide, began in 1759 (registering the year 1758) and was printed by R. and J. Dodsley in Pall Mall. For most of our period, it was published by Rivingtons (taken over by Longmans, Green and Co., that great Victorian publisher, for the 1890 volume, published 1891). This invaluable survey has been consulted by me far more often than would be guessed at from the reference notes. It gave me my sense of pace, seeing the different events of each year so clearly spelled out side by side. References to it appear as *The Annual Register* followed by a year and a page number.

In referring to the works of the Victorians themselves, I have been conscious of the multiplicity of editions available to different readers. Sometimes a modern edition of a poet – most notably that of Tennyson by Christopher Ricks – is so good that it seems almost a necessity to consult that rather than an earlier version. Sometimes I refer to first editions, but more often simply to a volume which happens to be to hand. I try to guide the reader as carefully as I can by reference to chapter or section-numbers of books, as well as to the page numbers of the works cited. This is especially necessary in the case of the two giants. I refer to thirty-nine volumes of *The Works of John Ruskin*, edited by E.T. Cook and Alexander Wedderburn, because it is the standard edition to which all Ruskin scholars refer, and to the thirty volumes of the Edinburgh Edition of *The Complete Works of Thomas Carlyle*, published in New York in 1903 by Charles Scribner's Sons, because it happens to be the edition on my own shelves. (How we British visitors miss Scribner's beautiful shop in Fifth Avenue!)

1 The Little Old Woman Britannia

1 Cocks, p. 13.
2 Dickens, *Speeches*, ed. Fielding, p. 205.
3 Clapham, p. 53.

2 Victoria's Inheritance

1 Woodham-Smith (1972), p. 139.
2 David Cecil, p. 391.
3 Woodham-Smith (1972), p. 140.
4 Ibid., p. 141.
5 Victoria (1912), II, p. 144.
6 Anstruther (1984), p. 35.
7 David Roberts, pp. 97–107.

3 The Charter

1 Douglas Browne, p. 83.
2 Finer, p. 30.
3 Halévy, p. 510.
4 Philip Thurmond Smith, p. 18.
5 Ibid., p. 85.
6 Ibid., p. 44.
7 Ascoli, p. 83.
8 Woodward, p. 79.
9 Gash (1927), p. 214.
10 Thomas Carlyle, *Chartism 1839* (Critical & Miscellaneous Essays, vol. IV, *Works*, vol. XXIX, p. 153).
11 McDonall, *Chartist and Republican Journal*, quoted in Slosson, p. 59.
12 Dorothy Thompson, p. 58.
13 Woodward, p. 127.
14 Ibid., p. 130.
15 Dorothy Thompson, p. 338.
16 Dorothy Thompson, p. 31.

4 Typhoon Coming On

1 Woodward, p. 357.
2 Bethell, p. 329.
3 Ridley, p. 259.
4 See Hewison *et al.*, p. 71.
5 A.J. Newman, p. 102.
6 See Heuman, *Between Black and White. Race, Politics and the Free Coloureds in Jamaica, 1792–1865.*
7 Fulford (1949), p. 106.
8 Weintraub (1997), p. 99.

5 The Age of Peel

1 Read, p. 61.
2 There are three superb historians of this for which I largely rely for what follows. Robert Blake (1985), Donald Read and Norman Gash (1976 & 1977).
3 Hastings, p. 104.
4 A.C. Benson (1899), I, p. 47.
5 Dunn (1961), p. 420.
6 For all previous see Anstruther (1963).
7 Sheila M. Smith, Introduction to Disraeli (1982), p. xiii.
8 Read, p. 138.

9 Ibid., p. 139.
10 Gash (1977), p. 248.
11 Blake (1985), p. 59.
12 Woodward, p. 120.
13 Clapham, p. 454.
14 Blake (1985), p. 67.

6 Famine in Ireland

1 Quoted in Gray, p. 76.
2 Clapham, p. 391.
3 Hoppen, p. 570.
4 Dunn (1961), p. 69.
5 De Beaumont, quoted in Saville, p. 31.
6 Hoppen, p. 63.
7 Woodham-Smith (1962), p. 21.
8 Saville (1987), p. 6.
9 Percival, pp. 72–3.
10 Saville (1987), p. 16.
11 Woodham-Smith (1962), p. 167.
12 Berkeley, ed. Jessop, vol. 6, p. 243.
13 Woodham-Smith (1962), p. 165.
14 Ibid., p. 375.
15 Ibid., p. 409.

7 Doubt

1 *The Leisure Hour*, September 1849.
2 Altick (1978), p. 318.
3 Ibid., p. 317.
4 Janet Browne, pp. 462–3.
5 De Beer, p. 32.
6 Ibid., p. 25.
7 Lyell, p. 407.
8 Robert Chambers, pp. 25–6.
9 Ibid., p. 157.
10 Quoted in de Beer, p. 12.
11 Robert Chambers, p. 231.
12 See Milton Malthauser, *Just Before Darwin*, Wesleyan University Press, Middleton, Ct, 1954, p. 36.
13 Robert Chambers, p. 203.
14 John Henry Newman (1974), p.107.
15 See Appleyard, *Henry Francis Lyte*.
16 Quoted in Erikson, *Phrenology and Physical Anthropology*, p. 51.
17 See Storer, p. 7.
18 See Jonathan Miller, 'A Gower Street Scandal', pp. 183ff.
19 Kaplan, p. 235. See also Crabtree, *From Mesmer to Freud*.

8 The Failed Revolution

1 For the many significant textual and notional differences between the 1848 first edition (German) and the 1888 English version, see Fisher (1984).
2 Saville (1987), p. 81.
3 Ibid., p. 110.
4 Ibid., p. 112.
5 Dorothy Thompson, pp. 341–68.
6 Woodward, p. 131. Fisher pp. 16, 96.

9 The Great Exhibition

1 Smith & Spear, p. 664.
2 Stanmore Papers, BL Add. MS 49,131, f. 73.
3 Ibid., f. 46.
4 Olive Anderson, p. 211.
5 Auerbach, pp. 63, 64.
6 Lees-Milne, p. 131.
7 Ibid., p. 154.
8 Auerbach, p. 45.
9 Bird, p. 111.
10 Auerbach, p. 104.
11 Ibid., p. 106.
12 Auerbach, p. 171.
13 John Ruskin, 'The Opening of the Crystal Palace Considered in some of its Relations to the Prospects of Art, 1854', quoted in Beaver, p. 59.
14 Longford (1972), p. 478.
15 Tennyson, 'Ode on the Death of the Duke of Wellington', *Poems*, ed. Ricks, p. 412.
16 Woodward, p. 249.
17 Eyck, p. 152.
18 Longford (1972), p. 484.

10 Marx – Ruskin – Pre-Raphaelites

1 Woodward, p. 144, and for most of supra.
2 Martineau (1855), p. 23.
3 Marx (1857), p. 289.
4 Ibid., p. 292.
5 Ibid., p. 247.
6 Longford (1964), p. 372.
7 *The Cambridge World History of Disease*, ed. Kiple, p. 648.
8 Ibid.
9 Mary Bennett, in Bowness, p. 163.
10 Hamlin, p. 333.
11 Carlyle, *Past and Present*, in *Works*, X, pp. 24, 31.
12 Marsh (1999), p. 119, Bowness, p. 86.
13 Quoted in Marsh (1999), p. 210.
14 Amor, p. 10.
15 Diana Holman Hunt, p. 69.
16 Ibid., p. 52.
17 Diana Holman Hunt, p. 106.
18 Hilton (1965), p. 156.
19 Ibid., p. 118.
20 Froude (1884), I, p. 97.
21 Haight, p. 101.
22 Fulford (1933), p. 293.

11 The Crimean War

1 Soyer (1987), p. 142.
2 The above quotes from Seacole, pp. 90, 121.
3 Ibid., p. 137.
4 A.J.P. Taylor (1954), p. 81, characteristic of an English historian of a certain

age, does not mention the Turkish casualties, which I have been unable to locate in any work of reference.

5   William Howard Russell (1995), p. 38.
6   Ibid., p. 50.
7   Ibid., p. 53.
8   Royle (1999), p. 130.
9   William Howard Russell (1995), p. 103.
10 Royle (1999), p. 269.
11 Ibid., p. 276.
12 Ibid., p. 290.
13 Quoted ibid., p. 126.
14 Tennyson, *Poems*, ed. Ricks, p. 1034.
15 Ibid., p. 1308.
16 A.J.P. Taylor (1954), p. 75.
17 Olive Anderson, p. 76.
18 *DNB*, XV, p. 1013.
19 Quoted in Ridley, p. 433.
20 Southgate, p. 339.
21 Fitzroy, p. 65.
22 Apperson, p. 164.
23 Alford, p. 28.
24 Lawrence James (1981), p. 10.
25 Ibid., p. 136.

12   India 1857–9

1   Sen, p. 42.
2   Hansard 1st series, XXVI, p. 164, 22 June 1813.
3   Chaudhuri, p. 116
4   Hibbert (1978), p. 80.
5   Sen, p. 59.
6   Ibid., p. 61.
7   *Source material for a History of the Freedom Movement in India*, vol. II, 1885–1920, Bombay, 1958, p. 192.
8   Srivastava, p. 157.
9   Nanuk, 1858.
10 Smith & Spear, p. 668.
11 Quoted by Eric Stokes (1959), p. 3.
12 Hibbert (1978), p. 90.
13 Ibid., p. 111.
14 Lawrence James (1997), p. 287.
15 Rotton, p. 6.
16 Hibbert (1978), p. 173.
17 Having protested against his loss of privileges – permission to maintain his own army, for example, or exemption from the jurisdiction of civil courts – Nana Sahib bided his time, to all outward signs on cordial terms with the British authorities. Srivastava, p. 14.
18 Eric Stokes (1986), p. 53.
19 Ibid., p. 56.
20 Quoted in P.J.O. Taylor (1996), p. 53.
21 Sen, pp. 147, 159.
22 Taylor (1992), p. 51.
23 Ibid., p. 81.
24 Ibid., pp. 6, 1.
25 Edward Thompson, p. 46.

26 Ibid., p. 48.
27 Sir J.W. Kaye, *A History of the Sepoy War*, II, quoted Edward Thompson, p. 70.
28 Coopland, p. 33.
29 Oldenburg, p. 3.
30 Ibid., p. 11.
31 Hibbert (1978), p. 223.
32 Iddesleigh Papers, BL Add. MS 37,151, f. 6.
33 Hibbert (1978), p. 350.
34 Ibid., p. 424.
35 *Illustrated London News*, 9 October 1858.
36 Canning, quoted in Maclagan, p. 140.
37 IHibbert (1978), p. 386.

13   Clinging to Life

1   *DNB*, 1912–1921, p. 547.
2   Quoted Bowlby, p. 74.
3   Janet Browne, p. 447.
4   Irvine, p. 68.
5   White & Gribbin, p. 30. See also Gribbin, *In the Beginning*.
6   Darwin (1951), p. 73.
7   J.R. Moore, p. 82.
8   Hoppen, p. 200.
9   See Barzun, *Darwin, Marx, Wagner. Critique of a Heritage*.
10 Fulford (1949), p. 234.
11 Ibid., p. 242.
12 Fulford, ed. (1964), p. 14.
13 Fulford (1949), p. 238.
14 Eyck, *The Prince Consort. A Political Biography*, especially pp. 66–100.
15 Ibid., p. 72.
16 Ibid., p. 94.
17 Longford (1964), p. 398.
18 For a statement of the case on both sides see *The Schleswig-Holstein Question and its Place in History* by Max Müller and the Danish View of the Schleswig-Holstein Question by Dr A.D. Jörgensen, Spottiswoode & Co., 1897.
19 Longford (1964), p. 400.
20 Fulford (1949), p. 261.
21 Hibbert (2000), p. 185.
22 Fulford, ed. (1964), p. 144.
23 Ibid., p. 245.
24 ('I am sure you will be benefitting all Germany if they could be generally introduced') ibid., p. 171.
25 Weintraub, p. 407.
26 Hibbert (2000), p. 279.
27 Fulford, ed. (1964), p. 171.
28 Hibbert (2000), p. 281.

14   The Beloved – Uncle Tom – and Governor Eyre

1   R. Arthur Arnold, p. 11.
2   Ibid., p. 38.
3   Morley (1912), II, p. 77.
4   Adams, II, pp. 304–5.
5   Robert Blake (1966), p. 419.
6   Brian Jenkins, II, p. 394.
7   Ibid., I, p. 235.
8   R. Arthur Arnold, p. 109.
9   Brian Jenkins, I, p. 761.
10 Ibid., p. 167.
11 Morley (1912), II, p. 55.
12 Robert Blake (1966), p. 579.
13 Devereux Jones, p. 275.
14 Sainsbury, pp. 196–7.
15 Marsh (1999), p. 292.
16 Banks, p. 48.
17 Burn, p. 92.
18 H. Oliver Horne, p. 201.
19 Burn, p. 17.
20 Banks, p. 91.
21 Olivier, p. 125.
22 Charles Tennyson, p. 359.

15   The World of School

1   Hughes, *Tom Brown's Schooldays*, p. 164.
2   Ibid., p. 175.
3   Prothero, I, p. 41.
4   Hoppen, p. 312.
5   Mack, p. 23.
6   Hansard, 183, pp. 1925, 1926. 5 June 1866.
7   Kirk, p. 24.
8   Ibid., p. 39.
9   Nick Davies, p. 102.
10 Armytage, p. 130.
11 Scrimgeour, p. 72.
12 Gathorne-Hardy, p. 87.
13 Scott, in Simon & Bradley, ed., p. 35.
14 Stanmore Papers, BL Add. MS 35,226.

16   Goblin Market and the Cause

1   Elizabeth Garrett, p. 6.
2   Butler, p. 82.
3   Dorothy Porter, in *Companion Encyclopedia of the History of Medicine*, p. 1248.
4   Kiple *et al.*, ed., p. 1268.
5   Elizabeth Garrett, p. 8.
6   Finnegan, p. 3.
7   Walkowitz, p. 70.
8   Ray Strachey, p. 107.
9   Weintraub, p. 103.
10 Marsh (1994), p. 237.
11 Marsh (1999), p. 220.
12 Ibid., p. 241.
13 Ibid., pp. 374–9.

14 Davidoff, *Journal of Social History*, vol. 7, 1984, p. 410.
15 Ibid., p. 412.

17 Wonderland
1 Hacking, p. 36.
2 Bartram, p. 134.
3 Cohen, p. 170.
4 Quoted ibid., p. 101.
5 Ibid., p. 102.
6 Cohen, p. 77.
7 Rose G. Kingsley's introduction to *The Water-Babies*, 1908 edition, Dent.
8 Kendall, p. 137.
9 Ibid., p. 249.

18 Some Deaths
1 Brian Doyle (1968), p. 254.
2 Woodward, p. 179.
3 Robert Blake (1985), p. 98.
4 Ibid., p. 100.
5 G.K. Chesterton, Introduction to *Great Expectations*, Everyman, 1907.

19 Gladstone's First Premiership
1 Horne, p. 505. See also Michael Howard, *The Franco-Prussian War*.
2 Ensor, p. 6.
3 Fulford (1977), pp. 16–17.
4 Fulford (1971), p. 317.
5 Matthew, p. 133.
6 Shannon (1999), p. 62.
7 Beeler, p. 76.
8 Morley (1912), II, p. 41.
9 Spiers, pp. 2–24.
10 Spiers, pp. 14 & 17.
11 Spiers, p. 15.
12 Robert Blake (1993), p. 15.
13 Shannon (1999), p. 92.

20 The Side of the Angels
1 Lowder, p. 38.
2 Menzies, p. 10.
3 Ibid., p. 33.
4 Ibid., p. 183.
5 *DNB*, XIX, W.H. Fremantle, 'Archibald Campbell Tait', p. 292.
6 Lowder, pp. 214–15.
7 Monypenny & Buckle, V, p. 58.
8 Fulford, ed. (1971), p. 161.
9 Fulford, ed. (1964), p. 173.
10 E.A.T., p. 137.
11 J.H. Newman (1875), p. 66.
12 Darwin (1874), p. 619.
13 Ibid., p. 1171.
14 Ibid., p. 719.
15 Ibid., p. 45.
16 Alfred Tennyson, 'Locksley Hall, Sixty Years After', ed. Ricks, p. 1362.
17 C.A. Russell, p. 290.

18 Hoppen, p. 459.
19 Robert Blake (1966), p. 504.
20 Ibid., p. 505

21 The End of Lord Beaconsfield
1 Ensor, p. 38, Robert Blake (1966), p. 582.
2 Rothschild, p. 47.
3 Ibid., p. 47.
4 Ibid., p. 46.
5 Robert Blake (1966), p. 581.
6 Ibid., p. 587.
7 Pamuk, p. 123.
8 Ibid., p. 83.
9 Kasaba, p. 47.
10 Ibid., p. 48.
11 Mansel, p. 17.
12 Shaw & Shaw, pp. 77–9; 666–73.
13 Ibid., p. 158.
14 A.J.P. Taylor (1954), p. 233.
15 Shaw & Shaw, p. 162. William Miller, p. 366, places the Bulgarian casualties at 12,000 that summer.
16 Matthew (1995), p. 33.
17 William Miller, p. 376.
18 Hoppen, p. 627.
19 Quoted in Robert Blake (1966), p. 613.
20 Dodwell, V, p. 418.
21 Headlam, p. 483.
22 Froude (1890), p. 251; Headlam, pp. 486–9.
23 Quoted in Robert Blake (1966), p. 610.
24 Quoted ibid., p. 612.
25 Quoted ibid., p. 607.
26 Robert Blake (1966), p. 679.
27 Ibid., p. 646.
28 Ibid., p. 649.
29 Ibid., p. 566.
30 Quoted ibid., p. 712.
31 Morley (1912), II, p. 451.
32 *The Times*, 23 January 1905, p. 9.
33 Haight, pp. 470–3.

22 Wagner – Gilbert and Sullivan
1 Vamplew, p. 35.
2 Mason, p. 15.
3 Ibid., p. 25.
4 Ibid., p. 30.
5 Ibid., pp. 138–9.
6 Adburgham, p. 208 *passim*.
7 *The Complete Annotated Gilbert and Sullivan*, Oxford, 1996, ed. Ian Bradley, p. 43. Hereafter, Bradley.
8 Jacobs, pp. 71, 106.
9 Rothman & Rothman, ed. p. 29.
10 Olsen, p. 149.
11 Bradley, p. 485.
12 Merrill, p. 130.
13 Bradley, p. 137.

14 Padfield, p. 158.
15 Beeler, pp. 261, 266, 267.

23 Country Parishes – Hardy
1 Chambers & Mingay, p. 162.
2 Ensor, p. 115.
3 Ibid., p. 116.
4 Chambers & Mingay, p. 179.
5 Orwin & Whetham, p. 244.
6 Chambers & Mingay, p. 178.
7 Ibid., p. 182.
8 Ibid., p. 185.
9 Hoppen, p. 21.
10 Orwin & Whetham, p. 207.
11 George Edwards MP, *From Crow-Scaring to Westminster*, 1992, p. 22.
12 Orwin & Whetham, p. 216.
13 Chambers & Mingay, p. 188.
14 Ensor, p. 117.
15 Stewart, p. 21.
16 The examples are quoted in Stewart, p. 26.
17 Seymour-Smith (1994), p. 20.
18 Ibid., p. 136.
19 Stewart, p. 45.
20 Seymour-Smith (1994), p. 422.
21 Stewart, p. 22.
22 Ibid.

24 A Crazy Decade
1 Jeffrey, p. 71.
2 Russell & Goldfarb, p. 128.
3 Glendinning, ed., p. 10. See also Patterson, *100 Years of Spirit Photography*.
4 Dostoyevsky, II.i, p. 3.

25 The Plight of the Poor
1 Quoted Kynaston, p. 72.
2 Nightingale Papers LXIII, BL Add. MS 45,801.
3 Quoted Saville (1988), p. 9
4 Sims, p. 107.
5 Jay, p. 77.
6 Hoppen, pp. 70, 606.
7 Kynaston, p. 121.
8 Quoted MacCarthy, p. 466.
9 Ensor, p. 88.
10 Arnstein, p. 28.
11 Hoppen, p. 325.
12 Arnstein, p. 287.

26 The Rise of Parnell
1 Neary, pp. 11, 12.
2 Andrew Roberts, p. 471.
3 Kee, p. 370.
4 Ensor, p. 72.
5 Kee, pp. 75, 383.
6 Matthew, p. 231.

7 Roy Jenkins (1958), p. 239.
8 Ibid., p. 356.
9 Ibid., p. 352.

27 The Fourth Estate – Gordon of
Khartoum – The Maiden Tribute
of Babylon

1 Hoppen, p. 633. See also Brown,
Victorian News and Newspapers, and
Alan J. Lee, *The Origins of the
Popular Press 1855–1914*.
2 Ensor, p. 51.
3 *DNB*, XXII, p. 507.
4 Quoted in Pierce Jones, p. 17.
5 Farwell, p. 257.
6 Ibid., pp. 266–7.
7 Hoppen, p. 661; Farwell, p. 269.
8 Ensor, p. 80.
9 Zetland, p. 89.
10 Allen, p. 183.
11 Ibid., p. 194.
12 Ibid., p. 195.
13 The idea began with W.S. Blunt in
Gordon at Khartoum and is repeated
in *Eminent Victorians* by Lytton
Strachey and *After Puritanism* by
Hugh Kingsmill.
14 Allen, p. 213.
15 Ibid., p. 215.
16 Ibid., p. 271.
17 Lytton Strachey (1993), p. 301.
18 Ensor, p. 83.
19 Williamson, p. 80.
20 Pierce Jones, p. 26.
21 Quoted in Roy Jenkins (1958), p. 241.

28 Politics of the Late 1880s

1 Roy Jenkins (1995), p. 560.
2 Hoppen, p. 265.
3 Ibid.

29 Into Africa

1 *Annual Register*, 1885, p. 60.
2 Dawson, p. 441.
3 Ibid., p. 359.
4 Sundkler & Steed, p. 1007.
5 Pakenham (1991), p. xxiii.
6 Andrew Roberts, p. 518.
7 Hoppen, p. 664.
8 Pakenham (1991), p. 25.
9 Ibid., p. 13.
10 Ibid., p. 22.
11 Ensor, p. 192.

30 Kipling's India

1 *Annual Register*, 1885, p. 60.
2 Field, 'Internal Combustion Engines',
p. 164.
3 Field, 'Mechanical Road Vehicles',
p. 427.

4 McLuhan, p. 90.
5 McGrath, p. 293.
6 Kipling (1990), 'McAndrew's Hymn', p.
98.
7 Ibid., p. 103.
8 Ibid., p. 338.
9 Raine, p. 1.
10 Kipling (1990), 'The White Man's
Burden', p. 261.
11 Quoted R.J. Moore, p. 435.
12 R.J. Moore, p. 428.

31 Jubilee – and the Munshi

1 Fabb, p. 58.
2 Chapman & Raben. No pagination.
3 Ibid.
4 Andrew Roberts, p. 612.
5 Van der Kiste (1986), pp. 109–11.
6 Ponsonby, p. 95.
7 Ibid.
8 Michaela Reid, p. 132.
9 Ibid., p. 128.
10 Ponsonby, pp. 13–15.
11 Longford (1961), p. 676.

32 The Dock Strike

1 Andrew Roberts, p. 462.
2 Mackenzie & Mackenzie, ed., *The
Diary of Beatrice Webb*, vol. 1, p. 58.
3 Ibid., p. 150.
4 Andrew Roberts, p. 470.
5 Fiona MacCarthy, pp. 566–74; Mackail,
p. 201; Ensor, pp. 180–1.
6 MacCarthy, p. 570.
7 Anne Taylor, p. 196.
8 Ibid., p. 197.
9 Quoted in Fiona MacCarthy, p. 573.
10 Webb, vol. 1, p. 290.
11 Anne Taylor, pp. 205–10.
12 H. Llewellyn Smith & Vaughan Nash,
*The Story of the Dockers' Strike Told
by Two East Londoners*, 1889,
pp. 22–3.
13 Kent, p. 13.
14 Ibid., p. 20.
15 Illustrated in Terry McCarthy, ed.,
facing p. 97.

33 The Scarlet Thread of Murder

1 A.E. Wilson, p. 212.
2 Ibid., p. 201.
3 Farson, p. 121.
4 Ibid., p. 75.
5 Brandreth, p. 55.
6 Ibid., p. 46.
7 Ibid., p. 31.
8 Ian Gibson, *The Erotomaniac*.
9 Doyle, *A Study in Scarlet*, ed.
Edwards, p. xlvii.
10 Ibid., pp. 18–19.

11 Ibid., p. 19.
12 Ibid., p. 13.
13 Quoted in Doyle, *The Sign of Four*, ed.
Lancelyn Green, p. xxxiii.

34 The Fall of Parnell

1 Andrew Roberts, p. 445.
2 Quoted ibid., p. 261.
3 Conor Cruise O'Brien, p. 207.
4 Andrew Roberts, p. 447.
5 Ensor, p. 180.
6 Conor Cruise O'Brien, p. 232.
7 Ibid., p. 279.
8 Ibid., p. 346.
9 Foster (1989), p. 424.

35 The Victorian Way of Death

1 Litten, p. 170.
2 Ibid., p. 141. A photograph of 'the
funeral of a London shopkeeper'
seems to be half filling one side of
Regent's Park.
3 Croker Papers, Bodleian Library, MS
Eng. Lett. 2.367, f. 215.
4 Stephen White, 'A burning issue', *New
Law Journal*, 10 August 1990, p. 1145.
5 Jupp, p. 16.
6 Stephen White, p. 1157.
7 *The Law Journal*, June 1884, p. 141.
8 Ibid.

36 Appearance and Reality

1 Anne Taylor, pp. 60–1.
2 'The best female public speaker I ever
heard' – eyewitness to author. Beatrice
Webb said Annie's voice was 'neither
female nor male but "the voice of a
beautiful soul"' – Anne Taylor, p. 55.
3 Ibid., p. 199.
4 Ibid., p. 59.
5 Ibid., p. 240.
6 Ibid., p. 257.
7 Washington, pp. 58–9.
8 Ibid., p. 67.
9 Ibid., p. 89.
10 Yeats (1955), p. 167.
11 Ibid., p. 302.
12 Yeats, ed. (1936), p. 1.
13 Yeats (1955), p. 130.
14 Raby, p. 20.
15 Ibid., p. 105.
16 Quoted Mackay, p. 15.
17 Keefe & Keefe, p. 50.
18 Mackay, p. 14.
19 Abdy & Gere, p. 54.
20 Egremont (1977), pp. 185–6.
21 Yeats (1955), p. 165.
22 Ibid., p. 165.
23 Hyde, ed., p. 85.
24 Ellmann, p. 412.

25 Brian Roberts (1981), pp. 185–6.
26 Hart-Davis, ed., p. 423.
27 Hyde, ed., p. 65.
28 Ibid., p. 133.
29 Ibid., p. 94.

37 Utopia: The Decline of the
    Aristocracy
1   Ensor, p. 222.
2   Webb (1979), p. 381.
3   Ibid., p. 389.
4   Ensor, p. 203.
5   Alfred Tennyson, 'Locksley Hall', ed.
    Ricks, p. 692.
6   Alfred Tennyson, 'Locksley Hall Sixty
    Years After', ibid., p. 1369.
7   Ibid., p. 1368.
8   S.J. Taylor, p. 31.
9   Keynes (1933), pp. 36, 37.
10 Grigg (1973), p. 44.

38 The Boer War
1   *DNB*, 1901–11, p. 184.
2   Rotberg, p. 285.
3   Ibid., p. 102.
4   Chesterton (1913), p. 181.
5   Webb (1948), p. 190.
6   Pakenham (1991), p. 1.
7   'We seem to have conquered and peo-
    pled half the world in a fit of absence
    of mind.' J.R. Seeley, *Expansion of
    England*, 1883.
8   Warner, p. 82.
9   Ibid., p. 98.
10 Quoted in Ensor, p. 211. Unless other-
    wise stated my chief sources for the
    following pages are Ensor, Le May,
    Pakenham and Emanoel Lee.
11 Emanoel Lee, p. 49.
12 Ibid., p. 57.
13 Quoted Le May, p. 107.
14 Ibid., p. 153.
15 Ensor, p. 251.

16 Ibid., p. 252.
17 Ibid., p. 254.
18 Le May, p. 119.
19 Warner, p. 124.
20 Ibid., p. 135.
21 See Emanoel Lee, p. 181.

39 Vale
1   Arthur Bigge, writing to Arthur
    Ponsonby. Ponsonby Papers, MS Eng.
    Hist. c651, f. 43.
2   Ponsonby, p. 26.
3   Michaela Reid, p. 201.
4   Ponsonby, p. 26.
5   Ibid., p. 25.
6   Michaela Reid, p. 215.
7   Ibid., p. 215.
8   Ibid.
9   Ibid., p. 217.
10 Grigg (1978), p. 270.
11 Ibid., p. 51.
12 Packard, p. 241.

Bibliography

The place of publication is London unless otherwise stated.

The names of publishers are only given where the title might otherwise be difficult to locate.

Abdy, Jane, & Gere, Charlotte, *The Souls*, 1984

Adams, Ephraim Douglass, *Great Britain and the American Civil War*, 2 vols, 1925

Adburgham, Alison, *Shops and Shopping 1800–1914. Where and in what manner the well-dressed Englishwoman bought her clothes*, 1989

Adelman, Paul, *Gladstone, Disraeli & Later Victorian Politics*, 3rd edn, 1997

Adrian, Arthur A., *Mark Lemon. First Editor of Punch*, 1966

Alcott, William A., *The Physical and Moral Effects of Using Tobacco as a Luxury*, New York, 1853

Alexander, Lt. Col. W. Gordon, *Recollection of a Highland Subaltern*, Edward Arnold, 1898

Alexander, Ziggi, & Audrey Denjee, *Mary Seacole*, Brent Library Service, 1982

Alford, B.W.E., *W D & H O Wills and the Development of the UK Tobacco Industry, 1706–1965*, 1973

Allan, Mea, *Palgrave of Arabia*, 1972

Allen, Bernard M., *Gordon and the Sudan*, 1931

A London Physician, *Emotional Goodness or Moody and Sankey Reviewed*, Dean & Son, 1875

Altick, R.D., *The Shows of London*, 1978

Amor, Anne Clark, *William Holman Hunt. The True Pre-Raphaelite*, 1989

Anderson, Olive, *A Liberal State at War. English Politics and Economics during the Crimean War*, New York, 1967

Anderson, Robert, *The Potteries Martyrs*, Stoke-on-Trent, 1993

Anon, *Charles Lowder. A Biography*, 'By the author of the Life of St Teresa', 1881

Anstruther, Ian, *The Knight and the Umbrella*, 1963

——, *The Scandal of Andover Workhouse*, 1984

Apperson, G.L., *The Social History of Smoking*, 1914

Appleyard, John, *Henry Francis Lyte M.A.*, 1939

Archives of the Independent Labour Party (held at London School of Economics), Harvester Press, 1984

Armytage, W.H.G., *Four Hundred Years of English Education*, Cambridge, 1970

Arnold, Matthew, *Letters of Matthew Arnold, Collected and Arranged by George W.E. Russell*, 2 vols, 1895

Arnould, Joseph, *Memorial Lines on Sir Robert Peel*, 1850

Arnstein, Walter L., *The Bradlaugh Case*, New York, 1965 (reprinted University of Missouri Press, Columbia, 1983)

Ascoli, David, *The Queen's Police*, 1979

Ashton, Rosemary, *G.H. Lewes. A Life*, Clarendon Press, Oxford, 1991

Askwith, Betty, *Two Victorian Families*, 1973

Auerbach, J.A., *The Great Exhibition of 1851. A Nation on Display*, Yale UP, 1999

Ayres, Harry Morgan, *Carroll's Alice*, Columbia University Press, New York, 1936

Bagehot, Walter, *The Works of Walter Bagehot, with Memoirs by R.H. Hutton*, ed. Forest Morgan, 5 vols, 1889

Baker, Diane, *Workhouses in the Potteries*, Stoke-on-Trent, 1977

Balfour, Arthur James, *The Foundations of Belief*, 1895

Balfour, Jean, 'The Palm Sunday Case', *Proceedings of the Society for Psychical Research*, vol. 52, part 189, February 1960.

Ball, Charles, *The History of the Indian Mutiny*, 2 vols, 1858

Banks, J.A., *Prosperity and Parenthood. A Study of Family Planning Among the Victorian Middle Classes*, 1954

Barbay, James, *The Crimean War*, Harmondsworth, 1975

Barker, Alan, *The Civil War in America*, 1977

Barker, Felix, *Highgate Cemetery. Victorian Valhalla*, 1984, Friends of Highgate Cemetery, London, 1984

Barrow, Logie, & Bullock, Ian, *Democratic Ideas and the British Labour Movement 1880–1914*, Cambridge, 1996

Bartram, Michael, *The Pre Raphaelite Camera*, 1985

Barzun, Jacques, *Darwin, Marx, Wagner. Critique of a Heritage*, 1942

Bassalle, George *et al*,. ed., *Victorian Science. A Self-Portrait from the Presidential Addresses of the British Association for the Advancement of Science*, New York, 1970

Battiscombe, Georgina, *Christina Rossetti. A Divided Life*, 1981

——, *Shaftesbury. A Biography of the Seventh Earl*, 1974

Beale, Dorothea, *Work and Play in Girls' Schools*, 1898

Beaver, Patrick, *The Crystal Palace. The Great Exhibition*, J.A. Auerbach (Yale), 1999

Beeler, John F., *British Naval Policy in the Gladstone–Disraeli Era 1866–1880*, Stanford University Press, Stanford, California, 1997

Begg, Paul, *Jack the Ripper. The Uncensored Facts*, 1988

Behe, Michael J., *Darwin's Black Box*, New York, 1996

Bell, H.C.F., *Life of Palmerston*, 1936

Benians, E.A., *et al*., ed., *The Cambridge History of the British Empire. Vol. III. The Empire-Commonwealth, 1870–1919*, Cambridge, 1959

Bennett, J.A., *Science at the Great Exhibition*, 1983

Benson, A.C., *The Upton Letters*, 1905

——, *The Life of Edward White Benson*, 2 vols, 1899

——, & Viscount Esher, ed., *The Letters of Queen Victoria* (3 vols), 1908

Benson, E.F., *Mother*, 1925

Berkeley, George, *The Works of George Berkeley*, ed. T.E. Jessop, 6 vols, 1953

Bertouch, Beatrice de, Baroness, *The Life of Father Ignatius, OSB, the Monk of Llanthony*, 1904

Bethell, Leslie, *The Brazilian Slave Trade – Britain, Brazil and the Slave Trade Question*, Cambridge, 1970

Bird, Anthony, *Paxton's Palace*, 1976

Blackburn, Douglas, *Thought-reading or Modern Mysteries Explained, being Chapters on Thought-Reading, Occultism, Mesmerism etc.*, 1884

Blake, Laurel, *et al.*, ed., *Investigating Victorian Journalism*, 1990

Blake, Robert, *Disraeli*, 1966

——, 'Disraeli and Gladstone. The Leslie Stephen Lecture, 1969', Cambridge University Press, 1969

——, *The Conservative Party from Peel to Thatcher*, 1985

——, *Gladstone, Disraeli and Queen Victoria* (Romanes Lecture, Oxford, 1993)

Bowlby, John, *Charles Darwin. A Biography*, 1990

Bowness, Alan, ed., *The Pre-Raphaelites* (catalogue of Tate Gallery Exhibition), 1989

Bradley, F.H., *Appearance and Reality*, Clarendon Press, Oxford, 1893

Bradley, Ian, ed., *The Complete Annotated Gilbert and Sullivan*, Oxford, 1996

Brandreth, Gyles, *The Funniest Man on Earth. The Story of Dan Leno*, 1977

Bridges, Yseult, *Saint – With Red Hands?*, 1954

Brogan, Hugh, *Mowgli's Sons. Kipling and Baden-Powell's Scouts*, 1987

Brontë, Charlotte, *Jane Eyre* (first pub. 1847), ed. Margaret Smith, Oxford, 1976

Brooke-Shepherd, Gordon, *Royal Sunset. The Dynasties of Europe and the Great War*, 1987

Brown, Lucy, *Victorian News and Newspapers*, Clarendon Press, Oxford, 1985

Browne, Douglas, *The Rise of Scotland Yard*, 1956

Browne, Janet, *Voyaging*, 1995

Browning, Robert, *Poetical Works, 1833–1864*, ed. Ian Jack, Oxford, 1970

Burn, William Lawrence, *The Age of Equipoise. A study of the mid-Victorian generation*, 1964

Burne, Maj. Gen. Sir Owen Tudor, KCSI, *Clyde & Strathnairn*, Oxford at Clarendon Press, 1891

Burne-Jones, Georgiana, *Memorials of Edward Burne-Jones*, 2 vols, 1904

Butler, A.S.G., *Portrait of Josephine Butler*, 1954

Butt, John, & Tillotson, Kathleen, *Dickens at Work*, 1957

Calder-Marshall, Arthur, *The Enthusiast. An enquiry into the life, beliefs and character of the Rev. Joseph Leycester Lyne, alias Father Ignatius*, 1962

Callender, Sir Geoffrey, & Hinsley, F.H., *The Naval Side of British History*, 1952

Campbell, Sir George, *Memories of my Indian Career*, 1893

Cannadine, David, *The Decline and Fall of the British Aristocracy*, Yale University Press, New Haven, 1992 (revised)

Carlyle, Thomas, *The Complete Works*, New York, Charles Scribner, 30 vols, 1904

Carpenter, William Boyd, *The Venture of Faith*, 1898

——, *The Hidden Life. A sermon preached January 29th, 1899 in commemoration of the death of General Gordon*, 1899

Cecil, David, *Melbourne*, 1965

Cecil, Lady Gwendolen, *Life of Robert Marquis of Salisbury*, 2 vols, Hodder & Stoughton, 1921

Chadwick, Owen, *The Victorian Church*, 2 vols, 1966 & 1970

Chambers, J.D., & Mingay, G.E., *The Agricultural Revolution, 1750–1880*, 1966

Chambers, Robert, *Vestiges of the Natural History of Creation* (1844), ed. with introduction James A. Secord, Chicago, 1994

Chapman, Caroline, & Raben, Paul, *Debrett's Queen Victoria's Jubilee, 1887 & 1897*, 1997

Chaudhuri, S.B., *Civil Disturbances during the British Rule in India, 1757–1857*, Collected from Bombay Governor Records. Source Material for a History of the Freedom Movement in India, vol. 1, 1818–1885. Bombay, 1957

——, *Theories of the Indian Mutiny (1857–9)*, The World Press Private Ltd, Calcutta, 1965

Chedzoy, Alan, *William Barnes – A Life of the Dorset Poet*, 1985

Chesney, Kellow, *Crimean War Reader*, 1960

Chesterton, G.K., *Robert Browning*, Macmillan, 1903

——, *G.F. Watts*, Duckworth, 1904

——, *The Victorian Age in Literature*, Williams and Norgate, 1913

Chinn, Carl, *Better Betting with a Decent Feller. Bookmaking, Betting and the British Working Class, 1750–1990*, Harvester NY, 1991

Chitty, Susan, *The Beast and the Monk*, 1975

Christie, O.F., *The Transition to Democracy, 1867–1914*, George Routledge & Sons, 1934

Churchill, Peregrine, & Mitchell, Julian, ed., *Jennie. Lady Randolph Churchill*, 1974

Churchill, Winston S., *My Early Life* (1930), 1989

Clapham, J.H., *The Early Railway Age 1820–1850*, Cambridge, 1950

Clark, Rufus W., *The Work of God in Great Britain under Messrs. Moody and Sankey 1873 to 1875*, Harper & Brothers, New York, 1875

Clarke, A.K., *A History of Cheltenham Ladies College*, 1963

Coates, James, *Has W.T. Stead Returned?*, L.N. Fowler & Co., 1913

Cocks, Barnett, *Mid-Victorian Masterpiece*, 1977

Cohen, Morton, *Lewis Carroll: A Biography*, 1995.

Compton, Piers, *The Last Days of General Gordon*, 1974

Coopland, Mrs, *A Lady's Escape from Gwalior*, 1859

Cotton Minchin, J.G., *Our Public Schools*, 1901

Cowen, Anne & Roger, *Victorian Jews through British Eyes*, 1986

Cowling, Maurice, *1867 Disraeli, Gladstone and Revolution. The Passing of the Second Reform Bill*, Cambridge, 1967

——, *Religion and Public Debate in Modern England*, Cambridge, 1980

Crabtree, Adam, *From Mesmer to Freud. Magnetic Sleep and the Roots of Psychological Healing*, New Haven, 1993

Craven, Margaret J., *The effects of the American Civil War upon the people of Bolton, Lancashire*, Chorley Day Training College, Lancashire, 1964

Creer, Edwin, *A Popular Treatise on Human Hair*, 1865

Crook, J. Mordaunt, *William Burges and the High Victorian Dream*, 1981

——, *The Rise of the Nouveaux Riches*, 1999

Crosby, Travis L., *The Two Mr Gladstones*, Yale University Press, New Haven, 1997

Crowther, M.A., *The Workhouse System 1834–1929*, 1981

Cullen, Tom, *Autumn of Terror*, 1965

Cunningham, Suzanne, *Philosophy and the Darwinian Legacy*, Rochester, New York, 1996

Curl, James Stevens, *A celebration of death, an introduction to some of the buildings, monuments and settings of funerary architecture in the Western European tradition*, 1993

Darnton, Robert, *Mesmerism and the End of the Enlightenment in France*, Harvard, 1968

Darwin, Charles, *The Origin of Species* (1859), 1951

——, *The Descent of Man* (1871), 1874

——, *The Voyage of a Naturalist*, 1905

Davidoff, L., 'Mastered for Life', in *Journal of Social History*, vol. 7, pp. 406–28, 1984

Davies, Nick, *The School Report*, 2000

Davis, Mary, *Comrade or Brother? A History of the British Labour Movement, 1789–1951*, Pluto Press, Boulder, Colorado

Dawson, E.C., *James Hannington. First Bishop of East Equatorial Africa*, Seeley & Co, 1887

de Beer, Gavin, introduction to Robert Chambers, *Vestiges of Creation*, Leicester & New York, 1969

Dennett, Daniel C., *Darwin's Dangerous Idea*, NY, 1996

Depositions taken at Cawnpore under the Direction of Lieut.-Colonel [*sic*] G.W. Williams, Allahabad(?), 1858

Desmond, Adrian, & Moore, James, *Darwin*, 1991

Dickens, Charles, *Speech of Charles Dickens Esq., delivered at the Meeting of the Administrative Reform Association at the Theatre Royal, Drury Lane, June 27, 1855*, 1855

——, *The Works of Charles Dickens*, 1880

——, *The Speeches of Charles Dickens*, ed. K.J. Fielding, Hemel Hempstead & Atlantic Highlands, NJ, 1988

Disraeli, Benjamin, *Coningsby* (1844), Oxford, 1982

——, *Sybil* (1845), Harmondsworth, 1980

——, *Lothair* (1870), ed. Vernon Bogdanor, Oxford University Press, 1975

Dods, John Boree, *Lectures on the Philosophy of Mesmerism*

Dodwell, H.H., ed., *The Cambridge History of India*, vols V and VIII, *British India 1497–1858* (1929)

——, ed., *The Cambridge History of the British Empire*, V, *The Indian Empire 1858–1918*, ch. XXIII, Dodwell, 'Central Asia', Cambridge, 1932

Dostoyevsky, F.M., *The Devils*, trans. & ed. Michael R. Katz, Oxford, 1992

Doyle, Arthur Conan, *The Sign of Four*, ed. Roger Lancelyn Green, Oxford, 1993

——, *A Study in Scarlet*, ed. Owen Dudley Edwards, Oxford, 1993

Doyle, Brian, *The Who's Who of Children's Literature*, 1968

Dudley, Edwards Owen, *Macaulay*, 1988

Dunbar, Janet, *The Early Victorian Woman. Some Aspects of her Life*, 1953

Dunn, Waldo Hilary, *James Anthony Froude. A Biography (1818–1856)*, Oxford, 1961

——, *James Anthony Froude. A Biography (1857–1894)*, Oxford, 1963

Durant, John, *Darwinism and Divinity*, Oxford, 1985

Durey, Michael, *The Return of the Plague. British Society and the Cholera 1831–2*, Dublin, 1979

Dutt, Romesh (Ramesachandra Datta), *India in the Victorian Age*, 1904

Eames, Elizabeth Ramsden, *Bertrand Russell's Dialogue with his Contemporaries*, Southern Illinois University Press, Carbondale and Edwardsville, 1969

E.A.T., *Alexander Heriot Mackonochie. A Memoir*, 1890

Edwardes, Michael, *A History of India* (revised, 1967)

Edwards, Owen Dudley, *Macaulay*, 1988

Egremont, Max, *The Cousins*, 1977

——, *Balfour*, 1980

Ehrlich, Paul, *The Population Bomb*, New York, 1968

Eliot, George, *Daniel Deronda* (1877), ed. with Introduction by Graham Handley, 1988

Ellmann, Richard, *Oscar Wilde*, 1987

Encyclopedia Britannica (13th edn), London and New York, 1926

Ensor, R.C.K., *England, 1870–1914*, Oxford at the Clarendon Press, 1936

Erikson, Paul A., *Phrenology and Physical Anthropology: The George Combe Connection*, St Mary's University, Nova Scotia, 1979

Esher, Viscount, *The Girlhood of Queen Victoria*, 1912

Evans, Martin Marix, *Encyclopedia of the Boer War*, ABC-CLIO, Santa Barbara, California, 2000

Eyck, Frank, *The Prince Consort, A Political Biography*, 1959

Fabb, John, *The Victorian and Edwardian Army from old photographs*, 1975

Faber, Geoffrey, *Oxford Apostles*, 1933

Farrar, Frederic W., *St Winifred's, or, the World of School*, 1908

Farson, Daniel, *Marie Lloyd & Music Hall*, Tom Stacey, 1972

Farwell, Byron, *Queen Victoria's Little Wars*, 1973

Fawcett, Millicent G., & Turner, E.M., *Josephine Butler*, The Association for Moral & Social Hygiene, 1927

Field, D.C., 'Internal Combustion Engines' (Singer *et al.*, 1958, pp. 157–77)

——, 'Mechanical Road Vehicles' (Singer *et al.*, 1958, pp. 414–38)

Finer, S.E., *The Life and Times of Sir Edwin Chadwick*, 1952

Finnegan, F., *Poverty and Prostitution*, Cambridge, 1979

Fisher, Hal, *The Annotated Communist Manifesto*, Berkeley, CA, 1984

Fitzroy, Almeric, *History of the Travellers' Club*, 1927

Forbes, Duncan, 'James Mill and India', *Cambridge Journal*, vol. V, 1951–2

Ford, Colin, & Harrison, Brian, *A Hundred Years Ago. Britain in the 1880s in Words and Photographs*, 1983

Foster, R.F., *Lord Randolph Churchill. A Political Life*, 1981

——, *Modern Ireland 1600–1972*, 1989

Froude, J.A., *The English in Ireland in the Eighteenth Century*, 3 vols, 1872–4

——, *The English in Ireland*, 1881

——, *Thomas Carlyle. A History of the First Forty Years of his Life*, 2 vols, 1882

——, *Thomas Carlyle. A History of his Life in London, 1834–1881*, 2 vols, 1884

——, *Lord Beaconsfield*, 1890

Fulford, Roger, *Royal Dukes. The father and uncles of Queen Victoria*, 1933

——, *The Prince Consort*, 1949

——, ed., *Dearest Child. Letters between Queen Victoria and the Princess Royal, 1858–1861*, 1964

——, ed., *Dearest Mama. Letters between Queen Victoria and the Crown Princess of Prussia, 1861–1864*, 1977

——, ed., *Your Dear Letter, private correspondence of Queen Victoria and the Crown Princess of Prussia, 1865–1871*, 1971

Fuller, Robert C., *Mesmerism and the American Cure of Souls*, 1982

Gardner, Martin, ed., *Lewis Carroll. The Annotated Alice*, Harmondsworth, 1965

Garrett, Elizabeth L.S.A., *An Enquiry into the Character of the Contagious Diseases Act*, 1870 (pamphlet, reprinted for the *Pall Mall Gazette*)

Garrett, Richard, *General Gordon*, Arthur Barker Ltd, 1974

Gash, Norman, *Peel*, 1976

——, *Politics in the Age of Peel*, 2nd edn, 1977

Gathorne-Hardy, Jonathan, *The Public School Phenomenon*, Penguin, 1979

Gatrell, V.A.C., *The Hanging Tree. Execution and the English People*, 1770–1868, Oxford, 1994

Gaunt, William, *The Pre-Raphaelite Tragedy* (1942), London, 1988

Gernsheim, Helmut, *Julia Margaret Cameron*, 1975

——, (Introduction), *Lewis Carroll Victorian Photographer*, 1980

Gibson, Ian, *The English Vice*, 1978

——, *The Erotomaniac*, 2001

Gilbert, Sir W.S., *The Savoy Operas*, 1939

Girard, Louis, *Napoléon III*, Fayard, Paris, 1986

Girouard, Mark, *Life in the English Country House*, Yale University Press, New Haven, 1978

——, *The Victorian Country House*, Revised, Yale University Press, New Haven, 1979

Gladstone, W.E., *The State in its Relations with the Church*, 1838

——, *The Church of England and Ritualism*, 1875

——, *The Vatican Decrees in their Bearing on Civil Allegiance*, 1874

Glendinning, Andrew, ed., *The Veil Lifted. Modern Developments in Spirit Photography*, 1894

Glick, Thomas F., ed., *The Comparative Reception of Darwinism*, Chicago, 1988

Goodway, David, *London Chartism 1838–1848*, Cambridge, 1982

Goodwin, Jason, *Lords of the Horizons*, 1999

Gordon, Colin, *Beyond the Looking-Glass*, 1982

Gorham, D., *The Victorian Girl and the Feminine Ideal*, Bloomington, Indiana, 1982

Graves, Richard Perceval, *A.E. Housman. The Scholar-Poet*, 1979

Gray, P., 'Potatoes and Providence: British Government Responses to the Great Famine', *Bullán: An Irish Studies Journal*, No. 1, 1994

Green, Thomas Hill, *Works*, ed. by R.L. Nettleship, 3 vols, 1885

Greengarten, I.M., *Thomas Hill Green and the Development of Liberal-Democratic Thought*, University of Toronto Press, 1981, Toronto

Gregorio, Mario A.D., & Gill, N.W., ed., *Charles Darwin's Marginalia*, vol. I, New York, 1990

Greville, Charles Cavendish Folke, *The Greville Memoirs, 1814–1860*, ed. Lytton Strachey & Roger Fulford, 8 vols, 1938

Gribbin, John, *In the Beginning, the birth of the living universe*, 1993

Griffin, Nicholas, *Russell's Idealist Apprenticeship*, Clarendon Press, Oxford, 1991

Grigg, John, *The Young Lloyd George*, 1973

——, *Lloyd George: The People's Champion 1902–11*, 1978

Groom, Helen M.I., *With Havelock from Allahabad to Lucknow, 1857*, 1894

Gurd, Eric, *Prologue to Cigarettes*. Issued by the Cartophilic Society of Great Britain (no date)

Hacking, Juliet, *Princes of Victorian Bohemia*, Prestel, Munich, London, New York, 2000

Haggard, H. Rider, *King Solomon's Mines* (1885), 1956

Haight, Gordon S., *George Eliot*, Oxford at The Clarendon Press, 1968

Halévy, Elie, *The Growth of Philosophical Radicalism*, Boston, 1955

Hamburger, Joseph, *Macaulay and the Whig Tradition*, Chicago, 1976

Hamilton, James, *Turner. A Life*, 1977

Hamilton, S.B., 'Building Materials and Techniques' (Singer *et al.*, 1958, pp. 466–99)

Hamlin, Christopher, *Public Health and Social Justice in the Age of Chadwick, Britain 1850–1854*, Cambridge, 1998

Hannary, John, *The Camera goes to War – Photographs from the Crimean War*, Edinburgh, 1974

Hare, Augustus, *The Story of My Life* (6 vols), 1885

Hart-Davis, Rupert, ed., *The Letters of Oscar Wilde*, New York, 1962

Hasler, August Bernhard, *How the Pope Became Infallible*, Doubleday & Co Inc, New York, 1981

Hastings, Maurice, *Parliament House*, 1950

Hastings, Selina, *Evelyn Waugh, a biography*, 1994

Hayter, Althea, *A Sultry Month*, Faber & Faber Ltd, 1965

Headlam, Cecil, 'The Failure of Confederation, 1871–1881', ch. XVIII in Eric Walker, ed., *The Cambridge History of the British Empire*, vol. VIII, *South Africa, Rhodesia and the High Commission Territories*, Cambridge, 1963

Hennessy, Alastair, 'Penrhyn Castle', in *History Today*, vol. 45(1), January 1995

Hennessy, James Pope, *Anthony Trollope*, Jonathan Cape, 1971

Henty, G.A., *Through the Sikh War. A Tale of the Conquest of the Punjaub*, 1894

Heuman, Gad J., *Between Black and White. Race, Politics and the Free Coloureds in Jamaica 1792–1865*, Westport, Connecticut

Hewison, Robert *et al.*, *Ruskin, Turner and the Pre-Raphaelites*, 2000

Hewitt, Margaret, *Wives and Mothers in Victorian Industry*, 1958

Hibbert, Christopher, *The Great Mutiny India 1857*, 1978

——, *Queen Victoria. A Personal History*, 2000

Hilton, Tim, *John Ruskin, The Early Years, 1819–1859*, New Haven, 1985

——, *John Ruskin, The Later Years*, New Haven, 2000

Hinchliff, Peter, *Benjamin Jowett and the Christian Religion*, Clarendon Press, Oxford, 1987

Hinton, James, *Labour and Socialism*, Wheatsheaf Books, Brighton, 1983

Hirst, F.W., 'Viscount Morley of Blackburn', *Dictionary of National Biography, 1922–1930*

Holland, Bernard C.B., *The Life of Spencer Compton, Eighth Duke of Devonshire*, 2 vols, 1911

Holloway, Richard, 'Holiness Plus Laughter', *Church Times*, 18 December 1987

Hopkins, Pat, & Dugmore, Heather, *The Boy. Baden-Powell and the Siege of Mafeking*, Zebra, Rivonia, SA, 1999

Hoppen, K. Theodore, *The Mid-Victorian Generation 1846–1886*, Oxford, 1998

——, *Ireland Since 1800* (2nd edn), 1999

Horn, Pamela, *Pleasures and Pastimes in Victorian Britain*, Sutton Publishing, Stroud, 1999

Horne, Alistair, *The Fall of Paris. The Siege and the Commune 1870–1*, 1965

Horne, H. Oliver, *A History of Savings Banks*, London/New York, 1947

Horrut, Claude, *Frederic Lugard et la Pensée Coloniale Britannique*, Institut d'Études politiques de Bordeaux, 1970

House, Humphry, *The Dickens World*, 1941

Howard, Michael, *The Franco-Prussian War*, 1961

Hudson, Derek, *Munby, Man of Two Worlds*, 1972

Hughes, Thomas, *Tom Brown's Schooldays*, 1948

Humpherys, Anne (sic), *Travels into the Poor Man's Country. The Work of Henry Mayhew*, 1977

Hunt, Diana Holman, *My Grandfather. His Wives and Loves* (1969), 1987

Hunt, Peter, ed., *Children's Literature. An Illustrated History*, Oxford, New York, 1995

Hunter Blair, The Right Rev. Sir David, Bt OSB, *John Patrick, Third Marquess of Bute K.T. (1847–1900)*, 1921

Huntley, Eric, *Two Lives. Florence Nightingale and Mary Seacole*, Bogle L'Ouverture, 1993

Huxley, Gervas, *Victorian Duke. The Life of Hugh Lupus Grosvenor, First Duke of Westminster*, Oxford, 1967

Huxley, Julian Sorell, 'Alfred Russel Wallace', in *DNB, 1912–1921*, 1927

Hyde, H. Montgomery, ed., *The Trials of Oscar Wilde*, William Hodge & Co Ltd, 1948

Hylton, Peter, *Russell, Idealism and the Emergence of Analytic Philosophy*, Clarendon Press, Oxford, 1990

Iliffe, John, *Africans. The History of a Continent*, Cambridge, 1995

Inglis, Hon. Julia Selina, *The Siege of Lucknow, A Diary*, 1892

Ionides, Luke, *Memories*, Paris, 1925

Irvine, William, *Apes, Angels and Victorians*, 1956

Irvine, William, & Honan, Park, *The Book, the Ring and the Poet*, The Bodley Head, 1975

Jacobs, Arthur, *Arthur Sullivan. A Victorian Musician*, 1984

Jamaica Addresses to his excellency Edward John Eyre, Esquire, 1865, 1866. M De Cordova & Co. Printers (Kingston, Jamaica)

James, David, Jowitt, Tony, & Laybourn, Keith, ed., *The Centennial History of the Independent Labour Party*, Ryburn Academic Publishing, 1993

James, Henry, *English Hours*, ed. A.L. Lowe, 1960

——, *The Princess Casamassima*, Everyman's Library (Introduction by Bernard Richards), 1991

James, Lawrence, *Crimea 1854–56. The war with Russia from Contemporary Photographs*, 1981

——, *The Rise and Fall of the British Empire*, 1994

——, *Raj. The Making and Unmaking of British India*, 1997

Jardine, N., Secord, J.A., & Sperry, G.C., ed., *Cultures of Natural History*, Cambridge, 1996

Jay, Richard, *Joseph Chamberlain. A Political Study*, Clarendon Press, Oxford, 1981

JCP, *Siege of Lucknow by a member of the Garrison, 1858* (no place of pub. or author)

Jeal, Tim, *Baden-Powell*, 1989

Jeffrey, Jan, *Photography. A Concise History*, 1981

Jenkins, Brian, *Britain and the War for the Union*, Montreal, 2 vols, 1974–80

Jenkins, Roy, *Sir Charles Dilke. A Victorian Tragedy*, 1958

——, *Gladstone*, 1995

Jenkins, T.A., *Disraeli and Victorian Conservatism*, St Martin's Press, New York, 1996

Johnson, Douglas J., 'The Death of Gordon. A Victorian Myth', *Journal of Imperial and Commonwealth History*, X (1982), pp. 285–310

Johnson, Rev. Paul, *An Epitome in Verse of the Life of His Royal Highness the Late Prince Consort*, 1883

Johnston, Valerie J., *Diet in Workhouses and Prisons, 1835–1895*, New York, 1985

Jones, Kathleen, *Learning Not to be First*, Windrush Press, Adlestrop, 1991

Jones, Wilbur Devereux, *Lord Derby and Victorian Conservatism*, 1956

Jowitt, J.A., & Taylor, R.K.S., ed., *Bradford 1890–1914: The Cradle of the Independent Labour Party*, Bradford Centre Occasional Paper, October 1908

Jupp, Peter, *From Dust to Ashes: the Replacement of Burial by Cremation in England, 1846–1967*, The Congregational Memorial Hall Trust, 1978

Kamm, Josephine, *Rapiers and Battleaxes*, 1966

Kaplan, Fred, *Dickens and Mesmerism*, 1975

Kapp, Yvonne, *Eleanor Marx*, vol. 1 (1972), 1979

——, *Eleanor Marx*, vol. 2 (1976), 1979

Karlin, Daniel, *The Courtship of Robert Browning and Elizabeth Barrett*, Oxford University Press, 1987

Kasaba, Resat, *The Ottoman Empire and the World Economy*, State University of New York, Albany, 1988

Kaye, Sir John William, *A History of the Sepoy War*, 4 vols, 1864–80

Kee, Robert, *The Laurel and the Ivy, the story of Charles Stuart Parnell and Irish nationalism*, 1993

Keefe, Robert & Janice A., *Walter Pater and the Gods of Disorder*, Ohio University Press, Athens, 1988

Kendall, Guy, *Charles Kingsley & His Ideas*, 1947

Kent, William, *John Burns. Labour's Lost Leader*, 1950

Keppel-Jones, Arthur, *Rhodes and Rhodesia*, University of Natal Press, Pietermaritzburg, 1983

Kermode, Frank, Introduction to Anthony Trollope's *The Way We Live Now*, 1994

Kerr, Donal A., *Peel Priest and Politics*, 1982

Keynes, J.M., *A Tract on Monetary Reform*, 1923

——, *Essays in Biography*, 1933

King, Peter, *The Viceroy's Fall, How Kitchener Destroyed Curzon*, 1986

Kinglake, Alexander William, *The Invasion of the Crimea*, 8 vols, 1863–87

Kingsley, Charles, *The Water-Babies*, 1863

——, *Alton Locke*, ed. with introduction by Elizabeth A. Cripps, Oxford, 1983

——, *Yeast*, Dover, 1984

Kingsley Martin, B., *The Triumph of Lord Palmerston*, 1924

Kingsmill, Hugh, *After Puritanism*, 1929

Kiple, Kenneth F. et al., ed., *The Cambridge World History of Human Disease*, 1993

Kipling, Rudyard, *Plain Tales from the Hills*, 1890

——, *Stalky and Co.*, 1930

——, *The Complete Verse*, 1990

Kirk, K.E., *The Story of the Woodard Schools*, The Abbey Press, Abingdon-on-Thames, 1952 (revised)

Klein, Viola, *The Feminine Character*, New York, 1949

Korg, Jacob, *Browning and Italy*, Ohio University Press, Asten, Ohio, 1983

Kruger, Rayne, *Goodbye Dolly Gray*, 1959

Kubicek, Robert, 'British Expansion, Empire and Technological

Change', in *The Oxford History of the British Empire*, ed. André Porter, Oxford University Press, 1999

Kurer, Oskar, *John Stuart Mill. The Politics of Progress*, New York, 1991

Kynaston, David, *King Labour*, 1976

Lawrence, T.E., *The Seven Pillars of Wisdom*, 1935

Leatherbarrow, W.J., ed., *Dostoevskii and Britain*, Berg, Oxford, Providence R.I., 1995

Lee, Alan J., *The Origins of the Popular Press, 1855–1914*, 1976

Lee, Emanoel, *To The Bitter End, a photographic history of the Boer War*, 1985

Lees-Milne, J., *The Bachelor-Duke. A Life of William Spencer Cavendish, 6th Duke of Devonshire*, 1991

Leithbridge, Robert, Introduction to *La Débâcle* by Emile Zola, Oxford, 2000

Le May, G.H.L., *The Afrikaners*, Oxford, 1995

Leo XIII, *Rerum Novarum. Encyclical Letter on the Condition of the Working Classes*, Catholic Truth Society, 1983

Leslie, Shane, *Henry Edward Manning, his life and labours*, 1921

Letwin, Shirley Robin, *The Pursuit of Certainty*, Cambridge, 1965

Lightman, Bernard, ed., *Victorian Science in Context*, 1997

Lindsay, Jack, *William Morris. His Life and Work*, 1975

——, *Turner the Man and his Art*, 1985

Litten, Julian, *The English Way of Death, The Common Funeral since 1450*, 1991

Lloyd, Arthur D.D., Bishop (Suffragan) of Thetford, *Enthusiasm, Confidence, Determination*, 1897

Longford, Elizabeth, *Victoria R.I.*, 1964

——, *Wellington, Pillar of State*, 1972

Longhurst, Arthur E.T., *The Diet of the European Soldier in India with the Effects of 'Tobacco Smoking' upon the Animal Economy*, Calcutta, R.C. Lepage & Co., 1862

Lovett, William, *Chartism: a new organization of the people, written in Warwick Gaol*, 1841

Lowder, C.F., *Twenty-one Years in St George's Mission*, 1877

Lugard, F.D., *The Rise of our East African Empire* (1893), reprint, 2 vols, 1968

Lycett, Andrew, *Rudyard Kipling*, 1999

Lyell, Charles, *The Geological Evidences of the Antiquity of Man*, 1863

Macaulay, Thomas Babington, *Prose and Poetry*, selected by G.M. Young, 1952

MacCarthy, Desmond, *Criticism*, 1932

MacCarthy, Fiona, *William Morris. A Life for our Time*, 1994

MacDonald, Robert, *Sons of the Empire. The Frontier and the Boy Scout Movement 1890–1918*, University of Toronto Press, Toronto, Buffalo, London, 1993

Macfie, A.L., *The Eastern Question*, Longman, 1989

Mack, Edward C., *Public Schools and British Opinion since 1860*, Columbia University Press, NY, 1941

Mackail, J.W., *The Life of William Morris* (1899), Oxford University Press, 1950

Mackay, Ruddock F., *Balfour, Intellectual Statesman*, Oxford University Press, Oxford, 1985

Mackechnie Jarvis, C., 'The Generation of Electricity' (1958, pp. 177–208)

MacKenzie, Norman & Jeanne, ed., *The Diary of Beatrice Webb*, vol. 1, *Glitter Around and Darkness Within*, 1982; vol. 2, *All the Good Things of Life*, 1983, in association with The London School of Economics and Political Science

Maclagan, Michael, *Clemency Canning*, 1962

McLuhan, Herbert Marshall, *Understanding Media: The Extensions of Man*, 1964

Majeed, Javed, *Ungoverned Imaginings: James Mill's History of India and Orientalism*, Oxford, 1992

Malthus, Thomas, *An Essay on the Principle of Population* (1806), ed. Geoffrey Gilbert, 1993

Manchester, Duke of, *Part of a Speech in the House of Lords Against the Maynooth Grant*, 1845

Mander, John, *Our German Cousins. Anglo-German relations in the 19th and 20th centuries*, John Murray, 1974

Mansel, Philip, *Sultans in Splendour*, André Deutsch, 1988

Manton, J., *Elizabeth Garrett Anderson*, 1965

Marsh, Jan, *Pre-Raphaelite Sisterhood*, 1985

——, *Pre-Raphaelite Women. Images of Femininity in Pre-Raphaelite Art*, 1987

——, *The Legend of Elizabeth Siddal*, 1989

——, *Christina Rossetti. A Literary Biography*, 1994

——, *Dante Gabriel Rossetti*, 1999

Martin, B. Kingsley, *The Triumph of Lord Palmerston*, 1924

Martin, Robert Bernard, *The Dust of Combat*, 1954

Martineau, Harriet, *Life in the Sick-Room. Essays by an invalid*, 1844

——, *Letters from Ireland, Reprinted from 'The Daily News'*, 1853

——, *The Factory Controversy*, 1855

Martyn, Edith How, & Breed, Mary, *The Birth Control Movement in England*, 1930

Marx, Karl, *The Eastern Question*, ed. E.M. & E. Aveling, 1897

——, *The Story of the Life of Lord Palmerston*, 1899

——, *The Russian Menace to Europe. A collection of articles etc.*, ed. Paul W. Blackstock, 1953

——, *Capital* (2 vols in one Everyman), 1957

——, *The Eighteenth Brumaire of Louis Bonaparte*, Moscow and London, 1984

——, & Engels, Friedrich, *The Communist Manifesto*, with introduction by A.J.P. Taylor, Harmondsworth, 1967

Marx, Roland, *Jack l'Eventreur et les fantasmes Victoriens*, Editions Complexe, Paris, 1989

Mason, Tony, *Association Football and English Society 1863–1915*, Harvester Press, Brighton, Sussex, Humanities Press, Atlantic Highlands, NJ

Masters, Brian, *The Life of E.F. Benson*, 1991

Matthew, H.C.G., *Gladstone 1809–1874*, Oxford University Press, 1988

——, *Gladstone 1875–1898*, OUP, 1995

Maurice, Frederick, *The Life of Frederick Denison Maurice Chiefly Told in his Own Letters*, 2 vols, 1889

Mayhew, Henry, *Mr and Mrs Sandboys and Family*, 1851

——, *London Labour and the London Poor* (first ed. 1851, enlarged ed. 4 vols 1861–2), 1967

Mazlish, Bruce, *James and John Stuart Mill. Father and Son in the Nineteenth Century*, 1975

McCarthy, Terry, ed., *The Great Dock Strike, 1889*, 1988

McClure, John A., *Kipling and Conrad. The Colonial Fiction*, Harvard University Press, Cambridge, Massachusetts, 1981

McCrum, Michael, *Thomas Arnold Headmaster*, Oxford, 1989

McGee, J.A., *'Thumping English Lies.' Froude's Slanders on Ireland and Irishmen*, New York, 1872

McGrath, J., 'Explosives' (Singer *et al.*, 1958, pp. 284–97)

McKean, John, *Crystal Palace. Joseph Paxton and Charles Fox*, Phaidon, 1994

Menzies, Lucy, *Father Wainwright. A Record*, 1947

Merrill, Linda, *A Pot of Paint. Aesthetics on Trial in Whistler v. Ruskin*, Smithsonian Institution Press, Washington DC, 1992

Metcalf, Thomas R., *Ideologies of the Raj*, Cambridge, 1994

Meyrick, Frederick, *But Isn't Kingsley Right After All?*, 1864

Mill, J.S., *A System of Logic*, 4th edn, 1865

——, *The Subjection of Women*, 1869

Miller, Jonathan, 'A Gower Street Scandal', *Journal of the Royal College of Physicians of London*, vol. 17, 1983

——, & Van Loon, Borin, *Darwin for Beginners*, Writers and Readers, 1982

Miller, William, *The Ottoman Empire and its Successors*, Cambridge, 1934

Millhauser, Milton, *Just Before Darwin*, Middleton Ct., 1959

Milner, John, *Art, War and Revolution in France 1870–1871*, Yale University Press, New Haven & London, 2000

Milton, Maj. Gen. Richard, *The Indian Mutiny. A Centenary History*, Hollis & Carter, 1957

Mitford, Nancy, *The Stanleys of Alderney*, 1939

Mokyr, J., *Why Ireland Starved*, 1985

Monk, Ray, *Bertrand Russell. The Spirit of Solitude*, 1996

Monypenny, W.F., & Buckle, George Earle, *The Life of Benjamin Disraeli, Earl of Beaconsfield*, 6 vols, 1910–20

Moore, Frederic, *The Zoological Gardens. A Handbook for Visitors*, 1838

Moore, J.R., *The Post Darwinian Controversies*, Cambridge, 1979

Moore, R.J., *Sir Charles Wood's Indian Policy (1853–66)*, Manchester University Press, 1966

Morgan, Kenneth, *Keir Hardie: Radical and Socialist*, 1975

Morley, John, *The Life of Cobden*, 1906

——, *The Life of William Ewart Gladstone* (1903), 3 vols, 1912

Morris, James, *Heaven's Command*, 1973

Morris, William, *News from Nowhere*, 1910

Mosley, Oswald Ernald Bart, *Wagner and Shaw. A Synthesis* (reprinted from *The European*), Sanctuary Press Ltd, 1956

——, *My Life*, 1968

Muddock, J.E., *The Great White Hand or the Tiger of Cawnpore*, 1896

Müller, Max, *The Schleswig-Holstein Question and its Place in History*, with Jörgensen, Dr A.D., *The Danish View of the Schleswig-Holstein Question*, 1897

Nanak, Chand, *Translation of a Narrative of Events at Cawnpore*, Allahabad(?), 1858

Neary, Tom, *I Saw Our Lady*, Knock, Co. Mayo, 1977

Netzer, Hans Joiachim, *Albert von Sachsen-Coburg und Gotha. Ein Deutscher Prinz in England*, München, 1988

Newbolt, Henry, *Selected Poems*, ed. Patric Dickinson, 1981

Newman, A.J., *The Times Geography and History of Jamaica*, Kingston, Jamaica, 1935

Newman, J.H., *A Letter to his Grace the Duke of Norfolk on the Occasion of Mr Gladstone's Recent Expostulation*, Pickering, 1875

——, *Apologia Pro Vita Sua* (1864), Everyman, 1955

——, *An Essay on the Development of Christian Doctrine*, Harmondsworth, 1974

Newsome, David, *The Convert Cardinals*, 1993

——, *The Victorian World Picture*, 1997

Nisbet, Hume, *The Queen's Desire*, F.W. White & Co., 1893

Norman, E.R., *The English Catholic Church in the Nineteenth Century*, Oxford, 1984

Norman, Colonel H.W., *A Lecture on the Relief of Lucknow*, Dalton and Lucy, 1867

O'Brien, Conor Cruise, *Parnell and his Party, 1880–1890*, Oxford at the Clarendon Press, 1957

O'Brien, James Bronterre, 'Ode to Lord Palmerston', 1856

O'Malley, Ida B., *Women in Subjection*, 1933

Oldenburg, Veena Talwar, *The Making of Colonial Lucknow 1856–1877*, Princeton, NJ, 1984

Olivier, Sydney, *The Myth of Governor Eyre*, 1933

Olsen, Kirstin, *Chronology of Women's History*, Greenwood Press, Westport, Conn., 1994

Orwin, Christabel, & Whetham, Edith H., *History of British Agriculture*, Newton Abbot, 1964

Packard, Jerrold M., *Farewell in Splendour*, Thrupp, Stroud, Gloucestershire, 2000

Packe, Michael St John, *The Life of John Stuart Mill*, 1954

Padfield, Peter, *Rule Britannia. The Victorian and Edwardian Navy*, 1981

Pafford, Mark, *Kipling's Indian Fiction*, 1989

Page, Norman, *A Kipling Companion*, 1984

Pakenham, Thomas, *The Boer War*, 1979

——, *The Scramble for Africa, 1876–1912*, 1991

Paley, Bruce, *Jack the Ripper. The Simple Truth*, 1996

Palgrave, William Gifford, *Essays on Eastern Questions*, 1872

Pamuk, Sevket, *The Ottoman Empire and European Capitalism, 1820–1913*, Cambridge, 1987

Pares, Bernard, *A History of Russia*, Cape, 1955

Parry, J.P., *Democracy and Religion. Gladstone & The Liberal Party, 1867–1875*, Cambridge, 1986

Patmore, Coventry, *The Angel in the House*, Oxford (3rd edn), 1860

Patterson, Major Tom, *100 Years of Spirit Photography*, 1965

Pattison, Mark, *Memoirs* (1885), Fontwell, 1969

Payne, Robert, *Dostoyevsky. A Human Portrait*, Alfred A. Knopf, NY, 1967

——, *Marx*, 1968

Pearson, Hesketh, *Gilbert and Sullivan*, Hamish Hamilton, 1935

Percival, John, *The Great Famine*, 1995

Pereiro, James, *Cardinal Manning. An Intellectual Biography*, Clarendon Press, Oxford, 1988

Perham, Margery, ed., *The Diaries of Lord Lugard* (4 vols), 1959

Perkin, Harold, *The Origins of Modern English Society. 1780–1880*, 1969

Pierce Jones, Victor, *Saint or Sensationalist. The Story of W.T. Stead*, Gooday Publishers, East Wittering, W. Sussex, 1988

Plomer, William, ed., *Kilvert's Diary, 1870–1879*, 1944

Plummer, Alfred, *Conversations with Dr Döllinger 1870–1890*, ed. Robrecht Boudens, Leuven University Press, 1985

Pocock, Tom, *Rider Haggard and the Lost Empire*, 1993

Poe, Edgar Allan, *Mesmerism*, 1846

Poirtier, Cathal, ed., *The Great Irish Famine*, Dublin, 1995

Politicus, *The Apparition of the late Lord Derby to Lord Beaconsfield*, Tubbs & Brook, Manchester, 1879

Pollock, John, *Shaftesbury. The Poor Man's Earl*, 1985

Ponsonby, Frederick (First Lord Sysonby), *Recollections of Three Reigns*, 1951

Pope-Hennessy, James, *Anthony Trollope*, 1971

Pope-Hennessy, Una, *Canon Charles Kingsley. A Biography*, 1948

——, *Charles Dickens* (1945), Penguin, Harmondsworth, 1970

Porter, Andrew, & Low, Alaine, ed., *The Oxford History of the British Empire.* vol. III, *The Nineteenth Century*, Oxford University Press, 1999

Porter, Andrew, ed., *The Oxford History of the British Empire*, Oxford, 1999, ch. 26, Christopher Saunders & Iain R Smith, 'Southern Africa 1795–1910'.

Porter, Dorothy, 'Public Health', in W.F. Bynum & Roy Porter, ed., *Companion Encyclopedia of the History of Medicine*, Routledge, London & New York, 1993

Potts, D.M., & Potts, W.T.W., *Queen Victoria's Gene*, 1999

Poulton, Edward Bagnall, 'Darwin', in *Encyclopedia Britannica*, 13th edn, New York & London, 1926

Pound, Ezra, *Selected Prose*, 1973

Prothero, Rowland, *The Life and Correspondence of Dean Stanley*, 2 vols, 1893

Pudney, John, *Lewis Carroll and his World*, 1976

Purcell, Edmund Sheridan, *Life of Cardinal Manning*, 2 vols, 1895

Quinton, Anthony, *Thoughts and Thinkers*, 1982

Raby, Peter, *Aubrey Beardsley and the Nineties*, 1998

Rahv, Philip, ed., *The Great Short Novels of Henry James*, Robinson Publishing, 1989

Raine, Craig, ed., *A Choice of Kipling's Prose*, 1987

Read, Donald, *Peel and the Victorians*, Oxford, 1987

Reboul, Marc, *Charles Kingsley, La formation d'une personnalité et son affirmation*, Paris, 1973

Reid, J.C., *The Mind and Art of Coventry Patmore*, 1957

Reid, Michaela, *Ask Sir James*, 1987

Rich, Norman, *Why the Crimean War? A Cautionary Tale*, University Press of New England, Hanover & London, 1985

Richter, Melvin, *The Politics of Conscience. T.H. Green and His Age*, University Press of America, Lanham, New York, 1983

Ricks, Christopher, ed., *The Poems of Tennyson*, 1969

——, ed., *A.E. Housman. Collected Poems and Selected Prose*, 1988

Ridley, Jasper, *Palmerston*, 1970

Roberts, Andrew, *Salisbury. Victorian Titan*, 1999

Roberts, Brian, *The Mad Bad Line*, 1981

——, *Cecil Rhodes. Flawed Colossus*, 1987

Roberts, David, 'How Cruel was the Victorian Poor Law?', *The Historical Journal*, pp. 97–107, 1963

Robertson Scott, J.W., *The Life and Death of a Newspaper*, 1952

Robinson, Gertrude, *David Urquhart*, 1920

Robinson, Jane, *Angels of Albion: Women of the Indian Mutiny*, 1996

Rotberg, Robert I., with Shore, Miles F., *The Founder. Cecil Rhodes and the Pursuit of Power*, Oxford University Press, New York, 1988

Rothman, David J. and Sheila M., ed., *The Dangers of Education*, Garland Publishing Inc., New York, 1987

Rothschild, Lord, '*You have it, Madam*', privately printed, London, 1980

Rotton, John Edward Wharton, *The Chaplain's Narrative of the Siege of Delhi*, 1858

Rowse, A.L., *Homosexuals in History*, 1977

Royle, Trevor, *The Kitchener Enigma*, 1985

——, *Crimea. The Great Crimean War, 1854–1856*, 1999

Ruskin, John, *The Works of John Ruskin*, ed. E.T. Cook & Alexander Wedderburn, 39 vols, 1903–12

Russell, Bertrand, *History of Western Philosophy*, 1946

——, *Autobiography*, vol. 1, 1967

Russell, C.A., *Cross Currents, Interactions between Science and Faith*, 1985

——, *John Stuart Mill. The Free Market and the State*, 1993

Russell, M., & Goldfarb, Clare R., *Spiritualism and Nineteenth-Century Letters*, Fairleigh Dickinson University Press, Associated University Presses Inc, Cranburg, NJ, 1978

Russell, William Howard, *My Indian Mutiny Diary*, 1957

——, ed. Roger Hudson, introduced by Max Hastings, *William Russell, Special Correspondent of The Times*, 1995

Ryan, Alan, *The Philosophy of John Stuart Mill*, 2nd edn, 1987

——, ed., *Mill*, A Norton Critical Edition, New York, 1997

Saintsbury, George, *The Earl of Derby*, 1906

Sarkar, Sumit, *Modern India, 1885–1947*, 2 vols, 1983 & 1989

Saville, John, *1848, The British State and the Chartist Movement*, Cambridge, 1987

——, *The Labour Movement in Britain, A Commentary*, 1988

Scott, Patrick, 'The School and the Novel. *Tom Brown's Schooldays*', in Brian Simon & Ian Bradley, ed., *The Victorian Public School*, 1975

Scrimgeour, R.M., ed., *The North London Collegiate School 1850–1950*, Oxford University Press, London, New York, 1950

Seacole, Mary, *Wonderful Adventures of Mrs Seacole in Many Lands* (first published 1857), OUP, New York, 1988

Semmel, Bernard, *The Governor Eyre Controversy*, 1962

Sen, Surendra Nath, *Eighteen fifty-seven*, The Publications Division, Ministry of Information & Broadcasting, Delhi, 1957

Seton-Watson, Hugh, *The Russian Empire 1801–1917*, Oxford at the Clarendon Press, 1967

Seymour-Smith, Martin, *Rudyard Kipling*, 1989

——, *Hardy*, 1994

Shannon, Richard, *Gladstone and the Bulgarian Agitation 1876*, 1963

——, *The Age of Disraeli, 1868–1881 The Rise of Tory Democracy*, Longman, 1992

——, *Gladstone: Heroic Minister 1865–1898*, 1999

Shaw, Bernard, *The Perfect Wagnerite. A Commentary on the Ring of the Nibelungs*, 1898

Shaw, Charles, *When I Was a Child* (1903), Caliban Books, 1977

Shaw, Stanford J., & Shaw, Ezel Kural, *History of The Ottoman Empire and Modern Turkey*, Cambridge, 1977

Simon, Julian, *The Ultimate Resource*, Princeton, NJ, 1981

Sims, George R., *How the Poor Live*, 1883

——, *Horrible London*, 1889

Singer, Charles, *et al.*, ed., *A History of Technology*, Oxford at the Clarendon Press, 1958

Singh, Shailenda Dhari, *Novels on the Indian Mutiny*, New Delhi, 1973

Skelley, Alan Ramsay, *The Victorian Army at Home*, London, McGill-Queen's University Press, Montreal, 1977

Skorupski, *John Stuart Mill*, 1989

Slosson, Preston William, *The Decline of the Chartist Movement*, 1916

Smiles, Samuel, *Self Help*, 1859

Smith, Iain R., *The Origins of the South African War 1899–1902*, 1996

Smith, Philip Thurmond, *Policing Victorian London*, Westport, CT, 1985

Smith, Vincent A., & Spear, Percival, *The Oxford History of India*, 1958

Soper, Kate, Introduction to Harriet Taylor Mill's *Enfranchisement of Women*, 1983

Source Material for a History of the Freedom Movement in India, Bombay, 1958

Southgate, David, *The Passing of the Whigs, 1832–1886*, 1962

Soyer, Alexis, *A Shilling Cookery for the People* (80th thousand), 1855

——, *The Selected Soyer. The writings of the legendary Victorian chef*, compiled by Andrew Langley, 1987

——, *A Culinary Campaign*, 1995

Spiers, Edward M., *The Late Victorian Army*, Manchester, 1992

Sprigge, T.L.S., *James and Bradley – American Truth and British Reality*, Open Court, Chicago and La Salle, Illinois, 1993

Srivastava, M.P., *The Indian Mutiny 1857*, Chugh Publications, Allahabad, 1979

Stamp, Gavin, *The Changing Metropolis*, 1984

Stamp, Robert M., *Royal Rebels. Princess Louise & The Marquis of Lorne*, Dundum Press, Toronto, 1988

Stanford, Derek, *Introduction to the Nineties*, Institut für Anglistik und Amerikanistik, Universität Salzburg, Austria, 1987

Stanley, Arthur Penrhyn, *Life and Correspondence of Thomas Arnold*, 2 vols, 1844

——, 'Charles Kingsley. A Sermon Preached in Westminster Abbey on January 31st 1875', 1875

——, *Historical Memorials of Canterbury Cathedral*, John Murray, 1900 (13th impression)

Stansky, Peter, *Redesigning the World. William Morris, the 1880s and the Arts and Crafts*, Princeton University Press, New Jersey, 1985

Stansky, Peter, *Gladstone. A Progress in Politics*, W.W. Norton, NY, 1979

Stedman Jones, Gareth, *Languages of Class*, Cambridge, 1983

Steele, David, *Lord Salisbury. A Political Biography*, 1999

Stevens Cox, J., ed., 'Hair Care in Late Victorian and Edwardian Days', St Peter Port, Guernsey, C.I., 1979

Stewart, J.I.M., *Eight Modern Writers*, Oxford at the Clarendon Press, 1963

Stokes, Eric, *The English Utilitarians and India*, Oxford, 1959

——, *The Peasant Armed. The Indian Revolt of 1857*, Oxford, 1986

Stokes, John, ed., *Eleanor Marx (1855–1898). Life, Work, Contacts*, Aldershot, Burlington USA, 2000

Storer, Henry, *Mesmerism in Disease: A Few Plain Facts*, 1845

Strachey, Lytton, *Queen Victoria* (1921), Harmondsworth, 1984

——, *Eminent Victorians* (1918), 1993

Strachey, Ray, *'The Cause'. A Short History of the Women's Movement in Great Britain*, 1928

Stubbs, C.W., *Charles Kingsley and the Christian Socialist Movement*, 1899

Sturgis, Matthew, *Aubrey Beardsley, a biography*, 1999

Sullivan, Zohreh T., *Narratives of Empire. The Fictions of Rudyard Kipling*, Cambridge, 1993

Sundkler, Bengt, & Steed, Christopher, ed., *A History of the Church in Africa*, Cambridge, 2000

Swartz, Marvin, *The Politics of British Foreign Policy in the Era of Disraeli and Gladstone*, 1985

Sykes, Christopher Simon, *Black Sheep*, 1982

——, *Private Palaces*, 1985

Taylor, A.J.P., *The Struggle for Mastery in Europe 1848–1918*, Oxford at the Clarendon Press, 1954

——, *English History, 1914–1945*, Oxford at the Clarendon Press, 1965

Taylor, Anne, *Annie Besant. A Biography*, Oxford, 1992

Taylor, Bernard, *Cruelly Murdered. Constant Kent and the Killing at Road Hill House*, 1989

Taylor, D.J., *Thackeray*, 1999

Taylor, Lucy, *Sahib and Sepoy or Saving an Empire*, 1897

Taylor, Miles, 'The 1848 Revolutions and the British Empire', *Past and Present*, No. 166, February 2000, pp.146ff.

——, ed., *The European Diaries of Richard Cobden, 1846–9*, Aldershot, 1994

Taylor, P.J.O., *A Companion to vol. 1 Mutiny of 1857*, Delhi, 1996, *Chronicles of the Mutiny*, Delhi, 1992

Taylor, S.J., *The Great Outsiders. Northcliffe, Rothermere and the Daily Mail*, 1996

Tennyson, Alfred, *The Poems of Tennyson*, ed. Christopher Ricks, 1969

Tennyson, Charles, *Alfred Tennyson*, 1950

Thomas, Donald, *Lewis Carroll. A Portrait with Background*, 1996

Thompson, C.J., *A Handbook of Personal Hygiene*, 1894

Thompson, Dorothy, *The Chartists*, Aldershot, 1984

Thompson, Edward, *The Other Side of the Medal*, Leonard & V. Woolf at the Hogarth Press, 1925

Thompson, E.P., *William Morris. Romantic to Revolutionary*, New York, 1955

Thompson, E.P., & Yeo, Eileen, ed., *The Unknown Mayhew. Selections from the Morning Chronicle 1849–50*, 1971

Thompson, F.M.L., *English Landed Society in the Nineteenth Century*, 1963

Thompson, Paul, *The Work of William Morris*, 1991

Thornton, A.P., *The Imperial Idea and its Enemies*, 1959

Tillotson, Kathleen, *Novels of the Eighteen-Forties*, Oxford, 1954

Tolstoy, L.N., *What Then Must We Do?* (1886), OUP, trans. Aylmer Maude, 1925

Townshend, Chauncy Hare, *Mesmerism Proved True and the Quarterly Review Reviewed*, 1854

Traill, H.D., *Lord Cromer*, 1987

Trevelyan, G.M., *Sir George Otto Trevelyan: A Memoir*, 1932

Trevelyan, G.O., *The Life and Letters of Thomas Babington Macaulay*, 1876

Tsuzuki, Chushichi, *The Life of Eleanor Marx 1855–1898. A Socialist Tragedy*, Clarendon Press, Oxford, 1967

Tyerman, Christopher, *A History of Harrow School*, Oxford University Press, 2000

Tyler, Colin, *Thomas Hill Green (1836–1882) and the Philosophical Foundations of Politics*, The Edwin Mellen Press, Lewiston, New York, 1997

Vamplew, Wray, *The Turf. A Social and Economic History of Horse Racing*, Allen Lane, 1976

Van der Kiste, John, *Queen Victoria's Children*, Allan Sutton, 1986

——, *Kaiser Wilhelm II*, Sutton Publishing, 1999

Van Riper, A. Bowdoin, *Men Among the Mammoths*, Chicago, 1993

Victoria, Queen, *The Letters of Queen Victoria*, ed. A.C. Benson & Viscount Esher, 1908

——, *The Girlhood of Queen Victoria*, ed. Viscount Esher, 2 vols, 1912

Vidler, Alec R., *F.D. Maurice and Company*, SCM, 1966

—— (ed.), *A Century of Social Catholicism, 1820–1920*, 1964

Vox Clamantis, *A History of Ritualism*, The Open Road Publishing Co., 1907

Walkowitz, Judith R., *Prostitution and Victorian Society*, Cambridge, 1980

Wallace, Richard, *The Agony of Lewis Carroll*, Gemini Press, Melrose, MA, 1990

Walsh, Walter, *The Secret History of the Oxford Movement*, 1897

Ward, Wilfrid, *The Life of John Henry Cardinal Newman*, 2 vols, 1912

Warner, Philip, *Kitchener. The Man behind the Legend*, 1985

Washington, Peter, *Madame Blavatsky's Baboon, Theosophy and the Emergence of the Western Guru*, 1993

Webb, Beatrice, *Our Partnership*, 1948

——, *My Apprenticeship* (1926), Cambridge, 1979

Weinreb, Ben, & Hibbert, Christopher, *The London Encyclopaedia*, 1983

Weintraub, Stanley, *Four Rossettis*, Weybright & Tatley NY, 1977

——, *Albert Uncrowned King*, 1997

Weldon's Christmas Annual, *Dizzi-Ben-Dizzi or The Orphan of Baghdad*, 1878

West, E.G., *Education and the State*, 1965

West, John, *The History of Tasmania*, 1971

Wheen, Francis, *Karl Marx. A Life*, 1999

White, Michael, & Gribbin, John, *Darwin. A Life in Science*, 1995

White, Stephen, 'A burning issue', *New Law Journal*, 10 August 1990

Whitehouse, J. Howard, *Vindication of Ruskin*, 1950

Whyte, F.W., 'William Thomas Stead', *DNB* 1912–1921

Williams, George Walter, *Depositions taken at Cawnpore under the Direction of Lieut. Colonel G.W.W. etc.*, Allahabad (?), 1858

Williamson, Joseph, *Josephine Butler. The Forgotten Saint*, 1977

Wilson, A.E., *East End Entertainment*, 1954

Wilson, A.N., *Hilaire Belloc*, 1984

——, *God's Funeral*, 1999

Wilson, Angus, *The Strange Ride of Rudyard Kipling*, 1977

Wilson, Colin, & Odell, Robin, *Jack the Ripper. Summing Up and Verdict*, Bantam Press, 1987

Winter, Barry, *The I.L.P. Past and Present*, 1993

Wise, Michael, & Gribbin, John, *Darwin. A Life in Science*, 1995

Wolfreys, Julian, *Being English*, State of New York Press, Albany NY, 1994

Woodham-Smith, Cecil, *The Great Hunger, Ireland 1845–9*, 1962

——, *Queen Victoria: Her Life and Times*, 1972

Woodward, E.L., *The Age of Reform, 1815–1870*, Oxford, 1949 (revised)

Worder, Nigel, *The Making of Modern South Africa: Conquest, Segregation and Apartheid*, Oxford, 1994

Wordsworth, William, *The Prelude* (1850), Harmondsworth, 1971

Wright, Brian, *A Fire in the House* (pamphlet, no name of publisher, no date), 1986? in BL catalogue

Wurgaft, Lewis D., *The Imperial Imagination: Magic and Myth in Kipling's India*, Wesleyan University Press, Middletown, Conn.

Yeats, W.B., *Autobiographies*, Macmillan, 1955

——, *Poems [Revised]*, ed. Richard J. Finneran, Macmillan, 1993

——, ed., *The Oxford Book of Modern Verse*, Oxford at the Clarendon Press, 1936

Young, G.M., *Portrait of an Age*, 1936

Young, Robert M., *Darwin's Metaphor*, Cambridge, 1985

Zetland, The Marquess of (Laurence Dundas), *Lord Cromer*, 1932

Zinn, Howard, *A People's History of the United States From 1492 to the Present* (second edn), 1996

Periodicals consulted

British Journal of the History of Science
Bullán, An Irish Studies Journal
Eliza Cook's Journal
Gentleman's Magazine
Hansard
History Today
Illustrated London News
Jamaican Historical Review
Journal of Social History
Journal of the History of Medicine and Allied Sciences
Journal of Imperial and Commonwealth History
Judy, or The London Serio-Comic Journal
New Law Journal
Notes and Queries
Pall Mall Gazette
Punch
Quarterly Review
The Historical Journal
The Illustrated London News
The Journal of the Royal College of Physicians of London
The Lancet
The Law Journal
The Leisure Hour
The Nineteenth Century
The Spectator
The Times

Manuscript collections

Reference to specific Manuscript numbers is in the notes. In the British Library I benefited from being able to read:

Balfour Papers (Additional MSS 49683–49962)
Burns Papers (Additional MSS 46286–94)
Dilke Papers (Additional MSS 43874–43967 and 49610–12)
Gladstone Papers (Additional MSS 44086–44835, 44900–1, 45724, 5644–53)
Iddlesleigh Papers (Additional MSS 50041)
(Florence) Nightingale Papers (Additional MSS 43393–43403, 45750–45849, 47714–47767, 68882–90)
Layard Papers (Additional MSS 38931–39164-, 46153–70, 58223–3)
Morley Papers (Additional MSS 48218–48301)
Morris Papers (Additional MSS 45298–45337)
Stanmore Papers (Additional MSS 49199–49285)
In the Bodleian Library, I consulted:
Benson Papers
Croker Papers
Ponsonby Papers

Illustrations

pp 1–3 Derby Day (oil on canvas) by Frith, William Powell (1819–1909) (after) (© *Private Collection/ Photo © Bonhams, London, UK/The Bridgeman Art Library*)

pp 4–5 Crowded beach and promenade at Margate, 1900 (*Getty Images*)

pp 6–7 Oxford Circus, London, *c.*1880 (*Getty Images*)

p. 8 'The Pleasures of the Rail Road – Caught in the Railway!', *c.*1840 (hand coloured etching) by Heath, H. (19th century) (© *Science Museum, London, UK/The Bridgeman Art Library*)

p. 10 *The Burning of the Houses of Parliament* (w/c on paper) by Turner, Joseph Mallord William (1775–1851) (© *Private Collection/© Agnew's, London, UK/The Bridgeman Art Library*)

pp 11–12 The Homes of the London Poor, from *The Builder Magazine*, 1854 (© *Guildhall Library, City of London/The Bridgeman Art Library*)

p. 15 Illustration by George Cruikshank from the first edition of *Oliver Twist* by Charles Dickens, 1836 (*Mary Evans Picture Library*)

p. 17 Queen Victoria (1837–1901) 1842 (oil on canvas) by Winterhalter, Franz Xavier (1806–73) (© *Chateau de Versailles, France/Lauros/Giraudon/The Bridgeman Art Library*)

p. 18 A Cabinet Lecture, Queen Victoria with Lord Melbourne, 1840 (engraving) by English School, (19th century) (© *British Museum, London, UK/The Bridgeman Art Library*)

p. 19 Poor Law poster, 1832 (*National Archives*)

p. 21 'John Bull caught between two humbugs', anonymous cartoon (*Mary Evans Picture Library*)

p. 22 'Peelers' *c.* 1835 (*Getty Images*)

p. 23 Drawing of Panopticon prison design from Jeremy Bentham's *Management of the Poor*, 1796 (*Getty Images*)

p. 27 Street fights between the Chartists and military in Newport, 1839. Woodcut, *c.* 1890 (*akg-images*)

p. 28 Two British officers of the East India Company entertained by music, Mogul School, *c.* 1820 (*akg-images*)

p. 30 *Slave Ship (Slavers Throwing Overboard the Dead and Dying, Typhoon Coming On)* 1840 (oil on canvas), Turner, Joseph Mallord William (1775–1851) (*Museum of Fine Arts, Boston, Massachusetts, USA, Henry Lillie Pierce Fund/The Bridgeman Art Library*)

p. 33 Victoria and Albert, 1854 (*Getty Images*)

p. 34 *Queen Victoria in the House of Lords* by Nash, Joseph (1809–78) (© *Houses of Parliament, Westminster, London, UK/The Bridgeman Art Library*)

p. 37 Floor design for the Houses of Parliament (gouache & pencil on paper) by Pugin, Augustus Welby Northmore (1812–52) (© *Victoria & Albert Museum, London, UK/The Bridgeman Art Library*)

p. 38 'Popery or No Popery?', 1850 (engraving) (b/w photo) by English School, (19th century) (after) (© *Private Collection/The Bridgeman Art Library*)

p. 42 Irish tenant farmers in the Duke of Devonshire's photographic studio, Lismore Castle, County Waterford, 1853 (*Getty Images*)

p. 45 Satirical Cartoon About the State of Ireland in the 1830s, from *McLean's Monthly Sheet of Caricatures*, Number 19 (engraving) by English School, (19th century) (© *Private Collection/ The Bridgeman Art Library*)

p. 48 The Monkey House at the Zoological Gardens, Regent's Park, engraved and pub. by the artist, printed by Charles Hullmandel (1789–1850), 1835 (colour litho) by Scharf, George the Elder (1788–1860) (© *City of Westminster Archive Centre, London, UK/The Bridgeman Art Library*)

p. 51 'Awful changes', 1830, drawn and engraved by H.T. de la Beche (*Getty Images*)

p. 53 Satire on mesmerism, *c.* 1830 (*Mary Evans Picture Library*)

p. 55 British Prime Minister John Russell greets a Chartist, from *Punch*, 1848 (*Getty Images*)

pp 56–7 Chartist demonstration on Kennington Common, 10 April 1848 (*Crown Copyright*)

pp 60–61 Crowds outside the Crystal Palace in Hyde Park for the Great Exhibition, 1851. Drawing and lithograph by Augustus Butler (*Getty Images*)

p. 62 Ilustration by George Cruikshank from Henry Mayhew's novel *Mr and Mrs Sandboys and Family*, 1851 (*Mary Evans Picture Library*)

p. 67 Great Exhibition, 1851: first sketch for the building, 1850 (ink on blotting paper) by Paxton, Sir Joseph (1801–65) (© *Victoria & Albert Museum, London, UK/The Bridgeman Art Library*)

p. 68 A display of machinery at the Great Exhibition in Hyde Park, 1851 (*Getty Images*)

p. 70 A variety of stalls at the Great Exhibition, 1851 (*Getty Images*)

pp 72–3 *Work*, 1863 (oil on canvas) by Brown, Ford Madox (1821–93) (© *Birmingham Museums and Art Gallery/The Bridgeman Art Library*)

p. 75 'The Cheap Tailor and His Workmen' by John Leech from *Punch*, *c.* 1870 (*Getty Images*)

p. 76 *The Light of the World*, *c.*1851–53 (oil on canvas), Hunt, William Holman (1827–1910) (*Keble College, Oxford, UK/The Bridgeman Art Library*)

p. 77 Elizabeth Siddal: Study for *Ophelia*, 1852 (pencil on paper) by Millais, Sir John Everett (1829–96) (© *Birmingham Museums and Art Gallery/The Bridgeman Art Library*)

p. 78 *Beata Beatrix*, *c.*1864–70 (oil on canvas), Rossetti, Dante Charles Gabriel (1828-82) (© *National Gallery of Scotland, Edinburgh, Scotland/The Bridgeman Art Library*)

Index

Cardwell, Edward, 1st Viscount, 178
Carjat, Étienne, 221
Carlyle, Thomas, 14, 15, 31, 76, 131,
    163,
    The French Revolution, 14
    Past and Present, 76
Carnarvon, Henry Howard Molyneux
    Herbert, 4th Earl of, 138, 162
carriages, 68, 98, 99, 112, 132, 133,
    195, 202, 255, 279, 324
Carroll, Lewis (Charles Lutwidge
    Dodgson), 156, 233
    Alice's Adventures Underground,
    154
    Alice's Adventures in Wonderland,
    154, 156, 161
    Through the Looking Glass, 154
Carson, Edward Henry (*later* Baron),
    297
Catholic Church, 52
    see also Maynooth; Mortara, Edgar;
    Oxford Movement; Papal
    Infallibility; Pius IX, Pope;
    Vatican Council, First
Catholic emancipation, 35
cattle plague, 213
Cause, the *see* feminism
Cavagnari, Sir Louis, 198
Cavendish, Lord Frederick, 232, 274
Cawnpore *see* Kanpur
cemeteries, 151, 281, 262, 281, 282
Cetewayo, Zulu Chief, 198, 199
Ceylon: unrest in, 64, 104, 287
Chadwick, Edwin, 22, 75, 146
    Preventive Policing, 22
Chamberlain, Joseph, 178, 226, 228,
    234, 235, 245, 246, 261, 306, 309,
    312, 314, 315
Chambers, Robert: *Vestiges of the
    Natural History of Creation*, 50,
    52
Chand, Nanak: *Narrative of Events
    at Cawnpore*, 104
Chapman, John, 81
Charlotte, Princess (George IV's
    daughter), 17
Charterhouse School, 138
Chartists, 24, 25, 26, 32, 35, 40, 55, 56,
    58, 59, 64, 66, 102, 227, 262
Chatsworth, Derbyshire, 47, 66
'Chatsworth Stove', 66, 70
Chaudhuri, S.B., 102
Chester Castle, 231
Chesterton, Gilbert Keith, 82, 164,
    217, 312
child labour, 126, 214
childhood, 131, 132, 143, 164
chloroform, 54
cholera, 21, 43, 47, 75, 88, 90, 106, 110,
    146, 183
Christian Science, 286
Christianity, 15, 73, 81, 101, 130, 138,
    148, 159, 173, 183, 202, 203, 279,
    287, 312
    see also Catholic Church; Church of
    England; religion
Church of England, 52, 178, 182, 183,
    189, 216, 279
    see also Christianity; religion
Church in Wales, 306
Churchill, Lord Randolph, 229
cigarette-makers, 97, 98
Clarence, Albert Victor, Duke of, 270
Clarendon Commission on public
    schools (1861–4), 138
Clarendon, George William Frederick
    Villiers, 4th Earl of, 46, 47, 94, 119,
    138
Clarke, General Sir Andrew, 240
class (social), *see* aristocracy; middle
    classes; working classes
Clergy Daughters' School, Casterton,
    141
Clerkenwell: Fenian bomb in, 165
Clifden, Nellie, 120
coal, 14, 75, 126, 178, 195
Cobbett, William, 25
Cobden, Richard, 38, 40, 59, 65, 213
Coburg family and dynasty, 32, 118,
    120

Cole, Sir Henry, 65, 66
Colenso, John William, Bishop of
    Natal, 199
colonies, 27, 29, 63, 64, 65, 176, 312
    see also empire
commerce *see* trade
communism, 55, 56, 73, 117, 130, 169,
    215, 265
Conder, Charles, 289
Condition of England question, 31, 35
Congo, 240, 249, 251
Congregationalists, 225
Conrad, Joseph, 205
    The Secret Agent, 227
Conroy, Sir John, 17
Conservative Party, 40, 162, 163, 199,
    200, 203, 299
    see also Tory Party
constituencies (Parliamentary):
    newly-formed, 162, 245, 299, 306
Constitution (British), 18, 33
Contagious Diseases Acts (1864–86),
    145, 146, 184, 242
Contemporary Review, 281
Co-operative Movement, 301
Cope Brothers (tobacco
    manufacturers), 98
corn, 40, 41, 43, 44, 46, 213
    see also Corn Laws
Corn Laws, 26, 35, 36, 38, 40, 41, 44,
    64, 199, 213, 215
    see also Free Trade
Cornforth, Fanny, 77, 80
Corry, Montague Lowry (*later* 1st
    Baron Rowton), 191, 198
Corsica, 41
Corvo, Baron *see* Rolfe, Frederick,
    289
cost of living, 41
cotton, 35, 73, 125, 126, 128, 129, 181,
    195, 264
Cotton, Sir Henry, 109
county councils, 303
Cowper, Francis Thomas de Grey, 7th
    Earl, 232
Cox, Rev. Bell, 184
Crawford, Donald amd Virginia, 234,
    235
Crawford v. Crawford and Dilke
    (lawsuit), 234, 235
creation, 50, 52, 115, 116, 187
    see also evolution, theory of
cremation, 281, 282
Cremation Society, 281
cricket, 143, 281, 304, 314
crime, 22, 24, 45, 47, 146, 164, 196, 267,
    270, 273, 274, 304
Crimean War (1854–5), 44, 69, 82, 85,
    86, 88, 93, 96, 97, 98, 99, 109, 119,
    195, 197, 281
    see also individual actions and
    participants
criminal code, 22
Criminal Law Amendment Act (1885),
    229, 298
Cripps, Sir Stafford, 130
Cromer, Evelyn Baring, 1st Earl of,
    238, 239, 240, 242, 314
Cromwell, John, 274
Crystal Palace, 69, 70, 71
    see also Great Exhibition (1851)
Cubitt, Thomas, 65
Curzon, George Nathaniel, Marquess
    Curzon of Kedleston, 254, 293
Cust, Harry, 293
Cyprus: occupied, 198, 202

Daily Chronicle, 237
Daily Mail, 304
Daily Mirror, 304
Daily News, 171, 196, 197, 237
Daily Telegraph, 206, 231, 237
Daimler, Gottlieb, 251
Dale, Rev. Thomas Pelham, 184
Dannreuther, Chariclea and Edward,
    206
Dante Alighieri, 117
    Paradiso, 117
Darwin, Charles, 118, 159, 186, 187,
    287, 293
    The Descent of Man, 186

On the Origin of Species, 115
    Voyage of a Naturalist, 186
    see also evolution, theory of; natural
    selection
Davidson, John, 289
Davidson, Randall, Bishop of
    Winchester (*later* Archbishop of
    Canterbury), 321
Davies, Emily, 141, 148
Davitt, Michael, 231, 233, 274, 275
Dawkins, Richard, 117
Dawson, Rev. E.C., 247
death *see* funerals
death certificates *see* Bills of
    Mortality
death duties, 303
Decadence, 289
Delane, John Thadeus, 237
Delhi: in Indian Mutiny, 103, 104, 105,
    106, 108, 109, 112
Delhi Declaration (1857), 104
democracy, 12, 19, 24, 25, 38, 59, 130,
    164, 246, 250, 267, 299, 300, 324,
    325
Democratic Federation, 227
demos, 32, 54, 147, 195, 261, 262
Demuth, Freddy, 264
Denmark, 119, 174, 324
Dennett, Daniel C., 117
dentistry, 145
Derby Day, 1–3, 243
Derby, Edward George Geoffrey
    Smith Stanley, 14th Earl of
    (*earlier* Lord Stanley), 71, 94, 130,
    135, 146, 162
Derby, Edward George Smith Stanley,
    13th Earl of (*earlier* Lord
    Stanley), 38, 40, 55, 65
Derby, Edward Henry Stanley, 15th
    Earl of (*earlier* Lord Stanley),
    191, 195
Dervishes (Sudan), 239, 241, 242, 314
Desborough, Ethel Anne Priscilla,
    Lady ('Ettie'), 293
design, 36, 65, 66, 70, 80, 251, 271, 281,
    290
determinism, 217
Devastation, HMS, 211
Devonshire, Spencer Compton
    Cavendish, 8th Duke of (*earlier*
    Marquess of Hartington), 232, 234
Devonshire, William George Spencer
    Cavendish, 6th Duke of, 47, 66
Dhondu Pant (Nana Sahib), 106
Dickens, Charles, 16, 18, 142, 157, 163,
    164, 306
    A Christmas Carol, 16
    David Copperfield, 157, 164
    Little Dorrit, 164
    Nicholas Nickleby, 142
    Oliver Twist, 18
    Our Mutual Friend, 16
    The Pickwick Papers, 16
    Sketches by Boz, 164
Diderot, Denis, 51
Dilke, Sir Charles, 178, 226, 228, 234,
    274, 279
Dillon, John, 274
Disraeli, Benjamin (*later* Earl of
    Beaconsfield), 19, 38, 40, 41, 71,
    118, 126, 128, 130, 156, 161, 162,
    171, 174, 178, 183, 185, 187, 189,
    191, 192, 193, 195, 197, 198, 199,
    200, 201, 202, 203, 210, 211, 215,
    220, 238, 259, 265
    Coningsby, 38
    Endymion, 203
    Sybil, 38
    Tancred, 38
    *Vindication of the English
    Constitution*, 38
Disraeli, Mary Anne (*later*
    Viscountess Beaconsfield), 202
divorce, 117, 177, 234, 273, 274 *see also*
    Matrimonial Causes Bill
dock strike (1889), 263, 265, 279
doctors, 21, 74, 120, 146, 187, 256
Dodgson, Charles Lutwidge *see*
    Carroll, Lewis
Dodson, Charles, 20

Dostoyevsky, Fyodor Mikhailovich,
    215, 223
    The Devils, 223, 227
doubt, religious *see* religion
Douglas, Lord Alfred ('Bosie'), 297
Dowson, Ernest, 289
Doyle, Sir Arthur Conan, 271
    The Sign of Four, 271
    A Study in Scarlet, 271
    see also Holmes, Sherlock
D'Oyly Carte, Richard, 206, 208
    see also Gilbert and Sullivan operas
drainage, 75
Dreikaiserbund, 191, 195
drink *see* alcohol
Drumlanrig, Francis Archibald
    Douglas, Viscount, 297
Duckworth, Rev. Robinson, 156
Dugdale, Blanche, 292
Duncan, Rev. Henry, 132
Dundas, Admiral Sir Richard
    Saunders, 88
Durnford, Lieut.-Colonel, 198
Dyer, Brigadier-General Reginald
    Edward Harry, 254

East India Company, 22, 29, 63, 64,
    101, 102, 104, 105, 106, 111, 112,
    131
    see also India; Indian Mutiny
'Eastern Question' *see* Ottoman
    Empire, 176, 194, 195
eccentricity: in upper classes, 88
economic depression, 19
    see also unemployment
Eddy, Mary Baker, 286
Edgar, William, 205
Edinburgh Review, 171
education, 14, 59, 137, 138, 139, 140,
    148, 151, 164, 173, 176, 179, 208,
    209, 225, 228, 301, 311
    see also public schools; schools
Education Act (Forster's; 1870), 140,
    179
Edward, Prince of Wales (*later* King
    Edward VII) *see* Albert Edward,
    Prince of Wales
Edward, Prince of Wales (*later* King
    Edward VIII), 40
Edwards, Colonel, 240
Edwards, George, 215
Effingham Theatre, London, 264
Eglinton, Archibald Montgomerie,
    13th Earl of: Tournament, 53
Egypt, 31, 137, 174, 193, 195, 228, 238,
    239, 240, 245, 287
Elcho, Hugo Charteris, Viscount, 293
Elcho, Mary, Lady (*later* Countess of
    Wemyss), 54, 293
electoral districts: organization of, 26
electoral reform, 40, 161, 246
    see also Reform Acts; suffrage
electoral systems, 25, 304
electric light, 208
Elgar, Sir Edward, 206
Eliot, George (Marian Evans), 16, 81,
    82, 120, 187, 203, 206
    Daniel Deronda, 203
    Middlemarch, 169
Eliot, Thomas Stearns, 268, 269, 271
Elkington & Co. (cabinet makers), 70
Ellenborough, Edward Law, 1st Earl
    of, 138
Elliotson, John, 54
Ellis, Sir Henry, 58
Ellis, William, 66
Elphinstone, Sir Howard, 121
employment, 47, 74
    see also unemployment
Engels, Friedrich, 55, 56, 58, 262, 301
    see also Marx, Karl
English Co-operative Society, 301
Enraght, Rev. R.W., 184
Erdmann, Johann Eduard, 173
Erzerum, Armenia, 194
Esher, Reginald Brett, 2nd Viscount,
    238
Etwall, Ralph, 20
Eugénie, Empress of Napoleon III,
    169, 199